THE WITNEY COURT B

The Oxfordshire Record Society

CALENDAR
OF THE
COURT BOOKS
OF THE
BOROUGH OF WITNEY
1538–1610

Edited by James L. Bolton
and Marjorie M. Maslen

VOLUME LIV
Issued for the years 1981 and 1982

1985

Produced for the Society by
Alan Sutton Publishing, Gloucester
and printed in Great Britain

TABLE OF CONTENTS

GENERAL EDITOR'S PREFACE

The publication of this volume (the last of eight to be published as a result of my tenure of the office of General Editor of the Oxfordshire Record Society) has been assisted by grants from The Publications Committee of Queen Mary College, University of London, The Twenty-Seven Foundation, the Isobel Thornley Bequest, the University Grants Committee of New Zealand, the research fund of the University of Otago, and the Pasold Research Fund. The members of the Society and the editors of this volume are most grateful for this generous help.

October 1984

J.F.A. MASON
General Editor, O.R.S.,
vols. xlvii–liv

EDITOR'S PREFACE

Witney's blankets have long been known world wide, so it is perhaps fitting that work on its borough records should be undertaken in two hemispheres, in England and New Zealand. We are indebted to many people, perhaps most of all to our families, for help in jointly editing these court books at a distance of 12,000 miles from each other. We have received generous support from our respective Universities in London and Otago, in the form of study leave, facilities and research grants. We have received willing advice and assistance from the Bodleian Library, Oxford, the British Library, the Library of Queen Mary College, London, the General Assembly Library and the National Library in New Zealand and the University of Otago Library, from the Hampshire Record Office, Oxfordshire Record Office and, of course, from the Public Record Office, London. Of the many people who have assisted us we must particularly thank Miss Shirley Barnes, Dr Molly Barratt, Mr Richard Early, Brigadier F.R.L. Goadby, Mr Jeremy Hammington, Mrs Flora Kirby, Miss Jean McLennan, the Duke of Marlborough (who gave us permission to use the records of the Blenheim estate office), Miss Irene Marshall, Dr John Mason the Society's General Editor, Mr J.R. Mayo of the Geography Department, Queen Mary College, who drew the maps, Miss Laurie Smith, Mr Hugh Walton and Mr J. Welsh. Finally, this edition would not have been possible without the Rector and Vestry of Witney Parish church who allowed us to use the court books and their other records.

Queen Mary College, University of London Jim Bolton
University of Otago, Dunedin Marjorie Maslen
April 1984

LIST OF ABBREVIATIONS

Bodl.	Bodleian Library, Oxford.
Cal. Charter	*Calendar of Charter Rolls* (H.M.S.O.)
Cal. Close	*Calendar of Close Rolls* (H.M.S.O.)
Cal. Fine	*Calendar of Fine Rolls* (H.M.S.O.)
Cal. I.P.M.	*Calendar of Inquisitions Post Mortem* (H.M.S.O.)
Cal. Pat.	*Calendar of Patent Rolls* (H.M.S.O.)
Cal. S.P.Dom.	*Calendar of State Papers Domestic* (H.M.S.O.)
churchwardens' accts.	Witney churchwardens' accounts 1569–1720, Bodl. D.D. Par. Witney c 9.
D.D. Par. Witney	Witney parish records (some uncatalogued) deposited in Bodl.
DNB	*Dictionary of National Biography*
Eccl.	Archives of the Bishopric of Winchester in the Hampshire Record Office.
Econ.H.R.	*Economic History Review*
E.P.N.S.	English Place-Name Society
L.&P. For. and Dom. Hen. VIII	*Letters and Papers of Henry VIII, Foreign and Domestic* (H.M.S.O.)
Misc.Je I/1	Court book of the manor of Witney in O.R.O.
Oldfield, Clerus Oxon.	W.J. Oldfield, 'Clerus Diocesis Oxoniensis, 1542–1908' (MS Index in Bodl.)
O.R.O.	Oxfordshire County Record Office
O.R.S.	Oxfordshire Record Society
Oxon. Inventories	*Household and Farm Inventories in Oxfordshire 1550–1590*, ed. M.A. Havinden, O.R.S.xliv (1965)
Par. Coll.	*Parochial Collections*, made by Anthony à Wood and Richard Rawlinson, ed. F.N. Davis, O.R.S. ii, iv, xi (1920, 1922, 1929)
P.C.C.	Prerogative Court of Canterbury
P.R.O.	Public Record Office. The chief documents used are:
C 1	Early Chancery Proceedings
C 3	Chancery Proceedings
C 54	Close Rolls
CP 25(2)	Court of Common Pleas, Feet of Fines
E 159	Exchequer, King's Remembrancer, Memoranda Rolls
E 179	Exchequer, King's Remembrancer, Subsidy Rolls
Prob	Wills proved in the P.C.C.
Req.	Court of Requests

Top. Oxon. d 210–212	Topographical collections for Witney made by William Langford of Eynsham in the 19th century and now in Bodl.
V.C.H.	*Victoria County History*
Visit. Oxon.	*The Visitation of the County of Oxford*, ed. W.H. Turner, Harleian Society, v (1871)
Wills Oxon.	Original Oxfordshire wills in Bodl.

INTRODUCTION

PART ONE: THE WITNEY COURT

The Borough of Witney and its Courts

This volume is a calendar in modern English of the two sixteenth-century court books of the borough of Witney in Oxfordshire. They were kept for many years with the parish records in Witney and have recently been deposited by the church authorities in the Bodleian library, but in origin they are manorial records and the sole surviving documents from the townsmen's own court.[1]

By the sixteenth century the borough court had been in existence for nearly 300 years. The bishops of Winchester had held the lordship of Witney for some two centuries when bishop Peter des Roches formed the borough out of the existing village in the early years of his episcopate between 1205 and 1208. He had perhaps already granted rights to the townsfolk by 1210 when certain townsmen paid him 40s. for a charter.[2] Apart from having a new town they acquired a grant of fairs in 1202 and 1231 and of freedom from the payment of toll, passage money and murage in 1232, rights all of which point to a body of tradesmen with specialized needs.[3] No charter survives to record precisely when and on what terms they gained a borough court but in 1256, when a later bishop granted a charter to another new town, Newton, Isle of Wight, he gave it all the liberties and free customs of his burgesses of Taunton, Witney, Alresford and Farnham.[4] These privileges were rehearsed in a Farnham charter of 1249 as being the right to do suit at their own court and before their own bailiffs, the right to make all attachments and distraints and to be free from attendance at any other of the bishop's courts except his twice-yearly hundred courts, the right to hold the assizes of bread and ale and to take the penalties, but not to have the fines from the use of the pillory and tumbril, which were reserved to the bishop.[5] Such rights accord with the system in Witney in the thirteenth century and later. In 1219 the bishop repaired his pillory and tumbril, and pleas and perquisites were entered in

[1] The court books are now D.D. Par. Witney d 1 and 2; for a record of the curate lending the books in 1861 see Top. Oxon. d 215, f.70
[2] *The Pipe Roll of the Bishopric of Winchester 1208-9*, ed. H.Hall (London, 1903), p.17; and for 1210-11, ed. N.R.Holt (Manchester, 1964), pp.63,64; M.W.Beresford and H.P.R.Finberg, *English Medieval Boroughs* (Newton Abbot, 1973), p.149.
[3] *Cal. Charter 1226-57*, p.140; *1300-26*, p.349; *Cal. Close 1227-31*, p.571.
[4] A.Ballard and J.Tait, *British Borough Charters, 1216-1307* (Cambridge, 1923), p.22.
[5] Ibid. pp.lxxxiv, lxxxvi; E.Robo, *Medieval Farnham* (Farnham, 1935), pp.175-80.

his accounts for the borough by 1232: in later years they were specified as for mêlées, hue and cry, unclean meat, offences against the assize of bread, and, of particular interest for tradesmen, for recovering debts and for defaults of pledge; in 1302 they were taken from fourteen courts for the borough during the year.[6]

The borough was a separate unit in the bishopric records from 1218. In the thirteenth and fourteenth centuries it was run by two local reeves who were allowed 3s. a year by the bishop for their office. But the bishop also had a bailiff in charge of the several manors, i.e. Witney, Adderbury, Brightwell and Harwell, in a bailiwick for Oxfordshire and North Berkshire, and this is the bailiff who accounted with the reeves for the borough in the bishops' Pipe Rolls of this period. By the fifteenth century the two local reeves had been transmuted into two bailiffs, who were likewise allowed 3s. rent a year.[7] The local officers farmed or leased the borough from the bishop on several occasions in the thirteenth century and from the fourteenth century on.[8] By this arrangement they were still paying in the sixteenth century a fixed rent of £9 8s. 10¾d., but a similar arrangement whereby they paid 18s. for farm of the toll of the fairs, 18s. for the stallage and 20s. for the seldage, i.e. for the stalls in the market and fair, had run into difficulties in the fifteenth century when the burgesses refused to pay. In the 1503 valuation the sums were entered among the arrears and allowances because the bailiffs swore on oath that they could not collect them, and in the later Pipe Rolls of the sixteenth century only 2s. to 3s. was received at the bishop's Exchequer for the toll of the fairs.[9]

The town was never incorporated and it remained a seignorial or mesne borough with the bishop by the sixteenth century still keeping a remote but real interest in it. In Edward VI's reign when the assault on the Church and its lands was at its height, John Ponet, who replaced the Catholic Gardiner as bishop of Winchester, was persuaded to grant his bishopric lands to the crown in 1551 in return for an annuity. This was to the profit of Northumberland's brother Sir Andrew Dudley, soldier and gentleman of the Privy Chamber (d.1559), who was given the Oxfordshire lands in 1552 including Witney manor and borough.[10] Fortunately for the borough he does not seem to have been able to increase his income from it and the rent remained as it had been in the Middle Ages

[6] Eccl. 2/159276, 159283, 159290, 159312, 159320.

[7] *Cal. Fine 1445-52*, p.27; Eccl. 2/155648.

[8] An account of the borough in the Middle Ages is given in A.Ballard, 'The Black Death at Witney', *Oxford Archaeological Society Reports*, 1909; P.Hyde, 'The borough of Witney', *Oxfordshire Hundred Rolls of 1279*, O.R.S. xlvi (1968), 89-90; and her thesis, Bodl. Ms. B.Litt. d 473.

[9] Eccl. 2/155648, 155885 etc.

[10] *Cal. Pat. 1550-53*, p.153; *DNB*. and J.D.Mackie, *The Earlier Tudors* (Oxford, 1952), under Dudley, Ponet and Gardiner.

and was also a century later.[11] Although Dudley was disgraced on Mary's accession and Bishop Gardiner was restored to Winchester, they made an arrangement for Dudley to enjoy the profits of Witney and it was not until the very end of the reign in June 1558 that the next bishop (John White) was able to get a regrant of his lands including Witney manor and borough.[12] There was a similar loss of episcopal lands almost one hundred years later in 1647 and under the Commonwealth.[13] Again the bishop managed to recover his property at the Restoration and remained Witney's lord until the nineteenth century. Finally in 1862 the Duke of Marlborough bought the reversion of the lease of the manor and borough, and the bishop of Winchester's long lordship came to an end.[14]

The bishop appears in the court books as lord of the manor or lord of the franchise (i, ff. 88r, 102v). By the sixteenth century his interest was mainly financial and the bailiffs' chief duty to him was to see that his rents and dues were collected and his rights observed.

The bishop's direct interest in the area had diminished with the various leases made of episcopal land from the late fourteenth century.[15] He leased demesne lands of Witney manor to a local yeoman family, the Brices, from the late fifteenth century but retained the court profits and the timber rights.[16] The borough was not farmed to a lessee until 1583 when Robert Dudley, Earl of Leicester, had an 80-year lease for £141 19s. ¼d. and accounted at the bishop's Exchequer instead of the bailiffs of the borough. His tenure was brief, though during it he patronized local industry by buying quilts and blankets for Kenilworth castle.[17] After Dudley's death in the year of the Armada, Mr. Stephen Brice, who had succeeded to his father's lease of the manor when he came of age in 1553, took over the borough lease in 1589. He made the same payment and later it went to his son who held it well into the seventeenth century.[18]

The lessee was known as the 'farmer' and it was with him and his steward that the town now had to deal, a situation causing particular problems when the lease passed to other and more powerful lords like the Earls of Rochester or Lord Cornbury in the eighteenth century, although

---

[11] Hyde, B.Litt.: analysis of the bishop's receipts from the Winchester Pipe Rolls; and Top. Oxon. d 211, f.130 for 1647 revenue.

[12] Cal. Pat. 1557-8, p.147 the arrangements are described in a court case: Req. 2/61/57.

[13] C 54/3418, mm. 39-40, n. 5; Top. Oxon. d 211, f.130. The customary and rental of the manor in 1646 and 1647 are presumably connected with this: Bodl. Ms. Rolls Oxon. 59; and D.D.Ravenor d 10.

[14] Blenheim Palace muniments, schedule of deeds relating to the purchase.

[15] A.Ballard, 'The manors of Witney, Brightwell and Downton', Oxfordshire Studies in Social and Legal History, v, no.9 (Oxford, 1916).

[16] Eccl. 2/155648 and Pipe Rolls; Misc. Je I/1, ff. 18r, 35Av, 40v, 43v.

[17] Eccl. 2/155891; Historical Mss. Commission Report, De L'Isle and Dudley Mss. i (London, 1925), pp.297-8. For him see DNB; he died at Cornbury near Witney.

[18] Eccl. 2/155891 to 159517; and see below, p.xlvii.

of one of them, Lord Clarendon, it was said that 'in his disorder he was overfond of his tenants of the Manor of Witney' and paid some dues to the bishop instead of them.[19] In 1751 the Duke of Marlborough, the most powerful nobleman in the region, bought the lease from Lord Clarendon and Lord Hyde.[20]

Contact with the townsfolk was by the steward, a man of importance in the administration of the episcopal lands, although when there was a lessee of the borough the steward for the borough was appointed by the lessee.[21] Between 1578 and 1589 William Sleepe, gentleman, was steward and frequently sat in the borough court with the chief officers though not, of course, himself presiding (i, ff. 183v, 267r). On one occasion he swore in an officer and it may be that his presence there in October courts was connected with this business. When another steward Francis Serle, gentleman, was in the borough court in 1590 he was evidently safeguarding the lord's interests since he received a declaration about the willing of property which was recorded in the book (i, f. 273r). The steward himself often had strong local interests and at the end of the century Leonard Yate, gentleman, from a local clothier family and connected with the lessees, was steward (i, ff. 298r, 304r).

The main reason for the steward's being in Witney, however, was to hold the bishop's courts for the manor and borough. In the sixteenth century there were two sets of manorial and hundred courts in Witney, corresponding to the division between town and countryside. The villagers of Hailey, Crawley and Curbridge attended the bishop's joint manorial and hundred court for Witney Manor twice a year, when the steward came round for the Hocktide turn in March or April and for the St Martin's turn in September or October.[22] The townsfolk had their own manorial court, i.e. the court calendared here, held monthly by their own officers, but they also attended the bishop's hundred or lawday court for Witney Borough, held twice a year by his steward. The bishop's courts for Witney Manor and Witney Borough were quite distinct from each other and appear as such in the bishopric archives.[23] The steward might hold them on the same day and the same inhabitants of the parish appear in both as jurors, officers and suitors, but the lists of jurors, the presentments and orders and final entry were separate. There was also a distinction in that the courts for Witney Manor dealt largely with transfers of copyhold land and regulation of agriculture, while the hundred court for the borough mainly concerned itself with town regulations. The one

---

[19] Blenheim Palace mun., Witney court books and bundle called 'Bishop's foreknowledge'. For a rental of 1716 for the Earl of Rochester see Bodl. Ms. Rolls. Oxon. 60.
[20] Blenheim Palace mun., schedule.
[21] Ibid., statement of customs and court books.
[22] There are records of the courts in Eccl. 1/73/1-6 and Misc. Je I/1.
[23] e.g. Eccl. 1/86/4,5 and box 90, ff.59, 81.

overlap in their business was that the leasing of the bishop's waste in the
market place and Corn Street in the borough was dealt with in the Witney
Manor court and not in the borough hundred court.[24]

The hundred court for the borough had various names in its long
history: it is the great portmoot or the 'turn' in the Winchester records, or
the lawday in the court books below (i, ff. 93v, 162v) and the court leet of
later times. It was a more important element in the lives of the townsfolk
than may seem from the occasional references in the borough court. At
Witney, as in another of the bishop's manors at Taunton, it had a
regulating authority and although never very profitable financially to the
bishop it was important to the borough as validating the actions of its own
court and lending it authority.[25] The lawday court examined the bishop's
franchise in the borough and saw that all men were in their wards, the
borough equivalent of the tithings of the manorial court; it looked into the
bishop's rights over bakers and brewers and collected his fines if they did
not grind their grain at his mill; it enforced regulations about boundaries
and muckhills and wandering pigs, received presentments of wardsmen
and jurors, and settled minor disputes and breaches of the peace.[26] Many
of these matters also appear below in the townsfolk's frequent courts. The
interaction of the two courts is illustrated in the court books in an order of
27 July 1565 to a tenant to make a boundary mound as appointed on the
last lawday (i, f. 93v),or in the many appearances of Anthony Larden in
the borough courts in the 1560s which eventually led to the jurors
presenting him in the lawday court as a barrator, or common bringer of
law suits and troublemaker (i, ff. 91r to 95r).[27]

One distinction between the lawday and town court was in the
summonses for attendance. There was a general summons for all suitors to
the lawday court and essoins and fines for non-attendance were particular
items, whereas the borough's own portmoot had no such general
summons, only a duty laid on the officers to be present and a specific
summons to those involved in cases. The lawday court was the only court
with jurors for the Crown who checked the presentments of the
wardsmen, but the borough's court had a greater range of business
especially in dealing with cases of debt and trespass between private
individuals and in functions laid on it by government.[28] There may have
been some reapportionment of work between the two courts in later
years, but this is impossible to check as the record of only a few lawday

[24] Misc. Je I/1, ff. 69v, 87Ar, 92r.
[25] cf. R.G.H.Whitty, *The Court of Taunton in the Sixteenth and Seventeenth Centuries* (Taunton,
1934), pp.51, 101. Whitty's discussion of those courts is very illuminating on a number of
points for comparison with Witney.
[26] Eccl. 1/86/4,5; and box 90, ff. 59, 81: lawday records for 1563, 1564, 1565.
[27] Eccl. 1/86/5; box 90, ff. 81r,v.
[28] cf. Whitty, *Taunton*, pp.81-114.

courts (those of the 1560s) has survived from the sixteenth century. It is noticeable that there are very few cases of breaches of the peace and minor boundary orders in the later borough courts; perhaps more of this work, if it was done, came into the lawday court or into the hands of the Justices of the Peace, whose records again do not survive.

That the lawday court remained important to the town is shown in its later history. The borough court did not survive long into the seventeenth century but the lawday court now called the court leet continued up to 1925.[29] The records preserved at Blenheim Palace for this court from 1649 to 1925 record elections of jurors for the King and presentments of offences such as failure to scour watercourses, the cutting down of trees, erecting stalls in the market place without licence and offences against regulations for weights and measures.[30] They also record the election of borough officers which in the sixteenth century had been the prerogative of the townsfolk's own court. There is only one record of a debt case in this court in 1653, however. It is evident that when the borough court disappeared in the seventeenth century some of its official business, though not the personal actions, was taken over into the lawday court which thereby had additional reason for survival.

The Borough Court in the Sixteenth and Seventeenth Centuries

In the sixteenth century, however, the borough court was flourishing perhaps more than ever before. The court books are the only ones of their kind for the court so that we cannot make a comparison with its business in earlier centuries: though the courts are mentioned in the bishop's account rolls in the Middle Ages there is not enough detail to judge the scale of their activities. Despite the setback of the Black Death and economic recession of the later Middle Ages, the town and its court with a securer basis in the wool trade may have been more prosperous and active than the surrounding countryside.[31] It was, however, the expanding economy and growing government interference in society which enabled the court to play such an important part in Witney's life in the sixteenth century. The court books below confirm the picture, suspected elsewhere, of the continuing vitality of certain small manorial and local courts in this period.[32]

[29] Blenheim Palace mun.; and information from Mr. J. Welsh, Clerk to Witney U.D.C. in 1973.
[30] Blenheim Palace mun. These are the records reported as being at Witney in the mid-nineteenth century and comprising 40 volumes: J.A. Giles, *History of Witney* (London, 1852), p.24. There are about 40 volumes at Blenheim relating to Witney manor and to the borough lawday or leet courts. The more interesting are described in Top. Oxon. d 215, and in W.J. Monk, *History of Witney* (Witney, 1894). Estreats and fines of the 1628 court are in D.D.Par. Witney, and Top. Oxon. d 211, ff. 95-7.
[31] See below, pp.liii–iv.
[32] cf. Whitty, *Taunton*, pp.120–21; and W.Holdsworth, *History of English Law*, i (7th ed., London, 1956), 137.

The government's exploitation of the court was the newest factor in the development of the borough court which in the sixteenth century went beyond its manorial origins and took on many of the functions imposed by the Tudor government on civil parishes and corporate towns. National legislation was often ambivalent, refering either to municipal authorities or to the parish.[33] The emphasis was increasingly on the parish but not immediately: in Banbury, for example, the town corporation was more important than the Vestry and in Witney the borough court administered the poor law until the seventeenth century.[34] The Witney Vestry appointed the churchwardens and surveyors of the highway but all other local officers served in the town court. There was no real competition between the two bodies, however, because the same people ran both. The churchwardens were present in the court on occasion and in 1599 the surveyors had their appointment confirmed there (i, ff. 257v, 267r; ii, f. 3v). In some ways the court had certain advantages in that it met more frequently than the Vestry, it had experience and was flexible enough to take on new functions whereas the later history of local government in England demonstrated the problems of government by Vestry.

Tudor legislation gave the town other duties too. The court appointed its leather and cloth searchers and supervised military equipment, registered the licensing of ale houses and enrolled apprentices. In the early 1600s like the Burford Court[35] it recorded the names of those liable for the subsidy and even distrained for its non-payment (ii, ff. 23v, 50r, 73r).

The new functions inevitably brought closer contact with the outside authority of the Justices of the Peace as against the older authority of the bishop. The record in the court books adds to what little is known of the sixteenth-century Oxfordshire Justices, since the Quarter Session records of the county only survive from 1687.[36] They appear in the court books as licensing authorities, regulating the ale houses and taverns of Witney, and presumably the constables presented their bills to them as they did in the later seventeenth century.

Despite this closer co-operation with the government, Witney borough still retained its independence from various kinds of interference. A rough note of this period concerning 'the liberties of Witney' maintained that the sheriff's bailiff should serve no writ upon any man within the borough but should deliver it to the bailiffs for serving. Likewise no summoner for the Church should serve any citation upon any person within the church or town only the vicar or his deputy. If they did so 'you may make him ette it for his so enterprysing against your liberties to brake the franchise'. If

[33] E.M.Leonard, The early history of English Poor Relief (Cambridge, 1900), p.56.
[34] V.C.H. Oxon. x.77; and below, p.xxv.
[35] R.H.Gretton, Burford Records (Oxford, 1920), pp.544-5.
[36] M.S.Gretton, Oxfordshire Justices of the Peace in the Seventeenth Century, O.R.S. xvi(1934), p.ix.

the royal Clerk of the Market came, it was permissible to let him sit and deliver his charge to a 'quest' but no verdict was to be given and no measure sold or fine taken 'for that apertayneth to your offise'. Any conviction to take up men had to be directed to the bailiffs or to the constable, and they need only take them to the other side of the borough 'for you nede goo no further'.[37]

Some in the town clearly wanted to formalize practice and procedure and purchase the town a charter of incorporation as in other towns. In 1626 when incorporation for towns was under discussion Mr John Clarke, clothier, bequeathed £6 13s. 4d. 'toward the obtaining of a corporation to the town of Witney', and in 1640 the Commissioners of Trade included Witney among the sixty chief clothing towns which would benefit by a grant of a corporation, but to no avail.[38] Trade was bad at this time and Witney men may have shared the view expressed at Bicester, likewise an unincorporated market town, that the freedom of such towns was their very attraction and their management less costly.[39] But by the end of the century, when they were again complaining as in 1693 to Quarter Sesssions of the 'deadness of trade' and the problem of the poor flocking into the town, opinion seems to have come round to the necessity of a 'more settled government' in the town. In 1670 they said it would preserve trade and keep out foreigners from it, and at last in 1711 with the incorporation of the Blanket Weavers Company they obtained what they hoped would be some form of protection and regulation of industry.[40]

The complaints of 1670 suggest that the borough court was no longer in existence by that date since, as Dr Plummer points out, there is no reference in the petition to any guild or form of control or government in the town. Various factors contributed to the decline of such local courts in the seventeenth century. There were problems in the cloth trade soon after 1610,[41] the last date for which we have entries in the Witney court books, and traders may not have found the court of much use in their difficulties. One of its chief services to them had been in the matter of small claims but already in the early 1600s the court books indicate that not many debt cases were being prosecuted successfully through the court. Debt collection was a general problem in Stuart England and other local courts connected with it likewise disappeared; the court at Banbury, for example,

[37] D.D.Par. Witney: undated but the writing and the interest in resisting the Clerk of the Market point to the late sixteenth or early seventeenth century. For a return of writs by the Witney bailiffs in 1446 see Cal. Fine 1445-52, p.27.
[38] Prob 11/151 21 Skynner; The Witney Blanket Industry, ed. A.Plummer (London, 1934), pp.12-13.
[39] V.C.H.Oxon. vi.37.
[40] O.R.O., Quarter Sessions, Epiphany 1693; Witney Blanket Industry, p.13.
[41] G.D.Ramsay, The Wiltshire Woollen Industry in the Sixteenth and Seventeenth Centuries (2nd ed., London, 1965), pp.71ff.

and the Taunton court, which had paralleled Witney so closely in its origins and business, while the Bristol Staple court, drawing on a similar region to Witney, declined and had fewer debt cases.[42]

A further reason for decline lay in the government's attitude to small local courts.[43] The Stuart government placed more emphasis for seeking out statutory offences on the Justices and Quarter Sessions, and it is relevant that there was a more settled Quarter Sessions with regular record keeping in Oxfordshire in the second half of the seventeenth century.

As at Taunton, however, there seem to be more local reasons for the decline of the Witney court, in the changes of lordship, when the bishops ceased to deal directly with the townsfolk through their stewards and the town bailiffs and leased the borough to an intermediary. In the late sixteenth century this may have been beneficial since there was a close connexion between the Witney lessee, Mr Stephen Brice and his uncle Richard Brice, the clerk of the borough court, but in the seventeenth century the new lessees were unsympathetic to the town court and its privileges. It is in the courts leet for the borough held for William Lenthall, Speaker of the House of Commons, that we first see the officers being sworn in the lawday court of 1654 and from 1661 they were elected in these courts, and we can presume that the town's own court had disappeared.[44] Interestingly enough, Lenthall was lord of Burford, which had also lost its borough court and privileges in the 1620s under an unsympathetic resident lord, Sir Laurence Tanfield.[45] Lenthall may have taken a similar view in dealing with his Witney burgesses. The townsfolk did not lose their rights without a protest, albeit belated. In 1742, perhaps inspired by a similar move at Burford, they prepared an affidavit challenging Lord Cornbury, the lessee, in his claim 'to use and enjoy . . . the franchise of holding . . . a court moot in and for the town and borough of Witney and to elect a jury . . . and to cause to administer the oaths taken by said bailiffs, constables and other annual officers elected'. By 1748, however, they had to drop their case which they had prepared for King's Bench and 'in the end they submitted and renounced'.[46] There was no further hope of reviving the Witney separate borough court.

The borough came under the influence of the Marlboroughs in 1751 like Woodstock and Oxford itself. The borough officers continued to be

[42] *V.C.H.Oxon.* x.77; Whitty, *Taunton*, p.118; E.E.Rich, *The Staple Court Books of Bristol*, Bristol Rec. Soc. v (1934), p.63; Holdsworth, i. 143; and below, p.xxxvii.
[43] Whitty, *Taunton*, p.122.
[44] Blenheim Palace mun., Witney court minute book, 1649–1710.
[45] *Burford Records*, pp.53ff.
[46] Ibid., pp.73–4; Blenheim Palace mun. Witney court book 1705–42, annexed paper; Top. Oxon. d 215, f.131; Monk, *Witney*, p.119.

elected in the lawday or leet court and the oath administered there until 1925. It was by no means an unusual history for a small borough. Many like it or indeed more important were under pressure from local gentry and aristocracy in the late seventeenth and eighteenth centuries and found it hard to maintain their independence.[47] Witney at least had the compensation of a new incorporated company where although the High Steward was, in the first instance, the local lord, Henry, Earl of Rochester, the actual conduct of the chief Witney interest, the regulation of the blanket industry, was in their own hands.[48]

The Court and its Officers

In the Middle Ages the borough court seems to have met on a Friday and this was the practice in the sixteenth century. The meeting place was the town hall, also called the guild hall, the predecessor of the present eighteenth-century town hall (i, ff. 57r, 65v, 142r). The court was technically a three weekly one (i, f. 217r) and met on average about once a month and rarely with more than a six-week interval throughout the seventy-year period of the court books. In a full year there could have been ten to twelve courts, but there are often fewer in the earlier years, presumably because of a lack of business.

The bailiffs presided and gave judgements with the assitance of the other officers and chief citizens present (i, ff. 165r, 248r). This was one reason why the court was so anxious that ex-officers and worthies should attend since they were needed to help reinforce the bailiffs' authority and there was no jury to hear cases. The bailiffs in later years were called the magistrates or the bench, or, with the chief officers, the masters of the borough, while others present were differentiated as the substantial men of the town or the commoners (i, ff. 183v, 192r, 248r; ii, f. 45r).

The fullest and chief sessions in the year were in October, since the officers of the court were elected and sworn in at the first Friday court after Michaelmas and it was usually at this court or the next that the tipplers were admitted and orders issued. Tudor courts of this kind always had a problem in compelling attendance and this is demonstrated at the other courts in the year. There was no general obligation to attend. The bellman or wardsmen gave notice of the courts but apparently only on the evening before (i, f. 286v; ii, f. 44r). Evidently this was not enough and, despite frequent threats and fines to try to compel past and present officers and even those supposed to attend for special purposes, like the ever-recalcitrant tipplers and bakers, it was often only the bailiffs,

---

[47] Blenheim Palace mun.; see *Crisis and Order in English Towns, 1500-1700*, ed. P.Clark and P.Slack (London, 1972), pp.24-5, 50-51.
[48] *Witney Blanket Industry*, p.19.

constables and sergeant who were there (i, ff. 57r, 86v, 135v, 142r; ii, f. 20r).

The officers were the most important element in the court. They fell into two groups. Some had come through from the medieval court: the two bailiffs, two constables, five wardsmen, two cardenars, two aletasters and the sergeant, of the list of 1539; and in 1542 the two chamberlains, who seem to belong to this group. In the two leather and two cloth searchers and two collectors for the poor, however, we can see the result of Tudor legislation for the regulation of industry and the poor. The virtual independence of the court from the bishop is indicated by the fact that the officers were elected and sworn in this court and did not appear in his lawday court until the following spring.

The names of the officers given in the court books show how far the government of the town was shared among various groups. The list of liberties emphasized the bailiffs' right to have the officers chosen and most officers were chosen in the court but the record rarely says how, save in the case of the chamberlains who were said to be chosen by the bailiffs with the consent of the benchers and the commoners (i, f. 192r). Election or nomination may have been in many cases a question of apportioning the duties to those willing to serve or with the appropriate skill. Some trade officers, such as the aletasters, cardenars, leather sealers and cloth searchers, were almost professional servants of the court and the same men served for a number of years, even though their appointment was recorded yearly. Oliver Ball, for example, who must have been a shoe-maker, was a leather sealer in the 1560s and 70s, Robert Kepe was aletaster from 1549 to 1563 and John Wylie, tailor, and Nicholas Gunne, clothier, were cloth searchers from 1573 to the 1590s. Such service to the court is well illustrated by the Maior family. William Maior appeared in the 1503 survey as sergeant for Witney[49] and a William Maior the younger, presumably his son, and Richard Maior, who may have been his grand-son, were sergeants mentioned in the court books between 1567 and 1608. William the younger, Nicholas and Richard Maior also occur in the books as aletasters, cardenars, wardsmen and collectors for the poor, while Richard was possibly the scribe for the court in the early 1600s.

Some officers, however, were changed each year and therefore more people were drawn into service for the court, as wardsmen, collectors of the poor, chamberlains and bailiffs. A man might serve twice as bailiff or even, like Thomas Taylor the tanner or Leonard Yate the clothier, serve seven or eight times, but it would not generally be in consecutive years. The posts of bailiff and chamberlain were evidently kept for the wealthiest and worthiest business men, but nonetheless were held by a number of such persons. There were some fifty-seven men who acted as bailiffs

[49] Eccl. 2/155648.

between 1539 and 1610; they came from thirty-seven families and involved most leading business and craftsmen: tanners like the Taylors, clothiers like the Yateses and Joneses, Rankells and Boxes, or mercers like the Daltons. There was a limited progression through the offices: constables and chamberlains often moved on to become bailiffs, whereas the wardsmen who were usually from the lower strata of small masters did not, usually, though even here you could sometimes find a future bailiff.

The work of these officers embraced all aspects of town life. The bailiffs were the chief officers and the defenders of the town's 'liberties' or rights against the officers of the Church or the Queen: in 1573 the ex-bailiffs were distrained before the Queen's court to answer for the price of the goods belonging to Thomas Vawse convicted of felony, which they had apparently claimed for the bishop's court.[50] In the Witney court they were the presiding officers, sitting usually together but sometimes singly or by deputy. They gave decisions, issued orders, imposed fines or amercements, allocated payments, examined apprentices, admitted tipplers, gave possessions of land and generally acted as the chief judicial and executive officers of the town as well as of the bishop, for whose rents and dues they were responsible.

The sergeant was the court's general officer and was called the sergeant of the mace, which was the bailiff's symbol of office.[51] He was responsible for collecting fines and distraining on property to enforce payment, but he also witnessed the grant of land in the court and the enrollment of apprentices, while in the 1570s he was involved with the collection of money for the poor (i, ff. 30v, 75r, 139r). His was not an appointment made in court and the names of only five sergeants occur in the court books. Presumably his close association from medieval times with the bishop's administration meant that he was chosen by the bishop.

The constables were technically the agents for keeping the peace in a local community and were detailed under Tudor law to supervise vagrants, apprentices, tipplers and other potential trouble-makers as well as seeing to the general maintenance of law and order and supporting other officers. Much of their work was administrative rather than judicial and although they appear in the courts perhaps more frequently than any other officer apart from the bailiff there is little information on what they were doing. They are found as witnesses to land transfers, and arresting strays within the town and in a case of suspected felony (e.g. i, ff. 10r, 30v, 83r, 339r). Their duties seem to overlap with the work which we find the wardsmen doing in court, a duplication of responsibility common in Tudor local government.

---

[50] Giles, *Witney*, appendix 1, from T.Madox, *Firma Burgi* (London, 1726).
[51] The eighteenth-century mace, inscribed with the bailiffs' names, was in Witney U.D.C. in 1973.

The wardsmen were the equivalent of the tithingmen of the manor or the aldermen of the greater towns and cities. Witney was divided into wards by the end of the thirteenth century and there were five by the time of these court books. Their bounds are not given at any period but the general location can be established, in part from the bounds of tenements mentioned in grants. Paternoster Ward was on the west side of Church Green and Market Place; East Ward on the east side of the same area and possibly taking in part of High St. as well; West Ward was on the west of High St. and took in Corn St.; Middle Ward most of High St.; and finally the ward beyond or beneath the bridge and the Windrush taking in West End (e.g. i, ff. 39v, 167r).[52] Wardsmen were generally responsible for presenting nuisances and offences in their wards both in the lawday and borough courts: offences against the assizes of bread and ale, rowdy houses, minor breaches of the peace, blockage of roads with mounds or dung heaps or wandering pigs. They often served in court as appraisers of goods taken by distraint and witnessed the land transfers in court for their individual wards (e.g. i, ff. 10r, 12r, 15v, 81v, 96r, 105v, 195r).

The town's finances were in the hands of at first two chamberlains, though from the 1570s there was apparently only one. Their appointment was recorded at infrequent intervals but they occur among the officers of the court from the early days of the court books in 1542 (i, ff. 11v, 87v). Witney borough had its own property, the town houses and the town close, all let at rents which were collected into the Chamber (i, ff. 82v, 169v). The chamberlains presented their accounts in court on a few occasions (i, f. 95v, 139r), and in 1563 their receipts amounted to £4 7s. 6d. (i, f. 87v) in the hands of various individuals. The sums were never large, under £5, and expenditure was small. One of the more interesting items and perhaps a major reason for presenting accounts was the bailiffs' expenditure on equipment for the muster, the military obligation demanded by the government from every vill: money on harness in 1542 and 1573 and a black corslett with furniture in 1581 (i, ff. 12r, 139r, 210r); in 1542 this was clearly connected with the returns of musters to government from all over the country.

Much of the supervisory work of the court officers was to maintain standards in the town industries and, in particular, to ensure good food and drink supplies. The ale tasters and the cardeners were two sets of officers of long standing, similar in some ways to the modern inspector of weights and measures and the public health inspectors, but chosen from local tradesmen. The ale tasters visited each brewer to taste his ale and see that it was 'good and wholesome', a vital task when there was no supplied clean water and ale and beer were the regular drink.

[52] For wards in 1751 see D.D.Par. Witney and Top. Oxon. d 212, pp.78ff. Giles, *Witney*, p.45, lists six wards in 19th-century Witney.

They also weighed bread (ii, f. 120r) and made presentments in court for baking too light. The cardenars' job was similar: to inspect the meat and fish offered for sale and see that it was fit for human consumption. (i, f. 12r).

From the mid–sixteenth century other officers appear in the court books. The leather searchers and sealers were elected in 1542 and made sporadic appearances in the court books until 1562, thereafter appearing regularly among the officers elected at the October court. This was presumably because of the statute of 1563 which laid down regulations for the tanning of leather. They had to mark properly tanned leather with a seal and search for and confiscate badly tanned hides.[53] The cloth searchers and sealers had similar duties. In 1602, for example, they were sworn for all narrow cloth, friezes, and all other cloth sold in the market (ii, f. 62r). Witney had its own seal for cloth sealing, as a result of government legislation, which since the late fifteenth century had attempted to move some of the responsibility for checking cloth from the royal official, the aulnager, to the cloth towns. In 1483 lead seals were to be made to seal cloth in every city or county where it was made, and faulty cloth was to be seized in towns by the mayors or bailiffs, who were to retain the third part for corporate use.[54] Presumably this was the seal mentioned on the first page of the court books in 1538. By the act of 1552 not only was every borough or town corporate to use its seal for cloth sealing but searchers and sealers were to be appointed to inspect the cloth and search premises.[55] The Witney cloth searchers are first recorded in the court book ten years later and there are several references to the seal being handed to them (i, ff. 199v, 208v). It is not clear whether both cloth and leather officers were new creations of this period in Witney, but their regular appearance in the October courts was undoubtedly the result of intensified government interest in trade and industry. The trade offences arising from these searches were not presented in the court books. The only reference is a memorandum in 1599 of the appearance of Peter Yate before the bailiffs in connexion with two cloths (i, f. 347v). In Wiltshire at this time the manufacturers of defective cloth appeared before Quarter Sessions and perhaps this was the case in Witney.[56]

The latest officers to appear in these books were the collectors for the poor who were 'elected and nominated' by the bailiffs for a year in 1583 at a December court and thereafter at irregular intervals at December courts up to 1608 in the same terms (i, ff. 226v; ii, f. 138r). They represent early attempts of the Tudors to deal with the increasing problems of poverty

---

[53] Act 5 Eliz.c.8.
[54] Act 1 Ric.III c.8. For the aulnager see Ramsay, *Wilts. Woollen Industry*, pp.52 ff.
[55] Act 5 and 6 Ed.VI c.6. There are drawings of Witney seals in the British Library Harleian Mss. 1095,f.2r and 1412,f.76r, and in Giles, *Witney*, opp. p.38.
[56] Ramsay, p.63.

and the poor: in 1536 an act ordered the mayors or head officers of every
city, borough and corporate town and the churchwardens or two others of
each parish to collect alms and provides boxes for them every Sunday,
Holy day and festival day for the relief of the impotent poor; by an act of
1552 they were to appoint two yearly collectors of the alms who were to
gather and distribute the money and to account quarterly to the mayor,
bailiffs or other officers: any surplus was to be put in the common chest of
the church. In 1563 there was to be a compulsory levy and in 1572 all
justices, mayors, sheriffs and bailiffs were to levy a reasonable rate and to
appoint collectors and overseers for the poor.[57]The sergeant in Witney
may have been responsible at first for collecting the money and the bailiffs
for the distribution, for in 1573 William Maior who was sergeant at this
period paid 2s. 10d. to the bailiff for the use of the poor and was
discharged in his annexed paper (i, f. 139r). Special collectors do not
appear in the records for another ten years, and no mention is made in
Witney of overseers of the poor until the 1630s, although they were
supposed to be drawn from the churchwardens and two to four other
substantial householders under the Poor Law Acts of 1597 and 1601.[58] The
dual responsibility of town and Vestry was seen in local wills where either
churchwardens or bailiffs could be directed to administer money for the
poor. In 1590, for example, Thomas Bishoppe alias Marten of Witney left
40s. for the poor to the bailiffs for them to distribute as they thought
useful.[59] Ashcombe's will of 1606 gave £10 to the poor to be distributed
by the bailiffs and various rents to the churchwardens to disburse to the
most distressed people of the town, and another £100 for a perpetual stock
for the yearly relief of the poor to the bailiffs who were to appoint two of
the best men of the town to administer it.[60] Details of some of these
arrangements appear in the second court book (ii, ff. 27v, 113r, 140r), and
one reason for the continued involvement of court and bailiffs in the poor
law was undoubtedly that they administered these charities. Although in
1597 the churchwardens' accounts show that the Vestry made an enquiry
into certain money left for the poor, it did not appoint the collectors for
the tithings until 1613 or for the borough until 1620. Similarly the bailiffs
were responsible for levying bastardy bonds until the mid-seventeenth
century when the Vestry replaced them in such documents.[61]

In the court books, therefore, it is the bailiffs who were made responsible in 1600 for the quarterly payments for the relief of a bastard child so
that the mother could discharge the town of its relief (ii, f. 26r), and in

[57] Acts, 27 Hen.VIII c.25; 5 and 6 Ed.VI c.2;2 and 3 P. and M. c.5; 5 Eliz.c.3; 14 Eliz.c.5.
[58] Churchwardens' accts.; Acts, 39 Eliz. c.3; 43 Eliz.c.2; and above. Overseers occur in
apprenticeship indentures in 1632 and in the churchwardens' accts. in 1681:D.D.Par.Witney.
[59] Wills Oxon.3/2/75.
[60] Copy in D.D.Par.Witney; Top. Oxon. d 210, p.80: and see O.R.O. T.C.III/iii.
[61] Churchwardens' accts. ff.23r,36r,43r; and bonds in D.D.Par.Witney.

1607 they took a bastardy bond to save the town the cost of maintaining an illegitimate child (ii, f. 121r). There is no record of rates being levied, but the poor men's box was mentioned frequently in wills from 1547 and in 1580 certain fines in court were to go to it (i, ff. 195v, 201v, 202r). The collectors accounted in court in 1605 and 1606 for the sums, 21s. 5½d. and 41s. 3d. respectively, remaining in the box (ii, ff. 111r, 118v), but the record is brief and the details on separate papers are lost. In 1596 a court entry concerning 'poor children part of the town charge' implies a problem but there was only one payment of 2s. 6d. to widow Jones for a child following it (i, f. 307r). The extent of poverty is better gauged from the wills, charities and the setting up of the County House of Correction in Witney, the Bridewell, in 1611.[62]

There was another official who appears only once in the court book. This was William Arden, clerk of the market, who gave orders for prices in 1552. He was not a local official: the local clerks of the market were perhaps the bailiffs in the sixteenth century and in the later seventeenth century two local clerks of the market were elected in the court leets. William of Arden or Ardern was the royal Clerk of the Market belonging to the Household, who periodically visited trading centres to check prices and to fine those who charged too much. His visits were usually not welcomed in towns, especially in the seventeenth century when the early Stuart government used the office to put pressure on local privilege: it is notable that the other mention of this officer in Witney is in the seventeenth-century list of liberties which insists on local rights.[63]

Finally, there is no mention of the method of appointment of two officers who were important for the calling and recording of the court. The bellman or town crier gave notice of the court beforehand (i, ff. 132r, 286v) and was perhaps appointed in the hundred court. The clerk of the court or town clerk was perhaps a nominee of the bailiffs and is discussed below as the scribe of the court.

The Business of the Court

For convenience the business of the court can be considered under various headings though no such division is made in the court book.

One of the chief reasons for the survival of manorial courts in Tudor and later times was the necessity to record the tranfer of copyhold land, the tenure which had emerged from the old villein tenure. There was copyhold land in Witney, according to the court book entries, in Corn Street, High Street, near Newlands Lane and Woodgreen and in West End beyond the bridge. It was not a great deal, but, such as it was, it was dealt

---

[62] Top. Oxon. d 211,f.88. We are indebted to Dr. D.M.Barratt for this reference
[63] *Cal. Pat. 1554-5*, p.349; cf. *L. & P. Hen.VIII*, xvi,1540-1, p.464. References were pointed out by Mr C.J.Kitching of P.R.O. See also above, p.xvii. For the office see *Agrarian History of England and Wales*, iv(ed. J.Thirsk, Cambridge, 1967), 578.

with in the borough court, where the bailiffs acted as the officers of the lord of the manor in accepting the surrender of the property from the previous tenant and granting it to the new one. It is termed a possession in the court books and was carried out in accordance with 'the custom of the borough', as for example, on 29 November 1602 when property was conveyed by a twig and a turf (ii, f. 60v). There were often other deeds and fines drawn up between the parties; these were not entered in the court books (ii, f. 134r; i, ff. 30v, 128v, 220r) but are occasionally found elsewhere.[64]

The town's own property was also granted in court, and in 1585 the bailiffs and inhabitants granted ground for houses to be built in Corn Street. One house was apparently by the Quarry at the western end; and another three were near Well Close (i, ff. 176r, 236r, 237r, 237v). These were part of the property in the town charity in the nineteenth century.[65]

It was largely through such local courts that control was kept in the sixteenth century over the food trades and public health and cleanliness. In Witney there was not the volume of orders or fines found in larger towns, but as elsewhere the most important regulations dealt with the food trades and reflect the policy of regulating prices in the interest of the poorer classes as well as maintaining the demarcation between tradesmen. Prices for the brewer, i.e. the wholesaler, to sell to the tippler, and for the tipplers and alesellers to sell on the premises or as 'off-licence' were fixed regularly by virtue of the right to the assize of ale (i, f. 51v). Bakers had to produce their loaves for weighing and were not, for example, allowed to sell more than 13 to the dozen. There were attempts to protect tradesmen: only licenced victuallers could sell bread and ale, i.e. the common bakers and brewers (i, ff. 49r, 88r, 151v); tipplers were not to bake bread or sell bread or cakes to their customers or horse bread, which was made of beans and bran and was unfit for human consumption, nor were they to brew ale to sell without a brewer's licence. The court made special mention of a brewer to brew for the poor, presumably providing a cheaper grade of ale (i, f. 27r).

According to the list of liberties, the bailiffs and burgesses were to approve of anyone setting up in an occupation or taking up a shop. There is one case in court of their allowing a Cirencester haberdasher to take over a piece of stall ground if no local man wanted it (i, f. 307v). There are, however, very few shop regulations recorded. In 1554 the butchers were ordered to remove their stalls off the street except on market days, and it may be this problem that in 1555 led to the unanimous demand of bailiffs and inhabitants for the removal of a local butcher's shop 'found to be a great annoyance' (i, ff. 51r, 55v). In the interests of the Church the

[64] D.D.Par. Witney. Fines were levied in the Court of Common Pleas.
[65] Bodl. Tithe award 1840;O.R.O. TC III.

inhabitants were forbidden in 1580 to keep their shop doors or windows open on the Sabbath during service (i, f. 195v).

There is no detail in the court books about the two Witney fairs held each year or about the markets, although the Chantry Commissioners of 1546 described Witney as a great market town and the market was held regularly from the Middle Ages to modern times on Thursdays.[66] We are only given some insight by the regulations against pigs in the streets on market days (i, f. 165r) and in the enrolments of sales of horses or cattle: in 1608, for example, a grey ambling mare was sold in the market and the sale and vouchees were recorded in the court book (ii, f. 135r). A number of the debt cases before the court must also have arisen from market day transactions.

Every Tudor town had its quota of obstructions and nuisances in its streets and it was traditionally the job of the local court to try to clear them. The Witney court made orders for dungheaps and mounds and blocks to be removed from the streets and attempted to control the pigs and dogs wandering in the streets as was common in any town (i, f. 46v). Pigs were supposed to be ringed through the nose to stop them rooting in the roads; mastiffs had to be muzzled and bitches on heat, or 'assaulte', were to be kept indoors, while stray horses and cattle were to be impounded (i, ff. 38r, 148v).

Other risks of Tudor life appear in the books. The fear of fire led to the order of 1582 whereby tubs of water were to be set outside every householder's door (i, f. 214r). The risk of plague led to the order of 1593 whereby no victualler or innholder was to lodge persons carrying infection from Burford, Eynsham or Abingdon (i, f. 291r). The town seems to have escaped lightly that time but in 1597 the plague struck again and the church register records many dead from it, some of them familiar names from the court books. The regulations against undertenants and lodgers indicate the contemporary worry about the poor and vagrant and the fear of the townsfolk that they might have to support them (i, ff. 98r, 146r); in 1574, for example, undertenants who had not lived in the town for a year were to be expelled, perhaps because two tenants had been taken the year before for breaking hedges (i, ff. 137v, 146r).

The bailiffs played an important role in running the various charitable bequests made by local residents. The first mentioned in the court books was a mere 30s. given to the town for the use of poor artificers and craftsmen by Mr John Atwell, described variously as a person or parson of Cornwall or Devon (ii, ff. 27v, 140r). The bailiffs were to hold this sum and to deliver it to their successors for ever. With others, they were given the responsibility of managing the very much more substantial bequest of

---

[66] *Oxfordshire Chantry Certificates*, ed. Rose Graham, O.R.S.i (1919), 48; *Par.Coll.* p.342; S.Lewis, *Topographical Dictionary* (London, 1849).

George Tomson, a Bampton yeoman. Tomson died in 1603, seised of moveable property valued at £951. In his will he left £30 to the poor of Burford, £44 to the poor of Bampton, Lew and Weald, and £40 to the poor of Witney. The will specified that the money was to be delivered to the bailiffs and the constable of Hailey and six others chosen at a public assembly of the parishioners held at the court. These 'trustees' were to lease out £10 yearly to be divided among four young 'occupiers' or beginners, that is young craftsmen of tradesmen, for a year at a time.[67] This was done and the yearly workings of the charity are recorded in the second court book (ii, f. 117r). Lastly, and most substantial of all, was Richard Ascombe's money. Ascombe or Ashcombe was a gentleman of Curbridge who in 1606 left £100 and a house to the poor of Witney.[68] The charity was the subject of a decree by the Lord Chancellor and the rent of the house and the interest on the £100 were delivered to the bailiffs, but how they employed the money is not specified here.[69] Thus, in all, the court helped administer charities worth over £140, a substantial sum for a small up-country town and a responsibility for the bailiffs.

Minor breaches of the peace could be brought before the borough court, but only a few cases of petty assault are recorded, which may reflect the activity of other courts rather than a peaceful society in Witney. The borough court played an essential part in the regulating of alehouses which were regarded and treated by the government as potential centres of trouble and even sedition. From the late fifteenth century the Justices were empowered to reduce their numbers; in 1541 they could search for unlawful games and gamesters in the alehouses; and in 1552 when a general reformation of alehouses was envisaged it was laid down that two Justices should licence every alehouse.[70] The court books reflect this anxiety. The bailiffs acted closely with the Justices, as agents of the government. The Witney tippler was obliged not only to appear before the Justices in their informal or petty sessions (i, f. 286r), but also to appear in the borough court with his licence and his sureties to be admitted by the bailiffs. The record of their court appearance begins in 1547, when all tipplers were to bring sureties for good order in their houses. Recognizances are mentioned in 1563 and in 1569 the appointment of two sureties was said to be done 'according to the statute' (i, ff. 21v, 86v, 115r). The sureties were bound in a certain sum: in 1582 a tippler was admitted whose sureties were bound in £5 to be paid to the bailiffs for the use of the Queen (i, f. 218r). The Justices of the Peace who licenced the tipplers are named in the court books from 1592 (i, f. 286r), and it is

[67] Wills Oxon. 191,f.414r.
[68] See above; and *Par.Coll.*, p.342.
[69] For decrees and cases about the charities in the late 17th century see D.D.Par.Witney; and Top. Oxon. d 211,ff.132-36v.
[70] Acts, 27 Hen.VIII c.25; 33 Hen.VIII c.9; 5 and 6 Ed.VI c.25.

evident that the process of control was a joint concern.[71] In 1584 the bailiffs refused to admit tipplers unless they purchased and produced a licence from the Justices of the Peace. In 1595 the justices charged that only alehouses allowed by the bailiffs should operate and in 1596 sent a warrant to the bailiffs for the closing of certain ones (i, ff. 232r, 298v, 312r). The number of tipplers appointed in the court varied according to the number who could be rounded up to appear. It was often about a dozen, but at peak periods it could be twenty as in 1579, a number approached only in 1598 and 1605 when there were eighteen (i, ff. 192v, 343r; ii, f. 110v). The policing of alehouses fell to the court. In 1567 the court forbade gaming in alehouses, and it was writen into apprenticeship records that the apprentice should not frequent alehouses or play illegal games (i, ff. 107r, 341v). Keeping an unruly house was an offence presented at lawday courts in 1563; in 1566 an alehouse keeper lost his licence temporarily for lodging evil disposed persons without the knowledge of the officers (i, f. 98r); and there was evidently a round-up of offenders in 1607 when eleven offenders were presented for misdemeanours at four alehouses (ii, f. 126r).

There are 105 covenanted servants in the court books, most of them young apprentices being bound for the first time with a few journeymen and other servants. Witney was not a chartered town, and was not obliged to record all indentures, but government legislation probably encouraged the practice: the Weaver's Act of 1555 required that no one should weave woollen cloth unless they had served a seven years' apprenticeship and the great Statute of Artificers of 1563 attempted to regulate apprenticeship and confine industry to the towns.[72] The Witney enrolments began in 1560. Earlier apprentices are seen in local wills: in 1547, for example, John Boxe provided for his son to be apprenticed to a local clothier until he was twenty to learn weaving, and in 1560 the most noted clothier of the town, Walter Jones, left 40s. to each of his apprentices dwelling with him.[73] The first covenants in the court book were themselves retrospective, one of them to 1558 (i, f. 76v), and refer to an already established 'custom of the borough', while there is an unexplained reference in 1571 to an agreement being recorded earlier in a Weaver's Court Book (i, f. 128r). This may mean that there was some other method of recording indentures in Witney or perhaps elsewhere, but there is no further evidence for this. There is no record of a weaver's guild in Witney, nor does anything else in the court book suggest that some agreements were recorded after 1560 in one place and some in another.

This impression is reinforced by the fact that the enrolments in the borough court were mainly for broadweavers' servants, and two-thirds of

---

[71] See Gretton, *Oxon. Justices*, pp.xxviii ff. for examples of licensing.
[72] Acts, 2 and 3 P. and M. c.11; 5 Eliz. c.4. By this last act enrolment was necessary in market towns as well for apprentices to mercantile trade, i.e. drapers, mercers and clothiers.
[73] Wills Oxon. 179, f.232v; Prob 11/44 20 Loftes.

the covenants were for the cloth industry, i.e. fifty-six to broadweavers, six to clothiers, three or four to tuckers, and one to a dyer. The pressure to enrol was not solely on broadweavers. Among the first entries there is a covenant between a shoemaker and his servant for which at that stage there was no legal compulsion (i, f. 77r). In all there were twelve covenants with shoemakers, four with tailors, two with rough masons, and single ones with a butcher, baker, cooper, chandler, currier, and bone lacemaker. There are only two domestic servants but local wills show many more in Witney households. Two enrolments only were with artisans outside the town. The custom of the borough is not referred to after 1563 perhaps because the Artificer's Act enjoined London custom.

It is clear that the enrolments did not represent all the covenanted servants in the town over 50 years. A small Oxfordshire town could not, of course, be expected to have the number of apprentices found in Worcester in the sixteenth century, where as a group apprentices are said to have run 'into hundreds at any one time' and the annual totals of enrolments could be sixty to a hundred; nor could it be compared with Bristol which had 1450 apprentices in the decade 1532 to 1542, or even with Southampton with a more modest hundred enrolments a decade in the early seventeenth century.[74] Witney, though, was a flourishing town with many small family businesses. This may partly explain the discrepancy since a son was able to serve with his own father without a formal indenture. It is possible, too, that the court and its officers were not always active in enforcing enrolment in those years when there are none in the court books, as in the late 1560s and 70s. There was more pressure generally in the early seventeenth century.[75] At Witney whereas between 1560 and 1598 the first court book records only forty-seven enrolments, there were a further fifty-two in the second volume for the ten years between 1599 and 1609. The increase may reflect the court's renewed activity and government pressure, but also perhaps the need to acquire servants after the deaths from plague in the 1590s.

The enrolments show someting of the process of indenture and the terms, although there is a variation in the amount of detail given, which is generally more in later years. The agreements did not have to be brought into open court, but could be enrolled at other times. A number were purely formal enrolments of accomplished fact (i, f. 159r). Late enrolment, after the apprenticeship had been engaged in for over a year, is found in about 10 per cent of the cases. They were perhaps made because of a demand for evidence of an apprentice's service or a query about the presence of out-

[74] A.D.Dyer, *The City of Worcester in the Sixteenth Century* (Leicester, 1973), p.154; *A Calendar of Southampton Apprenticeship Registers, 1609 to 1740*, ed. A.J.Willis (with introduction by A.L.Merson), Southampton Records 12 (1968), 15; *Calendar of Bristol Apprentice Books, 1532 to 1565*, pt i, 1532-42, ed. D.Hollis, Bristol Record Soc. xiv (1949).
[75] cf. *Southampton Regs.* p.xiii; Ramsay, *Wilts. Woollen Industry*, p.61.

siders in the town. Most others were retrospective only for a few weeks, and about a quarter were for a future date, again usually only a few weeks away. The change in enrolment in the early 1600s is shown by the fact that more then were for a future date and thirteen covenants date from the 'present', i.e. the date of enrolment.

Enrolments, however, involved more than a formal record. The covenant on p.83 (i, f. 178r) has been left in fuller detail to show the major elements involved. These were: appearance in court; consent of the servant and of his parent or guardian; examination of the servant by the bailiffs; the payment of covenant pence by the master to bind him and which in other covenants is clearly paid in court; the servant's covenant to be a covenanted servant, i.e. bound, and to dwell with and serve his master as a servant; the master's covenant to teach and maintain and at the end of the term of years to give him double apparel and generally, though not in the covenant on p.83, wages; on p.83 the exceptional extra is the payment of 40s. to the master.

It is clear, therefore, that the young apprentice had to appear in court or before the bailiffs and assent freely: in the second book there are more enrolments out of court but one or other of the bailiffs is usually said to examine the servant. The covenant on p.83 speaks of the sealing and signing of the covenant presumably of the original but on occasions both parties signed or made their mark in the book and the court officials witnessed the agreement: the implication is that the document was drawn up before them as well as enrolled or indeed that the court record was perhaps the only document (i, ff. 253r, 319r). Parties under twenty-one could not be sued for breach of covenant and so an apprentice was bound by his father, or, if he were dead, which was not uncommon in apprenticeship records, he was bound by his nearest relative, the mother (ii, f. 138v) or step-father, or the executors of the father's will (i, f. 245r). Some boys were under the commonly accepted age of 14, one was bound when he was eleven and the period of apprenticeship in his case seems to have been correspondingly lengthened to ten years, which would have released him at the age of twenty one (i, f. 319r,v). The age of the boys is not given often enough for us to see if twenty one was the customary age in Witney for the end of the term, as it was in Southampton in the seventeenth century, rather than the statutory age of twenty four. It is evident that it was not easy to impose standard practices in the indentures. The length of apprenticeship was supposed to be seven years, but only twenty-four covenants in the court books were for that period and fifteen of these were from after 1600, when this practice was becoming accepted elsewhere.[76] Often the term of eight years was favoured and there were cases of four,

---

[76] See *Southampton Regs.*; and J.S.Morrill in *Archives*, xii (1976), 194, review of *Kingston upon Thames Register of Apprentices 1563-1713*, ed. A.Daly, Surrey Rec. Soc. xxviii (1974).

five, six, nine and eleven years (i, ff. 76v, 77v, 78r; ii, 20v). The variation can be accounted for in some instances, as in the four transfers of apprenticeships from one master to another, or for the three journeymen whom William Clempson took into his shoemaking business in the 1580s (i, ff. 244r, 244v, 253r). Otherwise the Witney record confirms the difficulty of imposing regulations on tradesmen.

The terms of the covenants were the customary ones found in other towns. The young apprentice was expected to live with his master and be provided with food, bedding and clothing and adequate care in sickness and health (i, f. 155r). The details are rather fuller in later covenants but this may reflect not so much a change in the covenant as in the practice of the recording clerk since similar injunctions are found in 14th century London indentures.[77] However, towards the end of the century the details put down in the enrolments seem to reflect certain Tudor preoccupations in emphasizing the interests of the master and the authorities. In 1598 a lengthy list of what the apprentice must not do said that he was not to marry, not to frequent alehouses or taverns, except about his master's business, nor to play his master's goods at unlawful games, later defined as dice and cards. He was to eschew deceit, falsehood and fornication and, as a positive injunction, he was to keep his master's secrets 'lawful and honest' (i, f. 341v). The covenant payment of 1d. a year was perhaps a local peculiarity; it has not been noticed elsewhere or indeed in later Witney indentures. It was paid in court before the bailiffs by the master to the servant to bind him as 'earnest money'. On p.171 (ii, f. 34r) indeed it was received 'in earnest according to the statute herein provided', but there is no national legislation enjoining this and it was probably a town custom. Wages during service were not usual though some covenants specified the payment of one or more pence a quarter, sometimes increasing as the apprenticeship progressed (i, f. 78r). One agreement, where the apprentice was to be paid 30s. for the first four years and £3 for the last three, was quite exceptional (i, f. 337v), and was probably to be explained by the fact that the last two years at least were to follow his apprenticeship. At the end of his term, however, the servant was given a sum of 'wages' perhaps to help set him up. The usual amount was 26s. 8d., a sum which can be related to a journeyman's wage for a year.[78] A rough mason's servant, however, in 1572 was to be given only 10s., but tools as well, i.e. a trowel, stone hammer, plumb rule and other working tools (i, f. 132v; cf. 77r, 253r). The custom of the borough, as in other towns, was also to give the covenanted servant two suits at the end of his term, one for Holy Days and one for working days, 'fit for a journeyman of that occupation': the quality of the clothes was prescribed by Tudor sumptuary laws. In Witney

[77] S.Thrupp, *The Merchant Class of Medieval London* (Chicago, 1962 ed.) p.169.
[78] See rates in *V.C.H.Wilts.* iv.150.

in 1581 a servant covenanted to a currier was to receive a jerkin and breeches of cheaper grey freize and two shirts for working days and a locram shirt and a jerkin of medley russet for Holy Days, with 'the like nether stockings, good shoes, a seemly fair doublet and a felt hat' (i, f. 204v).

The name of the father is recorded in the court book enrolment, but there is no note of the statutory requirement of his wealth, i.e. the ruling that merchants and weavers in non-corporate towns could only take apprentices whose fathers owned freehold estates worth at least £3 a year. There is, too, no information about the payment of premiums which are in any case entered on the back of original indentures or in a separate bond in seventeenth century examples in the parish chest. In fact there was no obligation for craftsmen to demand a premium and it may be that it was not asked for from a local man's son. Payment towards keep in some instances, probably because the father was dead, is suggested by the provision on p. 83 in 1578 that 40s. 'further consideration' be paid, but 20s. of it was to be returned if the master died within a year. In another agreement, the master was given £5 of the dead father's goods to bring the boy up and train him, and at the end of the eleven years the boy was to receive back 30s. from the £5 as well, apparently, as 40s. wages (i, 309r, v).

It is not clear what pressure the court itself could put on parties either to enroll or to observe the terms, other than by offering them the safeguard of the court book record. The parties could sue in court but as there were only a few instances in the court cases of such action, the necessity to do so seems to have arisen infrequently (i, ff. 128r, 157r, 190r, 195v).

The record also gives the place and occupation of the father and shows that both the geographical and social origins of the apprentices and the few journeymen were typical of a country town in being drawn predominantly from local craftsmen and tradesmen; maps I and II show the places of origin of these indentured servants. Over half [58] were sons of Witney men being indentured to another townsman or in a few instances to their own parent (i, ff. 106r, 146r, 157v). Most of the others came from nearby villages within the county and only a dozen from outside, from neigh-bouring counties of Gloucestershire, Berkshire, Northamptonshire and Buckinghamshire. Business connexions could explain the presence of some of the boys from outside the county for nine of them were bound to broadweavers/clothiers, men who travelled and had these links like Harry Jones and John Clarke. There was evidently a business or family connexion involved when Clarke, for example, took Richard Makepeace of Chipping Warden in 1595: the last entry in the first court book records a £50 debt owed by Walter Clarke and George Makepeace to John Clarke (i, ff. 300v, 348v). In another case the relationship is clearer when an uncle by marriage, Peter Rankell, clothier, took his wife's nephew from Reading as apprentice (ii, f. 33r). The son of the minister of Gillingham, Dorset, came from further afield but his father was dead and the trade of mercer and bone-lacemaker was evidently considered respectable enough by his uncle, another minister who bound him (i, f. 245r). There were only four clergy binding their sons or the one daughter mentioned, Alice, daughter of the Witney clerk, Edward Fluraunc (ii, f. 74v). Seven apprentices came from farming families, four had fathers who were labourers, but the rest were from craft or trade.

It is perhaps curious that so few came from agriculture, when at Bristol in the 1530s and at Southampton as late as the 1610s there was a high proportion of farmers' sons enrolled. It is hardly likely that the restrictive clauses of the Statute of Artificers of 1563, debarring all save sons of townsmen or of forty-shilling freeholders from apprenticeship to most crafts, would inhibit Witney men more than anybody else; the reason may be that their own sons could in fact provide the boys needed without drawing greatly on the countryside. In general, from these few figures for apprenticeships it seems that Witney did not attract apprentices from a wide area and in this respect is unlike not only towns with a 'national' pull, such as its own county town of Oxford or the nearby regional centre of Bristol but also unlike small centres near London, i.e. the Kent towns and Kingston on Thames, all of which have been shown to draw apprentices from quite distant places.[79] Like some of the East Anglian towns which have been studied, Witney's region was very localized, effectively to within eight to twenty miles.

Much of the court's popularity arose from its usefulness as a court where townsfolk could sue for small personal claims. Small debts have always been difficult and expensive to recover and there have been many experiments over the centuries with county, manor and special merchant and staple courts in the Middle Ages and later with local Courts of Request in the seventeenth and eighteenth centuries, new County Courts in the nineteenth and experimental small claim courts in the twentieth century.[80] In the sixteenth century the Witney businessman was served by his own borough court, which offered a cheap and fairly speedy service. The minor courts of the county, borough and manor became courts for such business when the Statute of Gloucester in 1278 forbade the central courts to take cognizance of trespasses under 40s.[81] By the sixteenth

---

[79] cf. J.Patten, 'Patterns of migration and movement of labour to three pre-industrial East Anglian towns', *Journal of Historical Geography*, 2 (1976); and refs. above for Southampton, Bristol and Kingston. Oxford's apprentices came from 23 counties: Oxford City Records, Mayor's court, A.5.3 *passim*.
[80] See H.Smith, 'The resurgent County Court in Victorian Britain', *American Journal of Legal History*, 1969; H.D.Winder, 'The Court of Requests', *Law Quarterly Review*, lii (1936); *Cheshire and Fifoot's Law of Contract* (9th ed., ed. M.P. Furmston, London, 1976). pp.3-12.
[81] Act 6 Ed.I c.8.

century the sheriff's county court apparently no longer met in Oxfordshire
and the hundred courts were held too infrequently to be useful for debt
cases. Bampton hundred court, indeed, is mentioned in the court books as
a court where cases were heard (i, ff. 110v, 277v), but the bishop's
hundred or lawday court for Witney borough did not deal with debt and
there are only a few cases in his hundred courts for the tithings.[82]
Oxfordshire businessmen had to look to town courts and there were
courts dealing with debts in Burford, Banbury, Witney, Woodstock and
in Oxford which had both the mayor's court and the Chancellor's court.[83]

The sum of 40s. was a sizeable one, taken as equivalent to £20 in the
nineteenth century and £80 to £100 in the mid-twentieth century;[84] in the
sixteenth century it must be considered against a wage rate of some £2 to
£3 a year for a chief craftsman or tradesman in neighbouring Wiltshire and
the modest wealth shown in inventories.[85] Most claims in the Witney
court were for well under the 40s. maximum, more than half for 10s. and
under. One twelfth of the claims, some 140 cases, were for 30s. to 39s.
11d. with about half of these for the maximum of 39s. to 39s. 11d.
Because of the cost of sueing in the central court or assizes, suitors could
be tempted to try to split a larger debt into several parts and bring it to a
local court, even though such practice was in fact forbidden and laid the
case open to a writ of transfer.[86] There seems to be some two dozen split
debts in the Witney court but taken over the years they do not impair its
essential character as a small claim court.

There were about one hundred cases a decade in the first thirty years of
the court books but from the 1560s they increased to 300 a decade for the
last forty years.[87] In all there were about 1,700 plaints recorded in the
books and about £1,200 was sought through the court. A conservative
estimate would be that a quarter of the money, about £328, was recovered, assuming that the awards, orders and agreements were carried
out.[88] This can be considered against an estimate that in the
mid-nineteenth century about half the total amount claimed through the
new County courts, likewise small claim courts, was recovered.[89] There

[82] e.g. Misc. Je I/1, ff.42v,60v.

[83] Halsbury, *Laws of England*, x (4th ed., London, 1975), 467ff.; Oxford City Records, court
books; Bodl. University archives; *Burford Records*, pp.523–46. See also M.Underwood, 'The
structure and operation of the Oxford Chancellor's court from the sixteenth to the early
eighteenth century', *Journal of the Society of Archivists*, April 1978.

[84] Smith, 'Resurgent County Court', p.128, fn.9; Halsbury, *Laws* (3rd ed. 1956), p.506 note.

[85] *V.C.H.Wilts*.iv. *150*.

[86] G.Jacob, *Compleat Court Keeper; or Land Steward's Assistant* (London, 1713), p.219.

[87] cf. the 70 to 80 cases in 1595 and 1596 in Bristol and Burford: Rich, *Staple Court of Bristol*,
pp.173–99; *Burford Records*, pp.523–46.

[88] We are indebted to Mrs L.Smith of Dunedin for help with calculations. The figures have
been rounded up.

[89] Smith, 'Resurgent County Court', p.128.

are besides this a number of cases in the Witney books where there is no record of the outcome of the case. The claim may have been withdrawn or it is conceivable that sometimes the threat of court action was sufficient to lead to payment out of court, as in 1593 when Christopher Bancroft withdrew his claim for 21s. when he was paid 20s. without further court action (i, f. 289r). It is noteworthy that most information on the course of cases comes from the 1560s to the 1590s when there were active and careful clerks of the court. For example, in 1576 there were thirty-three actions with notes on the outcome for twenty-three, whereas in 1606 there is only information on the outcome of one of the eleven cases. The lack of comment perhaps also reflected the difficulty the court found in securing action, a problem which would have contributed to its demise.

Cases could be transferred to a higher court because the borough court was not a royal court and therefore not a court of record.[90] As there is only one case of transfer (i, f. 190v) to a higher court recorded, in contrast to the tithings' court,[91] its judgements were perhaps thought to be as satisfactory as could be expected for the time and price.

The vast majority of cases were for straightforward debt in a fixed sum, and other actions were infrequent.[92] Detinue (twenty cases) went closely with debt as the wrongful withholding of goods and money, as when William Bradshawe of Curbridge accused George Dey of detaining a calf and certain money (i, f. 179v). Trespass (twenty-three cases) and in two instances trespass on the case, or special trespass, was pleaded for damage actually done, as when a broadweaver killed a pig with his cart (i, f. 137r) or else for damages alleged through the withholding of goods or money. It appeared sometimes as a counter action to a debt case (i, f. 118r). It was difficult in medieval courts to sue for breach of promise but there is one case of covenant broken in 1552 (i, f. 36r), and nine cases of assumpsit between 1574 and 1599, an action involving the assumption that a promise or covenant has been broken. Its appearance reflects the fact that this promissory action was being developed in the higher courts at this time. It was suitable in the Witney court when action was brought against a pledge and in 1586 it was pleaded by a joiner of Bristol in his suit against a tailor of Witney who had stood pledge to his debtor (i, f. 243r; cf. f. 239r). On another occasion it was used by a pledge against his principal because he had been distrained for the debt (i, f. 198r). Two other actions appeared only late in the court books. There were nine cases of fugitive, i.e. debt where one of the parties has fled, brought between 1597 and 1604, although action of debt against fugitives occurred on a number of occasions earlier. Actions of account come only in the second book, where

[90] G.Jacob, *A New Law Dictionary* (London, 1782), under court.
[91] e.g. Misc. Je I/1, ff. 35r, v, 37v, 46v.
[92] Useful descriptions of actions are found in Jacob, *Law Dict.*; A.W.B.Simpson, *A History of the Common Law of Contract; the Rise of the Action of Assumpsit* (Oxford, 1975).

there are eleven cases, all occurring in the four years between 1599 and 1602. Several were to claim payment of wages for service while one was for six and a half stones of tallow and another for spoiling a coverlet (ii, ff. 28r, 41v, 56r). Finally there is one stray case of maintenance, in fact a criminal offence since the fourteenth century and directed against unlawful influence in a law suit; it was pleaded in 1564 by Anthony Larden, a notorious 'barrator' in the court (i, f. 90r).

The places of origin of the suitors are shown on Maps II and III. In most cases either one or both parties was from Witney itself and only six per cent of cases had no apparent Witney interest. Nonetheless 21 per cent of people involved were outsiders and they took part in the cases from the early years of the court books (i, ff. 4r, 6v). They came predominantly from Witney's rural area in Bampton and Chadlington hundreds, from the Wychwood forest area to the north up to Charlbury and the Cotswold village of Chipping Norton. They also came from the neighbouring villages in the Cotswold area of Gloucestershire, from Gloucester itself and from the Berkshire and Wiltshire villages along the Thames valley from Abingdon to Cricklade. In the east of Oxfordshire only Oxford and on single occasions Thame and Islip (in the person of a chapman) occured in the cases: Witney's ties with the west are clear. Over the years a few cases involved people from other counties nearby, i.e. from Buckinghamshire, Hertfordshire, Northamptonshire and Warwickshire and from London; and on single occasions from Bristol and places in Somerset, Cambridgeshire, Herefordshire, Worcestershire, Staffordshire and even from Ambleside in Westmoreland. They were not, however, a regular feature and the court's role is clear from the cases: it served a local borough and market town and its hinterland.

Apart from being brought into court themselves, outsiders evidently found the court useful and they sued in it more frequently as the century went on. The local farmer and wool supplier in Cogges, Richard Bryan, for instance, made great use of the court and between 1577 and 1588 sued twenty Witney craftsmen and traders in it (i, ff. 168v *et seq.*).[93] Traders from the other market towns of Eynsham, Burford, Bampton and Chipping Norton feature frequently, either being sued or, like the Chipping Norton mercer, Thomas Cornish, in 1607 to 1608, using the court to collect debts (ii, ff. 119v *et seq.*).

Another use of the court is seen in the 104 cases between outsiders only. The first instance of this was in 1556 when the vicar of Shilton sued Nicholas Bladon of South Leigh (i, f. 64r). The practice became more popular towards the end of the century and two thirds of such cases come from the last twenty years between 1590 and 1609. Family connexions may sometimes explain this, as with Richard Clempson who had property

[93] For him see also below, p.lxxvii.

both in Witney and Abingdon[94] or the Cornishes of Chipping Norton and Witney, but it must have been the convenience and cheapness of the court which brought in cases, for example of a Charlbury butcher against a Spelsbury baker or when a Burford dyer prosecuted Mrs Anne Dormer of Farthinghoe in Northamptonshire or a Herefordshire husbandman sued a Chimney yeoman (i, ff. 158v, 206v; ii, f. 143v).

The parties were predominantly from business and trade, with some local farmers. The upper class and gentry from nearby, the Wenmans of Witney Park and Caswell, the Snapes of Standlake, the Untons of Bruern and Anthony Ashfield of Shipton,[95] came into court seeking debts or owing money to local tradesmen. Sir John Harrington brought cases in 1584 against three broadweavers, a tinker, tailor and carpenter, all of Witney, and against another tailor in 1586 (i, ff. 231r, 243v). This group makes up, however, only one per cent of the cases. At the other end of the social scale labourers involved in cases were equally few, though they appeared from Witney and from neighbouring villages (e.g. i, ff. 121v, 177r, 202v, 250r).

Perhaps the most tantalizing thing about the court books is that often they give little or no detail as to why the actions were brought. Some cases were said to concern the payment of wages and covenants, other were claims for rent or when the court officers sued for payment of amercements, and once for money due to a charity (i, ff. 157r, 190r, 274r, 323v; ii, f. 117v). Personal concerns are seen in the claim for money due on the date of a marriage or for the nursing and keeping of a child (i, ff. 152v, 279r). When many of the parties were in business or a craft it is tempting to supose that the cases involved their occupation, as we are told in the two cases over payment for looms and another over the hire of one (i, ff. 93v, 261v; ii, f. 40v). After 1571 when the trades of the parties were regularly given it is perhaps permissible to speculate that business reasons may have led a clothier to sue a flockman or have brought dyers and broadweavers into court or a quarrier and a slater, a tanner and a butcher and similar apparent trade connexions (i, ff. 165r, 190v, 232v, 233r, 254v).

The Court's Procedure in Personal Actions

Contemporary law books had elaborate rules for the conduct of cases, but little of this appeared in detail in the Witney record, where the clerk entered up only the briefest information. Fortunately for most of the period they adopted the practice of grouping everything about the case with the first entry of it or in the margin alongside. It is usually only necessary to search through subsequent courts for the cases up to 1557 and

---

[94] Prob 11/99 32 Montague; and see below, p.lxxxiv.
[95] For his activities as a wool patentee see P.J.Bowden, *The Wool Trade in Tudor and Stuart England* (London, 1962), pp.128, 129.

in the 1600s. As a rule details of the submissions were not included in the record and it was specifically said in some cases that there were loose papers (i, f. 190v). There is, nonetheless, sufficient detail, particularly in the fuller entries of 1553 and 1554, to show that the practice was similar to that of other borough and contemporary courts.[96]

The case began with the entry of the plea, or plaint, as it was technically since it was initiated without writ. The form in English was that AB took (or entered or commenced) an action of debt against CD upon the demand of a certain sum. In the latin courts the form was 'AB queritur versus CD in placito debiti super demand' and then an amount. The plaintiff could enter his plea whether the court was sitting or not; pleas entered out of court were distinguised by Md. and the appropriate date of entry.

Most plaintiffs appeared in person. It was usually the outsider who used an attorney or deputy and it is a practice found early in the books in 1545 when Rowland Treye of Eynsham acted by attorney (i, f. 18v). The Witney attornies were local men, tradesmen or businessmen or officers of the court, and were certainly not the professional attornies pleading for clients noted in other courts of the period[97]. Fees are mentioned in two or three cases and were specified as 6d. in a case in 1580, when the clerk of the court, Richard Bryce, was acting (i, ff. 270r, 196v).

By custom of the court the case was called for a maximum of three times after entry, a practice found in other courts. There are dots, circles or numerals in the margin to show the number of calls. The defendant usually waited to be called two or three times, but there are still a number of times where once was evidently enough. Where there are no indications in the margin it may mean that the case was heard immediately or that it was 'let fall' or withdrawn, or that the scribe did not record the calls. This last may be the explanation for many entries without calls in the second book.

The court could force the defendant to appear by licencing an arrest or attachment of property but it had no power of arrest of his person as it was not a court of record.[98] The arrest of property was also known as a distress and was made by the sergeant or on occasions the plaintiff carried it out with the bailiff's consent (i, ff. 296v, 206v). The goods were described in various cases, as in 1589 when a grey mare was arrested and in 1594 the overplus of a wagon (i, ff. 265r, 296v). It is often not possible to distinguish these distresses from the distraints for payment.

If the defendant was an outsider, arrest was either not possible or certain and in 1590 a case was lost because an attempt to arrest a sorrel mare of a

[96] cf. *Borough Customs*, ed. M.Bateson, Selden Soc. xviii, xxi (1904, 1906); T.Atkinson, *Elizabethan Winchester* (London, 1963), c.ix and especially pp.163-70; Rich, *Bristol Staple Court*, c.iv. There is more detail in the Burford records: *Burford Records*, pp.523-46.
[97] e.g. Rich, p.89.
[98] Jacob, *Law Dict.* under court.

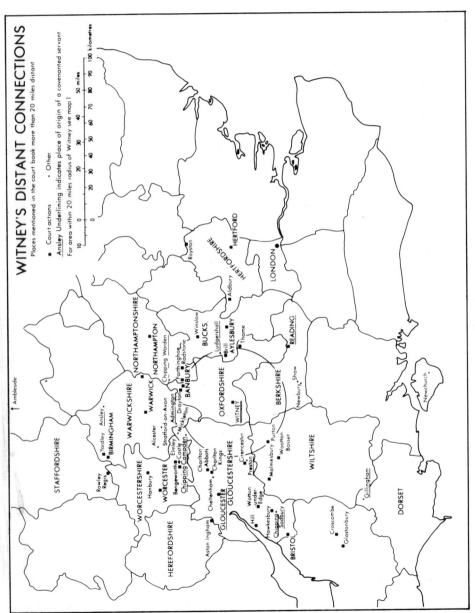

WITNEY'S DISTANT CONNECTIONS

Places mentioned in the court book more than 20 miles distant

■ Court actions   • Other

<u>Ansley</u> Underlining indicates place of origin of a covenanted servant

For area within 20 miles radius of Witney see map I

50 miles

10 0   10 20 30 40 50 60 70 80 90 100 kilometres

↑ Ambleside

STAFFORDSHIRE

Rowley Regis

Yardley   Ansley

BIRMINGHAM

WARWICKSHIRE

WARWICK

NORTHAMPTONSHIRE

NORTHAMPTON

Chipping Warden

Alcester

Stratford-on-Avon

Honbury

WORCESTER

WORCESTERSHIRE

Bengeworth   Elmley

Castle

Chipping Campden

Mickleton

Admington

Drayton

Farnthorpe

BANBURY

Radstone

Winslow

BUCKS.

Brill

Ludgershall

AYLESBURY

Thame

HEREFORDSHIRE

Aston Ingham

GLOUCESTER

Cheltenham

Charlton Kings

Charlton Abbots

OXFORDSHIRE

WITNEY

GLOUCESTERSHIRE

Hill

Wotton under-Edge

Hawkesbury

Chipping Sodbury

Cirencester

Preston

Purton

Malmesbury

Wootton Bassett

Newbury

Shaw

BERKSHIRE

READING

HERTFORDSHIRE

Royston

HERTFORD

Aldbury

LONDON

BRISTOL

Croxcombe

Glastonbury

WILTSHIRE

Gillingham

DORSET

Newchurch

Map I

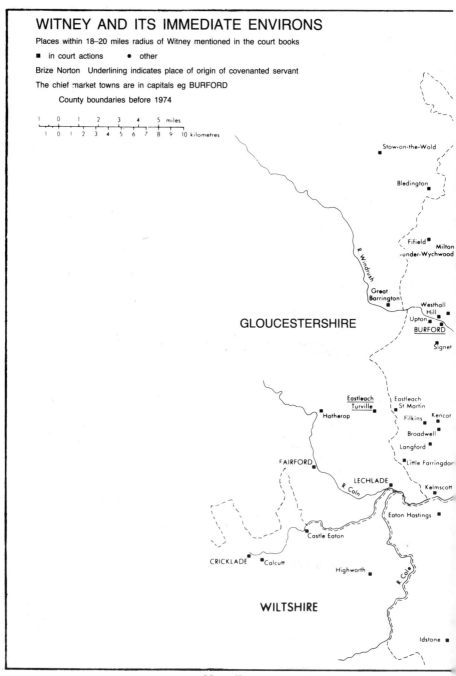

WITNEY AND ITS IMMEDIATE ENVIRONS

Places within 18–20 miles radius of Witney mentioned in the court books

■ in court actions   ● other

Brize Norton   Underlining indicates place of origin of covenanted servant

The chief market towns are in capitals eg BURFORD

County boundaries before 1974

```
1   0   1   2   3   4   5 miles
1   0   1   2   3   4   5   6   7   8   9   10 kilometres
```

Stow-on-the-Wold ■

Bledington ■

Fifield ■   Milton
-under-Wychwood ■

R. Windrush

Great
Barrington ■

Westhall
Hill ■
Upton ■ ■
BURFORD

GLOUCESTERSHIRE

Signet ■

Eastleach
Turville ■   ■ Eastleach
St Martin

Hatherop ●   Filkins ■   Kencot ■

Broadwell ■

Langford ■

Little Farringdon ●

FAIRFORD ■

LECHLADE ■   Kelmscott ■

R Coln

Eaton Hastings ■

Castle Eaton ■

CRICKLADE ■   ● Calcutt   Highworth ■   R Cole

WILTSHIRE

Idstone ■

Map II

WARWICKSHIRE

Adderbury •

Hook Norton

Barton-on-the-Heath

OXFORDSHIRE

N. Aston

CHIPPING NORTON

Sandford St. Martin

Churchill

Enstone

Lower Heyford

Chadlington

Bruern

Glympton

Spelsbury

Ascott
-under-
Wychwood

Chilson

CHARLBURY

Kirtlington

Shipton-under-Wychwood

Cornbury

Fawler

WOODSTOCK

Finstock

Wilcote

Combe

Thrupp

R. Cherwell

Langley

Leafield

Ramsden

Bladon

Kidlington

Islip

Field Assarts

Long Hanborough

Fulbrook

Asthall Leigh

Hailey

New Yatt

Church Hanborough

Water
Eaton

Horton

Swinbrook

Minster
Lovell

Crawley

N. Leigh

Yarnton

Wood Eaton

Asthall

Worsham

Woodgreen
Newland

Cassington

WITNEY

Shilton

Caswell

Curbridge

Cogges

S. Leigh

Eynsham

OXFORD

Brize Norton

Ducklington

R. Windrush

Lew

Cokethorpe

Sutton

Hardwick

Yelford

Stanton
Harcourt

Cumnor

Black Bourton

Brighthampton

Eaton

Alvescot

Aston
Cote

Northmoor

BAMPTON

Standlake

Clanfield

Weald

Shifford

R. Thames

Chimney

Dry Sandford

Longworth

Fyfield

Thrupp

Carswell

Buckland

Kingston Bagpuize

Wadley

Fyfield
Wick

ABINGDON

Marcham

FARINGDON

R. Thames

BERKSHIRE

WALLINGFORD

WANTAGE

East Hagbourne

E. & W. Lockinge

West Hagbourne

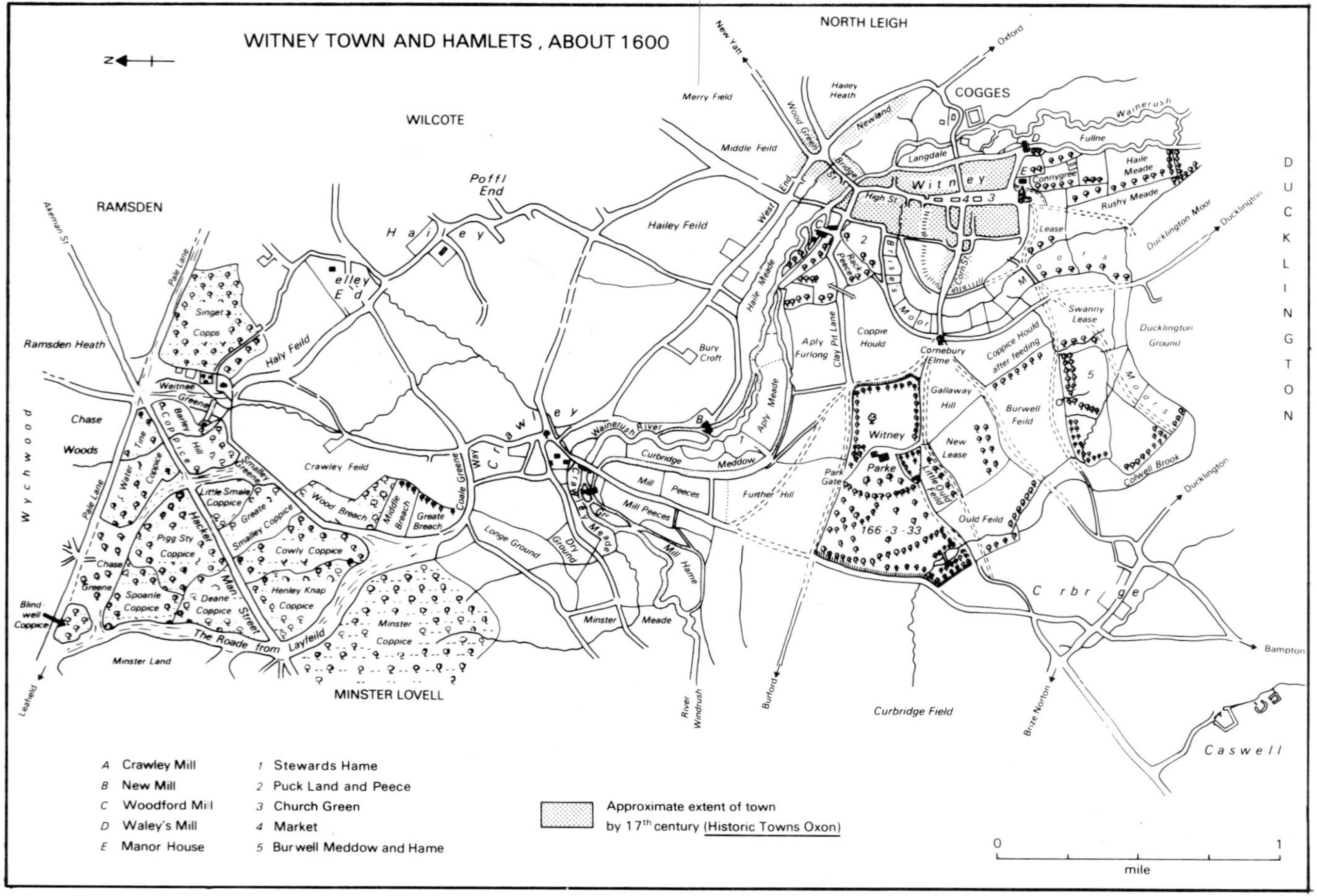

WITNEY TOWN AND HAMLETS, ABOUT 1600

Map III

N

Legend:

- Approximate extent of town by 17th century (Historic Towns Oxon)

1 Stewards Hame
2 Puck Land and Peece
3 Church Green
4 Market
5 Burwell Meddow and Hame

A Crawley Mill
B New Mill
C Woodford Mill
D Waley's Mill
E Manor House

0 ___ mile ___ 1

DUCKLINGTON

NORTH LEIGH

COGGES

WILCOTE

RAMSDEN

MINSTER LOVELL

Wychwood

Ramsden Heath

Akeman St

Chase Woods

Pale Lane

Water Lane

Blindwell Coppice

Leafield

Hailey Feild

Poffl End

Merry Field

Middle Feild

New Yatt

Wood Green

Hailey Heath

Hanly Heath

Oxford

Witney

Burford

Brize Norton

Caswell

Bampton

Curbridge Field

Ould Feild

New Lease

Burwell Feild

Swanny Lease

Duckington Moor

Waterrush

Fullwel

Haite Meade

Rudly Meade

Lease

High St

Langdale

Bridge

Corn St

Briseis Moto

Rack Peece

Clay Pit Lane

Aply Furlong

Coppice Hould

Cornebury Elme

Gallaway Hill

Little Feild

Parke

Parke Gate

Further Hill

Aply Meade

Hailr Meade

West

Bury Croft

Curbridge Medow

Mill Peece

Mill Hame

Mill Peece

Mill Meade

Minster Meade

Minster Land

Dry Ground

Lodge Ground

Haw Meade

Witham River

Coale Greene Way

Great Breach

Middle Breach

Wood Breach

Crawley Field

Hailey Eld

Singet

Coppice

Barley Hill

Pigg Sty Coppice

Wetnel Coppice

Hacket Coppice

Deane Coppice

Spoanle Coppice

Greene Coppice

Chase Coppice

Henley Knap

Cowly Coppice

Minster Coppice

Smaller Coppice

Man Street

The Roade from Layfield

River Windrush

Burford butcher failed when the mare turned out to belong to someone else (i, f. 270r). Therefore by the later sixteenth century the court often asked for pledges for answering from defendants from other places. These pledges were local Witney men, who would be known to the court. In 1595 a Witney man who was fugitive also had to produce a pledge for answering (i, f. 303v), but it was not normal procedure for Witney men.

When the defendant had been successfully brought to court, the plaintiff had to state his case in a *declaration*. They are only occasionally given in the record and it is not clear whether they were always presented in writing, although there is one instance where the plaintiff was ordered to make a sufficient written declaration (i, f. 209v). Examples in the latin courts of 1553 are evidently in a set form, and in several cases the plaintiff's declaration was that he had lent a certain specified sum at a specified time to the defendant and given a week to repay but that it was unjustly detained to his damage.

There is no indication in most debt cases that the plaintiff had to show proof of the debt other than by his word and there is no mention of bills or obligations being produced or of the device used in other courts of pledges to prosecute.[99] In certain promissory actions, however, witnesses were brought by the plaintiff, e.g. three lawful witnesses in a case of assumpsit in 1598 and two witnesses in a 1607 case about the working of the coal pit at Lew (i, f. 338v; ii, f. 120v).

If the plaintiff did not prosecute his suit or attend the court a non-suit was called and he could be amerced (i, ff. 118r, 302r). In a case in 1580 the plaintiff was also ordered to pay 2s. 6d. towards the defendant's trouble and expense within seven days (i, f. 200v).

The defendant had to appear personally and if he wished to avoid the case his most extreme action was to leave the town and be entered as a fugitive. If he also took away his goods and chattels he could not be attached by them and forced to appear before the court. In October 1590,for instance, Elizabeth Meryman lost her case for wages because the defendant was fugitive and had conveyed away his goods by night (i, f. 274r).

The defendant's death also led to the action being cut off though there are instances of actions being commenced against executors (i, ff. 47v, 127v, 226r).

Another choice before the defendant was to refuse to answer to the declaration in which case a non-response was entered and the case condemned and lost (i, f. 97v).

The defendant who contested the case could deny the whole or part of the debt and ask for a respite and day to wage his law, since there was no jury in the court for an alternative method in a contested case. In 1578 a

---

[99] cf. *Borough Customs*, i. 95; Rich, pp.80-81.

case was respited from 21 March to 23 May and then the next court was set as the day when the defendant could appear with his 'hands' to wage his law (i, f. 179v; cf. 181v). The hands were the honest men willing to support the defendant by their oaths, an ancient practice that survived in local courts without juries and in debt cases when they were not pleaded 'on the case'.[100] In Witney, as in the contemporary Winchester courts, three hands were required, i.e. the defendant and two others (i, ff. 42v, 44v). It was a legal device of value where the parties were well known, as in a small community such as Witney, and in 1588 a defendant was ordered by the court to wage his law or have the case condemned (i, f. 333v). Witnesses for the defence in the modern sense were rare, but in a 1583 case a defendant brought a witness to testify that he had bought a cow and had a right to the hide (i, f. 219r).

Often, however, the defendant came into court and acknowledged or confessed the whole or part of the debt; settlements by agreement are recorded frequently. The latin courts of 1553 have notes of licences to agree or make a settlement out of court (i, ff. 47v, 48r). Elsewhere cases are often annotated as 'agreed' with further details of arrangements. The agreement might be worked out between the parties or be an awarded agreement made by the bailiffs or arbitrators. One useful aspect of the court's practice is in the use of these arbitrators or daysmen as they are sometimes called (i, ff. 19v, 67r). They were usually two substantial men, ex-officers of the court or noted inhabitants, in whose hands the case was put, often 'to end the matter'. Both parties had to agree to abide by their decision (i, ff. 143v, 243r). On one occasion the agreement was said to cost 39s. apiece, although the debt was only 26s. 8d., but it would be surprising if this was the normal cost considering the usual cheapness of the court (i, f. 310v).

Orders, awards and judgements in the court were made by the bailiffs. Cases could be 'taken up', i.e. deferred, or 'assigned' which in the context seems to mean set over to a later court or to arbitration; or orders were made for discharge or for suitable payment. The agreements and orders usually concerned not only the amount but also the manner and date of payment. The court had some advantages over the common law courts in being able to make more flexible arrangements. It could award less than was claimed (i, ff. 149r, 154r) and it could arrange for deferred payment or payment by instalments on specified days, either weekly, monthly or quarterly. There are many examples of deferred instalments in the books, for example the payment of one groat a week in 1548 to pay off a debt of 6s. 8d., or the two agreements in 1587 to pay within three years (i, ff. 24r, 253v). Judgement could be peremptory, however, as in the case in 1580 when after the plaintiff's declaration to the court on 15 April that wood

[100] Simpson, *Law of Contract*, pp.137-8.

had been carried away, the defendant defaulted with a non-response at a court of 10 June 1580, but his pledge acknowledged the action and the bailiff in July ordered satisfaction to be made before the next court without any further delay (i, f. 190r).

To agree or get an order was one matter; to ensure payment was another. Local inhabitants could achieve it through the court's power to order the sergeant to distrain goods (i, f. 243r). In 1548 an agreement allowed for the payment of a debt on Midsummer Day and if it was not made then it was lawful for the plaintiff to take a distress against the defendant 'as he might have done at the day of making hereof' (i, f. 23v). On one occasion a loom distrained by one creditor was transferred to another and other goods seized ranged from brass and pewter pots and pans to cloth, sheets, blocks to support a stall in the market, a cart, corn and sheepskins. Goods were appraised by a group of qualified tradesmen or the wardsmen. There were limitations to the value of distraint as the goods apparently could not be sold,[101] although in one instance where the defendant did not appear the goods seized, presumably to compel his appearance, were delivered to the plaintiff (i, f. 326v). But distraint against outsiders, like arrest for appearance, was again difficult. In 1597 in a case between two outsiders it was agreed to bring in security to satisfy the action and other debts before the bailiff and three others (i, f. 321r).

A more usual procedure was to ask an outsider and on rarer occasions a native to provide pledges or sureties for payment who were local men (i, f. 216r). It was no idle undertaking for if the principal did not pay the pledge was obliged to satisfy the creditor (i, f. 239r). In 1578 Philip Box sued Anthony Larden for money paid out by suretyship and in 1579 Hew Rodes was given a respite of payment of 15s. 3d. to a Witney tailor so that he could go to Humfrey Berry in Worcestershire for whom he had acted as surety to try to collect the debt (i, ff. 181r, 187r). The burden is shown in a memorandum of 1564 whereby two pledges, one local and one from South Leigh, became sureties 'every man in the whole' to pay the sum (i, f. 91v).

Payments were frequently made into court or to the bailiffs who saw to the paying out (i, ff. 255v, 306r). In early years the clerk cancelled the cases when the debt had been paid and the court had finished with the case but this practice was not kept up after 1571. That an awarded settlement or agreement was not always the end of the matter is shown in 1581 when John Peacock of Shilton 'set away' the paper of agreement made in 1574 because it had not been carried out and threatened to sue in a higher court, even though the debt was only for 20s. 7d. (i, f. 190v).

Use of the court was encouraged by its cheapness and comparative speed. It was one great virtue that costs were low and conservative. None are specifically mentioned until 1575 and 1576, though it is likely that they

---

[101] Jacob, *Law Dict.*, under court baron.

were represented earlier by the odd 3d. on the end of many sums (cf. i, f. 91r, 93v). They were first detailed in two cases involving outsiders and in 1577 there was a charge of 3d. for entering the plea and a charge for an arrest (i, ff. 162v, 165r, 177r). By 1579 it is clear that the system applied to Witney people and 3d. entry and 4d. for an arrest and in 1582 another 4d. for bailiffs' fee was added separately to the sum claimed for both locals and outsiders (i, ff. 188v, 216v, 217v). The cost, therefore, was 11d. if all charges were incurred but often no arrest was necessary, especially for local people, and the bailiffs' fee was infrequent after 1584. The only increase over the period was to 4d. for the entry fee by the end of the century. The fees were presumably paid to the officers involved, the clerk, sergeant and bailiff. In addition there is occasional mention of payment to appraisers as in 1595 when they were paid 8d. and the clerk 2d. (i, f. 303v).

The speed of the case varied firstly according to the number of summonses or calls. An examination of the calls throughout the period shows that most cases waited for two or three months to get the defendant into court. In 1586, for example, out of thirteen cases where we can see the course of the action, only one was clearly settled at the initiating court, another after one call and eight after the third call. A respite or a contested case or arbitration could add another month or so and the case between Croftes and Jonson in that year was called three times from January, committed to arbitration for an award to be made by June and finally paid in July (i, ff. 242r, 243r). On occasion cases could take much longer but the general picture is that they could be settled in six months to a year in Witney as in Burford.[102]

The virtues of the local court were perhaps evident when the Box and Rankell families considered their lengthy wrangle with a relative John Hampshere of Eynsham over the tenure of two meadows and 40 acres of arable at Bury Crofts between 1572 and 1596, a case which led to local arbitration and to the Court of Requests in London, as well as to the spiritual court in Oxford when Thomas Boxe was accused of tearing a leaf out of the church book in order to falsify the age of his younger brother Leonard.[103]

In its sphere Witney court compared not unfavourably with others or indeed with modern courts. Essentially manorial in origin but firmly controlled by the townsmen, it showed in the sixteenth and early seventeenth centuries that it could both expand to meet the new demands of government and provide essential services for its local community.

The Court Books and their Keepers

The court books consist of two paper volumes, the first of 348 folios and the second of 146 folios, each folio page measuring about 270 by 185 mm.

---

[102] cf. *Burford Records*, p.523ff.
[103] Req.2/76/24.

Both books are sewn into parchment covers. The entries in the first volume run from 4 October 1538 to 1 June 1599 and there are also jottings of court business on the end cover. The volume has been damaged by damp and has crumbling edges on the first thirty folios and stains on all of the first sixty folios. In three places stubs show that a leaf has been torn out: between ff. 9v and 10r with possible entries for February to March 1542; between ff. 18v and 19r with possible entries for April 1545 to September 1546; and between ff. 64v and 65r with possible entries for January to September 1557.[104] Apparent gaps elsewhere probably indicate inactivity in the courts or else incomplete recording (i, ff. 6v, 7r). The second court book runs from 20 April 1599 to 24 February 1610. It appears to be complete, though with less systematic entering of court business on occasions (e.g. ii, ff. 67r,v, 68r,v). Additional papers 'annexed' are mentioned in the text but there are none attached to either volume (e.g. i, f. 190v). The language used in the court books was English except for the latin in courts of 1553–4 and in court headings and annotations in a period of uncertainty at the end of Mary's reign and the beginning of Elizabeth's in the years 1557 to 1559.

In 1575 the book was called the 'town book' (i, f. 163r); and both books at times contained matters of more general interest than strictly court business. However, the books are best described as court record books, since this was their main business and it was evidently the intention only to enter an abbreviated record, not to minute details of pleadings and cases. It is clear that most entries were made either before or after the court sitting, but agreements and covenants with signatures and notes that they were recorded 'in the face of the court' indicate that they must be regarded as contemporary records written up close to or in the court meeting (e.g. i, f. 134r). The courts were entered in chronological order but after the first few years the subsequent course of a case was written besides the first entry. Entries of grants for 1548 and 1549, which are apparently out of order after the 1552 courts, are, in fact, in the hand of the scribe of 1548 and he obviously chose to write them up away from his court entries (see i, ff. 22r, 39r,v, 40r,v). In the second book there is more variation in the order of entries and it is clearer that they were written up from memoranda and after the court.

The appearance and neatness of the court books was due entirely to the habits of the writers and there is naturally much variability. From the handwriting and style about fifteen main scribes seem to have kept the book over the 70 year period, as well as a number of others occasionally making entries. Up to 1560 there was a different scribe every one or two years: from 1538 to 1541 (i, ff. 1r to 11r); 1542 to 1544 (ff. 11v to 17r); 1544 to 1546 (ff. 17r to 19r); 1546 to 1547 (ff. 19r to 20v); 1547 to 1549,

---

[104] We are indebted to Dr D.M.Barratt of the Bodleian Library for her advice on the mss.

1554, 1555, 1556 (ff. 20v to 28r; 39r to 40v; notes on 41v, 42r; 51r and v; 54v, 61v to 63r); 1549 to 1550 (ff. 29r to 30r); 1550 to 1553 (ff. 30v to 38r; 41r to 45r); 1553 to 1555 (ff. 46r; 52r to v; 53v to 54r, 55r to v); for the latin courts of 1553 to 1554 (ff. 46v to 50v), 1555 to 1556 (ff. 56r to 61v); 30 Oct. 1556 (ff. 63v to 64r); 1556 to 1559 (ff. 64v to 72v). The next fifty years saw more continuity. There is one hand from 1560 to 1570 (i, ff. 73v to 119r), and the one writer named in the book, Richard Brice or Bryce, made the entries from 1571 to 1596 (i, ff. 119v to 309r). The man who succeeded him in 1596 wrote from the end of the first book well into the second up to 1605 (i, f. 309r to ii, f. 108r). There is no certain evidence as to who he was but a mention of a case 'assigned . . . to me Richard Maior' in 1606 may mean that the broadweaver Richard Maior, deputy to the sergeant and in 1608 sergeant himself, was the clerk compiling the record; a comparison of his signature and the hand in the book also suggests this (ii, ff. 1r, 99v, 100v, 101v). The next writer in the book from 1605 to 1609 (ii, ff. 109r to 146v) is also unnamed but similar evidence indicates that he may have been Thomas Willsheer, shoemaker, who had been constable in 1600 (ii, ff. 7r, 119r, 121r, 133r). Both men like Brice frequently witnessed agreements.

The general form of abbreviated entry was already established at the beginning of the first court book and this suggests that it had predecessors which have not survived. Variations in the style of entry and annotation reflect the idiosyncracies of the various scribes rather than a change in court procedure. Early entries in the 1540s and 50s vary, for example, between describing a case as 'taken' or 'entered' and between using dots or circles or arabic or Roman numerals in the margin to indicate the number of summonses (e.g. i, ff. 2r, 30v, 44v, 55v, 65v). Again, some scribes cancelled completed cases with bold lines drawn through them (e.g. i, ff. 29v to 36v), whereas others left no record of the ending of a case. The court records were best kept in Elizabeth's reign. The man who wrote the book up between 1560 and 1570 had not a particularly attractive or neat hand, but he kept the entries in an orderly fashion with appropriate annotations alongside the cases of the number of summonses and the course of the action. His successor was exemplary.

Richard Brice with thirty-five years of record keeping had most impact on the record. He had a particularly elegant and distinctive secretary hand and took a keen interest in the business of record keeping, describing himself as the 'keeper of the court book' or 'the writer of these present' and even as 'the town clerk' (i, ff. 153r, 155v, 163r, 272r, 274v). He was in fact the local scribe and can be found writing local wills and deeds from the late 1550s and the churchwardens' accounts from 1569 to 1594 with the same pride in his calling.[105] He belonged to a local family and was

---

[105] Prob 11/71 62 Spencer; Wills Oxon. 131/1/13; ibid. 183, f.317r; churchwardens' accts. ff.4–10r. Dr. D.M.Barratt has identified his hand in the churchwardens' accts. and notes a gap 1594–7.

probably the Richard Brice, whose brother Thomas, yeoman of Curbridge, and lessee of the manor, died in 1547, leaving him the reversion of the fulling mill and 'my bargain and sale with my uncle Leonard Yate for two houses and a barn on the north side of the bridge in Witney borough'.[106] Their mother Alice was a Yate herself and when she died in 1553 worth £71, she left the residue of her property in the parish to Richard.[107] He and his wife Anne were therefore established in Witney in the second half of the century, and they are found dealing with property in Witney and Hailey and were perhaps in business, for in 1587 when the local clothier Nicholas Ifeelde died his will forgave Richard Bryce all debts owned by him by specialty.[108] The Brice family had close connexions with the parish and Richard's nephew Stephen Brice, gentleman, the son of his brother Thomas, was also lessee of the manor and borough.[109] These connexions and ties with local families perhaps explain Richard's interest in keeping the records of the borough and even the survival of the court books from this period.

Richard acted for the court before he took charge of the books. In 1558 he was constable and later he was an attorney, twice an arbitrator for the court and in 1574 deputy for the sergeant (i, ff. 70r, 101v, 123r, 149r). He may have written in the court book as early as 1554 when there is a hand similar to his, but headings and dates before 1571 in his hand were perhaps added later, when he went back over the earlier entries, as a clerk in charge of the records for a long time might do (e.g. i, ff. 89r to 90r). From 1571, when he took over, there is a marked improvement in the record. The main entries were separated and bracketed with the sum at the end of each entry. In time he carefully distinguished the various ways in which the sums and the court charges were made up. He gave more explanations of the course of cases and careful annotations in the margin or under the first entry of each case. By 1574 (i, f. 146v) he had opted for describing a case as 'commenced' as against the earlier variations and he settled from the beginning for abandoning the cancelling system and for using arabic numerals in the margin for summonses. He died in April 1596 some months before the plague which carried off so many of his fellows.[110]

The two later scribes did not keep up his careful annotation of cases or chronological entries and the record deteriorated in the last fourteen years between 1596 and 1610 in neatness, style and detail.

[106] Wills Oxon. 179, f.266r.
[107] Ibid. 180, f.176r; cf. ibid. 75/3/3, where Joan Yates left sheets and other bequests to her cousin Richard Brice and his wife.
[108] CP 25 (2) Hilary 1 Eliz. and Easter 16 Eliz.; Prob 11/71 62 Spencer.
[109] See above, p.xiii.
[110] D.D.Par.Witney d 3, f. 34r. Another Richard Brice, broadweaver, of 1593 in the court books may have been the son of John Brice, broadweaver, and a member of another Curbridge family: Wills Oxon. 184, f.13. The parish baptismal register records only Alice, Joan and Henry as the children of Richard Brice: D.D.Par. Witney c 1, ff.2v, 5v, 12r.

PART TWO: THE SOCIETY AND ECONOMY OF WITNEY

The Topography of Witney

Behind the court books lay the society of a thriving Tudor town and it possible to read them with greater enjoyment with some knowledge of the progress of Witney in the sixteenth century. Bishop des Roches chose a good industrial site when he put his new Oxfordshire town not in his manor of Adderbury near the hard waters of the Cherwell but in Witney besides the Windrush, a good mill stream with soft water, in a parish near the Cotswold wool supplies, with good communication to Oxford, London and to the south via Abingdon to Southampton. He was a man with a good eye for making money and in administration as his work for King John testified, and the wool and cloth markets had been flourishing in the inflationary years of the late twelfth century.[1] He laid out his town with a market square and new street, set out plots for new buildings, paid for shops and stalls to be set up and attracted tenants from surrounding villages with privileges for the town and with small holdings carved out of Hailey and his demesne, the assart or sart land, as it was still known in the sixteenth century.[2] The town expanded in the thirteenth century and the bishopric accounts show money paid for new land by townsfolk over a number of years: by 1219 for example there were sixteen messuages in the meadow next to Cogges bridge.[3] The mills were a vital part of the venture: in 1210 money was paid out to restore one or more of them and in the following years £17 to £18 was paid for their lease or 'farm'.[4] In 1223 there were not only three grain but also three fulling mills, evidently in the same position as the sixteenth-century mills for two already bore their sixteenth century names of Woodford Mill (mentioned in 1219) and Waleys Mill in Curbridge (called after a certain 'Walensis' or Welshman who held it in 1223–4) while there was the third fulling mill already in Crawley[5]: in the sixteenth century these mills were a source of wealth for the Bishop and Box families who feature in the court books.

The bishop's plan was still the pattern for Witney in the sixteenth century. The chief features of the town are shown in Map III. The market

[1] P.Harvey, 'The English Inflation of 1180-1220', *Past and Present*, no. 61 (Nov. 1973).
[2] See above, p.xi; and Eccl. 2/159771, 159278, for example of seldage and town plots.
[3] Eccl. 2/159276.
[4] Ibid. 159370A, 159272.
[5] Ibid. 159276-8, 159287.

place was the town centre with the town or guild hall and the cross.
Businessmen made bequests for town buildings though perhaps not all
were fulfilled. In 1514 Richard Martin left 5s. towards the building of the
'yeld hall' and in 1560 Walter Jones left £20 for the building of a market
house in the market place at Witney, if it could be built within 12 months,
while in 1606 Richard Ashcombe left £50 to build a house over and above
the cross.[6] The land was still part of the bishop's 'waste' and when
William Hunte junior, son of the local cardmaker, set up a butcher's shop
it was described as on the lord's waste in the market place of Witney and
he paid for it in the manor court.[7] This was a favourite area for butchers:
Thomas Hands and Thomas Shaw and later his former apprentice, Robert
James, all had their butchers' shops in the area backing on West Crofts and
Corn Street (i, ff. 281r, 332r, 336r). The 'possessions' in the court book
show other tradesmen, either occupying shops here like Robert Surell the
haberdasher and Robert Taylor or Cakebred, innkeeper, or owning
property which they may once have occupied but were now leasing, like
the Daltons, mercers and tailors of Witney and London, the Clempsons,
mercers in Witney and Abingdon, the Willsheares, local shoemakers and
the Rings the chandlers (i, ff. 332r, 336r).[8] In 1602 William Hunte, cardmaker, had two tenements here described as having halls, parlours,
chambers, stables as well as shops (ii, f. 66r).

Brice's manor house was near the church, presumably where Mount
House was later built[9] and the houses of some of the wealthier clothiers
and woolmen flanked Church Green. Dame Emmote Fermor bought a
house here in 1494; in 1591 Harry Jones, clothier and bailiff of the town in
1561 and later, was tenant of the Wenmans' house next to Shaw the
butcher (i, f. 281r), and another clothier and bailiff, Nicholas Gunne, had a
shop on the north side of Church House.[10] Tenements belonging to other
clothiers were in High Street and the business community of victuallers,
tailors, woollen-drapers, carpenters and clothiers stretched down towards
the bridge. In 1501 one Wenman and two Fermor houses in High Street
were bequeathed in Dame Emmote's will[11] and in 1549 Thomas Wenman
had a tenement lying on the west side. Both this and tenements belonging
to Leonard Yate and Robert Adeane next to it were described as being on
the town ditch, and there was apparently another ditch on the other side
(i, ff. 40r, 40v). It is not easy to identify properties but Nicholas Hill's
ownership of the Plough Inn on the east side of High Street is certain,[12]

[6] Prob 11/17 29 Fetiplace, 44/20 Loftes and 107/47 Stafford.
[7] Misc. Je I/1, f.69v.
[8] Ibid. ff. 35r, 92r.
[9] C 54/3418,mm. 39–40, no. 5.
[10] Top. Oxon. d 210, f.114; D.D.Par. Witney; Misc. Je 1/1, f. 90v.
[11] *Some Oxfordshire Wills 1393-1510*, ed. J.R.H.Weaver and A.Beardwood, O.R.S. xxxix
(1958), 70.
[12] Wills Oxon. 188, f.15r.

and alongside him were the Yates the clothiers and Edward Ashfield the glover; close to them was Adeane property held by Giles Palmer, broad-weaver, and next to him the Rankells, again a clothier family providing bailiffs of the town at the end of this century (i, ff. 128v, 266r, 155v).

As might be expected the tenement of the wealthy dyer, Richard Humfrey, bailiff in 1540, lay near the river; he left 10s. for the repair of Witney High Bridge over the Windrush in his will in 1568.[13] There were a number of properties in this area described as beyond or beneath the bridge (i, ff. 74v, 97r, 39v). In West End there was the town close, and the Hornes and Wheelers, both carpenter families, had tenements here, as did Richard Bishop or Martin, the local miller, and bailiff in 1598 (i, f. 97r, 344v, 82v).

Perhaps the most interesting development was in Corn or Corndell Street. There were houses belonging to wealthy clothiers, the Joneses, Yateses and Bringfields; there were the town's own houses and the Chantry Hall messuage belonging to the chantry dissolved in 1546; and there were the broadweavers' houses, evidence of the industrial expansion of the town (i, ff. 30v, 39r, 39v, 153r). The street was still the bishop's 'waste' and the manor court recorded increments for rents there and licences for new cottages. In 1558, for instance, Margaret White was granted a parcel of waste in the street measuring eighteen feet by twenty in order to build a cottage at the new rent of 4d., and John Cosborne was similarly granted waste sixteen feet by fourteen.[14] In the court books below the bailiffs give permission to a labourer, a broadweaver and two tailors to build cottages in Corn Street (i, ff. 236r, 237r, v). One was in the quarry at the end of Corn Street from which stone for the substantial building in the town came (i, f. 176r), as well perhaps as from Down Hill where stone was quarried.[15]

Such houses or cottages must have been very much like that of Gregory Merryman, a poor broadweaver who died in 1596. It consisted of a hall or living room furnished simply with a table, bench and form, a cupboard and a chair, but with glass in the window valued at 13d. Probably leading off this room, but possibly reached by a ladder was the chamber or bed-room, with a little chamber leading off. In the main room was a joined bedstead, a press or clothes cupboard and an old coffer, whilst in the little chamber there was a bedstead, a flock bed, a pair of hempen sheets, two pillows, a pair of blankets and a white coverlet, with an old red mantle. The buttery and little kitchen contained a few pots and dishes and Merryman's wearing apparel consisted only of a cloak, a coat, a doublet and a pair of breeches. Like many others in Witney, Merryman can only

[13] Ibid. 185, f.36v.
[14] Misc. Je I/1, ff. 27r, 28r, 39v, 44r, 54r for further examples.
[15] *Historic Towns in Oxfordshire*, ed. K.Rodwell (Oxford Archaeological Unit Survey no. 3; Oxford, 1975), p.181; Misc. Je I/1, f.59r.

have lived simply, even frugally, with only glass in the window to add a touch of luxury. Other, better-off broadweavers, ironmongers and bakers lived more comfortably in houses with more than one storey and more in the way of furnishings and pewter and even, in one case, a bible and other books.[16]

The building of new houses was not confined to poorer cottages. Though refronted in later times many surviving houses in the town centre have a sixteenth or seventeenth-century 'core' and were built or extended by the prosperous clothiers of this period. Richard Clempson, mercer, spoke in his will (February 1601) of his new house, lately built with glass in it, and the increased comfort of houses is shown in the number of rooms and fitments listed in inventories. Thomas Taylor, (d. 1583) a yeoman and tanner, had an inner and outer court in his town house with twenty-four separate rooms, chambers and service houses, and he had glass windows in various rooms and in his stairs windows; his descendent Robert Taylor, innholder, also recorded the glass in all windows of his house in his will, while in 1602 Nicholas Gunne, clothier, had specified that his widow should enjoy the house and leave the glass windows in as good a state as when she entered.[17]

Gunne lived in some style. His house had two main living rooms on the ground floor, with a separate buttery, kitchen and dairy house, a shop where he kept three looms and a warping house for the preparation of the yarn. Upstairs there were two main bedrooms, but it is not so much the size of the house as its furnishings which give the impression of comfortable living. The hall had a carpet on the floor, wainscot on the walls, a set of ten joined stools and Gunne's or the town's arms were displayed there, two black bills, a headpiece and jack, a sword with a girdle, a sheaf of arrows and a calaver, an early form of musket. But it is from the kitchen where the pewter was kept that the impression of a good life really comes. There were kept 25 large pewter platters, two and a half dozen of a lesser sort, a dozen dishes, half a dozen plates, half a dozen porringers, half a dozen saucers great and small, 'my pewter chamber pot' valued at 4s., fifteen candlesticks, numerous brass pots, pans and kettles, five dozen trenchers, four spits and a furnace [oven]. There was a great deal of cooking and eating done in this house, and later the master and mistress at least could retire to a comfortable feather bed made up with one pair of the twenty sheets, fine and coarse, listed and with feather pillows and bolster.

Witney town was set in a typical Oxfordshire landscape of the sixteenth century, a landscape of open field and enclosure. The tithe awards of 1840 to 1842, drawn up before later boundary alterations, show nearly 189 acres in the town as against 2, 827 acres for Hailey, 3,076 acres for Curbridge

[16] Wills Oxon 170/1/7; cf. 30/4/11; 66/1/5. For sixteenth-century housing see *Oxon. Inventories*, pp.16, 19.
[17] Prob 11/99 32 Montague; *Oxon. Inventories*, no. 107; Wills Oxon. 65/3/30, 25/2/25.

and 1,116 acres for Crawley. In the sixteenth century, surveys describe the parish in medieval terms as comprising thirty yardlands in Curbridge, ten in Crawley and assart, or land cleared mainly in the thirteenth century: there were 1,488 acres of assart in Hailey, 70 acres in Curbridge and 22a.3rood in Crawley. Besides this there were 115 demesne acres in Curbridge now in the hands of tenants, of course, and 2a.3rood of purpresture, again cleared land, in Crawley.[18] Most of the yardlands and assart would have been in open field in the earlier Middle Ages, but by the sixteenth century there had been considerable enclosure. Witney Park in Curbridge was enclosed for the bishop in the thirteenth century,[19] but other enclosure came from tenant sheep farmers in the fifteenth century and later; some is recorded but much took place silently. Richard Wenman enclosed Caswell in Henry VII's reign, and William Brice, lessee of the manor, enclosed three messuages and perhaps as many virgates about the same time.[20] This was in Curbridge near Witney township and was probably the land described as Brices leases and other enclosures in the sixteenth-century manor court book and on the later seventeenth-century map.[21] Nonetheless, though the Curbridge land near Witney itself was enclosed, there were still open fields in Curbridge towards Minster Lovell and 910 acres were open field as late as 1845.[22] In Hailey the Martins were active enclosures. They called themselves alias Bishop in the sixteenth century and appear as millers and bailiffs in the court books. In 1429, however, John Martin of Witney was described as a husbandman or woolmonger, and his descendant Richard Martin was described as butcher, woolman or yeoman, in 1509 when he was pardoned his debt to a London stockfishmonger.[23] The family's interests explain why Richard was presented in the bishop's courts in the early sixteenth century for overloading pasture in Hailey with 300 sheep and for trespassing in Witney Park with his cattle, and to the Inclosure Commissioners for enclosing 76 acres in Hailey in the same period and depopulation. He was not the only one responsible. Thomas Hill or Hull, Henry Smyth and John Wheeler, all with family names important in sixteenth-century Witney, were likewise accused in the bishop's court of over-loading pasture with their sheep and four other men, among them William Hanks of Cogges, again a name occurring among the sixteenth-century bailiffs, were accused before the Commissioners of enclosing 78

[18] Misc. Je I/1, f.13r; Bodl. Tithe award.
[19] *Oxfordshire Hundred Rolls*, ed. E.Stone, O.R.S. xlvi (1968), 71.
[20] *The Domesday of Inclosures, 1517-18*, ed. I.S.Leadam (London, 1897), i.346-7, 365.
[21] Misc. Je I/1, ff.8v, 10v and passim; Top. Oxon. d 212, p.12; and cf. sale of manor in 1649: C54/3418,mm. 39-40, no. 5.
[22] R.Davis, *Map of the County of Oxford* (1797); O.R.O. inclosure award; and see H.L. Gray, *The English Field Systems* (Harvard reprint, 1959), p.541.
[23] *Cal. Pat. 1429-36*, p.169; *1494-1509*, p.600.

acres in Hailey.[24] There must have been more unrecorded enclosing in
Crawley where there were enclosed 'breaches' mentioned in the sixteenth
and seventeenth centuries and by 1824 there were only 502 acres of open
field left in Hailey and Crawley.[25] Much of this altered look of the Witney
landscape dates back to the fifteenth and sixteenth centuries when local
men were looking for wool supplies. Resentment is reflected in the town
court book's reference to undertenants who were 'common hedgebreakers'
(i, f. 137v) and in the manor bylaws against overloading pasture.[26]

Wealth and Population

The early fourteenth-century subsidies show that the wealth of the parish
was largely in the town and already concentrated in a few hands. It is clear
that the rural areas met problems in the later Middle Ages not only
because of the decline in population after visitations of the Black Death but
also because of the poor returns from the land broken in or assarted in the
thirteenth century.[27] The town may have suffered too, but perhaps revived
more quickly because of its connexion with wool. Cotswold wool was
much in demand and Witney's participation in the trade must have been
encouraged by the fact that the bishopric wool from this area was stored in
Witney from 1370 sometimes for a number of years while waiting sale.[27]
The bishops had given up their interests in farming, even of sheep, by
1453 [28] but there were energetic local merchants profiting from the brisk
wool trade along the Cotswolds. Local woolmen, the Elises of Thame and
the Standlake family who later held Caswell appear in the town in the
1327 subsidy; in 1429 the local woolman was John Hood of Witney,[29] and
the Wenmans and the Fermors flourished as woolmen in the later fifteenth
century. There had always been weavers, fullers and dyers in Witney,[30]
though whether in any number is uncertain, but by the late fourteenth
century a new interest in the cloth trade was general, and the opportunity

---

[24] Eccl. 1/73/2 and 3; *Domesday of Inclosures*, i.345-6.
[25] See entry fines in Misc. Je I/1, ff.23v and 47r and v, 51r, 57v, 61v; map in Top. Oxon. d
212; Gray, *Field Systems*, p.542.
[26] Misc. Je I/1, ff. 46r, 49r, 89r.
[27] A.Ballard, 'The manors of Witney . . .', p.192; J.Z.Titow, *Winchester Yields* (Cambridge,
1972), p.32; and K.Scott, 'Oxfordshire Fourteenth-Century Subsidies' (dissertation, History
Dept, University of Otago, N.Z.)
[27a] T.H.Lloyd, *The English Wool Trade in the Middle Ages* (Cambridge, 1977), pp.311-12.
[28] Ballard, 'The manors of Witney . . .', p.202.
[29] *Cal. Fine 1422-30*, p.292. A John Hood exported cloth from Bristol to Prussia in 1391 (*The
Overseas Trade of Bristol*, ed. E.M.Carus-Wilson, Bristol Rec. Soc. vii (1937), 196), and a man
of this name was a merchant of the Staple trading from Boston (Lincs.) in the mid-fifteenth
century (*Cal.Pat.*1452-61) pp.135, 213. But whether these references indicate one, two or
three men is uncertain.
[30] e.g. see dyers and weavers in 1256 in Eccl. 2/159292; and *c.* 1279 in Hyde, 'The borough of
Witney', pp.102, 104.

of buying bishopric wool when it was unsold on the export market may have stimulated the local cloth industry in Witney. John Dier in the 1390s and Henry Dier alias Moundevyle, bailiff in the 1440s, for example, may have laid the fortunes of the Humfreys, alias Dier family, the prosperous dyers who appear in the court books.[31] A new lease of the fulling mill in 1460 and the brisker trade in land in the court books with new fines and entry fees in the late fifteenth century suggest quickening economic life.[32]

The greatest growth may not have come until the sixteenth century was well under way and perhaps not until the 1530s and 1540s, the boom years of the English cloth trade before the mid-century collapse of the Antwerp market. Though great woolmen, Staplers trading mainly in raw wool, dominate the parish tax records, these were the years when a thriving cloth industry would have encouraged growth in the town. Tax and communicant returns give some support to this. In 1524 the great merchant of the Staple, Richard Wenman, paid four-fifths of the tax, £43 6s. 8d. and was assessed on £1,200.[33] He provides a prime example of the concentration of wealth and capital which has been noted in several towns in this subsidy, as in Lavenham, Coventry, Leicester and Canterbury. His wealth is comparable with that of only a few merchants in England, like the Springs of Lavenham or Jannys an alderman of Norwich, and when he died ten years later he made cash legacies of over £2,000, as well as leaving property.[34] Because of Wenman's assessment Witney paid £55 3s. 8d., the highest subsidy for any town in the county outside Oxford, and on a level with the prospering town of Abingdon in Berkshire, which paid £53 12s. 10d.[35] In both the payments show a change in the ranking since the 1334 subsidies and suggest growth and prosperity.[36]

But in terms of tax-payers and, therefore, the distribution of capital, Witney had only half of Abingdon's numbers. Within Oxfordshire it ranked as tenth among the towns for the first payment to the subsidy and sixth for the second payment, with Banbury, Bicester, Burford and Eynsham well ahead with ninety to one hundred tax-payers. Although there were ninety-four contributions in all in the parish the picture is of a small market town with a third of its population in the surrounding villages, whereas Banbury, Bicester and Burford had most of the parish population concentrated in the market town. In terms of population, the

---

[31] Cal. Pat. 1391-6, p.461; 1429-36, p.10; Cal. Close 1441-7, p.440; and for Humfrey alias Dyer, E179/162/370. For other families see below.

[32] Hyde, B.Litt.

[33] E 179/161/172.

[34] W.G.Hoskins, Provincial England (London, 1964), pp.74-7; cf. P.Slack and P.Clark, English Towns in Transition (Oxford, 1976), p.106; Wills Oxon. 181, ff. 15v-18v.

[35] Historic Towns Oxon., p.201.

[36] Ibid. The value of direct comparisons of payments in 1334 and 1524 is now questioned, but see A.R. Bridbury, Economic Growth: England in the Later Middle Ages (London, 1962), pp.112-3.

tax-paying figures suggest that Witney like Burford and Bicester fell into
the well-recognized class of market towns in England with under 1,000
inhabitants: only Oxford, Henley and Banbury were certainly above that
level in the county. Its growth since the Middle Ages is in line with the
view that Oxfordshire, like much of the rest of England, was slow in
making up its population in the fifteenth century.[37] Nonetheless, Witney
was an important urban centre in its area, where the depopulation of the
fifteenth century is marked in the low return of forty-seven tax-payers for
the once dominant parish of Bampton in 1524.[38]

That there had been changes by the 1540s is suggested by the Chantry
Commissioners' description of the town as 'replenished with much
people', and though this may only be a general remark the communicant
figures explain why it may have more substance. The 1544 subsidy had
the same number of tax-payers as for the second payment of 1524, but the
Wenmans now paid their tax with the tithing of Curbridge where their
chief property lay. The woolman Edward Wilmot was the wealthiest
contributor in the town assessed on £60 work of goods but nowhere near
Wenman's wealth of 1524. The chantry returns, however, show an
increase in the parish to over 1,000, for even if the 1545 return of 1,100
communicants is discounted as exaggerated the 1547 return is reasonable.
Then there were 800 'houseling people' or communicants about the age of
fifteen or over in the parish as a whole, and if distributed as in the lay
subsidies this would mean about 500 in Witney itself and 320 in the
hamlets. This puts the town on a par with Burford with 544 communicants. The more interesting comparison is with the surrounding villages
where there were 184 'houseling' people in Chadlington, 180 at Eynsham,
162 at Brize Norton but only 80 in North Leigh, 60 in Cogges, 49 in
Charlbury and 46 in South Leigh. Witney was now clearly much larger
than the villages in the countryside around it. The muster returns of 1542
likewise showed that Burford with 88 men and Witney with 70 and six
more provided by Wenman were well above the other parishes in the three
hundreds of Chadlington, Bampton and Wootton, where Chipping
Norton, for example, was to provide 34 men, Woodstock 36 and others
many fewer. The general impression of a 'replenished town' is borne out
by the baptismal registers of the early 1550s which suggest a possible
population of 1,200 or more for the parish, whilst the court books and
wills show numbers of people connected with the cloth industry in the
town and new housing.[39]

Thereafter Witney grey steadily like many other market towns, which

[37] J.Cornwall, 'English Population in the early Sixteenth Century', *Ec.H.R.*, 2nd series xxiii
(1970); 'English Country Towns in the Fifteen Twenties', ibid. xv (1962-3).
[38] cf. K.J.Allison *et al.*, *The Deserted Villages of Oxfordshire* (Leicester, 1966), especially pp.22-3.
[39] *L. and P. For. and Dom. Hen, VIII*, xvii, 1542, pp.506-7; and see Table I.

INTRODUCTION

TABLE I

Witney Population and Wealth

	Tax payers (a)				Communicants (b)	
	1327	1377	1524	1544	1545 (i)	1547 (ii)
Crawley	19			6		
Curbridge	32		14	17		
Hailey	47		17	22		
Witney town	47		63	72		
Total Parish	145	434	94	107	1100	800
Population estimate (c) town			315	360		
parish			470	535	1375	1000

	Births in parish (d)				
	1551–4	1564–71	1586–93	1594–99	1600–11
Average per year	47	53	74	57	64
Population estimate between	1175/ 2115	1325/ 2385	1850/ 3330	1425/ 2565	1600/ 2880

Taxable Wealth 1334 and 1524

	1334 (15th)		1524	
	Paid	*Assessed*	*Paid*	*Assessed*
	£ s d	£ s d	£ s d	£ s d
Crawley	1 19 4	29 10 0		
Curbridge	3 13 0	54 15 0	1 19 4	47 13 4
Hailey	5 11 5	83 11 3	1 3 10	47 0 0
Witney town	11 18 6	178 17 6	55 3 8	1,538 0 0

Distribution of Goods in Subsidy, 1524/5 (e)

Number of Taxpayers

	£0–2	£2	£3–5	£6–9	£10–19	£20–39	£40–99	£100+	Total
Witney	21	14	14	5	3	3	2	1	63
Burford	17	31	15	20	9	3	3	3	101
Value of goods in 1524 (to nearest £) (e)									
Witney	17	28	52	32	42	42	125	1200	£1,538

(a) Compiled from E 179/161/9, 13, 177, 173 and 162/233 and with reference to: J. Cooper, 'Comparative Wealth and size of Oxfordshire market towns', in *Historic Towns Oxon.*, pp.202–3.

(b) *Chantry Certs.*, pp. 17, 48, and Intro. p. xiv; E 301/38 mm. 2r, v, 3r, 4r, v, 5r, v.

profited from the political stability and growth of internal trade in Elizabeth's reign. In a country parish, too, it may have been freer from the 'dearths' of food which led to higher death rates in big towns. In the Witney registers there were high birth rates in the late 1560s and late 1580s, as well as an exceptionally low death rate in the 1580s which would account for the population peak of 2,000 in the late 1580s and early 1590s; the period, too, of the greatest activity in the court books below. One indication of this growth is in the family sizes revealed by local wills; they show only a small part of the population but explain why some families and their businesses prospered. In nineteen out of sixty wills proved locally between 1545 and 1604 four to five children were named, the lowest figure for those families, since some would die before their parents and some not be mentioned. Ten wills, or sixteen per cent of the sample, mention more. Thomas Ring, the chandler, for example, left seven children in 1557; Leonard Penny, the clothier, nine children in 1567; Richard Humfrey, the dyer, eight in 1568; Richard Bishop, alias Martin, the tucker and miller, eleven in 1599, while Leonard Yates, clothier (de. 1601), married twice and had fifteen children surviving.[40]

The last decade of the sixteenth century saw a setback with the 'sickness', probably the plague which had infected Burford in 1593 and led to 30 deaths in Witney in 1594, and with the more serious visitation of plague in 1597 which affected many towns and led to 187 deaths in Witney: no less than 140 were between December and April when the burial register recorded 'the unknown disease which the Lord has inflicted on us'. There was dearth, too, in these years, brought about by harvest failure in 1596 and 1597, although it was blamed as usual on enclosures. It brought political trouble close to Witney, for John Steere and Vincent Rankell, weavers of Witney, were involved in the planned rebellion in

---

(c) Estimates offered only tentatively and based on a calculation of one third omission of poor and others in 1524, and of equal numbers of women and 40 per cent for children in 1546: this may be too low a figure in the later year but the value of the chantry returns is very debatable and it is safer to err with a lower estimate. The calculations are based on factors suggested by J. Cornwall, 'English Country Towns in the Fifteen Twenties', *Ec.H.R.* 2nd series xv (1962–3), and 'English Population in the early Sixteenth Century', *ibid.* xxiii (1970); and J. Patten, 'Village and Town: an Occupational Study', *Agricultural H.R.* xx (1972).

(d) With acknowledgement to the Cambridge Local Population Studies Group and to Brigadier Goadby. We have extended their suggestions and must take responsibility for any errors. The estimates are based on calculations of 1 to 25, 1 to 35 and 1 to 45 as a possible relation of births to population. Since the register of baptisms is defective the calculations must be very tentative.

(e) cf. tables in Cornwall, 'English Country Towns', p. 62.

[40] Wills Oxon. 181, f.210; 184, f.395v; 185, f.36v; 3/4/55; 75/3/7.

West Oxfordshire in these years, and it was alleged that one hundred men were coming from Witney to meet with others on Enslow Heath and then to spoil the houses of various gentry.[41] It was an abortive attempt and the truth of the Witney allegations cannot be established. The end of the period covered by the court books saw the population recovering a level of some 2,000 in the early seventeeth century, but without the swift growth of fifty years before. Burford, by comparison, grew more slowly over the sixteenth century to about 1,200 in the 1590s. By the time of the Hearth Tax returns of 1664 Witney had clearly established itself as the chief centre in this part of Oxfordshire, and fourth in ranking in the county behind Oxford, Henley and Banbury.[42]

The growth of the town brought new names and families to Witney. Although some of the growth was from natural increase, like other Tudor towns Witney was a target for immigration. One source was probably local, the casualties of the numerous enclosures not only within the parish where Brice's enclosure is said to have deprived six people and the Hailey enclosure sixteen, but also generally in the area.[43] There was enclosure in many nearby places: Wilcote, Widford, Brize Norton, Bampton, Yelford, Ducklington, Radcot, Leafield, Cokethorpe, for example, though it can only be guessed that deprived tenants would have made for the nearest town. Witney, moreover, lay on good routes between South Wales and the West Midlands and London and must have seen many moving through the town in the restless era of the migrant and vagabond depicted in Tudor records. Some must have stayed as workers, as, perhaps, John Blome, weaver, who in 1550 left a bequest to Joan Hemmyng of Feckenham, Worcestershire, 'my natural mother'.[44] There is evidence, too, in the court books and local wills of the numerous Welsh in the town who came along the routes from Gwent and Gloucester: the Joneses, Powells, Lewises, Williamses, Morrises and Johnsons in local business, as well as the itinerant chapman like Peter Powell and John Jenkins and the sieve maker or 'seevegar' William Monmouth, who came and went and left a child for whose nursing a carpenter's wife in Stanton Harcourt tried to get some payment (i, f. 279r).

Towards the end of the century there is a hint, though never much more, of the influx of poor into the town: in the arrangements for the poorbox and later the workhouse and mandates against undertenants as well as the statement in the 1597 riots of the town being full of poor people, as many as sixty.

---

[41] *Cal. S.P.Dom.* iv, 1595–97, pp.317, 319 etc.
[42] *Burford Records*, pp.189–91, 599–606; *Historic Towns Oxon.*, p.201.
[43] *Deserted Villages Oxon.*, gazeteer.
[44] Wills Oxon. 1/3/31.

Woolmen and Businessmen

It is easier to trace the origins of individual families in Witney than to track larger movements of population. The profits of enclosure and the wool trade attracted new people and enabled them to build up business and family, wealth and status. Some of the most noted woolmen feature only incidentally in the running of the town and clearly had wider horizons, though their wealth was important for the parish. This is very apparent with the Wenmans, Fermors and Wilmots. The Wenmans, the wealthiest of them, appear only casually in the grants registered in the court books (i, ff. 40r, 281r). The family was established in the parish in the second half of the fifteenth century with Henry Wenman, woolman. How he arrived is not certain. It may be, as Wood suggested later, that they were long-distance carters with 'wains'.[45] It is possible that Henry was the son of a John Wenman of London, a stockfishmonger in 1427 and a man who had transactions with a Bristol merchant in 1430, working, that is, in a business area which would have brought him to the Cotswold country.[46] Henry himself was said to be of Blewbery, Berks, and married a lady from the Welsh borderlands, Emmote, an heiress, daughter of Simkin Hervey of Herefordshire.[47] The family's Witney interests must have been well-established before his death, which occurred sometime between 1458, when he was dealing with London business as executor of a will, and the late 1470s when his wife had remarried and started her second family by another Witney merchant.[48]

Their son Richard[49] who was granted arms in 1509, clearly prospered on the busy wool trade of the Cotswolds as a woolbuyer, encloser and farmer in cattle and sheep. He held the bishop's land at Caswell by 1500 and leased Witney Park, and in his will, proved in December 1534, his investment in the neighbourhood is clear.[50] He bequeathed the parsonage of Cogges, the manor of Caswell and the occupation and profits of Witney Park and leases of tenements in Witney borough. His farming interests are particularly revealing: the bequests included the farm and cattle of Holwell, the farm, cattle and sheep of Lew and cattle and sheep on land at Weald and in Cogges. There is a reminder of the links between the Cotswolds and the wool trade in the bequest of his term of years in

---

[45] *Par. Coll.*, p.343. cf. John Bay of Witney who in 1378 took wool from Henley to a Lombard merchant in London in his wain: *Cal. Close 1377-81*, p.211.
[46] *Cal. Close 1422-29*, p.333; *1429-35*, p.102.
[47] *DNB* (Fermor); and *Visit. Oxon.*, p.176.
[48] *Cal. Close, 1454-61*, p.292; and see below, p.lx.
[49] Or grandson, if the heralds' (and Wood's) date of 1500 for the death of Henry's son Richard is correct; but it is at variance with the heralds' other evidence and with the mention in the will of Richard Wenman (1534) of his Fermor half-brothers: *Visit. Oxon.*, pp.145, 176; *Par. Coll.*, p.345.
[50] *L. and P. For. and Dom. Hen. VIII*, i, pt. 1, 1509-13, p.75; Wills Oxon. 181, ff.15v-18v.

Sevenhampton (Gloucs.) and of all cattle and sheep on his farm there: in
the fifteenth century Southampton carts had regularly lumbered up to
Oxford and along to Gloucester past Witney with their wine and alum,
returning with Cotswold wool, though with the pull of London in the
sixteenth century this link was weakening.[51] Richard left money to repair
the highway between Newland and Witney and between Milton and
Abingdon on the routes. Like a good woolman gifts of wool featured
among his bequests to poor maidens of Witney married the year after his
death 'to make a garment against their marriage', and he left tods of wool
to his servants. Other interests were shown in his arrangements for his
funeral, prayers and charities: bequests to the four orders of friars in
Oxford, to poor prisoners in Oxford castle and to the provost, masters
and scholars of Eton, while he left the term of years of the parsonage of
Evenley, Northants., to the churchwardens of Witney for his obit in
Witney Church where he was to be buried. The family's interests are also
reflected in the will of his wife, Anne, daughter of John Bushe of
Northleach, which was proved in March 1538. To her grandson, Henry
Wenman, she left all her sheep at Taynton, where her own side of the
family seems to have owned a sheep farm.[52] The Bushes were also noted
woolmen and her brother Thomas Bushe, a merchant of the Staple like
her own husband, had earlier let his farm at Taynton to yet another
stapler. Anne's further bequest of 20s. to 'brother' Thomas Midwinter and
of £10 to his son William was again in the same circle of trade, for the
Midwinters of Northleach are well known for their association with the
London wool merchants, the Celys.[53]

Richard and Anne both mention only one son in their wills, Sir Thomas
Wenman of Caswell, M.P. for Oxfordshire in 1555. His children made
profitable marriages and with the alliance of his son Richard to the
daughter of Sir John Williams of Thame, the man who made his fortune
out of the Dissolution of the Oxfordshire monasteries, the family continued its move up in wealth and status and eventually into the nobility.[54]
Those interests again account for their non-appearance in the petty court
business of the town in the later sixteenth century, though they were still
at Caswell and Witney Park. They had left a gap in the local business
world, however, of which other men were able take advantage.

The Fermors were closely connected with the Wenmans, through Dame
Emmote's second marriage to Thomas Fermor (d. 1485), another woolman, who is buried in the church with her and his first wife.[55] He was
clearly of Welsh ancestry, alias Richards and the son of Henry Richards

[51] C.Platt, *Medieval Southampton* (London, 1973), pp.157ff.
[52] Prob 11/27 15 Dyngeley; C.W. Fallows, *Northleach Brasses*, no. 7 (Northleach, n.d.).
[53] *The Cely Letters, 1472-88*, ed. A.Hanham (Oxford, 1975).
[54] *Visit. Oxon.*, pp.179, 308; *V.C.H.Oxon.* vii.177.
[55] *Visit. Oxon.*, p.46.

alias Fermere of Langford, a woolman who died in 1467.[56] Thomas
Fermor had extensive holdings in the area in Witney itself, in Hailey,
Cogges, Burford, Chadlington, Filkins and Langford.[57] His sons by
Emmote, like their Wenman half-brothers, prospered on trade and enclos-
ure, but although they continued to hold property in Witney they estab-
lished their families elsewhere.[58] Their share in the Oxfordshire wool trade
is well attested: Laurence and William were accused of enclosing in
Oxfordshire and William appeared among the greater woolmen in
England in a list of 1533 when he had 150 sacks of wool of his 'growing
and gatherying' in the Cotswolds.[59]

Edward Wilmot, who appears in the 1544 subsidy as the richest man in
the parish after Wenman, was perhaps the last of the woolmen dealing in
raw wool to prosper in Witney. Again his background was enclosure and
trade, since he was a younger son of John Wilmot of Abingdon, who was
a suitor in the court below in 1539 (i, f. 3v), and a member of the Wilmot
family which had enclosed in Stadhampton and Chislehampton earlier in
the century.[60] Edward seems to have moved into Witney sometime in the
1530s or 1540s perhaps at the instance of the Wenmans for in 1532 Richard
Wenman wrote to Cromwell urging him to grant Wilmot the lease of
Witney parsonage.[60a] His interest in woolbuying in the district is preserved
in a chancery case with Richard Bryan of Cogges, who had undertaken to
supply his wool at a fixed price and defaulted, perhaps in view of the
inflation.[61] Wilmot clearly prospered for he lent £570 to Sir Anthony Lee
in the 1540s on a bond of £100 and as a merchant of the Staple he traded
with the Johnson brothers at Calais and lent them £1,000 in 1542 at 12 per
cent.[62] When Calais was lost he was one of the merchants pardoned for
selling wool to Bruges.[63] He also exported other goods for in 1542 there
was a complaint about the treatment of a ship owned by a Dieppe man
and it was said that there was a little tallow, a pack or two or kerseys and a
horse in it belonging to Edward Wilmot of Southampton.[64] He was
presumably the Edward Wilmot who held the Dolphin inn in Southampton
in English street in 1548 and as merchant, late of Southampton, was

[56] *Some Oxon. Wills*, pp.26-7.
[57] Ibid. p.37; *Cal.I.P.M.Hen.VII*, i, nos. 169, 170.
[58] See *DNB*; *V.C.H.Oxon.* vi.292-3.
[59] *Domesday of Inclosures*, i. 348, 360; M.Beresford, *The Lost Villages of England* (London, 1954), p.193.
[60] *Complete Peerage*, xii, pt. ii, p.179; *V.C.H.Oxon.* vii.11,12,134; *Domesday of Inclosures*, i.340-1.
[60a] *L. and P. For. and Dom. Hen. VIII, Addenda*, i, pt.i, no.788.
[61] C 1/1279/45–7. and above, p.
[62] B.Winchester, *Tudor Family Portrait* (London, 1955), pp.216, 219; *L. and P. For. and Dom. Hen. VIII*, xiv, 1559, pt.ii, p.93; ibid. xix, 1544, pt.i, p.600; pt. ii, p.3; C 1/1241/28.
[63] *Cal. Pat. 1557-8*, p.300.
[64] *L. and P. For. and Dom. Hen. VIII*, xvii, 1542, p.672.

pardoned in the first year of Elizabeth's reign for treasons.[65] But he was clearly settled in Witney in the 1550s when his children were baptised there and he made charitable bequests to poor householders and poor maids on their marriage in Witney and like Wenman towards the mending of the highways.[66] By the time of his death in 1558 he had bought land in Marlow, Bucks. and Newent, Gloucestershire, and his children (i, f. 71r) did not stay in Witney or in trade.[67] There was a clause in his will that if his desperate debts came to £400 his legacies were to be abated, and it may be that his trading ventures had met difficulties, as indeed might well happen to anyone involved with the Johnson brothers and the Calais market. His grandson, too, moved into the peerage and his seventeenth-century descendents have been called 'the wild Wilmots' but they earned those distinctions through fighting in Ireland and service to the Stuarts.[68]

In contrast with the early woolmen the men who prospered in Witney in the days of the court books were those connected with the cloth trade, the clothiers, fullers and tanners. They were more interested in running the town, for though the clothiers, for example, were travellers collecting and reselling and putting out wool and marketing cloth, they were also broadweavers with looms, apprentices and premises in the town. Some were old denizens in the parish like the Gunnes, the early dissenters in Witney, the Colliers and Martins whose families appear in thirteenth-century records or the Newmans in the fourteenth century.[69] Others seem first to appear in the fifteenth century, a period from which a number of families in the later court books can be traced. Robert Temple, clothier and bailiff from 1541 to 1543, was from an original Leicestershire family which had been established in Witney for some four generations.[70] The Yates, clothiers, prominent again as bailiffs in the sixteenth century, moved in from Charney Basset, Berkshire, to Standlake and Witney.[71] One cannot always be sure of the family antecedents of sixteenth-century merchants but it must be significant that a number of families established in the cloth trade in sixteenth-century Witney have the names of families

---

[65] *Cal. Pat. 1548-9*, p.48; *1554-5*, p.128; *1558-60*, pp.177, 215.

[66] Prob 11/42A 9 Welles. Edward Wilmot's coat of arms in the church is noted in *Visit.Oxon.*, p.45.

[67] *V.C.H.Bucks*. iii.80; *V.C.H.Gloucs*. x.91; *Cal. Pat. 1555-7*, p.94. But Leonard Wilmot was said to have provided for the poor of Witney etc: O.R.O. D.Y. 11/i/1.

[68] *Complete Peerage*, xii, pt.ii, p.179; O. Barron, 'The Wild Wilmots', *The Ancestor*, no.xi (1904), pp.1-14.

[69] Eccl. 2/159319. For the sixteenth-century Gunnes see *L. and P. For. and Dom. Hen. VIII*, iv, pt. ii, 1526-8, p.1788.

[70] *The Visitation of the County of Leicester*, ed. J.Fetterston, Harleian Soc. ii (1870), 168; and information from Dr N.Alcock and Brigadier Goadby. His father Thomas had land in Hailey in 1508: Eccl. 1/73/2. Robert (d.1568) apparently left Witney, but his son Cuthbert was a clothier in Standlake: Prob 11/51 4 Sheffeld.

[71] *Visit.Oxon.*, p.158. See below p.xxvii.

prominent in the southern English wool trade of the fifteenth century. The Daltons, sixteenth-century mercers in Witney and London, may be from the fifteenth-century family of woolmen in Leicester.[72] It may be in the fifteenth century that the Boxes, Pennys, Taylors and Wiltshires who were trading out of Bristol in cloth, wine, woad and other commodities in 1479 established an interest in the parish.[73] There were Pennys or Pennes, too, in London, one a merchant stapler, in the fourteenth century and connected with Oxfordshire in 1416 when Thomas Stonor paid for cartage for the Flemings to a John Penne.[74] John Penny (d. 1554), the first bailiff in the court books, held 'Heylonds' of Sir Francis Stonor, and though he is given no trade in his will it is probably that like the other bailiffs he was originally a business man of the town, perhaps a clothier or a broadweaver like his son, Leonard (d. 1567).[75] The movement of business families into various towns was a natural one in an expanding community and continued. There were Bishops and Hannes and Johnsons among the bailiffs of both Burford and Witney;[76] at the end of the sixteenth century Richard Clempson, mercer, had property in Witney and Abingdon, and Nicholas Ifeelde of Witney (i, f. 241r), clothier, had property in Somerset and Witney when he died in 1587.[77] The advent of Thomas Cornish of Chipping Norton, mercer, bailiff of Witney in 1601, was marked by his marriage to the widow of Thomas Bishop alias Martin.[78]

The other side of this immigration into Witney was, of course, the migration out, especially to London and many Witney families had sons or relatives established there in the sixteenth century. Wills and references in the court books show that the Boxes, the Daltons, Hills, Johnsons, Kings and Laurences, to name a few, had close family links there (e.g. i, ff. 266r, 332r; ii, f. 134r).[79] This practice, whether by apprenticeship or other means, ensured a good business connexion with the chief centre of commerce in Britain, and rarely meant the complete loss of a business house to Witney. Like Henry Box, the founder of the grammar school in the seventeenth century, a number came back in old age or remembered

[72] *The Cely Letters, 1472-88*, index. For their later history see Monk, *Witney*, p.257.
[73] *Overseas Trade of Bristol*, pp.196, 207, 220 and index; cf. the Bristol connexions of Thomas Croft (d.1485) of Woodstock, who also had small holdings in Witney: *Some Oxon. Wills*, p.37; *Cal. Pat. 1461-67*, p.473. For the Bristol cloth trade and industry see *Atlas of Historic Towns*, ed. M.D.Lobel, ii (London, 1975), 10 ff.
[74] *Cal. Pat. 1429-36*, p.393; *Stonor L. and P.* i, ed. C.L.Kingsford, Camden Soc. 3rd. series, xxix(1919), 30; *Cal. Plea and Memoranda Rolls of the City of London, 1458-82*, ed. P.E.Jones (Cambridge, 1961), pp.143-4, 155; S.Thrupp, *Merchant Class of Medieval London*, pp.360, 383.
[75] Wills Oxon. 180, f.224v.
[76] *Burford Records*, p.96.
[77] Prob 11/99 32 Montague; 11/71 62 Spencer.
[78] Misc. Je I/1, f.77v.
[79] See index to P.C.C.Wills, and for the Boxes see M.Fleming, *Witney Grammar School 1660-1960* (Oxford, 1960). The building up of the Box property is seen in Misc. Je I/1 and in Req. 2/20/103, 36/98, 118, 61/57 etc.

their birth place in their wills. Oxford, curiously, seems to have exercised only a minor pull on Witney if we can rely on apprenticeship records which show only five clear enrolments in Oxford of Witney apprentices between 1514 and 1591.[79a]

It is clear that many factors led to success in starting a business: enterprise, luck, the market as well as family and business connexions. It looks very much as if the rise of the major families in Witney took place before the mid-sixteenth century and that they continued to dominate the town for many years. Though apprenticeship is a well known avenue, it is doubtful from the Witney records discussed above whether it was easy to break into established family businesses solely through this route by the later sixteenth century. Father and son seem to follow in the family businesses of, for example, the Yates or the Taylors or Clempsons, and this stability undoubtedly aided the prosperous growth of the town in this period. The leading families were closely interrelated and marriage and family 'clientage' was another important factor in securing a business and position in the town. It is hard to point to any leading family that was not in this circle of intermarriage. Thomas Taylor (d. 1549), for example, married one daughter to a Wenman and his son to Leonard Yate's daughter. When Thomas Taylor the younger's mother-in-law, Joan Yate, died in 1587 she made bequests to her relatives the Willsheares, the Bishops, the Rings and the Bryces. Branches of the Yates were related to the Cornish family and to the wealthy gentry family, the Ashcombes; the Brices were related to the Bishops and to Mr John Clarke, a prominent clothier, the Clempsons to the Daltons, and the Webleys to the Johnsons.[80]

Many of these points about the rise of Witney clothiers are well illustrated in the Jones family of Witney and the career of Walter Jones, perhaps the most noted clothier to appear in the court books. Walter Jones was a clothier, broadweaver, Merchant Adventurer of England and a bailiff of Witney in 1550 and 1558. He first appeared in the town records in the late 1540s together with his brothers Henry and Giles. All three served as town officers and became prominent business men. They are said to have been descendents of John Jones of Grosmont in Monmouthshire, and if we look for a trading background to account for their business interest in the Cotswolds it may be that they were connected with the Lewis Jones who was trading out of Bristol in 1479, and like the Boxes was sending cloth to Spain.[81] Nearer at hand there was a Jones family established in Burford in the 1520s; a John Jones paid taxes there and was burgess and bailiff of the town in the 1530s and took a lease of a Burford

[79a] Oxford City Records, Mayor's Court, A.5.3, ff. 26r, 26v, 31v, 102v, 130r.
[80] Wills Oxon. 179, f.324; 180, f.201v; 185, f.137; Prob 11/120 107 Fenner.
[81] M.Dickens, *Chastleton* (Banbury, 1938), pp.22-3; *Overseas Trade of Bristol*, pp.219-20.

fulling mill, and a Giles Jones appears in the 1542 muster.[82] A family
connexion might well account for Walter Jones' later bequests to the poor
in Burford. However, by 1548 he was a substantial contributer to the
subsidy in Witney and was assessed on £8 worth of goods while ten years
later he paid on £16 worth and his brother Henry on £2.[83]

Walter had a house in London beside Strand bridge, lands in
Oxfordshire and Berkshire and connexions, perhaps land again, in
Worcester where his sister Margaret had married a Strete, probably one of
the wealthy clothiers of that name there.[84] From the 1540s until his death
in 1560 or 1561, his centre was Witney where he was eventually buried.
He had three houses there, looms and apprentices and he made bequests to
his apprentices, tenants and to the poor weavers and spinners in Witney
and thereabouts with whom he must have had many dealings. Like other
prosperous dealers in cloth he had financial interests in local mills and was
able to leave various grain dues from Morton mill to his wife and his lease
of Crawley fulling mill to his brother Giles. His concern for the prosperity
of the district led him to leave £10 to rebuild Newbridge on the Thames
on the route to Abingdon which he must have often travelled, as well as
the money for the market house. Another £10 left for the repair of the
school house in Witney 'to the intent that the children may be taught and
brought up in learning' is a reminder of the importance of education to the
merchant and industrialist of the age; in 1612 Richard Lygon of Witney
left 10s. to repair it. Jones' trading connexions must have been a considerable asset for Witney's cloth industry and it is relevant that he left £50 as a
stock to the Merchant Adventurers of England to help two young
merchants 'to prosper and forward them in their trade'.[85]

His wealth was considerable: there is no inventory with his will but his
bequests totalled about £700 apart from the property he left and any debts
due to him. He had no children, at least when he died, but his influence
and money benefitted Witney long after 1561. He gave a helping hand to
his apprentices, relatives and tenants with bequests of money and looms in
his will: John Southern, Giles Palmer and Henry Johnson and Jones'
relatives, the Cooks and Allens,[86] were all broadweavers in Witney who
benefitted. The interrelation of business, marriage and apprenticeships is
very evident in his bequests to the Rankells. It may be guessed that there
was a close family connexion, perhaps the one that brought Walter into
Witney, with John Rankell the glover or tanner (d. 1565), a man established in Witney by 1544 when he was assessed on £20 worth of goods.

[82] *Burford Records.*, pp.96, 655, 658–60.
[83] E 179/162/263 and 320.
[84] Prob 11/44 20 Loftes; Dyer, *Worcester*, p.28.
[85] Prob 11/44 20 Loftes.
[86] Joan Cook was Jones' sister. For the Allens see also Thomas Cooke's will of 1567: Wills
Oxon. 184, f.83r.

Walter had one of his sons, Thomas Rankell, as an apprentice and left £4 each to seven of John's children and a house each to Anne Rankell who was his god-daughter and to her brother Peter. The Rankells were broadweavers and clothiers later in the court books. Peter was a chamberlain and bailiff of the town, as well, apparently, as being a some- what stormy man, said by his son-in-law Thomas Box to have been in both Oxford jail and the debtor's prison, the Marshalsea.[87]

Walter, however, made his young nephew and namesake his heir and gave major bequests to his own two brothers Giles and Henry. They were perhaps somewhat younger than he since they lived for another thirty years: both died in 1594, Giles of the plague and Henry possibly too.[88] Both played a large part in Witney life in Elizabeth's reign in the cloth industry and as leading citizens acting as bailiffs and vestrymen and churchwardens. Giles Jones, called a clothmaker below (i, f. 207r) was left Walter's interest in the fulling mill at Crawley and £180 for himself and other money for two daughters. Henry Jones, a clothier, had the lease of Walter's dwelling house after the widow's death. His own will demon- strates his involvement with Witney where he was to be buried next to his father and late wife in Witney Church. He bequeathed £20 to three poor men of any occupation within the borough for them to borrow for two years at a time with preference to clothiers. He also made bequests to his apprentices and forgave his workmen all sums of money they owed him. He left two of his looms and his house, presumably business premises, to his son-in-law Thomas Cave and two other looms to his grandson Henry Surbye, while his apprentices were to be transferred to his sons-in-law Cave or Boxe. His seven daughters had all been married off to local business men, including John Clarke, Thomas Cave and Richard Boxe, clothiers, and had presumably been endowed then, for his total bequests came to only about £160. He may have disposed of part of his wealth already or invested in property which largely went to his son and heir Walter Jones, who was clearly not going to carry on the clothier business.[89]

This Walter (II) Jones (i, ff. 190v, 296v) had already been well set up by his inheritance from his uncle at the age of ten. His career has been well charted. He went on to marry one of the Popes of Oxfordshire and to further his fortunes at Lincoln's Inn in a distinguished legal career and as town clerk of Worcester and M.P. for Worcestershire. He had property in Witney but his interests were elsewhere and in the end he settled his family away from both Witney and Worcester by buying Chastleton house in north west Oxfordshire in 1602.[90] The Joneses in Witney in the seven-

[87] Req. 2/36/118 and see above.
[88] Parish records: Brigadier Goadby's transcripts.
[89] Prob 11/83 10 Dixey.
[90] Dyer, *Worcester*, pp.200-201; Misc. Je I/1, ff. 37r and v, 42r.

teenth and eighteenth century were not connected with this main branch
which ceased as a business house after 1594. It is a pattern of history
already familiar from the early wool merchants, of migration into the
town, the establishment of a business fortune and then movement into the
gentry and out of Witney. In the course of it the life and prosperity of
Witney were enhanced.

Occupations and Wealth

Some of the people who appear in the early years of the court books had
also paid taxes in 1523 and 1524 and these sources together with local wills
can be used to study Witney society. In 1523-4 Witney was exceptional in
that the wealth of Richard Wenman made all other contributions such a
small proportion of the the the total paid: in other towns studied as much as a
third to a half might be paid by those assessed on under £20. Still, there
was a typical Tudor pattern in Witney society of a few moderately
wealthy men at the top, a group of middling masters and traders in
between, and a broader base of the not so prosperous to poor craftsmen
and servants. Those with under £1 were not assessed and we do not know
how many of these non-contributing poor there were in Witney. The
problem of the very poor may not have been the same as in larger towns
like Worcester, Coventry or Leicester, where they are estimated at a third
to a half of the population. There is not in Witney as large a proportion
assessed under £2 as even in nearby Burford; this suggests that poverty
was not so pressing and that there may have been prospects for work and
the tenure of the old assart land. It may be more profitable to compare
Witney and Bampton hundred with the region around Lavenham, the
rural and cloth-producing hundred of Babergh in East Anglia, where a
comparison of the tax returns and the 1522 musters puts the
non-contributing poor at ten to twenty per cent of the population.[91]

The comparative status of the various businesses in the town is seen in
the tax assessments in 1523. After Wenman, the lessee of the manor,
William Brice, a yeoman, headed the list, but later his family too paid in
Curbridge. The most prosperous business men operating within the town
were Thomas Taylor and Richard Humfreys both bailiffs in the 1540s.
Taylor (d. 1549) was called a yeoman in his will but was probably a tanner
like his son, Thomas (d. 1583), to whom he bequeathed his property.[92]

[91] Comparisons are based on J.Cornwall, 'English Country Towns', pp.63–4; and J.Patten,
'Village and Town: an occupational study', *Agricultural History Review* xx (1972), 1–15. For
recent summaries of work on class structure see W.G.Hoskins, *The Age of Plunder 1500-47*
(London, 1976), pp.96ff.; cf. J.Patten, *English Towns 1500-1700* (Folkestone, 1978), pp.189ff.
[92] *Oxon. Inventories*, no. 107. Unless otherwise stated the dates of death and details of the
wills are taken from the Bodleian Mss. Wills Oxon. and the call numbers are not given here:
they can be checked by the personal name index in the Library and in publication. For
occupational references see below.

Richard Humfreys (d. 1570) was the local dyer and like Taylor was related to the Wenmans: he was called 'cousin' Humfreys by Richard Wenman who left money to him and his son Fabian. The clothiers of the town, Leonard Yate (d. 1554) and Robert Temple (d. 1568) ranked lower in assessment but both were bailiffs in the 1540s. They were placed in the subsidy alongside Richard Millent, perhaps the Millington of Standlake (i, f. 147v), and Henry Smythe who may be the tailor of the 1550s (i, f. 42r), or one of the Smiths, farmers in Hailey. Beneath them again were the smaller masters and traders: William Gunne the tanner (d. 1550), John Banning the shoemaker (d. 1576), Thomas Hyat the tailor, William Box (d. 1549), miller in 1527 of Waleys mill; William Horne the carpenter, and Elizabeth and William Hill, the bakers.

The people who paid on £1 and £2 are often equated with the semi-independent craftsmen and apprentices and labourers. They included the sawyers Richard and Thomas Andrews who appear in the courts of Mary's time and several servants and labourers. The broadweaver Richard Webbe (d. 1547) also appears in this group, despite his later status in the town as a clothier with apprentices, and was perhaps just setting up. John Penny (d. 1554) who may have been a broadweaver and Roger Legge (d. 1557) the baker, who were the first bailiffs in the court books, were both also assessed on only £2 worth of goods; they too may have had to make good in business or alternatively had their investments elsewhere.

The 1544 subsidy in many ways gives a better picture of the standing of the business men in the court books, since both Wenmans and Brices were assessed in the rural areas of the parish and it is possible to see how some townsfolk have advanced in wealth. Wilmot, the woolman, with £60 paid on only twice as much as the four other leading business men, Humfreys the dyer, Taylor and his sons, Leonard Yate and the miller William Martin. Two leatherworkers William Gunne the tanner and John Rankell (d. 1565) the glover, and Thomas Ryng (d. 1558) the chandler and Robert Temple the clothier were close with £20 worth of goods. In the £10 tier were Richard Hannes (d. 1559) the shoemaker, William Box yeoman, one-time miller, the bakers Agnes Hill and Roger Legge and the wiredrawer William Byrde; and among those paying on £3 to £7 worth was the broadweaver-clothier Richard Webbe, the woollen draper William Elmer, the carpenter Harry Horne and the sawyer Roger Atkins. The £2 and under assessment covered a varied class of traders and craftsmen: the fuller Robert Mukell, the smith William Abley, the mercer William Dalton and the tippler and victualler Randel Margeries. Walter Jones's relatives were here too, the weavers the Cooks and the Allens. There must have been many more textile workers in these lower groups, like Thomas Colyer, servant, probably apprenticed, to William Martin the tucker or miller, and Thomas Glossope the dyer's servant.

The later subsidies are even less reliable as a guide to real wealth and have a low number of contributers in proportion to the population, but they show the leading business men of the community. In 1548 these were still Wilmot the woolman and Temple the clothier, Humfreys the dyer, Ryng the chandler, Bishop or Martin, the miller, with Yate and Taylor; and in 1558 the same group, with Wilmot's widow, and with Walter Jones and Philip Box, clothiers, paying larger contributions. The seventeenth century subsidies in the court books must be regarded with the same suspicion, but again they show a ranking of wealth and that the clothiers, millers and tanners are still the leading business men. Among the group chosen to assess their fellows in 1603 were John Clarke, then the most prosperous clothier, Richard and Thomas Box, clothier and tucking miller respectively, Thomas Taylor of the earlier tanning business, and William Clempson, mercer, whose ranking shows the growth of retail trade in the town (ii, ff. 50r, 73r, 83v, 115r).

The average tradesman did not expect to make the wealth of a Wenman or even of Wilmot or Walter Jones whose assets were held not only in Witney but also in London Southampton or Worcester. The wealth of those who held solely in Witney and Oxfordshire can be seen in 130 wills proved locally between 1545 and 1650, a range of years appropriate for people appearing in the court books.[93] In the first half of the period from 1545 to 1590 wills and inventories for seventy craftsmen and farmers in the whole parish show a range of wealth, from £1 10s. for Joan More in 1546 to £313 for John Penny in 1554, with a median value of £17; if craftsmen's and traders' wills alone are taken for the town the median is £15. These figures show Witney men with much the same wealth as elsewhere in

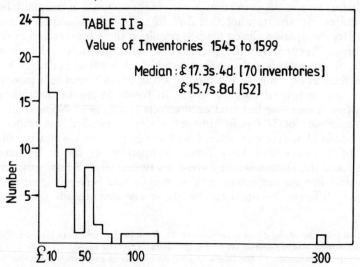

TABLE II a

Value of Inventories 1545 to 1599

Median : £17.3s.4d. [70 inventories]
£15.7s.8d. [52]

[93] The sample excludes those whose wills were proved in the P.C.C.

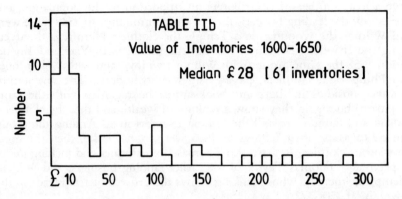

Oxfordshire, where a median of £22 for farmers and £15 for craftsmen has been established. They were markedly less prosperous, however, than Worcestershire traders with a median value for their wealth in inventories of £44. In the seventeenth century the Witney inventories have a median value of £28, which is roughly comparable with the £17 of the sixteenth century because of inflation. Again this is lower than in places outside Oxfordshire, where, for example, Lichfield has a median of £55 from 1600 to 1649, but it was perhaps a reasonable figure within Oxfordshire where it falls between the medians of £43 for Bicester and £14 for Banbury.[94]

The opportunities for making a living in sixteenth century Witney are shown by the occupations in the town (Table III) which are given not only in wills but also in the court books, where they appear occasionally before 1570 and nearly always after that date for officers and suitors. There are about fifty occupations listed for 540 people in these sources and in central government records for the period 1545 to 1610, only indeed a small sample of the total population but larger than is often available. Witney can be seen as offering a full range of occupations found in a prosperous market and industrial country town. In larger towns of the time there were often about one hundred occupations listed, as at Norwich in 1570 when a census of 504 poor showed ninety-seven different trades. But Witney should again be compared with the Suffolk area where the market town of Sudbury had forty listed occupations in the early sixteenth century and the cloth town of Lavenham twenty-five. At the other end of the period the market towns in East Anglia had between forty and one hundred different occupations by the early seventeenth century, and

[94] The comparisons are based on *Oxon. Inventories*, Introduction, and G.H.Dannatt, 'Bicester in the seventeeth and eighteenth centuries', *Oxoniensia* xxvi/xxvii (1961–2), 303–11, and her forthcoming introduction to the Banbury probate records in the Banbury Record Society publications. See also Dyer, *Worcester*, and *Agrarian History of England*, iv. 488 ff.

Table III

*Trade structure, Witney 1545 to 1609**

Cloth		Retailers	
Clothiers/weavers	196	Mercer, haberdasher	15
clothmen, clothmaker, coverlet maker,		ironmonger	1
		fishmonger	3
blanket maker	8	pearmonger	1
warper, woolwinder	2		—
cardmaker	1		20 = 4%
dyer	8	Services	
fullers (tuckers)	32	Carpenters	15
felt maker	1	Building [mason,	19
	—	joiner, glazier,	
	248 = 46%	plasterer, slater]	
Artisan retailers		millers	9
Tailors	27	barbers	2
tanners	3	surgeon	2
glovers	12	schoolmaster	3
saddlers	4	physician	1
shoemakers, cobblers	23		—
metalworkers [brasier,	13		51 = 9%
wiredrawers, tinkers,		Food and drink	
bellfounder, nailman]		Aquavyte man	2
smith	15	baker	17
currier	2	butcher	16
wheeler	4	licenced victualler	69
cooper	5	vintner	2
collar maker	1		—
hatter	1		106 = 20%
sievemaker	4		
fence maker, bowyer	2	Total	541
	—		—
	116 = 21%		

*This table is based on wills, inventories, court books and excludes the occupations of clerk, yeoman and one flockman.

Banbury wills showed thirty.[95] The occupation of yeoman or husbandman which, of course, was the most usual one for the rural parish is not shown in this list but it was often the status of the mill lessee like William Box or his grandson Thomas Box, of a retired clothier like John Penny or retired mercer like Christopher Drynge (i, ff. 24r, 43r) who was 'late' of Witney in 1559, alias of Buckland, Berks., yeoman.[96]

Witney evidently serviced the rural area in Bampton hundred: with its tailors and barbers, chandler, leather workers, builders, masons and inn-keepers and other retailers as well as the rural involvement in its cloth industry. Some indication of the connexions are shown in the debt cases in the court book. These show, for example, that the Witney smiths, coopers and wheelers worked mainly for local squires, yeomen and husbandmen as when George Warde, tinker had cases brought against him by Sir John Harrington in 1584 and also by suitors from Brize Norton, Bampton, Shifford and Weald (i, ff. 231v, 254r, 264r, 267r). The number of building and woodworkers in the town indicates that there was work available in the area and masons and carpenters in the court books have extensive dealings with yeomen and husbandmen in the surrounding villages of Cogges, Stanton Harcourt, Shipton, North Aston and in Burford and further afield: William Fawdrey or Fauthry, mason, was sued by a miller from Hatherop and a husbandman from Fairford, both in Gloucestershire, as well as by men from South Leigh and Burford and Witney itself, possibly for work as mason (ii, ff. 51r, 55v, 83r, 85r). This was the period of the 'great rebuilding' of rural England, when rising wealth was reflected in the renewal and improvement of houses and Witney craftsmen and traders were able to make a comfortable living out of it. The trade of plasterer or pargeter (ii, ff. 33v, 119v) reflects the fact that, while there is little of this work in present Witney, wooden buildings and Tudor orna-mental plaster work were once more common in the town and neighbour-hood. The glazier's work is shown in the proud recording of new glass windows in local wills, as well as in debt cases (ii, f. 68r).

Witney retailers concentrated on a local market, leaving the London market to the clothiers. They feature perhaps more frequently than any other class in the court books and this suggests a lively trade between them and inhabitants not only of Witney but also of the tithings and surrounding villages. They may even have brought goods in for sale from some distance for one of the cases of debt brought against Humfrey Malen, woollen draper, was by Ewen Jackson of Ambleside, and may have been for the special cloth of that town (i, f. 145v).

Conversely the rural area also supplied Witney with important raw

[95] cf. Hoskins, Age of Plunder, pp.91ff.; J.Patten, 'Urban occupations in pre-industrial England', Transactions of the Institute of British Geographers, n.s. 2 (1977), 296ff.
[96] Cal. Pat. 1558-60, p.243.

materials and labour. The clothiers and broadweavers had their spinners in the district and must have gathered some wool locally and from the fells brought in for local tanners and leatherworkers. The use of the court by tanners from outside, Nicholas Launce of Eynsham, for example, indicates such contacts (i, ff. 282v, 219r). Butchers in Witney and around were clearly an important link in this chain of dependence (i, f. 300r). The debt cases suggest that stock was bought in the neighbourhood, as when William Daube (Dalbe) butcher, was sued for debt by yeomen from Bladon, Bourton and South Leigh in the 1590s and Thomas Shawe, butcher, by yeomen from Ducklington and Crawley (i, ff. 304v, 310v, 325r; ii, f. 128v). Corn and flour again must have been bought locally, for Witney bakers, judging from their inventories, seemed neither to grow their own supplies nor to have stockpiled their corn as in the case of the Worcester bakers who have been investigated. Presumably they relied on local millers in Witney and nearby. The presence of carriers and far carters in the court books indicates the importance of local carrying trade (i, ff. 296v-308v).

Within Witney the distribution of trades followed a pattern seen in other county towns as well as showing some of the peculiarities of Witney's own position. Clothing, food and drink trades and building trades usually occupied 30 to 40 per cent of a town's population and Witney just falls within this range. The retailing percentage of distributive trades is perhaps lower than might be expected, whether of 'pure' retailers, i.e. mercers and haberdashers, or artisan retailers, but in this Witney could not be the same as a regional capital, like Coventry, York or Norwich where there was a growing emphasis on the town as the centre of luxury items. Leather and metal working engaged a moderate number of workers and there was evidently no specialization in these trades in the town, despite any individual wealth.

Most marked is the proportion of people in the cloth industry and in trades like tailoring dependent on it. Within Oxfordshire it is not, as yet, easy to point to another town where there was such a high percentage of cloth-workers within the town: in Banbury wills between 1590 and 1650 only some 16 per cent of the occupations was in the cloth trade and many weavers supplying the town are said to have been in the countryside around; the distinctive occupation in the town was leather working and especially shoemaking. Neither Henley nor Thame developed a weaving industry, while Bicester and Charlbury throve on the ordinary dealings of a market town. Burford from its history and position might have rivalled Witney but there is no evidence to suggest that there was this development in the sixteenth century. For a comparison further afield, in the Midlands only Worcester had the same concentration of textile workers with some 42 to 54 per cent in a sample of 620 wills and inventories over a seventy year period; Coventry had 33 per cent in the early sixteenth century and in

Northampton and Leicester the actual textile industry as opposed to cloth trades like tailoring, was of minor importance compared with leather working or the food and drink trades. Again the clearest comparison is with the Suffolk cloth producing area around Sudbury with 32 per cent working in textiles and 60 per cent in Lavenham in the early sixteenth century. Witney must be compared with these smaller towns, too, in the fact there was no rigid organization of its trades and crafts as in larger towns and no evidence of gilds in the town.

A classification of occupations, however, does not always show the diversity of occupation for one man in a small town. Thomas Taylor (d. 1583), for example, was termed a yeoman and had indeed malt, hops, cheese and wool in store; he had a warping house and probably provided Witney weavers with the spun yarn for the warp threads in their looms. But he was also a tanner and many people in neighbouring parishes owed him for leather and he probably sold his skin and hides for the glove makers not only in Witney but also in the Wychwood forest villages nearby. He also sold wood and laths for roofing, salt, lime and household stuff and in addition he was something of a money lender since twenty people had borrowed money from him. Taylor was successful according to his inventory, worth £162 in goods and chattels and £246 in debts owed to him or money on loan.[97] The court books and church wardens' accounts show his political power in the town. At the other end of the scale many a weaver or poor tradesman combined his trade with tippling.

The Witney Cloth Industry

The organization of industry in Witney is best seen in the cloth working of the town which was to become in the next century Witney's chief claim to fame. There are few references in the court books to anything other than broadweavers and broadcloths, though blankets were listed among household goods and in 1584 it was Collier of Witney, presumably John Collier the clothier, who supplied the blankets to Kenilworth castle. Blankets, made from the coarser fell wool, were a natural product of the broadcloth industry, but it looks as if Witney did not turn to specialization in this branch until the seventeenth century when circumstances, perhaps the easy availability of coarse wool and the fact that the Wiltshire weavers turned to making 'medleys', a finer dyed cloth, led the Witney weavers practically alone in the West of England cloth industry to keep to the blanket cloths.[98] It is not until 1624 that blanket yarn as such was listed in an inventory when Richard Budd's goods included eight score and sixteen

[97] *Oxon. Inventories*, pp.10–11.
[98] *Witney Blanket Industry*, pp.9–10; Ramsay, *Wilts. Woollen Industry*, pp.103–7; *V.C.H.Wilts.* iv. 148ff; N.Lowe, *The Lancashire Textile Industry in the Sixteenth Century*, Chetham Soc. 3rd series xx (1972), 96 ff.

lb of blanket yarn, while in 1634 Thomas Thompson, broadweaver, left his ware and blankets to his wife. By 1641 the weavers were specifically petitioning as blanketweavers.

Narrow cloth, made on a narrow loom and of finer quality, must also have been made in the town, though not in any quantity. In the court book the two narrow weavers both came from outside Witney from South Leigh and Aston (ii, ff. 18v, 40v) but one case concerned 7s. owed by Roger Babbe of Witney for a narrow loom and earlier in 1547 Richard Webbe of Witney, clothier, bequeathed two narrow looms with their harnesses to two servants: John Webbe, his kinsman, and Andrew Johnson. In 1602 the cloth searchers were specifically authorized to seek out narrow cloth and friezes in the market (ii, f. 62r), and the seven yards of narrow cloth that Thomas Slaymaker, carpenter, had in his house in 1612 may have been local.

Broadlooms could also be adapted to the weaving of linen and Slaymaker's goods included twenty-one lb of linen yarn and Thomas Taylor, tanner, in 1615 had linen yarn and two linen wheels. Linen wheels are occasionally found in other local inventories: both Nicholas Gunne, the clothier (d. 1602), and Nicholas Clempson, fuller (d. 1595) possessed them.

Broadcloth, the heavy felted cloth used for all kinds of clothing, covers, awnings, tilts and horse cloths, as Plot listed in the late seventeenth century, was, therefore, the staple cloth of Witney and its fortunes were very much part of the great West of England broadcloth industry in the sixteenth century. The clothiers of Witney had family connexions with Wiltshire: John Box of Witney, tucker, and brother-in-law to Henry Jones, clothier, was brother-in-law, too, of Thomas Eton of Malmesbury; and Leonard Yate (d. 1554) married Joan Presci of Bishopston.[99]

The cloth was usually white or undyed like the white cloths sold by Witney clothiers in London in the first years of Elizabeth's reign or produced in court in 1574 (i, f. 147v). Obviously some were dyed in the town and the three quarters of red cloth taken as a 'distress' in the court book may have been local (i, f. 92v). As in Wiltshire there are not many dyers but they were not poor men: the wealth and position of Richard Humfreys dyer has already been discussed and Richard Okeley who died in 1644 had 40 tod of wool and yarn worth £30 5s. and cloth worth £50 in his house.

Suppliers of wool were obviously in a strong position in the town. Although the matter of Witney's wool supply cannot be fully resolved, it is rather puzzling that there is not more evidence of contracts or the use of distant markets. After the decline of the wool export trade by the mid-century, many staplers turned to the internal market but it is not possible to point to one operating in Witney after the Wenmans and Wilmot,

[99] *Visit. Oxon.*, p.158; and Oxon. Wills.

although Anthony Ashfield, the wool patentee lived close by in Shipton and had been an active collector in the mid-century but for the foreign market and Leonard Yate, clothier in the court books, had shipped wool to Calais in the 1530s. In 1577, however, the Mayor of the Staple's collection of names of the chief buyers and broggers of wool in Oxfordshire did not include any Witney names although it included Robert Secole of Eynsham and Shugborough of Banbury, the latter 'who wekely selleth 60 tod', and who appears below as a clothier selling a broadloom. Other names from Banbury, Henley, Hinksey, Horton, Shenington and Woodstock, which had a liberty for stapling wool, all indicate where Witney men may have bought their wool.[100]

Local farmers in West Oxfordshire were an obvious source of wool especially with the early enclosure movement in the area and the development of sheep farming by such people as the Lees of Ditchley and Dormers of Rousham in the later sixteenth century. Much reliance must have been placed on quite modest flocks: the 1549 tax on sheep shows that there were fifty-five flocks within Bampton hundred with a median size of 155 sheep. There were ten people taxed on 2,300 sheep in Witney according to this return.[101] Wills and inventories indicate local sheep flocks, even when only small bequests were made to children and servants. John Haddon of Curbridge (d. 1553) left ten sheep, a cow and a heifer to his daughter and Robert Burdeye of Crawley (d. 1561) left instructions that the children were to have 'their ewes and lambs' when they were twelve. Thomas Taylor (d. 1549) left sheep to his grandchildren, Thomas Wenman's children, and his son Andrew (d. 1545) left sixty sheep in his bequests. John Newman of Curbridge (i, f. 4r) husbandman (d. 1548) also left bequests of some forty sheep. The names show clothier connexions. Philip Box (d. 1593), yeoman and ex-clothier, with land in Curbridge and Hailey, bequeathed one wether sheep and one ewe apiece to his grandchildren and to his overseers, and Maud Brice, widow (d. 1623) of the manorial lessee, had a flock of 200 ewes and rams and 100 tegs and old sheep, together worth £135. At the other end of the scale Richard Fuller of New Yatt (d. 1630) tailor left nine sheep worth 27s. Pasture was a valuable asset and was sold for 100 sheep at Ducklington in 1597 while fifty ewes were offered as a bribe to gain the lease of Bury Crofts in Hailey.[102]

Another source may have been the tithe wool for several of the richer clothiers held impropriate parsonages and wills and law suits suggest their value.[102a] Witney parsonage and the tithes in Hailey and Crawley were

---

[100] *L. & P. For. and Dom. Hen.VIII, Addenda*, i.pt.i, pp.244, 320; P.R.O. S.P.12. vol. cxiv, nos. 31, 34.
[101] M.Beresford, 'The Poll Tax and Census of Sheep, 1549', *Agricultural H.R.* ii (1954), 25ff.; and E *179/162/275*.
[102] Req. 2/76/24. For the property see below, p.lxxi.
[102a] This source of supply was suggested by Dr D.M.Barratt.

leased for a number of years to the Pennys of Witney. By the 1580s they were in other hands and in one law suit the Baylies, sons of the Queen's physician in ordinary, alleged that William Andrews and Thomas Box had dispossessed them of the property, including the tithes of lamb wool.[102b] The parsonage of Minster Lovell, held by the Rankells for a time, included most of the tithes as the vicar was paid only a stipend. For the Brices at Witney Park the commutation of their tithes for a small modus had the negative advantage that the wool they produced themselves would not be reduced by tithe payment.

In the court books Richard Bryan of Cogges was an obvious supplier of wool and in the case of Henry Broke, broadweaver, bailiff in 1607, it came from a Kelmscott yeoman who sued him for payment in 1600 (ii, f. 16v). Otherwise one can only guess that yeomen like Richard Blake of Wadley (Berks.) or gentlemen like Sir Henry Unton of Bruern were perhaps in debt cases over such supplies (i, ff. 279r, 287r). It is tempting to surmise that the Witney benefactor Richard Ashcombe made his wealth in this way and that his charity was some kind of return. He was a gentleman of Curbridge and appears in the court book not only for his bequests but also in debt cases when he sued five small broadweavers, a tailor, fuller and warper in 1590 (i, ff. 268v, 269r); in his will he held bonds from the Brices, Yates and Kings of Witney. Apart from his many bequests he left his wife £800 in ready cash 'in a little black trunk with a padlock on in my chamber at Witney' and was evidently financially very secure. His lands included Witney Farm in Curbridge and Holway grange or farm, and lands in Dorset settled on his wife and the parsonage of Pebworth and Marston in Gloucestershire, all useful connexions for Witney's wool supply.[103]

The larger clothiers and clothmen in the town were in an advantageous position as against the smaller broadweavers as they often had family connexions with the wealthier yeomen and local farmers and held land themselves. The Yates must have profited by their connexion with the Yates, farmers in Standlake and Witney (ii, f. 60v) as well as from their own lands in the parish and elsewhere, and Thomas Box, yeoman and miller, claimed to have supplied his father-in-law, Henry Rankell, with upwards of £200 worth of wool and yarn.[104] Inventories suggest that clothiers stockpiled wool themselves for resale. Richard Budde (d. 1624), clothier, had £40 10s. out of an estate of £104, consisting of the value of various kinds of yarn and wool, broadlist warp and woof, sorting warp and woof, fine yarn and blanket yarn, fleece and fell wool, middle and coarse wool, with a further £9 4s. 4d. worth of wool at the spinners. His

[102b] Req. 2/133/20.
[103] Prob 11/107 47 Stafford.
[104] Req. 2/36/118.

son Richard (d. 1640) had even more, with his wool and yarn worth about £100 compared with his fifteen cloths valued at £80. Both men were engaged in cloth production (cf.i, f. 299v) but the stocks suggest that they were dealers too.

Enclosed land is said in the end to have produced a wool unsuitable for broadcloth and this, together with the farmers finding more profit in grain, forced the cloth industry to look for other supplies.[105] There was the great market in the Cotswolds at Cirencester but the availability of fell wool, which the industry in Witney used in the later seventeenth century, was clearly bound up with the development of the tanning and glove industry in Oxfordshire and of the London market on which Witney came to depend. In the sixteenth century the importance of the local tanners, as seen in Thomas Taylor's inventory, indicates the local supplies of fell wool. Other leatherworkers, too, had supplies and in 1626 Richard Harris, glover, had 27lb of coarse wool, 23 lb of middle wool which had been sold to Goody Garner, and one tod and 9½ lb of fine wool in his house. There is reason to be suspicious about the activities of Robert Taylor alias Cakebread who died in 1611. He was involved in the victualling or food and drink trade. His name appears regularly in the lists of tipplers, he was described as a victualler of ale and in his will as an innholder. When he died his estate was valued at £311 and it becomes clear on reading the inventory that he drew his income from a variety of sources. There were two looms in the shop and wood worth £20. He was owed £97 10s. by leases and annuities, he had £20 in his purse and debts without security of £18 4s., wool and yarn worth £53 5s. and cloth valued at £33. The innkeeper's role in commerce and industry is gradually becoming better known and it seems likely that in Witney men like the Taylors had a vital part to play in the distribution of raw materials.

The cloth industry already showed the characteristics noted in the seventeenth and eighteenth century when the typical manufacturer in Witney as in Yorkshire was the independent master with only two or three looms, whereas the Wiltshire industry in contrast had been able to support some clothiers who were essentially organizers of the trade, supplying the raw material and selling the finished product, with a variety of workers for wages in between who produced the cloth.[106] The Witney clothier in the sixteenth century was more akin to the modest clothiers in Wiltshire and the north of England who were themselves broadweavers and shaded in terms of wealth into that class. Some were of considerable substance like Walter Jones or Leonard Yate, described as a man 'of great wealth', or like Nicholas Gunne (d. 1602), moderately prosperous with goods valued at £196 in his inventory and bequests of £200. But there

[105] Bowden, *Wool Trade*, pp.57 ff.
[106] *V.C.H.Wilts*.iv.144ff; *Witney Blanket Industry*, pp.15–17.

were the poor clothiers whom Henry Jones remembered in his will and beneath them the simple broadweaver like Edward Dodswell (d. 1588) worth some £10 and Gregory Meriman (d. 1596) with only £4 to £5 for probate.

About thirty-six men were operating as clothiers in Witney over the period of the court books and with them should be included the clothmen and clothmakers since Giles Jones, Richard Haskins and John Collier were called either one or the other (i, ff. 163v, 207r; ii, 104r). It is clear that the Witney clothiers were also broadweavers. Walter Jones owned five looms in his will, two in his shop and three in his house, and his brother Henry had four looms in his shop. Nicholas Ifeelde (d. 1587), had four looms and a shop[107] and Nicholas Gunne had a warping house and a shop with three looms worth £4. They had apprentices bound to them specifically to learn the art of broadweaving and only rarely as a clothier (ii, f. 111v).

Looms, however, were not exceptionally expensive and even modest broadweavers could own a couple and have an apprentice. Thomas Cooke (d. 1567) left one broadloom to his wife for life and the covenant of his servant was to be worked out with her, while his new broadloom was in the occupation of his brother. Where the clothier differed was in his larger capital and in his ability to store quantities of yarn and wool and to have cloth lying idle in the finishing processes or on sale at London and yet still keep his looms going. Anthony Yate (d. 1630) had a stock of 327 lb of yarn and 20 tod of coarse wool as well as nine broadcloths worth £77 while his three looms were valued at only £3 10s. Clothiers could also employ more labour. Richard Webbe had four servants in 1547, Walter Jones two apprentices, two servants and a 'late' servant in 1561 and Henry Jones who was taking apprentices early in the court books (i,f.76v) left money in his will to four apprentices and forgave all sums of money and debts owed by his seven workmen. John Clarke had three servants who had to take the oath of allegiance in 1597 (i, f. 326v). A clothier like Henry Rankell who in 1605 took on five apprentices at once should by statute have been employing a journeyman as well (ii, ff. 93r, 94r, 104v). In contrast Andrew Johnson had no servants but three sons who may have worked for their father at the looms which he left to them. The richer clothier, however, also had sons and his servants were in addition to the family workforce. Both Johnson and Cook were relatively prosperous and it is difficult to see how Gregory Meriman could have employed anyone. For Henry Gould of Woodgreen who died in 1604 worth only £8 6s. 8d. the case seems clearer for he apprenticed three of his five sons to other broadweavers some years before his death (ii, ff. 8r, 12r, 42r).

Although the independent broadweaver was a very strong part of the Witney industry there is some evidence for the way in which the richer

[107] Prob 11/71 62 Spencer.

clothiers kept control. 'Putting out', or the domestic system, is suggested in Walter Jones' will which left £5 to be distributed among the poor spinners and weavers in Witney and other towns thereabouts, a bequest typical of someone employing them as labour. Peter Rankell, clothier, had yarn and debts due to him from various spinners for yarn alleged to be of the value of £210.[108] They must have been in many of the poorer farming families in the area or among widows like Christine Levingstone of Witney who owed 12d. in 1584 to the cardmaker. Spinning wheels as against the distaff were mentioned in wills regularly. Bequests to the poor in other clothier wills may disguise more such relationships between a rich clothier and the poor weavers. It is clear that the clothiers often leased looms out as when Henry Jones leased a shop and loom for 6s. 8d. a year to Robert Weaver (i, f. 174r) and Roger Larden hired a loom from Nicholas Ifeelde (i, f. 261v) and it is suggested in Wiltshire studies that looms left in wills to servants may disguise some such hiring out.[109]

Where the clothiers most obviously controlled the industry was in their hold on the finishing processes. There was a separate class of shearmen and fullers, or tuckers as they were termed in the West country industry, and in this the Witney industry was unlike its North Country counterpart where the clothiers often undertook the finishing in their own homes. Most fullers and shearmen were men of modest wealth and indeed seem to have combined both finishing processes: Thomas Belwood, fuller and tippler, was called a shearman in his will, and in 1596 Nicholas Clempson, fuller, was worth £31 0s. 8d. and had shears, a shearboard, press and other tools worth 50s. in his inventory, while in 1600 Peter Ridare's tucking shears were distrained for payment of tax (i, ff. 118r, 148v; ii, f. 23v). But the ownership or lease of the fulling mills conferred wealth and control and the tuckers who held them were in a different class, acting like clothiers in organizing the trade. It has been noted for the Wiltshire industry that one member of the family might be the tucker or lessee of the mill and the other the clothier and such arrangements, though often troublesome for family harmony, can be seen in the Box family and with the Yates below (ii, f. 31v) and the Colliers, where John was the clothier in 1594 and Stephen the fuller.[110]

The lease of the mill or close family ties with millers or the yeomen owners was an evident factor in the rise of certain clothiers. Waleys mill, presumably where Farm Mill now stands, was held by the Brices, lessees of the manor, and various members of the family were connected with the cloth trade, as when Richard Brice offered cloth for sale in 1558. But they also leased it to others. William Box, presumably the later Bailiff Box,

[108] Req. 2/36/98, 118.
[109] V.C.H.Wilts. iv.145, 150.
[110] Ibid. p.143; Cal. S.P.Dom. iii, 1591-4, p.569.

held it in 1527 and in 1547 and 1553 it was held by Leonard Yate, senior, clothier, and bequeathed in his will.[111] The Bishops alias Martin had a long association with Woodford Mills in the fifteenth century and throughout the sixteenth century and appear as tuckers and clothiers.[112] Crawley mill was held by one branch of the Box family. In the 1540s there were two tuckers, John Box (d. 1547) and Richard (d. 1547) who both apprenticed their sons to clothiers, the one to Richard Webbe and the other to Cuthbert Temple of Standlake [113] Richard Box was the Crawley miller in 1535 and 1543, but it passed into the occupation of Giles Jones and Philip Box and by 1561 was held by Walter Jones, clothier. He bequeathed it for twelve years again to his brother Giles until his nephew Walter Jones was of age, and it was later listed in the bishop's records as a new built fulling mill in the tenure of Walter Jones.[114] The Philip Box who held it briefly, so it seems, was the descendant of the other Box family from William Box, bailiff. Their interest in mills is shown in the dispute over the lease of Bury Crofts in Hailey which Philip's son Thomas (d. 1596) wanted in order to build a tuck mill and which he used also as a jointure for his marriage to the daughter of Peter Rankell, clothier. It was clearly a prime site, said to be worth £400 and, in the course of the quarrel with both his own father and Rankell, it was claimed that an offer had been made to repay a debt of £200 by the dressing of ten cloths a week at the mill, which would equal £100 a year.[115] Thomas did built his tuck mill which was known thenceforth as New Mill and which later passed to his son Henry Box and then to Thomas Clarke by the mid-seventeenth century.[116]

After finishing came the process of selling. Access to the London market must also have been conducted largely through the clothiers. In the opening years of Elizabeth's reign attempts were made to stamp out the sale of defective cloth at the chief market in London, Blackwell Hall, and the records of the Exchequer court show which merchants were selling there. Yorkshire and Wiltshire clothiers were the most numerous but Oxfordshiremen were also to be found there from Oxford itself, Shipton under Wychwood, Wootton, Banbury and above all from Witney. In 1561-2 Thomas and John Collier, Peter Rankell, Henry and Giles Jones, Thomas Bishop and Thomas Yate and Richard Brice were offering cloths for sale, and in 1564 Martin Bishop of Witney, most specified as clothiers.[117] The relationship with London merchants is indicated by the record in the account book of John Isham, Merchant Adventurer of

---

[111] Eccl. 2/73/5; Wills Oxon, 180, f.201v.
[112] Misc. Je I/1, ff. 25v, 62r; and see above, p.lii.
[113] Wills Oxon. 179, ff.232v, 258v.
[114] Eccl. 2/73/2; Prob 11/44 20 Loftes; Misc. Je I/1, f.1r.
[115] Req. 2/76/24; and 176/52.
[116] C 54/3418, mm.39–40, no. 5.
[117] E 159/350 Recorda, Hilary Term, 7 Eliz., mm. 329(2), 330; E 179/355, m.206.

London, that in 1558 Robert Brysse of Oxfordshire, clothier, owed money for a certificate come from Flanders 'for faults of clothes of him bought'.[117a] The clothiers may have gone to London themselves or used an agent or factor. Philip Box, clothier, is noted in the court book as away in London (i, f. 123r), but Leonard Penny employed his brother-in-law, Peter Humfreys, to travel on his affairs.[118]

Other Industries and Trades

Many of these same characteristics are seen in the other industries and occupations in the town and it is important to recognise that other trades occupied a substantial section of its population.

In the leather industry the tanners stood out clearly above the others because of the high level of capital investment needed in vats, lime pits and oakbark to cure hides as well as in money tied up in stock passing through the tannery. Thomas Taylor and sons and the Gunnes have already been noted as some of the better-off business men throughout the century and the leaders of the community as bailiffs alongside the clothiers. Shoe-makers, cobblers and glovers had only a modest level of wealth in comparison. Edward and Jerome Hannes, shoemakers, both combined that trade with tippling. Jerome Hannes (d. 1588) the elder was one of the few shoemakers to make a will. He shared out his goods, beds, joined press, cutting knife and hammer among his seven children, but a major concern in the will was for his stock of oak timber carried off by John Crofts. The most prosperous shoemakers were those with connexions with sources of supply like the Taylors who appear as shoemakers (i, f. 346v) and the Willshears, both families related to the tanners. The Willshears or Wilkshears were the only shoemakers who apparently combined trade with farming.[119] William Clempson, who in 1586-7 took three servants into his shoemaking business, was clearly prosperous, but probably derived his status as bailiff in 1599 from his position as mercer and from his family connexions with other mercers (i, ff. 244r, 253r, 305v). He was able to apprentice a son in London and to leave a £100 apiece to his four children.[120] If apprentices were a sign of wealth Thomas Vawse and Thomas Warde could afford them (i, ff. 77r, 185r) though Vawse was later a felon and his goods claimed by the Queen.[121] The absence of wills and lack of status in the court books for most shoemakers and cobblers mentioned points to a proverbial group of poor craftsmen.

[117a] *John Isham, Mercer and Merchant Adventurer*, ed. G.D.Ramsay, Northants. Rec. Soc. xxi (1962), 1.
[118] Wills Oxon. 184, f.395v.
[119] cf. ibid. 79/3/1; Misc. Je I/1, ff.31, 35r.
[120] Prob 11/113 24 Dorset.
[121] Case cited in Giles, *Witney*, Appendix I, from Madox, *Firma Burgi*.

Perhaps because of competition from villages around or the nature of the trade, glovers had only moderate wealth, too, in Witney. John Rankell, bailiff in 1548, left his goods to his wife in 1565 with instruction that his son William should be able to buy the stock of gloves and skins from her: they included working gloves at 16d. the dozen and pointed gloves at 2s. 8d the dozen, and pointed deer, calf and dog gloves at 4s. the dozen and hedging cuffs and gloves; wrought leather at 20s. the hundred and leather in the lime pit at 13s. 4d. a hundred and box skins, doe skins, buck skins, calf skins and dog skins, bull hides and horse hides. The son was also to occupy the waterside and the shop. Nonetheless Rankell did not have a great deal in the way of working capital for his total inventory was £21 4s. 2d. The glover, John Lawrence (d. 1618), however, had only about one pound's worth of leather and skins, less than the value of his cow, mare and hay at £4 13s. 4d., and his total inventory, allowing for inflation was much less, at £18 19s. 4d., than Rankell's. On the other hand William Harris (d. 1576) was worth £68 and Edward Ashfeld paid on lands in the subsidy of 1601 (ii, f. 50r), though we have no details as to their stocks and goods. Harris' son Richard (d. 1618) was worth only £14 2s. 4d. and had a stock of seven dozen gloves worth 25s. and skins and hides valued at £4 19s.

There is a general impression, too, of a poor return for most in the metal and building trades. William Ably, smith (i, f. 1r), had at his death in 1546 estate of only £4 7s. 8d. which included his anvil and a bolster of iron, though he also owned his own house. A little further up the economic ladder was John Marryat of Hailey (d. 1601), worth £15 19s. 10d., who combined farming with smithing: his working tools were worth only 20s., less than his cow and only twice his stock of bees at 10s. Robert Clay (d. 1598) evidently found it better to combine smithing with tippling and his inventory reached £32 16s. 7d., but it also points to the low profits of the trade. The fact that there are no wills or inventories of the other metal trades again suggests that wiredrawers, nailors, and tinkers made little. In the building trade only two masons were wealthy enough to take apprentices, and John Sea, joiner, had to combine his trade with victualling, usually a sign of hard times (i, f. 285r; ii, ff. 119r, 123v). The principal woodworking families, the Hornes and the Wheelers, made a comfortable living on the level of the middling broadweaver, but in each case it seems to have been associated with the possession of some land (ii, f. 50r).[122] The plasterer, Thomas Constable, who died in 1612, had possessions worth £29, about the same as Davy Horne's, but the major part was the value of fifteen quarters of malt and barley worth £14 whilst his plasterer's tools were valued at only 5s.

There were sharp contrasts, too, among the retailers. The elite were the

[122] cf. Misc. Je I/1, ff. 2r, 40v, 47r, 63r.

lxxxiv INTRODUCTION

mercers–drapers–haberdashers, often related to clothiers, like Leonard
Dalton, nephew of Leonard Yate, clothier, or Nicholas Gunne,
tailor–draper, a nephew of Nicholas Gunne, clothier.[123] Some were long
established family concerns like the Brinkfields, father and son, who
operated from the 1540s, and others had a foothold in several towns, like
the Clempsons and Daltons of Witney and Abingdon. It is doubtful if any
achieved the levels of the Worcester mercers where inventories of £300 to
£400 were possible in the setting of a county capital. The shoemaker–
mercer, William Clempson was perhaps one of the wealthier and his
brother Richard Clempson (d. 1602) mercer, had property in both Witney
and Abingdon and bequeathed his two daughters one hundred marks
apiece.[124] The evidence of inventories is often deceptive. On the surface,
Thomas Pooll, chandler (d. 1616) would appear to have been a prosperous
man with an estate of £146 and yet a great deal of this was the value of his
stock, while Thomas Cornish (d. 1617) would seem to have been worse
off with an inventory of only £35 13s., but he owned three houses, all
leased out, and his wife who died within a few months of him was worth
£108. Actual trading premises were usually little more than a room with
storage space, part of the dwelling house. Nicholas Gunne's inventory of
his shop, for example, described the contents as 'one table board with a
frame, one hinged sideboard and a bedstead, worth 10s.' Investment in
stock varied. Thomas Pooll's weights and scales were valued at 40s. and
his stock consisted of four score and one quarter of malt, worth £96, made
tallow valued at £20 and 20 dozen made candles at £3; in all £119 out of a
total estate of £146. John Hartley, ironmonger, had wares worth £15 out
of a total inventory of £81. At the other end of the scale were the poorer
men combining business of draper and tippler like Humfrey Malen or of
tailor, draper, constable, clothsearcher and tippler like William Peto (i, ff.
117v, 119v, 122r, 127r, 133r, 134r, 217v).

Food and drink trades were important occupations, as the court book
regulations indicate. The Shaws, Goods and Colliers were established
butchers' families, and the consumption of meat was an indication of a
rising standard of living in Tudor Witney. Setting up as a butcher did not
take much in the way of capital as far as equipment and premises were
concerned. Thomas Hannes (d. 1629) had a slaughter house and shop with
his ropes, trees, axes, cleavers, knives, setters, and other equipment valued
at only 8s., while in Stephen Collier's shop the weights, scales, cleavers
and other implements were worth only 26s. Meat could, of course, be sold
from a stall as Collier did at Burford and Anthony Larden at Witney,
much to the annoyance of his neighbours (i, f. 55v). What required capital
was the purchase of stock for slaughter and of Collier's total inventory in

[123] See *Oxon Inventories*, pp.128–30; and Gunne wills.
[124] Prob 11/99 32 Montague. For Clempson relations see also the will of his son Richard, a
mercer of Abingdon (d.1612): Prob 11/120 107 Fenner.

1639 no less than £62 out of £150 was the value of five oxen, three heifers and a bull in the ground at Hailey. The butchers, therefore, could hope to make a reasonable living: Edward Goode (d. 1591) had estate of £52 and could afford to employ a servant, Robert James, who himself became an independent butcher with a lease in High Street. Thomas Hannes (d. 1629) was valued at £59. Richard Shaw (i, f. 282v, 303v) may have been a bad manager but the fact that he could borrow £60 from Leonard Yate and put his up house as security for repayment is an indication of his substance.[125] There were poor men too: Anthony Larden had to combine butchering with tippling and Mother Agnes Shaw the widow of a tippler and butcher followed the same callings. (i, ff. 74r, 122r, 133r, 134r, 146r, 151v).

There were a number of bakers in the town and there seem to have been plenty of customers for they lived comfortably. Robert Baker in 1594 baked bread by the bushel for Thomas Knight, broadweaver and Thomas Taylor, mason, and probably entered into regular contracts for baking with his customers, for the picture of self-sufficiency and home-baking in a pre-industrial society breaks down in an industrial town (i, f. 295v). Nicholas Hill, father and son, occupied the trade in Witney for thirty years from the 1550s to the 1580s and when Nicholas Hill junior died in 1589 he left three houses, one of which was leased out and two granted to Richard King, citizen and grocer of London, for £80 to be paid to Hill's assigns. His son Nicholas had been apprenticed to Edward Hannes, shoemaker, and had become a citizen and cordwainer of London, whilst he himself had had an apprentice (i, ff. 128v, 132r, 159r, 266r). Although there is no inventory to Hill's will there is little doubt that he was well-off. Others had more modest wealth: Thomas Beddall's inventory was nearly £21 in 1605, James Watts' £28 in 1619. It was not great but on a par with the prosperous broadweaver and carpenter. None of these, however, butcher or baker, was of sufficient status to become bailiff in the town.

Perhaps the final occupation which showed great difference of wealth was that of supplier of drink and lodging: the tipplers and innholders, though they in fact had little in common. The innholder beside catering for the respectable traveller played a vital commercial role as general dealer, money lender and commercial agent and a man like Taylor, whose will has been discussed above, was worth not only the £311 of his inventory but also the amount of his real property including two houses in High Street. No such capital investment was needed to follow the occupation of tippling which was viewed with great suspicion by the authorities. It could be a part-time occupation to be combined with all manner of other work from broadweaving to baking and could be carried out by both men and women. It could also be the sole occupation of some as with Randell Margeries, tailor perhaps by training but who seems to have done nothing else except wage his law incessantly and act on

[125] C 3/250/77.

occasion as informer (i, ff. 21v, 101r).[125a] It is difficult to say what level of wealth it produced since it was so often combined with other occupations. The answer is probably little or none, although many were glad to engage in it for the small return it might later bring.

The various occupations in Witney thus produced a broad spread of wealth, from affluence at the top to those just above or even below the poverty line at the bottom. How did this compare with the surrounding countryside? As the Wenmans and the other woolmen either withdrew or died, they were replaced in the tithings by men who described themselves in a variety of ways, gentleman, yeoman or husbandman. Some wealth there was, though perhaps not as great as the Wenmans', and comparisons are difficult because of the severe inflation of the sixteenth century. George Thompson of Bampton, yeoman, benefactor of Witney in 1603, was worth, for example, £951 9s. 0d. Richard Ashcombe of Curbridge the other benefactor may have been even wealthier but there is no inventory to his will and this lack in the wills proved in the Canterbury court undoubtedly hampers a proper appreciation of wealth at the top. Others, often men related to the clothiers, were of more moderate but still substantial wealth. Edward Bowman of Hailey, who described himself as a gentleman in his will and acted as a trustee of George Thompson's money between 1606 and 1609, died in 1612 with estate worth £352 15s. 11d., and Stephen Brice esquire, who farmed the manor, had estate valued at £261 7s. 2d. Inevitably, too, there were the Yates and Robert Yates, of Poffley End, gentleman (d. 1639) had goods and chattels worth £537 18s. 4s.[125b] Such wealth put them on a par with, if not above, the town clothiers. Below them wealth was, as usual, unevenly spread as the following sample from wills suggests:

Name	Rank	Date of Death	Place of Origin	Value of estate £ s. d.		
Henry Newman	Yeoman	1599	Curbridge	217	15	10
William Harris	Husbandman	1627	Hailey	151	5	6
Edward Chimney	Husbandman	1623	Hailey	106	5	6
William Ring	Yeoman	1602	Cogges	81	9	0
Henry Smyth	—	1571	Hailey	90	10	0
George Kempe	Yeoman	1601	Witney	62	14	5
Henry Harberd	Shepherd	1615	Curbridge	63	10	8
Richard Smyth	Husbandman	1563	Hailey	37	9	9
Robert Burdeye	Husbandman	1561	Crawley	15	16	0
William Lambert	Day Labourer	1575	Hailey	4	15	4

[125a] E 159/335, Recorda, Hilary Term, 2 and 3 P. and M.dorse m.69.
[125b] He was a Standlake Yate settled in Hailey: M.Toynbee in *Oxoniensia*, xxv (1960), 93; D.Sturdy, ibid.,xxviii(1963), 321.

There was, therefore, a very similar pattern in town and country of a few wealthy men, a substantial number of yeomen and husbandmen who were comfortably placed and the barely known mass of the poor.

Town and country inventories are, however, not strictly comparable. Town inventories usually list only the contents of the house and any monies owed the deceased. All too often no mention is made of stock in the shop or weaving house. Conversely the country inventories, where they survive, nearly always included substantial sums tied up in stock and crops. Thus, of Robert Yate's estate of £538, £288 represented the value of sheep and animals, corn and equipment. The contents of his house and his wearing apparel came to only £250. He was therefore more on a par with Nicholas Gunne, clothier, whose inventory of £196 contained virtually no stock or equipment, except three looms valued at only £4. Gunne was far wealthier in terms of material possessions than William Harris, husband-man, most of whose estate consisted of stock and crops valued at £96. Neither was Harris as well off in material terms as Thomas Taylor, tanner, whose household goods and furniture were valued at £105 10s 6d. in 1615. Where town inventories did include stock, the personal wealth of the man concerned was much less as shown in the case of Thomas Pooll above. On balance, however, despite the limitations of evidence, towns-men of substantial to middling wealth seem to have had more in the way of material possessions than countrymen.

Land and Credit

Two questions remain to be asked about the business community in sixteenth-century Witney: their relationship to land and their ease of access to capital and credit, both obviously connected to land since property was the best form of security.

Despite the original set-up of the town which seemed designed to let the trader have some small holding in Hailey there is little evidence that by the end of the Middle Ages the smaller trader benefitted from land holdings in the tithings. The early fourteenth-century subsidies seem to show that the assart land was not yielding much in comparison with the town, and later subsidies and manorial records indicate the engrossment of land into a few hands by the early sixteeth century. The possession of land and property, in fact, distinguished the richer business man from the poorer broad-weaver, shoemaker or tippler. Of the considerable number of broad-weavers, for example, named in the court books, only twenty-nine certainly held property and only four or five of these held it in the tithings as against in the town. These were men like William Box, William Bishop and Robert Horne, connected with major families, or like Henry Gould of Woodgreen, living on the outskirts of the town.[126] Weavers in the town

[126] Misc. Je I/1 ff.3v, 7r, 33r, 36r, 43v; below, ii f.60v.

sometimes owned houses but often rented: it can be seen below how Crescent Warner bought a house in Bridge Street from Thomas Box and Robert Baissley one in Corn Street from Thomas Bryan, while Richard Weaver was tenant of Clemence Jonson (i,ff.77v,272r; ii,ff.70r). Some had closes or gardens attached, and Robert Gryffeth, broadweaver, was able to assign a close attached to his house to pay a debt of 13s. 4d., but the cottages put up in Corn Street at this time, judging from the measures, must have been too small to support much gardening (i,ff.194r,236r). It is suggestive, too, that few wills and inventories of the smaller townsfolk show much if anything in the way of crops or stock.

In contrast the richer men acquired land and property. John Penny (d.1554) was able to give his son Leonard Penny, broadweaver, the lease of the parsonage of Witney and the tithes in Hailey and Crawley and Leonard passed these on to his son William, again a broadweaver. The Rankells had the parsonage of Minster Lovel and Thomas Yate (d.1591) the parsonage of Wootton, presumably near Abingdon.[127] The Boxes and Bishops were obviously well established in the tithings with their mills and it is hardly surprising that they built up their land holdings there, though other farmers and yeomen were distinct from the townsfolk. The Smiths and Bowmans were the chief yeomen in the tithings with the Brices and it was they who seem to have benefitted most by being able to take over Wenman land: the Brices, for example, took on the lease of Witney Park and built up Witney Park Farm and the manor court book shows Bowman and Smith holding Wenman land. It is not clear whether any Wenman land in the tithings came to townsfolk apart from their town houses which were let out, but the general turnover of assart land and closes seen in the manor court book enabled the richer business men to acquire holdings. The Daltons, Humfreys, Taylors, Gunnes, Yates are listed among its jurors and tenants; it is curious that no butchers seem to have bought there.[128] One inhibiting factor in the acquisition of land in the parish may have been that there was no monastic land. Henry Box of London was granted the chantry land which lay in Witney and Cogges but it was worth only some £7 a year and was already let out to twenty-one townsfolk.[129] Leonard Yate, clothier, tried to lease Eynsham Abbey site in Eynsham in the 1540s but was balked by another lessee. He and William Box, however, were engaged in the enclosure of Cokethorpe and the

---

[127] Req. 2/36/118; Prob 11/77 55 Sainberbe. Later descent of the parsonage of Witney and the tithes, one lease of which came to Thomas Box, is in Req. 2/133/20. There is no mention of Yate holding the parsonage of Wootton in *V.C.H.Berks.* iv, 403–4, but the rectory of Wootton (Oxon.) was not impropriated (ex inf. Dr. D.M. Barratt).

[128] Misc. Je I/1 ff. 55v, 84r and v; Dalton, ibid. 12r, 31v, 35r, 35Ar, 36r, 48v, 55v; Humfrey, ibid. 10r, 28v, 46v, 48v; Gunne, ibid. 37v; Taylor, ibid. 6v, 36v; Yate, ibid. 6v, 8r, 10r and *passim.*

[129] *Cal. Pat. 1547-8*, p.389; cf. *Chantry Certs.*, p.17.

demolition of its chapel in the 1550s.[130] Leonard's two sons Thomas and
Leonard can be seen building up property in the manor court rolls in the
second half of the century. The desire of local men to buy land for their
family is seen in the will of Thomas Ring, chandler (d.1558), bailiff in the
1550s. He left copyhold and freehold land which he had bought in Hailey
and Crawley and elsewhere for his son Augustin, who was to be put to
school 'until he had sufficient knowledge to be preferred and put to some
honest science and occupation'. He bought other land in Hailey for his son
Thomas and the elder son William was also established there while a
daughter was married to one of the Smiths, farmers in Hailey. At the end
of the century John Clarke, bailiff, apparently a newcomer, built up his
property by leasing the watercourse near Woodford Mills and acquiring
sixteen acres in Hailey and 127 acres of customary land and five of assart in
Curbridge: he did not farm it himself but leased it out. He built his
house, however, in Curbridge and received a grant of eight elms from the
bishop for it.[131]

Another source of property was, of course, town houses, and generally
in the sixteenth century there was greater interest in this property development. In Witney there were those who could at most only leave their
house or its lease like Roger Legge (d.1588), baker, who left his wife his
house 'with the standard' until his heir came of age. But again there were
the business men like the Taylors or Thomas Cornish who had rents from
leases of houses, though in Witney, unlike in some other towns, they
rarely seem to have had more than two or three such properties. A good
'case history' is seen in the Wheelers. Roger Wheeler, carpenter (d.1602)
acquired a tenement in West End in 1566 and another in High Street in
1583; he bought land in Corn Street in 1574 and by 1598 had two houses
there, one leased to a cobbler and the other to his son Thomas
(i,ff.97r,153r,331v). In his will, where he is described as a yeoman, he left
two houses in West End to his wife and his son Roger respectively and a
cottage elsewhere to his grandson. The family was evidently working
their way up the social scale and Roger Wheeler, junior, paid subsidy on
lands in 1601 (ii,f.50r).

Property was the major capital on which mortgages and credit could be
raised and its value to the business men is obvious. In 1588 Henry Brooke,
broadweaver, mortgaged six acres of an arable close in Hailey to Henry
Jones for £60. In 1590 Leonard Yate, senior, lent Richard Shawe, butcher,
£60 against the security of Shawe's house. If the debt was not repaid then
Yate was to have the house but lease it to Shawe for 21 years at an annual
rent of 40s. In another case recorded in the manor court book Leonard
Yate junior mortgaged 13½ acres and three closes containing 11 acres in

[130] C 1/1284/8; *Deserted Villages Oxon.*, p.36.
[131] Misc. Je I/1, f.69v.

Hailey to John Clarke for £100 in 1593, to be repaid in 1597 in the church porch at Witney so that all could see.[132]

Without this security the business man might resort to straight borrowing with the payment of interest or 'speciality' and rich landowners or merchants acted as money lenders and secured bonds or debts 'with specialities'. Richard Ashcombe of Curbridge clearly lent extensively and the sums owed him ranged from £5 to £68. In 1549 Richard Humfrey, dyer, lent John Barnabye £18 while in 1607 Henry and Richard Humfreys, broadweaver and dyer respectively, borrowed £16 from a member of the local gentry, Humfrey Willoughby of North Leigh.[133] Probate inventories show debts as a considerable part of the estate of some local men. John Poolle (d.1612), yeoman, had £140 in bonds and bills owing to him, the major part of his estate of £215, and Ann Petty (d.1622), widow first of John Petty and then of Thomas Webley (d.1610), the clothier, had debts by speciality of £178 10s. and without speciality of £19 in her estate of £269 4s. Some of this was probably from her husbands' debtors but widows in Witney as elsewhere were a source of money for borrowing. There was a desperate debt of £20 owing by bill in Maud Brice's inventory of 1623, and Margaret Cornish (d.1618), widow of Thomas Cornish (d.1617), mercer, likewise had £47 debts by speciality in her inventory, though her husband's inventory had mentioned none. One illuminating case in the Court of Requests shows how profitable lending could be. Margery Hanson of Witney, wife of William Hanson, dyer, lent £7 10s. to William Barkdale of Shaw, Berks., for which £12 had to be repaid, a rate of 60 per cent interest.[134] This profit is confirmed by the account which Joan, widow of Thomas Hannes, butcher, put in for her husband's debts in 1629. He owed some £46 on seven bonds taken out with various people and the bond was usually at double the money borrowed, e.g. a £40 bond for £20 borrowed from Thomas Humfreys of Witney.[135] Family relationships were particularly important in raising money and wills frequently mention debts owed by members of the family. The disputes they might cause is particularly seen in the Box-Rankell disputes already discussed.

The credit with which the court books were largely concerned, was, however, trade credit and debts owed for goods and services rendered. Much must have been on a larger scale than could be claimed in this local court. It is well known, for instance, that the wool and cloth industry worked from start to finish on credit sales and purchases. Peter Rankell

---

[132] Ibid. ff. 36v, 40v, 54v, 55r; Yate later mortgaged the same property to Thos. Cornish, ibid. ff.71v, 84v. He also mortgaged land in Curbridge and failed to make repayment at the due time: ibid. 87v. For Shawe see C 3/250/77.

[133] C 1/1285/4; C 3/294/67. For Ashcombe see above. p.xxix.

[134] Req. 2/172/18.

[135] Wills Oxon. 297/24. For the role of credit in rural society see B.A.Holderness, 'Credit in English Rural Society before the Nineteenth Century', *Agricultural H.R.* xxiv (1976).

(d.1594), clothier, settled all his goods and chattels on his son Henry when
he married with the agreement that Henry should take over his father's
debts 'for divers great sums of money', and it was alleged that as well as
himself owing money Peter was owed for yarn from various spinners and
from at least two mercers or woollen drapers, presumably for cloth.[136]
Rankell had a book of debts and so did other merchants, like Leonard
Dalton, chandler (d.1581), and Thomas Taylor, tanner: but none have
survived for the Witney trade, though their debtors can often be traced
through inventories. Dalton had some ten debtors as well as desperate
debts 'as appearethe by his booke' and they made up over half of the total
£59 of his inventory, though £15 was for the debt owed for the lease of a
close. John Hartley (d.1617) left £15 worth of debt owing by the book as
well as £10 on bond, and Andrew Hodson left £13 debts by bill out of his
total inventory of £31 7s. 8d., while Thomas Hannes himself was owed
desperate debts 'without speciality' of £8 from Sir Edward Stanley and £2
5s. from others. It might have been expected that more of these men's
debtors would have been cited in the local court than seem to appear. But
the good business man may have been better at getting paid than a man
like Anthony Larden, the butcher, who made such frequent use of the
court (i,ff.42r,57r, and *passim*). Butchers, bakers and retailers, indeed,
feature so often in the court that, even though the details of the cases are
not given, it looks as if what the books best illustrate is the widespread use
of credit in the Witney retail trade of the sixteenth century: we see business
men who had to collect in court and debtors who would not pay. In the
end those who never appeared in the court or made restrained use of it are
as important as those who made frequent resort to it if we are to assess the
health of the economy of Witney in the Tudor period.

[136] Req. 2/36/98,118.

EDITORIAL NOTE

Our main object has been to produce a readable calendar in modern English: the manuscripts are accessible in the Bodleian library or on microfilm for students who wish to study the detail, language and hands of the originals. The foliation of the manuscripts is discussed on pp.xlivff, but references to *blank folios* are omitted in the calendar; these can easily be identified and are listed below. *Editorial additions* are put in square brackets. *Illegible entries* or blanks in entries are shown by three dots (. . .).

In calendaring the business of the courts we have made the major divisions those between one court and the next; actions entered between courts are introduced by Md. (for Memorandum) and follow immediately the business of the earlier court, as in the manuscript. *Years* and *dates* have been put into modern style; as have the *Saints' days* commonly used in the original to date terms of payment or the beginning of apprenticeships; St Peter's Day is the only Saint's day left in the calendar, because of doubt whether it represents St Peter ad Vincula (1 August) or St Peter and St Paul (29 June). *Court headings* have been standardized; the names of the bailiffs who held the courts are given only once a year, normally for the October court where they were elected. The chief of *court officers* are given in the Appendix. We have sometimes rearranged *court business* for ease of calendaring, but only within a particular recto or verso. In court *actions for debt* and similar actions the words 'taken', 'commenced' and 'entered' have been left out; common form in entries concerning *covenanted servants* is given in the appropriate full versions on pp.83, 158, 165, 186.

One major rearrangement has been to put the *details from the margin* of the manuscript into the main text, where they immediately follow the actions; this was the practice of the scribes themselves where they had room, and eases printing. The number of times the case was called has been put in *round brackets* and replaced the scribal indications by dots or circles or numbers in the margin of the MS; the practice is discussed above. All *numerals* have been transcribed into arabic numerals; the variations of practice are given on p.xlvi.

The original spelling of *surnames* has been retained but the letters 'u' and 'v' have been given their modern position. *Christian names* have been put into a standard modern form except in cases of doubt. *Placenames* are likewise given their modern spelling unless the identification is unknown or doubtful. The counties are those before the 1974 reorganization; earlier changes are noted in the index.

We have not been able to afford to identify in footnotes the people in the text, although we have extensive material on them. However, many

notable families in sixteenth-century Witney are discussed in the introduction and many identifications, e.g. of clergy, are made in the index.

The *changes in handwriting* are many; they are not noted in the Calendar,
but are discussed above, pp.xlvi–ii.

The *blank folios* are: in volume i: 1v,28v,31v,32v,38v,45v,53r,56v,79v,
80v,160r,208r,212r,and   v,225v,238r,265v,273v,275r,325v,331r,336v,344r;
and in volume ii: 10v,11v,13r,andv,14v,28v,29r,38v,39v,42v,43v,47r,52v,
62v,65v,66v,70v,73v,76v,77v,79v,80v,81v,86v,89v,95r,102r,103v,107v,
108v,116v,136v.

Queen Mary College, University of London   J.L.B
University of Otago.   M.M

GLOSSARY

The definitions are taken from: *The Oxford English Dictionary;* R.E. Zupko,
A Dictionary of English Weights and Measures (Wisconsin, 1968); and *Select
Tracts and Table books relating to English Weights and Measures (1100-1742),*ed.
H.Hall and F.J. Nicholas, Camden Society, Misc. xv(1929). Legal terms
used in the Court Books are discussed above, pp.xxxix–xliv.

ale, dozen of: thirteen gallons, stale ale: ale which has stood long enough to
    clear, i.e. is old and strong; ale under the (hair) sieve: ale strained to
    remove impurities.

aqua vyte or aquayty man: an aqua vitae man, a maker or seller of spirits

assault, to go: to rut, seek the male

badger: a licensed tradesman or hawker under 5 & 6 Ed.VI c.14; or a
    licensed beggar under 5 Eliz. c.3.

bearing cloth: christening robe

bear ward: a bear keeper who leads a bear for public show

bedder: a bed maker, upholsterer

bonelace: made of linen thread on a pattern with bone bobbins

bowyer: a maker of bows

brake: toothed implement for breaking flax or hemp

brazier: a worker in brass

bread, halfpenny, penny or twopenny: bread of set price but varying in
    weight according to the assize, e.g. in 1517 a penny loaf weighed 10 ozs.
    (*Select Tracts,* p.52)

brinded: tawny or brownish

broadcloth: heavy fulled cloth made on a broad loom and 24 yards long and
    1½ to 2 yards wide

broadweaver: one who weaves broadcloth

bushel: standard measure for grain

byson man: perhaps a maker of basins

cardmaker: a maker of cards for carding wool

castar: cloak, or a castor, a hat of beaver or rabbit fur

chafer: small closed brazier for a chafing dish

chandler: a dealer in candles, oil, soap and groceries

chapman: a pedlar

cloth: *see* broadcloth, narrow cloth

corselet: body armour

cortell: a man's tunic

cowl: water tub with two ears, a cooler

currier: one who dresses or colours tanned leather

curtilage: the ground attached to a dwelling house

double apparel: one suit for working days and one for Sundays

ell: cloth measure of 45 inches

endman: a collector of refuse wool or ends

friezes: coarse woollen cloth with nap on one side

fuller: one who fulls cloth (i.e. soaks and beats it)

furniture: armour

gannaker: an alehouse keeper

gorgets: neck armour

gressilde: grey

ham: meadow

handles: fuller's, probably to hold teasles

harness: apparatus on loom to move warp sets

heriot: a due paid to the lord on the tenant's death, traditionally in Witney Manor 'his best one goods' (Giles, *Witney*, 1647 custumal).

holland: linen fabric from Holland

horse-bread: bread made of bran or beans

hose: leg covering

kerchief: head covering

kersey: coarse cloth woven from long staple wool

kever: cover

lattermath: the last mowing

lists, lysts: selvages, edges to cloth to prevent unravelling

loader: a carrier or a beggar

locram: coarse linen cloth

medley: cloth woven of wools of different colours

metalman: a worker or dealer in metal

mounds: hedges or fences to delineate property

nailman: a nailmaker

narrow cloth: cloth made on a narrow loom and finer than broadcloth (q.v.)

narrow weaver: a maker of narrow cloth

parater, pargeter, paritor: a plasterer doing pargetry work

peel: long-handled wooden or iron implement to put bread in oven

pell: pelt, sheepskin

plie: to work the ground

porringer: basin for porridge or soup

posnet: small metal pot with handles and three feet

pottel: standard measure for ale of two quarts

rough layer, rough mason: a mason who laid ashlar or walling stone as against fine work

saulte: on heat

sealed measure: standard measure stamped with seal as conforming to the King's standard

seevegar: probably a sieve maker

shears, fuller's or tucker's: used to shave nap on cloth

shred: to prune

shroud: lopping of trees

sley: implement to beat up weft of wool

small drink: weak beer

solar: upper room

tagged: tail tipped with white or other colour

tallow-chandler: a dealer in tallow

tawed: skins soaked in alum and salt solution in order to make leather

teg: sheep in its second year

thirdendell: standard measure for stale ale for innholders and tipplers, i.e. 3 pints 'for a peny potte accordyng to the thyrdendell in the kyng's escheker' (Select Tracts, p.50)

thrum: fringes of threads left on the loom, hence the occupation of thrum gatherer

tippler: an alehouse keeper

tod: wool weight of 28lb

tucker: a fuller

venetians: breeches

victualler, licensed: an innkeeper

warper: man who stretched warp thread on the loom

wheeler: a wheelwright

wine quart: standard measure of one pint

wiredrawer: a maker of wire

woolwinder: possibly one who wound wool to form the long threads for
the broadloom

wotmell maker: perhaps a worm or screw maker

yarndle: an appliance for winding a skein of yarn into a ball, hence
perhaps an outhouse where this was done

CALENDAR
OF THE WITNEY COURT BOOKS
VOLUME I, 1538–99

f.1r Court held 4 Oct. 1538 at which time being bailiffs . . .[1] and Roger Legg the
constable . . . Webb and William Abley, wardsmen . . . Margeris, John
Grene, John . . . Walton and Walter Shepard, cardenars . . . Fathers and
William Maior, ale tasters . . . Skargyn and Jeffrey Perte the sergeant . . .
Hiatt.

 Order: ale set at . . . the dozen.

 Action of debt : Richard Dyer against John Bachalar for . . .

 At the same court the town seal was in the hands of William Hyll.

 Court held 26 Oct. 1538 by John Peny and Roger Lege, bailiffs.

 Actions of debt : William Habley against Thomas Skopam for 20s. . . .
        Roger Fadyrs against Thomas Andrew for 5s. 4d.

f.2r Court held 22 Nov. [1538] by John Peny and Roger Lege, bailiffs.

 Action of debt : Brian Goddard against William Shepard for . . .

 Agreed: Mr Skopam to pay William Abley . . . 21 Dec 8s. 9d.; and . . . next
ensuing 8s. 9d.

 Court held 13 Dec. [1538] by the bailiffs.

 Court held 17 Feb. [1539] by the bailiffs.

 Action of debt : William Follar against William Colyns for 20s. 2d.

 Court held 6 Feb. [*sic*] [1539] by the bailiffs.

 Court held 28 Feb. [1539] by the bailiffs.

 Action of detinue: William Prodon against Thomas Horste.(3)

f.2v Court held 21 March [1539] by the bailiffs.

 Court held 11 April [1539] by the bailiffs.

 Action of debt : Ralph Legge against John Saton for 7s. 3d.

f.3r Court held 2 May [1539] by the bailiffs.

 Actions of debt : Richard Large against William Golsmyth for . . . (3)
        Ralph Aberstoke against Thomas Skopam for 20s.(3) To be
  paid on 1 Aug. next.

---

[1] In the first thiry folios some words at the end of each recto are missing because of damage;
see above, p.xlv.

1

Court held 23 May [1539] by the bailiffs.
Action of debt : Thomas Wauker against Thomas Meryman for 22 . . .

Court held 12 June [1539] by the bailiffs.
Action of debt : Robert Pryer against John Payne for a cortell, a kerchief, a castar, a pair of hose.(3)

f.3v   Court held 4 July [1539] by the bailiffs.
Amerced : Walter Shepard, 2d.
Action of debt : John Wylmot of Abingdon [Berks.] against Randell Margeros for 10s. 4d.

Court held 25 July [1539] by the bailiffs.
Actions of debt : Thomas Androw against John Horne for 3s. 7d.
                    John Horne against Thomas Androw for 13d.

Court held 22 Aug. [1539] by the baliffs.
Action of debt : Robert Pryer against Thomas Lowe for 2s. 4d.

f.4r   Court held 19 Sept. [1539] by the bailiffs.
Agreed: Thomas Meryman and Thomas Wauker for all manner of reckoning between them in times past.

Court held [*deleted*] Oct. [1539] by the bailiffs.

Court held 10 Oct. 1539.
Bailiffs: John Peny, Roger Legge.
Constables: Richard Webbe, John Marten.
Wardsmen: William Taylar, Harry Taylar, John Saly, William Walton, Thomas Horste.
Cardenars: Ralph Lege, William Golsmyth.
Ale tasters: John Cargyn, Jeffrey Perte.
Sergeant: Thomas Hyat.

Court held 30 Oct. [1539] by the bailiffs.
Action of debt : John Numan of Curbridge against Roger Faders for 6s. 7d.(I)

f.4v   Court held 21 Nov. [1539] by the bailiffs.
Action of debt : Thomas Brynfyld against Randell Margeris for 7s. 3d.(I)

Court held 9 Jan. [1540] by the bailiffs.
Action of debt : Richard Dyer against William Mager for 11s. 2d.

Court held 30 Jan. [1540] by the bailiffs.
Action of debt : John Grene of Curbridge against William Shepard for 7s. 10d.

Court held 21 Feb. [1540] by the bailiffs.

Actions of debt : Robert Pryer against Thomas Carlys for 2s.
        William Follar against Thomas Scopam for 20s. 2d.

f.5r   Court held 12 March [1540] by the bailiffs.
Action of debt : William Brykelbanke against Robert Quyer for 6 . . .

Court held 9 April [1540] by the bailiffs.
Actions of debt : John Wether against William Lopton for . . . 10 . . .
        Thomas More against William Belynford for . . .

Court held 30 April [1540] by the bailiffs.
Action of debt : William Gonne against Thomas Skopam for 10s. 10d.

f.5v   Court held 28 May [1540] by the bailiffs.
Action of debt : Mother Nylols against Harry Halle for 2s. 3d.
Agreed: Thomas Skopam to pay William Gonne four quarters of barley
    by 1 Nov.

Court held 18 June [1540] by the bailiffs.
Action of debt : William Borde against William Lopton for 22s. 10d.

f.6r   Court held 8 Oct. 1540.
Bailiffs: Thomas Tayler, Richard Umfrey.
Constables: Thomas Meriman, John Raynkyll.
Wardsmen: John Collyns, Nicholas Alyn, John Lun . . ., Richard Handes,
    Randell Margeris.
Cardenars: William Goulsmyth, Harry Delf.
Ale tasters: Jeffrey Pert, John Scargyn.
And in the hands of John Raynkyll . . . Thomas . . ., 3d. to pay [*line crossed
    out*].

Court held 29 Oct. [1540] by the bailiffs.
f.6v   Court held 19 Nov. [1540].

Court held 10 Dec. [1540].
Action of debt : Thomas Pemurton of Oxford against William Poufle for
    13s. 4d.(3)

f.7r   Court held 3 June [1541].

Court held 2 July [1541].
Order: ale set by the bailiffs at 20d. the dozen.

f.7v   Court held 27 July [1541].

Court held 19 Aug. [1541].
Action of debt : John Bacler of Hailey against William Loupton of Witney
    for 18s. Agreed: Lopton to pay Bachelar 10s. 8d. on 8 July next.

f.8r   Court held 7 Oct. 1541.
         Bailiffs: Richard Umfrey, Robert Tempull.
         Constables: Thomas Meriman, William Beyrd.
         Wardsmen: John Collyns, Morris Nayler, John Bouclound, Richard Hannys,
             Randell Margres.
         Cardenars: William Goulsmyth, Harry Delf.
         Ale tasters: John Scargyn, John Clarke [*crossed out*], Richard Parkar [*added*].
         Action of debt : John Peny against Walter Sheppard for 12s. 7d.

f.8v   Court held 4 Nov. [1541].
         Action of debt : Sir John Probyn against . . . Plommer for 18s. 3d.(3)
             Received in part payment, 10s.; the other 8s. to be paid on 25 March next.
             Md. Richard Dyar paid Sir John Probyn . . . for Plommer 8s. 4d.

         Court held 25 Nov. [1541].
         Action of debt : William Marten against Edward Peson for 7s. 3d.(2)

f.9r   Court held 16 Dec. [1541].
         Actions of debt : William Gonne against William Yngle for 2s. 3d.
             [3s. 7d. *crossed out*].
                         Thomas Brondshaw against Randell Margeris for 10s. 3d.
             Received 3s. 3d.

f.9v   Court held 13 Jan. [1542].
         Actions of debt : John Plommer against Walter Shepperd for 8s. 1d.
                         John Grene against Robert Bannyng for 21d.

f.10r   Court held 14 April [1542].[2]

         Court held 5 May [1542].
         Presented: John Boklonde, wardsman, that Robert Squyr made an outcry
             against one of the constables, Thomas Meryman, about ten of the clock at
             night; witnesses John Boklonde, William Lopton, Allan Harbar with divers
             other more. Also Walter Sheparde complained that Robert Squyr came into
             his house on 4 May and in the presence of Sir John Clarke, priest,[3] and
             Richard Kyncam, weaver, beat Shepard's wife; witnesses Robert Gouylde,
             Richard Ellyatt, William Heyram.
         Action of debt : William Brinkefyld against Thomas Andros, sawyer, for
             2s. 11d.

f.10v   Court held 26 May [542].
         Action of debt : John Raynkell against Walter Shepperd for 13s. 4d. Sheppard
             to pay 12d. a week from 14 July until paid.

---

[2]   A leaf is missing, and perhaps contained the courts between Feb. and March 1542: see
above, p.xlv.
[3]   Curate of Cogges in 1530: *Visitations in the Diocese of Lincoln 1517-31*, ed. A Hamilton
Thompson (Lincs. Rec. Soc. 35, 1944), p.56.

f.11r   Court held 1 Sept. [1542].
         Court held 22 Sept. [1542].

f.11v   Court held 6 Oct. 1542.
         Bailiffs: Robert Temple, William Bouysshyp.
         Constables: William Byrde, John Bally.
         Wardsmen: Ralph Leyge, William Beller, James Brokes, Richard Mewkell,
            William Lopton.
         Cardeners: William Brykellbaynke [*crossed out*], Robert Keyp, Harry Dellfe.
         Ale tasters: John Greyn, Robert Hykoxs.
         Chamberlains: William Goyn, Robert Leyge. Rests in their hands 15s. 8d.
         Leather searchers: Thomas Carlys, John Greyn.
         Complaint: John Coke against William Box concerning a mound between the
            said John and William Box, to be made by 1 Nov. next on pain of 3s. 4d.
f.12r   Presented: John Horyn presented for a 'streyt' [i.e. path] make and hedge to be
            made next to John Broke by 1 Nov. next on pain of 3s. 4d.
         Delivered to William Byrde and John Bally two pairs of harness for the town
            with gorgets.

         Court held 4 Nov. [1542].
         Presented: Cardenars William Brekyllbanke and Robert Keyp presented
            William Byrde and William Lopton for unlawful mutton that they sold.
            Neither of them to kill for sale such unlawful victuals on pain of 3s. 4d.
            apiece.
         William Hyll's white bread lacked of the assize 3s. 4d.;[4] no such fault to be made
            again on pain of 5s.
         Ralph Leyge, wardsman, presented John Parkar, servant to William
            Brekylbanke, for a bloodshed that he made upon John Horin 6d.
         John Horin presented for the fray also.

f.12v   Court held 24 Nov. [1542].

         Court held 15 Dec. [1542].
         Action of trespass: William Lopton against Roger Fathars. (3)

         Court held 5 Jan. [1543].
         Court held 26 Jan. [1543].

f.13r   Court held 16 Feb. [1543].
         Actions of debt : Robert Ryche against Randell Margerys for 3s. 7d.
                          Robert Pryar against Robert Coxs for 2s.
                          Robert Temple against John Plommar of Witney for 4s. 2d.
                          Richard Stokforde esq. of Rowley, Staffs., against Thomas
            Skoppam of Witney for 8s. 7d. John Peny and William Bryde have
            awarded Richard Stokford 4s. by agreement.
                          Thomas Mondy of Oxford, butcher, against Walter Sheparde
            of Witney for 12s. 3d.

         ⁴ i.e. not of the required weight under the assize; Hyll was therefore fined.

6
THE WITNEY COURT BOOKS, 1543

f.13v Court held 9 March [1543].
Actions of debt : . . . Horne against Thomas Isson for 2s.3d.
Thomas Hyatt of Burford against Thomas Ayndros of Witney, sawyer, for 2s 3d. (3)

f.14r Court held 30 March 1543.

Court held 20 April 1543.
Presented : James Brokes, wardsman, presented Roger Fatheres for his mound and Richard Dyar for a mound to be made by Ascension Day next on pain of 3s. 4d.
Robert Mukell presented John Horyn for a mound to be made between Margaret Wheyllar and the said Horyn, the mound to be made by Ascension Day on pain of 2s.
Actions of debt : John Penney against John Horyn for 5s. (3)
Anthony Tayllar against Robert Squeyr for 4s. 3d. (3)
Same against Edward Peyrsson for 15d. (3)
Same against Thomas Skoppam for 2s. 1d. (3)
Same against Margery Moyr for 3s . . .
f.14v William Greyn against William Loppton for 4s. 7d.
Robert Law against William Gouldesmeythe for 20s. 3d.
Agreed that Robert Pryar to pay Robert Law 7s. and one load of wood for William Gouldesmythe and 3s. 4d. on 24 June, 20d. on 29 Sept, and 2s. on 25 Dec.

Court held 11 May [1543].
Actions of debt : Margaret Skargell against Thomas Fouyrde of Ducklington for 2s. 7d.
Annys Hyll against Walter Sheparde for 7s. (3)
William Goyn against the same for 5s. 1d. (3)

f.15r Court held 1 June [1543].

Court held 22 June [1543].
Actions of debt : Fabian Humfrey against Thomas Cartar for 5s. (3)
Thomas Cartar against William Bryde for 5s. (3)

Court held 13 July [1543].
Action of debt : Thomas Tayllar against Walter Shepard for 6s. 8d. (3)

f.15v Court held 3 Aug. [1543] by Robert Tempoll and William Marten,[5] bailiffs.

Court held 7 Sept. [1543].
Presented: Robert Mewkell, wardsman, presented John Horin for his mound between Richard Hayns and Margaret Wheyllar to be made before 21 Sept. next on pain of 2s.

[5] Alias Bishop; see above, p.lii.

Action of debt : Stephen Crosly of Cassington against Roger Fathers of Witney for 6s. 11d. (3)

f.16r   Court held 9 Nov. [1543].
Actions of debt : William Lysson, clerk,[6] against John Horin of Witney for 8s. 3d. (3)
William Brynkfylde against John Plomar alias Powell, weaver, for 11s. 6d. (3)
Presented: Robert Mewkell, wardsman, presented William Box for a mound to be made between John Cooke and the said Box by 24 Nov. on pain of 2s.
Action of debt : William Goyn against Robert Coxs for 4s. 5d. (3)

Court held 14 March [1544] by Robert Tempoll and William Marten, bailiffs.[7]

f.16v   Court held 1 Feb. [1544].
Action of debt : Edmund Richardes against John Powell alias Plomar for 6s. 3d. (3)

Court held 22 Feb. [1544].
Court held 11 March [1544].

f.17r   Court held 2 May [1544].
Actions of debt : Harry Caykbred of Hanborough against Thomas Skoppam for 10s. 8d. (2)
John Baylly against William Box of Witney for 12s. 8d. (3)
Same against William Ably of Witney for 11s. 8d. (3)
William Dytton against Robert Squyr of Witney for 7s. (2)

Court held 18 July [1544].
Court held 12 Sept. [1544].

f.17v   Court held 23 Oct. 1544.
Bailiffs: Leonard Yate, Thomas Ryng.
Constables: Thomas Myryman, Ralph Legg.
Wardsmen: Edmund Rychardes, Leonard Pennye, John Plommar, John Larens, Roger Atkyns.
Cardenars: Harry Delff, Robert Kepe.
Ale tasters: John Buklond, William Brikillbank.
Action of debt : Robert Pryer against William Shepard for 7s. (3)

f.18r   Court held 14 Nov. 1544.
Actions of debt : Richard Oldfield against William Ritun for 3s. 3d.
Roger Raynold against Thomas Doyson for 8 . . . (2)
Order: ale set at 2s. 4d. the dozen.

6   Vicar of Cropredy, rector of Ducklington, d.1549/50: Oldfield, Clerus Oxon.
7   The Friday court; the court of 11 March on f. 16v seems an extra.

Court held 18 Dec. 1544.
Action of debt : William Rytyn against Robert Squyar for 5s. 7d.

f.18v   Court held 23 Jan. 1545.
        Actions of debt : Robert Kepe on behalf of Rowland Treye of Eynsham against
            John Payne for 10s. 3d., Roger Fathers for 4s., John Purson for 2s., and
            Thomas More for 12d.

Court held 13 Feb. 1545 by the bailiffs.

Court held 23 March 1545 by the bailiffs.
Actions of debt : John Loddard, servant to Sir Simon Harcourt, against William
    Belcher for 20s.
                Thomas Ryng against Walter Shepard for 10s. 10d.

f.19r   Court held 15 Oct. 1546[8]
        Bailiffs: William Box, John Peny.
        Constables: Walter Gonys, William Brynfylde.
        Wardsmen: Humfrey Malen, Thomas Hankys, John Larens, John Coke,
            Roger Raynolles.
        Cardenars: Harry Delfe, Robert Coxe.
        Ale tasters: Roger Faders, Robert Kepe.
        Actions of debt : William Elmar against Robert Greffyn for 6s. 8d. For lack of
            appearance, 2d.
                    Humfrey Malen against Richard Abley for 9s. 4d.

Court held 5 Nov. 1546 by the bailiffs.
Action of debt : Margaret Deson against Richard Abley for 2s. 9d. (2)
Order: ale set at 22d. the dozen.

f.19v   Court held 26 Nov. [1546] by the bailiffs.
        In bread all was well.[9]
        Sir John Rychardes and Randell [Margeris] chose two daysmen, John Fyllyppes
            and Thomas Hanks, to abide by their award upon paid of 3s. 4d.

Court held 7 Jan. [1547] by the bailiffs.
Actions of debt : Humfrey Malen against Randell Margeros for 22d.
                Robert Grefyth against the same for 14s.

Court held 29 Jan. [1547] by the bailiffs.

f.20r   Court held 18 Feb. [1547].
        Action of debt : John Horseley against Richard Grene for 2s. 4½d.

---

[8]   A leaf (or leaves) is missing and perhaps contained the courts between April 1545 and
Sept. 1546. It was noted as missing in the 19th century by the local historian William
Langford in a note attached to the Ms. See above, p.xlv.
    [9]   i.e. no breaches of the assize.

Court held 11 March [April *crossed out*] [1547].
Agreed: Randel Margeres to pay Robert Grefyt 3s. 4d. at Easter, 3s. 4d.
    at Whitsuntide and 6s. 8d. on 1 Aug. All well.

Court held 1 April [1547] by the bailiffs.
The same day Richard Grene did assign the court . . .

Court held 22 April [1547] by the bailiffs.
Action of trespass: Richard Grene against John Brone. The matter was put in
    the hands of Roger Legge and Walter Toker. Parties agreed and the court
    dismissed.

f.20v Court held 11 May [1547] by the bailiffs. All well.
       Court held 16 Sept. [1547] by the bailiffs. All well.

       Court held 7 Oct. [1547] by Roger Legge and Thomas Taylor, bailiffs.[10]
       Actions of debt : Humfrey Malyn against Richard Able for 7s.
                John Rede against John Plomar for 6s. 8d. due to Rede.
f.21r Agreed: Richard Able to pay Humfrey Malen the 6s. 4d. due to him on 23 Nov.
       next, or it shall be lawful for him to distrain.

       Court held 27 Oct. 1547 by the bailiffs.
       Actions of debt : Harry Bantyng of The Moors [in Ducklington] against Alice
       Crawly of South Leigh for 20d. Agreed 17 Nov.
                Nicholas Allen against Anthony Taylor for 6s. 8d.
f.21v Tipplers with their sureties: Thomas Hankkes for good order to be kept in
       Randell Margeras's house; Leonard Penny for Thomas Issund; Roger
       Raynowlles for John Kowks; John Koks for Roger Raynowlls.
       Order: by the bailiffs that all tipplers come to court the next court day and bring
       sureties for good order in their houses on pain of 3s. 4d.

f.22r Court held 18 Nov. [1547] by the bailiffs.
       Action of debt : Giles Jonnes against John Frene of Aston for 20s. 4d. Order
       taken between them 26 Dec.
       Tipplers with their sureties: Humfrey Malyn surety for William Gyllys; William
       Goodde for Walter Sheppard; Richard Umfrey for Roger Father; Thomas
       Klemssun for William Taylor; William Brynkffyld for Robert Cartar.

f.22v Court held 9 Dec. [1547] by the bailiffs.
       Actions of debt : John Hawlle of Crawley against Randell Marcheras for 2s.
                Humfrey Malyn against John Byrcott for 2s. 6d.

       Court held 23 Dec. [1547] by the bailiffs.
       Actions of debt : Roger Legge against William Taylor for 4s. 4d.
                Richard Able against Humfrey Malyn for 7½d.

---

[10]   Until this court roman numerals were used. There was a change to arabic until f.23r,
then to roman until the last entry on f.23r, then to arabic until f.29v (mixed); roman
numerals were used from f.30v.

f.23r   Court held 13 Jan. [1548] by the bailiffs.
         Actions of debt : Robert Tempull against Randell Margeris for 3s. 3d.
                          Leonard Penny against Robert Cokkes for 4s. 3d.
                          William Elmar against the same for 4s. 5d.

         Court held 3 Feb. [1548] by the bailiffs.

f.23v   Court held 2 March [1548] by the bailiffs.
         Actions of debt : William Malyn against Robert Hukwell for 15d.
                          Thomas Haynkkes against William Lowe for 3s. 3d.

         Court held 6 April [1548] by the bailiffs.
         Action of debt : William Gonne against Randell Margeras for 3s. 7d.
         Agreed between Robert Koxe and William Elmorre for 4s. 5d. due to Elmorre
             on the said day of entering. Elmorre is content to give Koxe day of pay-
             ment until 21 Dec; if Koxe does not pay, to be lawful for Elmorre to take a
             distress as he might have done at the day of making hereof.
f.24r   Action of debt : William Malyn against Robert Grevyth for 21d.

         Court held 4 May 1548 by the bailiffs.
         Actions of debt : James Darby in the name of Morris Smartt against Richard
             Harrys for 6s. 8d. John Grene entered the court on 10 Aug. and became
             surety for Richard Harrys with James Darby for such debts as Harrys owed
             Darby. One groat [i.e. 4d.] a week till it be paid.
                          Roger Legge against Robert Grevyth for 17s. 6d.
                          Christopher Drynge against William Yngle for 13s. 7d.

         Court held by the bailiffs [no date].

f.24v   Court held 15 June [1548] by the bailiffs.
         Action of debt : Master Kowke of Karsewell [i.e. Caswell, Berks.] against
             Richard Able for 20s. 3d.

         Court held 13 July [1548] by the bailiffs.
         Actions of debt : John Spysar of Charlbury against Randell Margeras for 9s. 4d.
                          Robert Hwkyns against Richard Able for 9s.

         Court held 10 Aug. [1548] by the bailiffs.
         Actions of debt : John Bolloke against William Horn for 2s 3d.
                          Same against William Shepard for 2s. 3d.

f.25r   Court held 7 Sept. 1548 by the bailiffs.

         Court held 5 Oct. 1548 by Thomas Taylor and John Raynkell, bailiffs.
         Action of debt : Humfrey Malyn against Walter Sheparde for 4s. 4½d.
             Agreed 15 March.

         Court held 8 Nov. 1548 by the bailiffs.

Actions of debt : Nicholas Hyll against Richard Able for 6s. . . . Agreed
    15 March.
                Robert Lowe against Robert Grevyth for 10s. 3d.
                Same against John Plommar for 7s. 9d.
Sureties: John Hawkyns and John Grene came into court and offered themselves
    as sureties for Richard Harrys for that Harrys was arrested by a Warrant of
    the Peace[11] before the face of the court. They stand bound in £5 apiece.
    [*Their marks affixed*]

f.25v Court held 7 Dec. 1548 by the bailiffs.[12]
      Actions of debt : Robert Carttar against Randell Margoras for 6s. 11d. Agreed
          15 March.
                  James Darby against Humfrey Malyn for 20s. 3d.
                  William Byrd against Richard Able for 16s. Agreed 18 Jan.

      Court held 18 Jan. [1549] by the bailiffs.
      Action of debt : Robert Tomson of Standlake against Richard Abley for 5s. 3d.

f.26r Court held 8 Feb. [1549] by the bailiffs.

      Court held 15 March 1549 by the bailiffs.
      Action of debt : John Barnabe against Richard Umfrey for 20s. 3d.
      Order: taken between Nicholas Hyll and John Bannyng for a mound between
          them which Bannyng shall make within ten days following, on pain of 3s.
          4d.

      Court held 19 April [1549] by the bailiffs.
      Actions of debt : Thomas Pryckyvans of Burford against Randell Margeras
          for 12s. 3d.
                  George Fry of Cricklade [Wilts.] against Robert Greyvthe
      for 3s. 3d.
f.26v Assize of ale: set at 20d the dozen for good and wholesome brewed ale.

      Court held 17 May [1549].
      Actions of debt : William Gonne against John Hawkyns for 12s. 3d.
                  George Kawkott of Standlake against Peter Wyrgge for 5s. 9d.
                  William Smythe of Hailey against Randell Margares for
      4s. 3d. Md. paid to William [*crossed out*].

f.27r Court held 2 Aug. [1549] by the bailiffs.
      Assize of ale: brewers to brew good and wholesome ale to sell from this day at
          2s. . . .d. the dozen and tipplers to sell one thirdendell of good ale for 1d.
          and half a thirdendell at ½d. Every brewer to provide for the comfort of
          the poor people good and wholesome drink and to allow a gallon and a

---

[11] i.e. issued by the Justices of the Peace.
[12] 1549 in the Ms. but the bailiffs named were in office from Oct 1548 to Oct 1549. The
year is not given again until f.27v.

half for 1d. and every brewer to allow of small drink for the brewing of a quarter of malt 12 'gawnes' [i.e. gallons].

f.27v Court held 7 June 1549 by the bailiffs.
Actions of debt : Robert Grevyth against Robert Sagar for 6s. 11d.
Same against John Grenne for 5s. 3d.
Arrest: taken against Robert Tomssun of Standlake [on account] of a certain restraint taken by Richard Able of 2s. 3d. and certain iron stuffs.

Court held 28 June 1549 by the bailiffs.
Order: for William Smyth of Hailey and Randell Margeras.
Margeras to pay Smyth 2s. at the last court and 2s. 3d. three weeks following. Md. paid 2 Aug.

f.28r Court held 31 Aug. [1549] by the bailiffs.
Assize of ale: brewers to brew good and wholesome ale for sale after this day at 22d. the dozen and tipplers for 2s. the dozen after the rate.
Action of debt : Richard Grene against Nicholas Allen for 2s. 8d.

f.29r Court held 11 Oct. 1549 by William Byshoppe and Thomas Yate, bailiffs.
Constables: Giles Jhones, John Lawrans.
Wardsmen: Richard Pryar, Anthony Taylar, William Mager, Robert Mukell, Richard Ridar.
Cardenars: Luke Leysam, Thomas Hyrste.
Ale tasters: Robert Kepe, John Hatherne.

Court held 31 Oct. 1549 by the bailiffs.
Assize of ale: brewers to brew good and wholesome ale to sell for 2s. 6d. the dozen. . .

f.29v Court held 21 Dec. 1549 by the bailiffs.
Action of debt : William Smythe of Hailey against Robert Cockes of Witney for 13s. 6d. Order taken 14 March. Cockes to pay 3s. 4d. on 24 June, and the same on 29 Sept., 25 Dec. and 25 March next. *Cancelled.*

Court held 21 Feb. 1550 by the bailiffs.
Actions of debt : Thomas Curtys against Randell Margeras for 10s.
Received of Randell on 2 May, 10s. 2d. *Cancelled.*
Same against Robert Grevyn for 10s.
Same against William Stubbes for 5s. Discharged with memorandum that he paid on 2 April. *Cancelled.*
f.30r   Humfrey Maylyn against Ralph Hayes for 5s. 7d.

Court held 10 April 1550 by the bailiffs.
Action of debt : John Howton against Randell Margerys for 37s.
Margerys paid in hand 6s. 8d. and agreed to pay the rest at 12d. a week.

Court held 2 April 1550 [*sic*] by the bailiffs.

Action of debt : Giles Jhones against Robert Kepe for 6s. 8d. *Cancelled.*

f.30v Court held 7 July 1550 by the bailiffs.
Action of debt : Laurence Wakur of South Leigh against Randell Margerys
for 11s. 8d.

Court held 27 Sept. 1550 by the bailiffs.
Md. a possession: given 5 July 1550 by Robert Harrys of Witney, weaver, of his
tenement in Crondell St. [i.e. Corn St.] to Walter Jones, his heirs and
assigns, for ever, according to a deed dated 5 July 1550. Possession given by
Thomas Ringe and Walter Jones, bailiffs, Philip Boxe and Matthew
Penney, constables, and Thomas Hankes, sergeant.[13]

f.31r Court held 10 Oct. 1550.
Bailiffs: Thomas Rynge, Walter Jones.
Constables: Matthew Penny, Philip Boxe.
Wardsmen: Richard Ryder, Richard Pryor, William Maior, Robert Mwekyll,
Anthony Taylor.
Cardenars: Luke Leysham, Thomas Hurste.
Ale tasters: Robert Kope, Richard Harryse.
Action of debt : Stephen Crosly of Cassington against Robert Fatherse for
6s. 11d. (3)[14]

Court held 14 Nov. 1550 by the bailiffs.
Md. a possession: given 7 Nov. by Thomas Hutchynse, by attorneys Richard
Homefre and John Lawrense, of a house with appurtenances in Witney in
the tenure of Anthony Taylor to Simon Wysdome of Burford and his heirs,
according to the purpose of a certain deed. *Cancelled.*

f.32r Court held 12 Dec. 1550 by the bailiffs.
Action of debt : Katherine Hale against Robert Kockes for 20s. 3d. (3)
Md. Laurence Waker received of Randell Margeris 4s.; Margeris promised to
pay 3s. 4d. more on 2 Feb. *Cancelled.*

Court held 9 Jan. 1551 by the bailiffs.
Actions of debt : Leonard Yate the elder against Thomas Elyot for 2s. 9d. (3)
Nothing found.
Nicholas Hyll against Thomas Mwkele for 4s. *Cancelled.* (3)

f.33r Court held 30 Jan. 1551 by the bailiffs.
Actions of debt : Thomas Meremane against John Lawrense for 19s. 6d.
Cancelled.
Nicholas Hylle against Henry Collyndon for 20d. *Cancelled.*(3)

[13] Since the bailiffs named were not in office until 10 Oct they must have given possession
after that date.
[14] The calls are recorded in arabic numerals from this point; see above p.xlvi.

Court held 20 Feb. 1551 by the bailiffs.
Actions of debt : William Loctone against Thomas Mwkyll for 16½d. *Cancelled.*
        Same against John Burkit for 12d. *Cancelled.* (3)
        Same against Robert Griffith for 12d. *Cancelled.* (3)
        Richard Greyne against Thomas Carter for 3s. 7d.
  Cancelled. (3)

f.33v   Same against Humfrey Baker for 3s. 4½d. *Cancelled.* (2)

Court held 20 March 1551 by the bailiffs.
Action of debt : John Baker against Richard Pryor for 2s. 10d. *Cancelled.* (3)

Court held 24 April 1551 by the bailiffs.
Action of debt : Robert Carter against John Pecocke for 21d. *Cancelled.* (2)

f.34r Court held 29 May 1551 by the bailiffs.
Actions of debt : William Brynkefeld against Randell Margerys for 37s. 3d. (3)
        Thomas Eleman against John Pecocke for 7s. 3d. *Cancelled.*

Court held 20 June 1551 by the bailiffs.
Court held 25 July 1551 by the bailiffs.

Court held 4 Sept. 1551 by the bailiffs.
Order: all brewsters in the town to sell a dozen of ale not above 2s. 8d.; and the gannaker to sell a thirdendell for 1d. indoors and outdoors.

f.34v Court held 9 Oct. 1551 by Thomas Ringe and William Brynkefeld, bailiffs.
Constables: John Barnaby, Edward Gune.
Wardsmen: John Saunders, William Malyne, Robert Fletcher, Roger Rydly, Roger Welar.
Cardenars: William Maior, Luke Leysame.
Ale tasters: Richard Harrys, Robert Kepe.
In candles forfeit 10lb 16 'wayte' [i.e. weight].[15]

f.35r Court held 30 Oct. 1551 by the bailiffs.
Actions of debt : Robert Carter against Thomas Mwkyll for 2s. *Cancelled.*
        Same against John Burket for 18d. *Cancelled.*

Court held 27 Nov. 1551 by the bailiffs.
Action of debt : William Malyne [Shepperd *crossed out*] against Walter Shepperd for 3s. 3d. *Cancelled.* (3)

Court held 18 Dec. 1551 by the bailiffs.
f.35v Actions of debt : Robert Lowe against Robert Griffithe for 6s. 3d. *Cancelled.* (2)
        William Loctone against John Horne for 3s. 3d. *Cancelled.*
        Eleanor Forde against William Taylor for 8s. 3d. *Cancelled.* (2)

[15] The meaning is not clear, but under 11 Hen.VI.c.12 wax candles etc. could only be sold at 3d in the pound beyond the price of plain wax on penalty of forfeiture.

Court held 22 Jan. 1551 by the bailiffs.
Action of debt : Thomas Clemston against Humfrey Baker for 18s. 1d. *Cancelled.* (3)

f.36r Court held 12 Feb. 1552 by the bailiffs.

Court held 11 March 1552 by the bailiffs.
Actions of debt : Thomas Yate against Margery Randals for 6s. 3d. (3)
          Griffith Grendom against John Powell for 3s. 7d. *Cancelled.* (3)
          William Maior against Harry Rugg for 3s. (3)
Action of covenant broken: Thomas Moore against John Peacock for 39s. 11d.

f.36v Court held 1 April 1552 by the bailiffs.
Action of debt : George Frye against Robert Gryffithe for 3s. 3d. (3)

Court held 29 April 1551 by the bailiffs.
Order: by the bailiffs. Brewsters to sell a dozen of ale for 22d. and the
    gannaker to sell a quart of good ale outdoors for ½d. and a thirdendell
    indoors for 1d. and a half thirdendell indoors for ½d.

f.37r Court held 20 May 1551 by the bailiffs.

Court held 17 June 1552 by the bailiffs.
Action of detinue: Andrew Plandon, schoolmaster, against Annese Mariges for
    withholding certain 'paye' of roofs to the value of 5s. (2)[16]
    Orders: by the bailiffs. No tippler nor aleseller to sell a quart of ale outdoors for
f.37v ½d. and a thirdendell indoors for 1d. and a half thirdendell for ½d.
    Brewsters to sell according to the decree made on pain of 6s. 6d. for each
    default. Tipplers likewise on pain of 3s. for default.

Court held 8 July 1552 by the bailiffs.
Actions of debt : John Wode against John Bradhorne for 3s.
          Leonard Penny against Anthony Larden for 13s. 3d.
Orders: brewers to sell a dozen of best ale for 2s. 8d.
    Tipplers to sell a thirdendell of ale outdoors for 1d. and a quart indoors at
    1d. on pain of 3s. 4d. for default. Brewsters selling above the said price and
    contrary to the decree to forfeit 6s. 8d.
f.38r   Mastiffs to be muzzled; not to go unmuzzled in the streets after 23 July
    next on pain of 10s. for each dog unmuzzled. No bitches to go assault about
    the town on pain of 3s. 4d. for each default.

Court held 9 Sept. 1552 by the bailiffs.

Court held 10 Feb. 1553 by William Brigefelde and William Burde, bailiffs.[17]

---

[16] Perhaps payment for work done.
[17] See also p.16.

f.39r   Md. possessions:[18] taken 24 Nov. 1547 by the bailiffs of William Burges of a house in Corn St., to the use of Leonard Yatte. Witnesses: Leonard Peny and Walter Jones, constables, Thomas Hankkes sergeant, William Good, William Beatrys and others.

Taken as above but of Thomas Slowe of a house in Corn St.

Taken 14 June 1548 as above but of Richard Kynge of a house in Crondawell St. [i.e. Corn St.].

f.39v   Taken 14 Sept. 1548 by the bailiffs of Edward Luddyatt by letter of attorney of one messuage in Crondawell St. [i.e. Corn St.]. next to James Mowdy on the west and one messuage of the Chantry Hall on the west [sic] to the use of Nicholas Allen. Witnesses: the constables, the sergeant, John Wyllsun, clerk, Robert Keppe, William Goode, Richard Pryor, Thomas Kartar and many others.

Taken 12 March 1549 by the bailiffs of Richard Bryan of Cogges of one tenement lying beneath the bridge late Ballowes, to the use of Elizabeth Raynowlds and her heirs for ever. Witnesses 'borres'[19] William Brynkfyld, Christopher Drng and Humfrey Malyn constables, Thomas Hanckes sergeant, John Cokke, Antony Stevyns, Henry Hornne and many others.

f.40r   Taken 14 April 1549 by the bailiffs of Margett Marbleston of one tenement on the east side of Witney between the tenement of Robert Adene on the north and the tenement of John Ranckkell on the south; and one tenement lying upon the town ditch on the west part of the town between the tenement of Thomas Wenman, esq., on the north and the tenement of Philip Box on the south; to the use of Richard Adene of Sandford [i.e. Sandford St. Martin], husbandman. Provision to allow his mother Margett Adene or her deputy quiet possession of the two tenements and the rent thereof as in her former estate; after her decease to remain in the hands of Adene and his heirs; if he has no heirs then to Adene for life with remainder to his brother Robert Adene and his heirs forever. Witnesses: the constables, the sergeant, Thomas Klemsun, Antony Taylor, John Hawkyns, Roger Raynowlls and many others.

f.40v   Taken the same day by the same bailiffs of Margett Marbleston of one tenement in High St. Witney on the west part of town between the tenement of Leonard Yatte on the south and tenement of Thomas Wenman, esq., on the north; and one tenement lying on the town ditch on the east part of the street between the tenement of Leonard Yatte on the north and the tenement of Richard Adene on the south; to the use of Robert Adene of Nether Guiting [i.e. Guiting Power], Gloucs., Yeoman. Provision for mother's or deputy's quiet possession in her lifetime and after her death to go to Robert Adene and his heirs. Witnesses as above.

f.41r   Court held 21 Oct. 1552 by William Brigfeild and William Burde, bailiffs. Orders: taken by William Arden, clerk of the market,[20] 16 Oct. 1552. Tallow

---

[18]   For the hands and placing of the entries on ff. 39r–40v see above p.xlv.
[19]   Possibly a corruption of 'borsholder', a head of a tithing or a parish officer.
[20]   The royal Clerk of the Market, on whom see above p.xxvi. Perhaps the repetition of orders by the bailiffs was an expression of their independence.

candles not to be sold above 2½d. per lb. Brewers not to sell a dozen of ale above 20d. and 13 gallons to the dozen. Item tipplers not to sell a quart of best ale or beer for ½d. , and a thirdendell indoors of best ale and beer for 1d. and a half thirdendell for ½d.

Orders: by the bailiffs. Brewsters not to sell above 20d. the dozen on pain of
f.41v 20s. to be levied on their goods and chattels. Tipplers not to sell less than a thirdendell of best ale or beer for 1d. indoors, or less than a quart of the same outdoors for ½d., and no better ale or beer indoors than out on pain of 5s.

Actions of debt : Robert Carter against Robert Cotyse, tailor, for 9s. *Cancelled.*
Same against Thomas Stougge for 23d. *Cancelled.*
William Selpe, smith, against Roger Harrys, smith, for 3s. 9d.
Cancelled.
William Loctone against John Bannynge for 3s. 3d. Agreed to
pay on 6 Jan. *Cancelled.*
f.42r Anthony Larden against Thomas Phillippes for 5s. (1)
Same against Lawrence Good for 20s. (1)
Same against John Chaundeler for 10s. (1)
William Brigfeild against Robert Cotyse, tailor, for 38s. 9d.
Cancelled.
Thomas Clempstone against Henry Smythe, tailor, for 10s.
8d. *Cancelled.* (1)
Same against Robert Cockes for 3s. 7d. Agreed to pay the debt
on 6 Jan. *Cancelled.* (1)
Same against Robert Gryffit for 2s. 3d. Agreed to pay by 6 Jan.
Cancelled. (1)
Same against Richard Pryer for 16s. *Cancelled.* (1) Agreed to
pay at 4d. a week, or else the court to stand assigned a bauble.
f.42v Same against Walter Shiltone, labourer, for 11s. 6d. *Cancelled.*
Awarded: John Horne to bring in his two hands and his own at the next court against Wodde.

f.43r Court held 11 Nov. [1552].
Action of debt : Thomas Davys against John Powell for 15d.

Court held 2 Dec. [1552].
Actions of debt : Elizabeth Shepperd [William Shepperd *crossed out*] against Christopher Drynge for 9s. 3d. (3)
Thomas Ison against John Box for 6s. 3d. (3)
Orders: by the bailiffs. No brewer to sell ale above 2s. 8d. a dozen; and 13 gallons to the dozen. Tipplers to sell a thirdendell of ale for 1d. outdoors and a quart for 1d. indoors.

f.43v Court held 23 Dec. 1552 by the bailiffs.

Court held 20 Jan. 1553.
Action of debt : John Rede against Thomas Yston for 4s. 3d. (3)

Court held 10 Feb. 1553 by the bailiffs.
Action of debt : William Brigefeld against John Powell alias Plommar for
16s. 9d. (2)

f.44r   Court held 3 March 1553 by the bailiffs.
Actions of debt : . . . Dey against John Dyckensone of Eynsham for 14s. 3d.
Cancelled.
Giles Jones against Luke Leysame for 12s. 9d. *Cancelled.* (3)

Court held 5 May 1553 by the bailiffs.
Action of debt : Steven Gylbart against John Kooke of Witney for 6s. 3d. (3)
At this court came John Dycinson and his witnesses John Popingey,
John Smythe.
Amerced: Nicholas Alen for a common baker. [21]

f.44v   Court held 2 June 1553 by the bailiffs.
Action of debt entered: Robert Warweke against John Laurans for 3s. 11d.(2)
Richard Grene allowed for a common baker.[22]
Awarded: Luke Leyssam to bring in his hands two honest men besides ownself.

f.45r   Court held 24 June 1553 by the bailiffs.
Actions of debt : Richard Okley against Christopher Dynge for 16s. 11d. (3)
Richard Wryte against Edward Goune for 20s. 3d. (1)
Nicholas Hyll against John Warom for 2s. 3d. (3)
William Bryan against William Daulton for 9s. 3d. (3)

Court held 4 Sept. 1553 by the bailiffs.

f.46r   Court held 20 Oct. 1553 by Philip Boxe and John Lawrans, bailiffs.
Constables: Robert Redewell, Nicholas Hill.
Wardsmen: William Waull, Robert More, William Meger the younger,
Robert Mugell, Randell Margeris.
Cardenars: William Mager, Luke Leasam.
Ale tasters: Robert Keape, Richard Harrys.

f.46v   Bailiffs' [hundred *crossed out*] court held 10 Nov. 1553.[23]
Presented: Walter Shepard to remove a muck hill in front of his door before the
next hundred [24] held here on pain of 6s. 8d.
William Lopton and William Deny not to pasture pigs in the royal
highway on pain of 3s. 4d. each.
Thomas Hankes twice broke the assize of bread [fined] 1s. To keep
the assize on pain of forfeiting his bread.

[21]   i.e. he was not licensed.
[22]   i.e. licensed to sell bread and cakes.
[23]   From this court until 16 June 1554 the entries are in Latin except for the memorandum of
debt on f. 48v, p.19. See above, p.xlv.
[24]   i.e. the bishop's lawday; see above p.xv.

f.47r   Actions of debt : Humfrey Malyn against Randell Margery for 10s. The
          defendant came to court and acknowledged the debt; given day to pay until
          1 Aug., paying each week 6d., or distraint to be taken for the whole debt.
          Pledge Philip Boxe. Licence to agree. To be levied.
                          Same against William Fylppes, fugitive, for 13s. 2d. Distress
          to be taken. To be levied.
          Order: brewers and bakers to keep the assize of bread and ale on pain of
          6s. 8d. each.

f.47v   Bailiffs' [hundred *crossed out*] court held 1 Dec. 1553.
          Action of debt : William Kyrby against William Androwes and Richard
          Androwes, administrators of the lands, goods and debts of Thomas
          Androwes late deceased, for 3s. 4d.
          Declaration: which he lent to Thomas on 17 Sept. 1552 in the presence of
          Roger Reynold and allowed a week to pay, but has not yet been paid.
          William Androwes agreed to pay the plaintiff 23d. at the next court held
          after Easter next. Licence to agree.

f.48r   Court held 12 Jan. 1554 by the bailiffs.
          Settlement: Richard Androwes paid 2s. to William Kyrby in part-payment of
          3s. 4d.; remaining 16d. to be paid within three weeks, Licence to agree.
          Action of debt : John Saunders against Randell Margery for 20s. 3d. Not to be
          levied. Licence to agree.

f.48v   Court held 2 March 1554 by the bailiffs.
          Md. 16 June 1554. William White, servant of Randell Margerys, presented
          before the masters bailiffs in the court by Thomas Clemson and Robert
          Tredwell and others at . . .

f.49r   Court held 16 March 1554 by the bailiffs.
          Actions of debt : Thomas Shawe against William Huntt for 5s. 10d.
          Declaration: which he lent to the defendant in Feb. 1554, viz. 2s. 10d. in
          silver and another 3s. in flesh at divers places, for which he allowed a week
          to repay, etc. Distraint to be made. The defendant acknowledged 5s. 2d. of
          the debt and to have [it] in court on pain of 10s.
                          Thomas Stegge against Randell Margery for 6s. 8d.
          Declaration: which he lent the defendant on 1 Dec. 1553 and allowed a
          week to pay, but which has not been paid and is unjustly detained to his
          damage to the value of 40d. and hence he makes his suit. Distraint to be
          made. Not defended.

f.49v   Court held 4 May 1554 by the bailiffs.
          Action of debt : William Elmer against Richard Pryor for 4s. 8d. The defendant
          came into court and acknowledged the debt; to pay 4d. a week until paid.
          Distraint to be made.

f.50r   Court held 24 May 1554 by the bailiffs.
          Action of debt : Thomas Carter against Randell Margery for 10s. 3d.

f.50v   Court held 16 June 1554 by the bailiffs. All well.

f.51r   Court held 5 Oct. 1554 by Richard Umfrey and Matthias Penny, bailiffs, Thomas Collyar and John Sawnders, constables, William Dowltun, sergeant, and others.
    Orders: butchers to remove stalls after Saturday next off the street on pain of 6s. 8d. for each default. Provided always that it should be lawful for the said butchers to set forth their stalls every market day and as soon as the market is done to remove them immediately and also for William Loptun to keep his room as is appointed to him by the lord's officers.

f.51v   brewers to sell their ale to the tipplers for 2s. 8d. the dozen and tipplers to sell their ale outdoors and in for 3s. 2d., i.e. a thirdendell for 1d. and a half thirdendell for ½d., on pain of 3s. 4d. for each default.
    Actions of debt : William Hucchyns, in the name of Thomas Nortun, against Luke Lessame for 9s. 3d.
                Lawrence Goode against Roger Harrysun, smith, for 12s. 11d.

f.52r   Court held 25 Oct. 1554 by the bailiffs, the constables and Alexander Raynesforde with others.

f.52v   Court held 16 Nov. 1554 by the bailiffs, the constables with others.
    Declaration: brought in by Thomas Norton of Langford against Luke Leasam for 9s. 3d.
    Action of debt : Lawrence Goode of Cogges against Roger Harryson, smith, for 12s. 11d.

f.53v   Court held 7 Dec. 1554 by the bailiffs and the constables with others.
    To the same court came William Maior the elder and brought with him to record of and upon a pair of indentures made between himself and Thomas More the elder and Thomas More the younger, which the aforesaid recorders Richard Brian of Cogges, John Waull and Luke Leysan of this same borough do testify and record that the aforesaid Thomas More the elder and Thomas More the younger did seal and deliver the foresaid indentures made between the parties in their presence as their one act and deed they recording thereunto the same.

f.54r   Court held 11 Jan. 1555 by the bailiffs and the constables with others.
    Actions of debt : Thomas Hanckes against Sir George,[25] schoolmaster, for 6s. 11d.
                William Duny against John Warran for 3s. 0½d.
                Walter Jhones against Walter Wasson for 31s. 8d.
    Orders: brewers to sell ale to tipplers for 3s. 8d. Tipplers to sell ale for 4s. good and stale the dozen, and other small drink for 1d. a gallon 'be it wholesome and good for mens bodies'.

[25]   A courtesy title.

f.54v   Court held 1 Feb. 1555 by Matthias Penny, bailiff, Roger Leg and Roger
          Raynold with others.
          Action of debt : John Carter against Randell Margery for 2s. 3d.

f.55r   Court held 3 May 1555 by the bailiffs and the constables.

f.55v   Court held 28 June 1555 by the bailiffs and the constables with divers others.
          Complaint: Thomas Tayloure, Thomas Yate, Leonard Yate, William
          Brinckfilde, Walter Jones, William Birde, Edward Gonne, John Lawrans,
          John Ranckell, Robert Tredwell, Thomas Clemson, William Elmer,
          Philip Boxe, Henry Jones, Thomas Merman with divers others for
          remedy to be made of a shop now in the tenure of Anthony Larden and
          found to be a great annoyance to the whole inhabitants of the whole
          borough and the town of Witney. It is thought good as well by us the
          bailiffs as the rest of the inhabitants that the said shop be removed and to
          stand in such form and sort as shall be thought good by the said parties for
          the avoiding of the aforesaid annoyance.
          Action of debt : William Lowdall against Richard Greyn for 13s.

f.56r   Court held 27 Sept. 1555 by the bailiffs with other brethren by whom an order
          is taken.
          Action of debt : Thomas Hanckes against William Taylor for 2s. 8d.

f.57r   Court held 25 Oct. 1555.
          Order: Richard Humfrey, Thomas Ring, Thomas Yate, Roger Legge, William
          Marten, Matthias Pennye, William Byrde, William Brynkfeld, John
          Rankell, Philip Boxe, John Lawrence, Thomas Merryman, Leonard Yate,
          each to appear at the town hall every court day therein accustomed to be
          held on pain of 12d. for every default. Likewise every wardsman and
          cardenar. Reasonable excuse to be accepted from friends assigned to answer
          for them.
          Actions of debt : Anthony Larden against John Horne for 5s. 8d. (2)
                            Same against John Powell alias Plumber for 11d. [33s. 11d.
          crossed out] (1)
                            Same against Robert Gryffen for 25s. 5d. (2)
                            William Maylyn against William Hearne for 2s. 11d.
                            Same against Thomas Bentlay for 2s. 9d.

f.57v   Court held 17 Nov. 1555
          Actions of debt : Harry Jonys against Randell Margeres for 28s. 3d. (3)
                            William Lopton against Richard Horswold for 2s. 8½d. (3)
                            Same against William Pita for 3s. 5d. (3)
                            Richard Hyckman against William Mayior for 3s. 11d.
          Agreed: between Anthony Larden and Nicholas Yfelde that, in contentment of
          such money and debt as was due to him by John Appowall, Yfelde shall pay
          him 20s. by next Whitsun.
          Order: John Meryman to pay Anthony Larden 20s., part payment of debt of
          25s. owed him by Robert Gryffen, by 25 Dec. next.

Action of debt : Md. 28 Nov. [1555] William Brynkefeld against John
Blacksman of Eynsham for 3s. 3d. (3)

f.58r Presented: Alexander Plumpber presents Andrew Byrde for selling flesh
contrary to the court order; cost of the action 3s. 4d.

Court held 6 Dec. 1555.
Richard Horrsald came to court and presented himself to answer William
Lupdon for his debt of 2s. 8½d. Within one month next after 25 Dec.
Presented: Robert Kepe presents Thomas Ring, Humfrey Maylen, Robert
Tredwell, Thomas Shawe, John Sawnders for allowing mastiffs and bitches
on the street against the court order.
Action of debt : Md. 24 Dec. 1555. Thomas Yate against John Brooke of Aston
for 2s. 3d. (1)

f.58v Court held 3 Jan. 1556 [sic] in the time of Thomas Taylor and Walter Jones,
bailiffs.
Tipplers with their sureties: for good order to be kept in their houses on pain of
10s. for default. Philip Boxe for the house of Robert Carter; Thomas
Hanckes for Roger Reynoldes; William Doulghton for Nicholas Hyll;
Thomas Hanckes for Randell Margeres; William Elmer for Emme Gyelles;
f.59r   Robert Tredwell for Walter Sheperd; Robert Sawgares for William Hayle;
William Dowlton for Thomas Yson; John Saunders for Thomas Shawe;
Anthony Larden for Nicholas Allen.
Distress taken: of John Hornnes commenced by Anthony Larden of the
following: two brass pots, four platters, one pewter dish, two saucers, one
skillet, one broad axe, valued in all at 20s.

f.59v Court held 24 Jan. 1556 [sic].
Action of debt : William Walle, in the name of William Hewens of Caswell,
against Anthony Larden for 30s. 11d.
The entrance of the matter between Barnaby and Fletcher.
Anthony Larden and Robert Moore came and said that they were at the
sealing of a pair of indentures between John Barnaby and Robert Fletcher,
at which time Robert Fletcher recited in the presence of the said parties to
understand whether it was the same lease that John Barnaby took at the
hand of Robert Rodborn of Standlake or not; and further recited the
covenant that he put the said Barnaby in trust thereon. Which Barnaby did
confess that they were and that if Fletcher were able to prove the contrary
he would be able [to show] him the lease that he took to Rodborn. In
witness whereof they have set their hands or marks, in the presence of the
court. [Marks]

f.60r Court held 14 Feb. 1556.
Actions of debt : Thomas Dyxon of Guiting [i.e. Guiting Power or Temple
Guiting], Gloucs., against Thomas Carter for 17s. 3d. (3)
Harry Chypnam of Oxford against Humfrey Maylen and
Thomas Clemson for 20s. 3d. Cancelled. (2)
Thomas Clempson against John Marttyn for 19d.

Same against Nicholas Fotherson for 6s. 3d. (3)

f.60v   Court held 6 March 1556.

Release of right: by Roger Raynoldes in an indenture or lease made between one Robert Deane of Nether Guiting [i.e. Guiting Power], Gloucs., gent., and the said Reynoldes of all rights in two tenements with appurtenances to the use of Nicholas Hyll and Christian his wife and their heirs and assigns during the term mentioned in the said indenture.

Actions of debt : Richard Raynoldes and John Cookes against Nicholas Jackson for 18s. 3d.

William Mason of Chadlington against Randell Margeris for 20s. 3d. Attorney for Mason, William Allan.

f.61r   Court held 26 March 1556.

Action of debt : Richard Raynoldes against Mr. Sharppe for 6s. *Cancelled*. (1)

Court held 23 April 1556.

Action of debt : Thomas Hanckes against Mr. Thomas Sharpe for 5s. 3d.

Court held 24 May 1556.

f.61v   Court held 12 June 1556.

Action of debt : Robert Lande against Robert Gryffethe alias Bodye for 3s. 11d. (3)

Court held 3 July [1556] by the bailiffs, William Elmore and William Huchyns, constables and others.

Actions of debt : John Wyllattes, nailman, by his attorney Robert Kepe, against Matthias Penny for 10s. 3d.(3)

Robert Bolloke of Cokethorpe, by his attorney Robert Kepe, against Nicholas Jakssun for 20s. 3d.(3)

f.62r   John Redbord of Curbridge, by his attorney Robert Kepe, against Randell Margeras for 20s. 3d. (3)

William Dunny against Walter Vahane for 2s. 4d. *Cancelled*. (3)

Court held by Thomas Taylor and Walter Jones, bailiffs, William Hucchynnes and William Elmore, constables, with others [No date; ? 24 July 1556].

Actions of debt : William Lopton, alias Bolchar, against Walter Shepard for 5s. 7d.(2)

f.62v   John Newman, by his attorney Robert Kepe, against Anthony Larden for 20s. 3d.(3)

Court held 14 Aug. 1556 by the bailiffs.

Actions of debt : Richard Perre, by his attorney Robert Kepe, against John Meryman for 22s. 4d.(3)

Md. 12 Sept. [1556] Richard Unfrey against John Smythe of Hailey for 12s. 3d. (1). Agreed at the same court for a reckoning between the parties. *Agreement cancelled.*

f.63r   Court held 18 Sept. [1556] by the bailiffs with worthies.
        Actions of debt : Anthony Larden against Edward Goode for 18s. 6d.(2)
                        Roger Rydle against Thomas Sharp for 4s. 8d.(3)
        Settled: John Smythe of Hailey for the debt of 12s. 3d. owed Richard Umfrey;
            acquitted for 6s. 8d. and one bushel of wheat to be paid on 1 Nov. 1557.

f.63v   Court held 30 Oct. 1556 by Leonard Yate and John Barnaby, bailiffs.
        Agreed: no man to let his mastiff go unmuzzled in the town on pain of 3s. 4d.
            No 'saulte' bitch to go in the town on pain of 3s. 4d. after ten days ensuing.
f.64r   Action of debt: Edmund Mashorader, vicar of Shilton, by his attorney
            Alexander Raynforde, against Nicholas Bladon of South Leigh for 11s. 6d.

f.64v   Court held 26 Nov. [1556] by the bailiffs.
        Actions of debt : Edward Goude against Anthony Larden for 15s. 1d.(2)
                        Thomas Clemson against Randell Margeris for 2s. 2½d.(2)

f.65r   Court held 20 Oct. 1557 by Thomas Ringe and Thomas Colier, bailiffs, with
            other brethren.[26]
        Orders: brewers to make good and wholesome ale and to sell at eight groats
            [i.e. 2s. 8d.] the dozen, 13 gallons to the dozen. Tipplers to sell a thirdendell
            for 1d. outdoors and an ale quart for 1d. indoors, on pain of 3s. 4d. for
            default. Brewers and tipplers to sell a gallon of small drink for 1d.
        Constables: Roger Raynoldes, Robert Warwike.
        Wardsmen: Nicholas Giles, Thomas Hurst, Anthony Watson, Roger Wheler,
            William Harryes.
        Ale tasters: Robert Keape, Richard Oldfild.
        Leather sealers:[27] Nicholas Aleyn, Richard Raynoldes.
        Cardenars: William Lopton, William Maior the elder.
f.65v   Actions of debt : Roger Hearnige of South Leigh against Anthony Larden
            for 12s. 3d.(3)
                        Thomas Clemsonne against Robert Fletcher for 13s. 10d.
            Cancelled.(2)
                        William Alleyn against Robert Bennet for 2s. 10d.
            Condemned. (3)
                        Philip Boxe against Edmund Cosyns for 8s. 3d.(3)

        Court held 11 Nov. 1557 by the bailiffs.
        Actions of debt : Robert Birdsey of Crawley against Robert Grffyn, alias Bodie,
            for 23d. Taken up until the next court day.(2)
                        Richard Hiet against Walter Barthelet of the Field [i.e.
            Leafield] for 19s. 9d.(3)

f.66r   Court held 3 Dec. 1557 by the bailiffs and others there assembled.

---

[26]   There is a leaf missing which possibly contained the courts between Dec. 1556 and Sept.
1557; see above, p.xlv.
        This is the first time they are so called; see above, p.xxiv.

Actions of debt : James Darbie against Thomas Coke of Corn St. Witney for 20s. 3d. Taken up until the next court day.(3)

> Jeremy Handes against Robert Fletcher for 7s. 3d. *Cancelled*
> Alexander Rayneford, on behalf of Margaret Keate of Brize Norton, against Thomas Ysonne for 7s.(2) *Cancelled.*
> Thomas Shawe against William Taylor for 6s. 7d.(3) *Cancelled.*

Court held 7 Jan. 1558 by the bailiffs, and others there assembled.
Actions of debt : Leonard Alleyn against William Wall for 2s. 3d.(1) *Cancelled.*

> Richard Raynoldes against John Coke for 23s. 7d.(3)

f.66v   Court held 4 Feb. 1558 by the bailiffs.

Orders: brewers to sell ale under the sieve at 20d. the dozen and 13 gallons to the dozen and to sell small drink at ½d. the gallon, brewing of both sorts good and wholesome ale and drink, on pain of 6s. 8d. for default. Tipplers to sell ale outdoors at a quart for ½d. and indoors a thirdendell for 1d.

Amerced: Thomas Hurst and Anthony Watson, wardsmen, 4d. apiece for non-appearance at the aforesaid court.

Actions of debt : William Elmore against Thomas Wayneman of Emley [i.e. Elmley Castle in Elmley Lovett, Worcs.?] for 9s. 7d. (3)[28]

> Anthony Larden against John Slowe for 28s.(3)
> Same against William Maior the younger for 12s. 3d.
> Same against Thomas Wisdome for 12s. 3d. Order taken until the next court day.(3)

f.67r   Court held 12 March 1558 by the bailiffs and other of the brethren assembled there.

Actions of debt : Ralph Longworth of Wolsone [i.e. Worsham] Mill[29] against Randolph Margeries for 7s. 3d. Put to daysmen until the next court day.(3)

> Thomas Wattes of South Leigh against Thomas Ysonne for 8s. 8d. Ordered that Ysonne to pay 8d. on the first court day after the action and 8d. every market day following until the debt is paid. To be omitted.(3)

Order: every inhabitant to carry and remove their muck hill from their door before Easter Day next on pain of 5s. for every default. *Cancelled.*

Actions of debt : Thomas Colier and William Daulton against Leonard Penye for 38s. 3d. Ask bailiff.(3)

> William Elmore against Augustine Waynman for 14s. 4d.
> Thomas Shawe against Alice Townesend of 'Brightenton' [i.e. Brighthampton], Standlake, for 37s. [*Marginalia cancelled;* 'delayed until further time' *entered*]. (3)
> Humfrey Malyne against Faith Hedgemen of Ducklington for 20s.(3)
> Faith Hedgeman against Humfrey Malyne for 6s. 6d.(3)

---

[28]   *V.C.H. Worcs.* does not mention Waynman at either Elmley Castle or Elmley Lovett.
[29]   Giles, *Witney*, p.53, mentions Wolmersham Mills, evidently the same. Worsham Mill was another of the Windrush mills to the west of Witney. See also Woolsham, p.204.

f.67v   Court held 15 April 1558 by the bailiffs.
         Actions of debt : Elizabeth Treadwell against John Purnell for 2s. (3)
                           John Wayte of Brize Norton against the same for 3s. 4d.(3)
                           Thomas Carter against William Andrews for 2s.(3)
                           William [Thomas crossed out] Rynge against Anthony Larden
         for 20s. Cancelled.(1)
                           Harry Jones against the same for 26s. Cancelled.(1)
                           Thomas Clemsonne against William Tayler for 35s. 11d.
         To be omitted(1)
                           Same against Peter Wirge for 17s. 11d.(3)
                           Same against John Ridley for 6s. 10d.(3)
         Order: every inhabitant to remove his much hill out of the street before Sunday
             next after Low Sunday [i.e. first Sunday after Easter] next on pain of 5s.
f.68r   Action of debt : Richard Colgrove of Glympton against Gregory Merymon
             for 14s. 1d. Held until Pentecost next.

         Court held 5 May 1558 by Thomas Colier, bailiff, Thomas Ringe the other
             bailiff now defunct.
         Orders in cases of action of debt : Richard Raynolds against John Coke for 23s.
             7d; to be paid 6s. 8d. at Pentecost next and 6s. 8d. on 29 Sept. next in full
             satisfaction of the debt.
                           Anthony Larden against William Maior the
             younger for 12s. 3d. to be paid on Whitsun next.
                           Same against John Slowe for 28s; to be paid
             20s. on 29 Sept. next and 8s. on 25 July.
         Action of debt : Roger Horne of Eynsham against Randolph Mergeries for
             6s. 11d. 3s. 4d. of debt paid. (3)

f.68v   Court held 27 May 1558 by Thomas Colier, bailiff, Thomas Ringe now
             defunct.
         Actions of debt : Harry Thomas of Bampton against Gregory Merymon for
             20s. 3d.(3)
                           Walter Kinges of Cogges against John Harte of South Leigh
             for 26s. 11d. Not to be called.

         Court held 1 July 1558 by Thomas Colier, bailiff, etc.
         Actions of debt : Robert Keape against Leonard Penye, William Rynge, William
             Lopton alias Bolcher and William Byrd for allowing their mastiffs to go
             unmuzzled against the court order. Penalty for each 3s. 4d.[30]
                           Mr Ashefild against Randolph Margerys for 15s. 3d. (2)
                           Same against Roger Smyth for 4s. 11d. [8d. crossed out.] (3)
f.69r   Same against Thomas Yson for 5s. 3d. (3)
                           Same against Anthony Larden for 19s. 3d. (3)
                           Robert Lond of Newland against Randolph Margerys for
             19d. (2)
                           Edmund Walker against Robert Fletcher for 3s. 7d. (2)

[30]   Amercements for breaches of the order on p.24.

Court held 29 July [1558] by Thomas Colyer, bailiff, etc.

Court held . . . Aug. 1558 by Thomas Colier, bailiff.
Action of debt : Mark Fathers against John Ratlif for 6s. 5d.(2)

f.69v   Court held 10 Sept. 1558 by the bailiff etc.

f.70r   Court held 4 Nov. 1558 by Thomas Yat and Walter Jones, bailiffs, Richard
         Brice and William Ryng, constables, and others congregated there.
         Wardsmen: John Collyer, John Slowe, Nicholas Maior, William Harrys,
         William Penye.
         Sergeant: William Dallton.
         Cardenars: Thomas Shawe, Edward Goodde.
         Ale tasters: Thomas Carter, Robert Keape.
         Sureties for honest rule and good order: Nicholas Hill of Witney, baker,
         for Elizabeth Raynolles.

f.70v   Court held 10 Feb. 1559 by the bailiffs and others congregated there.
         Orders: brewers and tipplers brewing ale to sell to send and give sufficient
         warning to the ale taster to taste their ale on pain of 3s. 4d. Brewers to sell
         outdoors a dozen of their best ale for 18d. Tipplers to sell outdoors a
         thirdendell for ½d.
         Actions of debt : Harry Thomas of Bampton against Gregory Meriman of
         Witney, broadweaver, for 20s. 6d. Paid, and quit. (3)
                     William Ring of Witney against William Harris of Witney,
         broadweaver, for 6s.

f.71r   Court held 3 March 1559 by the bailiffs and the constables with many others.
         Actions of debt : John Bannynge against Anthony Larden for 3s. *Cancelled.* (2)
                     Same against John Berell for 2s. 6d. *Cancelled.* (2)

         Court held 21 April 1559 by the bailiffs, the constables and others there.
         Action of debt : Mr Thomas Wilmote against Randell Margeries for 10s. . . . (3)

f.71v   Court held 12 May 1559 by the bailiffs.
         Actions of debt : Robert Carter against William Tayler for 10s. 3d. (1)
                     William Rynge, in the name of Harry Mawberley alias Tucker
         of Highworth, [Wilts.], against Richard Okeley for 20s. 3d. (3)
                     William Rynge against the same for 6s. 3d. (3)
                     Anthony Larden against John Bannyge for 3s. *Cancelled.*

         Court held 2 June 1559 by the bailiffs, the constables etc.
         Actions of debt : Agnes Davyes against Robert More for 7s. 3d. *Cancelled.*
                     Roger Horne of Eynsham against Randell Margeries for
         3s.6d. (3)
                     William Rynge, in the name and on behalf of Margery Alder
         of Abingdon, [Berks.], against William Arnold of Charlbury for 8s. 3d. (3)

f.72r Court held 7 July 1559 by the bailiffs and others.
Actions of debt : Thomas Barnard of Minster Lovell against Richard Raynoldes
for 4 nobles and 3d. [i.e. £1. 6s. 11d.] (3)
            Thomas Clemson against Thomas Hiestaye of Ramsden for
3s. 7d.

Court held 28 July [1559] by the bailiffs etc.
Award: Robert More to pay Agnes Davyes 6s. on 29 Sept. next; surety
Richard Raynoldes.
Actions of debt : John Frenche of Aston against Mundye of Bampton for 10s.
            Richard Wisdome, in the name and on behalf of Alice
Wisdome, against Anthony Larden, alias Bocher, for 7s. 3d.
Ordered and discharged in open court. (3)

f.72v Court held 16 Aug. [1559] by the bailiffs and others called together there.
Actions of debt : William Elmore against [Thomas] Hiestaye of Ramsden for
5s. 11d. *Cancelled.*
            Walter Jones against Robert Deene of Nether Guiting [i.e.
Guiting Power], Gloucs., for 39s. 11d.
            William Rynge against Edward Kyrby of Lechlade, Gloucs.,
for 39s. 11d. (3)

Court held 20 Oct. [1559] by Thomas Yate and Walter Jones, bailiffs.
Order: bakers to sell two horse loaves for 1d. and to the innholders 14 to
the dozen.

Court held 17 Nov. [1559] by Thomas Yate and Walter Jones, bailiffs.
Order: brewers to sell ale for 2d. the gallon, tipplers a wine quart for ½d. of
good ale.
Action of debt : James Merymon against Giles Jones of Witney for 12s. 3d. (1)

f.73r Court held 8 Dec. 1559 by the bailiffs.
Court held 10 Feb. 1560 by the bailiffs.

Court held 15 March 1560 by the bailiffs.
Actions of debt : John Ranckell against Randell Margeries for 3s. 3d. (3)
            Walter Jones of Witney against James Snoddam of Bampton
for 39s. 11¾d.
Sureties: William Mallen and Robert Stevens for good order in the house of
Edmund Proute on pain of £5 apiece for every default.

f.73v Court held 17 May 1560 by the bailiffs.
Actions of debt : William Harrys against John Dyssell for 6s. 3d.
            Robert Carpenter of Burford against Randell Margeryes for
2s. 7d.

f.74r Court held 11 Oct. 1560 by Thomas Taylor and Philip Boxe, bailiffs.
Constables: Harry Jones, Richard Hyett.

Wardsmen: Robert Stevens, Richard Weaver, John Dyssell, Thomas Alen, Arthur Browne.

Cardenars: Anthony Larden, Richard Ockley.

Ale tasters: William Walle, Robert Keepe.

Tipplers appointed: Robert Steven's ward: Emma Gyles, Thomas Shawe, William Hale alias Draycot. Richard Weaver's ward: Thomas Stagge, Marget Ison. Thomas Alen's ward: Anes Fathers. Arthur Browne's ward: Robert Carter, John Cook. John Dyssell's ward: Katherine Legg, Randell Margeryes, Anthony Larden.

f.74v Acknowledgement: John Barnaby came into court and confessed that whereas John Couke by his deed indented bearing date 14 March 1557 did demise and let to Barnaby one tenement beyond the bridge for certain years yet to come by virtue whereof Barnaby has hedged in for his own easement by estimation four yards in breadth and 25 yards in length of the backside of the said tenement and laid it to one other tenement which Barnaby holds of Mr Stratforde for term of years also. Whereas to avoid all doubt Barnaby confessed the same ground to be the said John Couk's and that on the end and expiration of his years Barnaby shall yield the said ground and tenement in every part to the said John Couke. And for the truth the said John Barnaby has hereunto set his hand. By me John Barnaby.[Mark]

Order: Richard Lawrens and Richard Reynolds to make sufficient mounds in their backsides before 1 Nov. next on pain of 3s. 4d. apiece. Penalty to be respited unto the next court. Discharged.

Covenanted servant: in court Roger Grene acknowledged receipt of eight pence and thereby bound himself to William Suche for eight years next ensuing; to be given at the end of eight years 5 nobles [i.e. £1. 13s. 4d.] and double apparel according to the custom of the borough.

f.75r Court held 31 Oct. 1560 by the bailiffs.

Order: by a common consent that Mr. Beckinsalle, Richard Humfraye, William Bysshipe alias Martin, Thomas Yeate, Walter Jones, Leonard Yeate, John Lawrence, John Barnabie, William Huchines, Thomas Martin, Thomas Clemson, William Elmer, William Brinckfild, John Ranckle, William Ringe, Thomas Coliare, John Coliare and Humfrey Maline, being lawfully warned by the wardsmen, are to associate with the bailiffs for and during the court, and having no lawful let to the contrary on pain of 6d. for default. To be levied and gathered by the sergeant to the use of the town houses. If they have lawful impediment, to assign some honest man to assign them and declare the cause to the contrary.

f.75v Action of debt : Thomas Clemson against Henry Alen for 14s. 5d.(3)

Court held 22 Nov. 1560 by the bailiffs.

Covenanted servant: in court John Irelond, son of James Irelond of Caswell, acknowledged receipt of sixpence and therefore bound himself to Richard Hyet of Witney for six years from 29 Sept. last past; to be given at the end of six years 20s. wages and double apparel according to the custom of the borough.

Order: brewers to sell ale for 2s. 8d. the gallon; tipplers for 3s.

Actions of debt : Marget Jonsons against John Ficchet of Hailey for 2s. 11d. (1)

f.76r   Thomas Pryddy of Fawler against William Wethered of Spelsbury for 11s. 7d. (3)

Thomas Shaw against Harry Banting of 'More' [i.e. The Moors, Ducklington], for 30s. 3d. (3)

Court held 13 Dec. 1560 by Philip Boxe, bailiff, and others.

Action of debt : John Hunnt of Standlake against William Harrys for 6s. 8d. (2)

Court held 3 Jan. 1561 by Thomas Taylor, bailiff, and others.

Action of debt : Harry Alen against Thomas Clemson for 12s. 3d.(2)

f.76v   Covenanted servants: in court Robert Higginges son of Thomas Higinges of Abingdon, Berks., acknowledged receipt of five pence and thereby bound himself to William Harrys of Witney, broadweaver, for five years from 1 Nov. 1558; to be given at the end of five years 26s. 8d. wages and double apparel according to the custom of the borough; the cloth of the best covenant coat to be 6s. 8d. the yard; and to be given 4d. every quarter during the last three years.

in court John Cannyng, son of Robert Canyng of Admington, Gloucs., acknowledged receipt of eight pence and thereby bound himself to Harry Jones of Witney, clothier, for eight years from 25 Dec. last past; to be given at the end of eight years 33s. 4d. wages and double apparel according to the custom of the borough.

f.77r   in court Paul Grove, son of Richard Grove of Campden, Gloucs., acknowledged receipt of nine pence and thereby bound himself to Harry Jones of Witney, clothier, for nine years from 29 Sept. last past; to be given at the end of nine years 33s. 4d. wages and double apparel according to the custom of the borough.

Court held 24 Jan. 1561 by Philip Boxe, bailiff, and others.

Covenanted servant: in court Richard Gryffyn received six pence and thereby bound himself to Thomas Vawes of Witney, shoemaker, for six years from 25 Dec. last past; to be given at the end of six years 10s. wages and double apparel according to the custom of the borough and such tools belonging to his occupation as shall be fit and necessary for a journeyman of that occupation to work withal.

f.77v   Court held 14 Feb. 1561 by the bailiffs.

Action of debt : Thomas Hycks against Harry Smyth of Hailey for 20s. 3d.

Lease: Clemence Jonson of Witney, widow, to Richard Weaver and Joan his wife of the house, backside and garden and appurtenances, now in Weaver's occupation for the term of her life for 10s. a year.

Covenanted servants: in court Fabian Payn acknowledged receipt of four pence and thereby bound himself to Thomas Stagg of Witney, broadweaver, for four years from 25 Dec. last past; to be given at the end of four years 20s. wages and double apparel according to the usage of the borough.

f.78r   in court Richard Lardner, son of John Lardner of

Finstock, received eight pence and thereby bound himself to Richard Weaver of Witney, broadweaver, for eight years from 12 Feb. last past; to be given at the end of eight years 26s. 8d. wages and double apparel according to the custom of the borough.

in court Richard Iles acknowledged receipt of eight pence and thereby bound himself to William Hodson of Witney, broadweaver, for eight years from Easter last past; to be given at the end of eight years 20s. wages and double apparel according to the custom of the borough; and in the first four years 2d. every quarter and in the last four years 4d. every quarter.

f.78v
in court James Hill acknowledged receipt of sixpence and thereby bound himself to John Lawrence of Witney, tucker, for six years from 25 Dec. last past; to be given at the end of six years 26s. 8d. wages and double apparel according to the custom of the borough.

in court James Margetes son of Martin Margetes of Spelsbury, received ten pence and thereby bound himself to William Harris of Witney, broadweaver, for ten years from 24 June last past; to be given at the end of ten years 26s. 8d. wages and double apparel according to the custom of the borough.

Action of debt : James Smyth against John Dyssell for 24d. [*sum crossed out*]

Court held 7 March 1561 by Philip Box, bailiff, with others.
Action of debt : Annes Taylor of Ducklington, widow, against William Pope, clerk,[31] for 30s. 3d.

f.79r Court held 27 March 1561 by the bailiffs with others.
Actions of debt : Richard Bekynshall against Thomas Stagg, Peter Wirge, Thomas Coke, Thomas Hurst, Philip Cakebred, Harry Alen, William Hodson, Alexander Harrys, Thomas Castellfoord and John Banyng for 3s. 4d. apiece for that they kept their swine going abroad contrary to the order of the court.[32]

Thomas Clemson against Gregory Meryman for 20s. 2d. (3)
William Elmar against Roger Wheler for 3s. 1d.(3) Ordered.
Same against Gregory Meryman for 34s. 7½d.
Harry Smyth of Hailey against Thomas Hickes for 8s. 3d. (3)

f.80r Court held 9 May 1561 by the bailiffs with others.
Action of debt : Hew Vaughan against Joan Meryman, a widow, for 5s. 11d. (3) Ordered.

Court held 6 May 1561 by Thomas Taylor, bailiff, with others.
Action of debt : Joan Meryman, widow, against Hew Vaughan for 6s. 3d. (3)

.Court held 4 July 1561 by Philip Boxe, bailiff, with others.

---

[31] Rector of Duckington 1558, d.1568: Oldfield, Clerus Oxon.
[32] Again breaches of a court order were treated as actions of debt.

Court held 22 Aug. [1561] by the bailiffs with others.
Action of debt : Harry Petye against James . . . for 6s. 11d.

f.81r Court held 10 Oct. 1561 by Thomas Taylor and Richard Beckynshaw, bailiffs.
Constables: John Colyar, Antony Watson.
Wardsmen: Robert Stevens, Hew Rodes, Thomas Vaus, Edward Goed, James Smyth.
Cardenars: Anthony Larden, Richard Ockley.
Ale tasters: John Bannyng, Robert Kepe.

Court held 19 Dec. 1561 by the bailiffs.
f.81v Orders: brewers to sell good and lawful ale at 2s. the dozen under the hair sieve; 13 gallons to the dozen. Tipplers to sell ale at ½d. the quart outdoors, on pain of 3s. 4d.

Court held 30 Jan. 1562 by the bailiffs with others.
Presented: James Smyth, wardsman, that Robert Carter and John Cok sell ale contrary to the court order, to the forfeit of 3s. 4d.
      Richard Horsall that Thomas Shaw and Andrew Byrd twice kept their shops open on the Sabbath at service time, to the forfeit of 3s. 4d.
Amerced: for keeping pigs going in the street contrary to court order, Humfrey Malen, William Maior, Thomas Shawe, William Elmar, Peter Payne, William Harrys, to the forfeit of 12d.

f.82r Actions of debt : Thomas Clemson against Robert Salye for 4s. 10d.(3)
      Same against Nicholas Maior for 9s. 9½d.(3)
      Same against John Meysie for 10s. 6d. (3)
      Same against Peter Wyrge for 5s. 8d.(3)

Court held 27 Feb. 1562 by the bailiffs with others.
Actions of debt : Thomas Adams of Bampton against Randell Margeryes for 16s. 8d. (3)
      William Elmar against Cyprian Collyns for 8s. 11d. (2)
f.82v Lease: granted by the bailiffs with the assent of Thomas Yate, Richard Umfrey, Leonard Yate, Philip Box, Harry Jones, John Rankell, John Colyar, Anthony Watson, William Brynkfyld, Humfrey Malen, Giles Jones, William Elmar, Thomas Clemson, and others, to Alice Hannes, widow, of the town close in the West End for her life at 2s. 8d. a year, over and above the chief rent; to be paid to the town chamberlains on 25 March and 29 Sept. Witnesses: [signatures of] Anthony Watson, Richard Bekinsaw, Thomas Taylor, Thomas Yate, Leonard Yate, Harry Jonys, William Brygfyld, Humfrey Malyn.
f.83r Md. a possession: taken 10 Jan. 1562 by the bailiffs of Peter Rankell of one tenement with curtilage and garden adjoining and one acre of arable land behind the tenement, in Witney in Corndelstreet [i.e. Corn St.] on the south side between the ground of Joan Yate, widow, on the east side and the tenement of John Box on the west side; to the use of Harry Jones of Witney, clothier. In the presence of the constables and Edward Walker, John Sowthan, Richard Weaver and others.

Court held 10 April 1562 by the bailiffs.

Actions of debt: Hew Sowthan against William Beane for 18s. 3d. (3) Ordered.

John Evans against Thomas Alen for 13s. 4d. Agreed to pay 5s. upon 1 Aug.

John Taylor against Thomas Hickes for 13s. 7d. To pay 6s. 8d. upon 21 July next.

f.83v Covenanted servant: in court Thomas Honyburne, son of Robert Honyburne of North Leigh, acknowledged receipt of eight pence and bound himself to John Horne of Witney, carpenter, for five years from 25 March last past; to be given for his service at the end of five years £3 6s. 8d. and double apparel, and 1d. every Sunday during the five years.

Court held 3 July 1562 by the bailiffs with others.

Actions of debt : John Busshe of Castle Eaton, [Wilts.], against Randell Margerys for 5s. 3d.

Thomas Clemson against Nicholas Huckwell for 16s.

f.84r Court held 23 Oct 1562 by Harry Jones and Thomas Busshop, bailiffs.

Constables: William Harris, Thomas Busshe.

Wardsmen: Robert Chapman, Leonard Rankell, Thomas Hickes, William Goold, James Smythe.

Cloth searchers: William Goold, Robert Stevens.

Cardenars: Anthony Larden, Richard Ockley.

Ale tasters: William Suche, Robert Kepe.

Leather sealers and searchers: Thomas Vaws, Oliver Ball

Orders: brewers to sell ale for 3s. 1d. the dozen. Tipplers to sell a quart of ale for 1d. indoors and 1d. the thirdendell outdoors on pain of 2s. 6d. for default.

Actions of debt : Thomas Colyar against William Andros for 2s. 3d. (3) Arrest.

Cyprian Collyns against Harry Rassell of Stratford on Avon, [Warws.], for 10s. 3d. Taken up.

Thomas Waters against Michael Pebworth for 7s. 5d. (3)

f.84v Court held 20 Nov. 1562 by the bailiffs with others.

Actions of debt : Thomas Lawrence against John Rackle for 2s. 11d. (3)

Edmund Bolt against Joan Meryman widow for 9s. 3d. (3) Thomas Clemson surety to pay 8s. on Whitsun eve next. Taken up with her.

Philip Box against Michael Pebworth for 12s. 3d.

Amerced: Thomas Shaw 12d. for not coming to court the same day. (3)

Court held 18 Dec. 1562 by the bailiffs.

Actions of debt : Hew Sowthen against William Beane for 12s. 11d. (2)

Richard Syms alias Thycket against Thomas Hurst for 4s. 3d. (1)

f.85r Court held 8 Jan. 1563 by the bailiffs with others.

Actions of debt : Thomas Busshe against Randel Margeries for 9s. 11d. (1) Taken up.

Actions of debt : Same against Richard Prior the elder for 7s. 3d. (3)
            Thomas Hanckes against Marget Ison for 22s. 3d. (3)
            William Kemster of South Leigh against Leonard Radley for
13s. 7d. (3)

Court held 29 Jan. [1563] by the bailiffs with others.
Order: brewers to sell ale for 3s. 6d. the dozen.
Actions of debt : Leonard Dalton against William Newman of Curbridge for
15s. 7d.
            Thomas Clemson against the same for 4s. 11d.

Court held 19 Feb. [1563] by the bailiffs with others. All well.

f.85v Court held 12 March [1563] by Harry Jones, bailiff, with others.
Court held 16 April [1563] by the bailiffs with others.
Court held 14 May 1563 by the bailiffs.

Court held 18 June 1563 by the bailiffs with others.
Actions of debt : Thomas Hicks against William Andros for 5s. 3d. (2)
            Justian Kenar alias Harper against Leonard Radley for
3s. 3d. (2)

Court held 30 July 1563 by the bailiffs with others.
Action of debt : Richard Reynolds against Thomas Shawe for 12s. 9d. (1)

Court held 20 Aug 1563 by the bailiffs with others.
Action of debt : Giles Jones against John Pyt of Hailey for 26s. 8d. (2)

f.86r Court held 8 Oct. 1563 by Leonard Yate and William Huchyns, bailiffs, with
others.
Constables: Nicholas Ifyld, Roger Rydley.
Wardsmen: Roger Coxe, William Petoo, William Cocke, William Rankell,
Roger Whelar.
Cardenars: Randell Margeryes, John Slowe.
Ale tasters: Roger Haryes, Robert Kepe.
Cloth searchers: John Slow, Roger Cox.
Leather searchers and sealers: Oliver Ball, Richard Oldfyld.
f.86v Tipplers with their sureties: Eme Gyles appointed and bound by recognizance
and for her William Ellmar and Thomas Hanckes; Thomas Hurst and for
him Harry Jones and Nicholas Hill; Thomas Stagg and for him John
Lawrence and Nicholas Hill; Thomas Barnard and for him Anthony
Larden and Richard Lewes; Annes Fathers and for her Richard Umfrey;
Anthony Larden and for him Thomas Bushop and John Barnabe; John
Coke and for him Robert Carter; Randell Margeryes, Katherine Legg,
Robert Carter, Thomas Shawe, William Hale. [*No sureties given.*]
Orders: brewers to sell ale under the sieve for 2s. the dozen. Tipplers to sell a
thirdendell outdoors for 1d., on pain of 3s. 4d. for default.
Wardsmen to attend each court day on pain of 6d. for default. Bakers
likewise on pain of 12d.

Action of debt : Jeremy Webbe against Randell Margeryes for 10s. 3d. *Cancelled.* Paid.

f.87r   Court held 29 Oct. 1563 by the bailiffs with others.

        Actions of debt : Thomas Clemson against Thomas Craftes for . . .

                  William Elmar against Leonard Ranckell for 16s. 7d. *Cancelled.* (1)

                      Randell Margeris against John Waren for 3s. 11d. *Cancelled.* (3)

        Order: brewers to sell ale under the sieve for 2s. 8d. the dozen on pain of 3s. 4d. for each default. Tipplers to sell a thirdendell outdoors and one quart of ale indoors on like pain; to brew as much to sell outdoors as indoors on pain of 3s. 4d. for default.

f.87v   Town Chamberlains: Thomas Clemson and Peter Ranckell appointed. Received at the same court in ready money 23s. 6d. More they have to receive now in the hands of William Brynckfyld, 30s: in the hands of Giles Jones, 18s; in the hands of Nicholas Hill, 14s. 8d; and in the hands of Alice Hands, widow, 16d. *All cancelled.* Paid. Sum £4. 7s. 6d. By me [signature of] Leonard Yate.

Court held 26 Nov. 1563 by the bailiffs with others.

Covenanted servant: James Whytley, servant with Antony Watson, covenanted to serve Watson from year to year and year after year during two years from 25 Dec. next; to be given at the end of two years 33s. 4d. wages and double apparel as usually given to such a servant.

Action of debt : Hew Pollyn, servant with William Busshop, against John Spyre of Standlake for 4s. [As]signed. (2)

f.88r   Order: no tippler to brew ale, beer or other drink to sell in- or outdoors after the next 14 days following save those common brewers appointed and licenced by the bailiffs on pain of 6s. 8d. for default to the use of the lord of the manor.

Common brewers appointed: Goodwife Gunne, Katherine Legg, Randell Margeryes, Leonard Ranckell, Thomas Stagg, William Hale, Robert Carter.

Court held 17 Dec. 1563 by the bailiffs with others.

Action of debt : Thomas Taylor against Thomas Shawe alias Bochar for 36s. 11d.

f.88v   Court held 7 Jan. 1564 by the bailiffs with others. All well.

Court held 18 Feb. 1564 by the bailiffs with the constables and others.

Actions of debt : Luke Leysam against William Such for 5s. 3d. (3)

                  Joan Meryman, widow, against Hew Sowtherne for 10s. 3d. (3)

                      Thomas Stagg against John Atkyns for 2s. 11d. (1) Agreed.

                      Richard Reynolds against John Purnell for 2s. (1) Agreed.

Court held 17 March 1564 by the bailiffs with the constable and others.

Actions of debt : William Harris against John Sturton, physician, for 39s. 11d. Agreed.

f.89r   Nicholas Hill against John Wall for 5s. 3d. (3)

Katherine Berell against Joan Meryman, widow, for 7s. 3d. (3) Ordered.

Marget Ryme, servant with John Steynton of Standlake, against John Magood for 5s. 3d. (3)

Court held 14 April 1564 by the bailiffs with the constables and others. All well.

Court held 19 May 1564 by the bailiffs with the constables and others.
Orders: brewers to sell ale under the hair sieve for 2s. 4d. the dozen on pain of 3s. 4d. for default. Tipplers to sell a thirdendell at 1d. outdoors and a quart of ale indoors upon like payment.
Action of debt : Thomas Elyot against Randell Margeryes for 5s. 8d. (1) Agreed.

f.89v Court held 16 June 1564 by the bailiffs with the constables and others.
Actions of debt : Thomas Harris of Ducklington against Anthony Larden for 24s. 11d. (3)

Thomas Howse of Minster [i.e. Minster Lovell] against Robert Whyte of Charlbury for 4s. 3d. Agreed.

Court held 14 July 1564 by the bailiffs with the constables and others.
Action of debt : Edmund Crosley of Hailey against Nicholas Huckwell for 8s. 3d.

Court held 4 Aug. 1564 by the bailiffs with the constables and others.
Actions of debt : Annes Camden of South Leigh, widow, against Marget Ison, widow, for 10s. 3d. (3)

William Elmar against Anthony Larden for 18s. (3) *Cancelled.*
Md. Larden to pay the whole sum at four equal payments, i.e. on 25 Dec., 25 Jan., 24 June, and 29 Sept. next. Paid.

f.90r   Robert Brewton of Burford against John Ockley for 39s. 2d. (1)

Court held 15 Sept. 1564 by the bailiffs with the constables and others.
Orders: brewers to sell ale under the hair sieve for 22d. the dozen. Tipplers to sell a quart of ale outdoors for ½d. and a thirdendell for 1d. on pain of 3s. 4d. for default.
Action of maintenance: Anthony Larden prayed an action against Thomas Clemson on behalf of the Queen's Majesty. (3)

Court held 6 Oct. 1564 by Thomas Hanckes and William Ellmar, bailiffs, with others.
Constables: Peter Ranckell, Jeremy Hannes.
Wardsmen: William Vawse, Thomas Foord, William Hodson, Gregory Meryman, John Berell.
Cardenars: Randell Margeries, William Taylor the elder.

Cloth searchers: Anthony Watson, William Taylor the younger.

Leather searchers: Richard Oldfyld, Oliver Ball.

Ale tasters: Roger Haryson, John Berell.

f.90v Action of debt : John Pyt of Hailey against Harry Bysshop for 2s. 3d. (3)

Court held 27 Oct. 1564 by the bailiffs with others.

Order: tipplers and brewers to sell ale as ordered in the last court order.

Tipplers with their sureties: Thomas Stagg appointed and for him John
Lawrence and Nicholas Hill; Thomas Hurst and for him Harry Jones and
Nicholas Hill; Randell Margeryes and for him William Malen and William
Vawse; Thomas Barnard and for him Anthony Larden and Richard
Lewes; Annes Fathers and for her Richard Umfrey and Philip Boxe;
William Gold and for him William Ryng and Robert Stevens; Eme Gyles
and for her Thomas Hanckes and William Ellmar; Katherine Legg and for
her Roger Ridley and Richard Weaver; Richard Kellyng and for him . . .;
John Cok and for him . . .; Leonard Rankell and for him John Rankell and
William Rankell; Thomas Shaw and for him Anthony Larden and Nicholas
Major.

Amerced: for not coming to court upon their warning. William Harrys,
Leonard Rankell, Thomas Shawe, John Coke, 12d. each.

f.91r Covenanted servant: in court William Phillips, servant with Robert Saly,
acknowledged himself bound to Saly for seven years from 29 Sept. last
past; to be taught the occupation he now uses, and to be given 2d. every
quarter for the first two years and 4d. for every quarter for the other five
years; and at the end of seven years 26s. 8d. for his wages and double
apparel meet and seemly for such a servant to have.

Actions of debt : Adam Greneway of Curbridge against Harry Busshop for
6s. 5d. To be paid on 2 Feb. next. (3)

George Dey of Finstock against Thomas Whyte of Charlbury
for 5s. 3d.

Thomas Hans against Hew Sowtherne for 18s. 3d. (3)
Ordered. Agreed to be paid on 14 Sept. next.

Court held 17 Nov. 1567 by the bailiffs.

Action of debt : Robert Brewton of Burford against Anthony Larden for 26s.
3d. Md. Larden confessed 23 March to pay 10s. to Thomas Taylor on 29
Sept. and 10s. on 25 Dec. next. (3) Ordered upon denying. Discharged.

Action of trespass: Anthony Larden against Robert Brewton of Burford for
39s. 11½d. (3) Ordered upon denying. Agreed 23 March.

f.91v Actions of debt : William Malen against John Rydley for 2s. 11d.

Md. 7 Dec. [1564], William Hurst of Combe against Richard
Androwes of Aston for 15s. 7d. Anthony Larden and Harry Wolbridge of
South Leigh became sureties every man in the whole to pay the said sum of
William Ellmar, bailiff, on Thursday next after the date of the present
court.

Court held 8 Dec. [1564] by the bailiffs, with the constables and others.

Action of debt : Thomas Busshop against William Ryng for 20s. 3d. Paid.

Action of debt : Walter Kyng of Cogges against Anthony Larden for 12s. 3d.
(3) Deferred until the next court day.

Action of trepass: Anthony Larden against Walter Kyng of Cogges for
39s. 11½d. (3) Void. *Cancelled.*

Action of debt : same againt the same for a hog for 15s. (3) Deferred until the
next court day. Md. 23 March Kyng discharged in that he and Walter
Lopton alias Belchar deposed that the plaintiff was satisfied for the hog.

f.92r   Court held 12 Jan. 1565 by the bailiffs.

Actions of debt : Hugh Sowtherne against Joan Meryman, widow, for 16s. 3d.
(3). Non suit.

William Ellmar against Edward Dowdeswell alias Whelar for
21d. (3) Day given till Whit Sunday.

Md. 30 Jan. [1565] Thomas Clemson against Alice Druet for
7s. 3d.

Court held 9 Feb. [1565] by the bailiffs with others.

Action of debt : Anthony Larden against Richard Lewes for 13s. (2) Agreed and
paid 15 June 1565.

Court held 2 March 1565 by the bailiffs with others.

Action of debt : Walter Kynges of Cogges against Anthony Larden for 12s. 3d.
Larden confessed 11s. and denied the rest and desired to wage his law
therein himself with his two hands at the next court.

f.92v   Action of trespass: Anthony Larden prayed an action against Walter Kynges of
Cogges for 10s. *Cancelled. Let fall.*

Distress taken of Anthony Larden: 3¾ broad yards of red cloth priced by Peter
Ranckell, William Ryng, Edward Gooed and others at 5s. the broad yard.

Court held 23 March [1565] by the bailiffs with others.

Action of debt : Clement Pemerton of Crawley against Anthony Pebworthe for
5s. 10d. (1)

Court held 13 April 1565 by the bailiffs with others. [*Marginalia erased and
illegible.*]

Order: Richard Lewes to pay Anthony Larden 8s. 8d. parcel of a debt of 13s.
before entered at or before the end of six weeks next ensuing and they are
to avoid the residue of the debt in the court by oath or otherwise as the
court orders.

Actions of debt : Davy Byat against Harry Busshop for 4s. 11d. (1) Agreed.

Md. 26 April [1565] John Magood against William Bolton of
Standlake for 15s. 9d. (2) Agreed 15 June 1565.

f.93r   Court held 4 May 1565 by the bailiffs.

Actions of debt : William Secoolle of Stanton [i.e. Stanton Harcourt] against
Randell Margeryes for 6s. 11d. (3)

Thomas Taylor against Richard Reynolds for 33s. 8d. (3)
Agreed.

Williams Ryng against William Denys for 10s. 3d. (3)

Court held 26 May 1565 by the bailiffs with others.
Actions of debt : William Ellmer against John Purnell for 2s. 7d. (1)
    Leonard Dalton against the same for 8s. 3d. (3)
    William Stevens against Richard Ockley for 4s. 4d. (2)
    Agreed.

f.93v Court held 15 June 1565 by the bailiffs with others.
Acknowledgement: by Hew Sowtherne of receipt from Thomas Hannes of 18s., part of the sum owed Sowtherne by William Shugborowe of Banbury[33] for one broadloom bought of Southerne.
Action of debt : Hew Sowtherne against Joan Meryman, widow, for 16s. 3d. (3) Agreed 5 Oct. 1565.
Action of trespass: William Denys against William Ryng for 39s. 11d. *Cancelled.* (3) William Ryng prayed a non suit for 31 Aug. 1565.

Court held 6 July 1565 by the bailiffs with others.

Court held 27 July 1565 by the bailiffs with others.
Order: William Androsse to make a good and sufficient mound between Cordwell and himself, as appointed on the last law day, on this side of 20 Aug. next on pain of 4s. 4d. for default.
f.94r Action of debt : Thomas Foord against Anthony Larden for 4s. 9d.

Court held 31 Aug. 1565 by the bailiffs.
Actions of debt : William Ryng against John Geffrees of Bampton for 9s. 7d. Agreed.
    Md. 27 Sept. [1565] Humfrey Malen against Geoffrey May of Alvescot for 12s. 9d.

f.94v Court held 5 Oct. 1565 by Humfrey Malen and Richard Hyet, bailiffs.
Constables: Edward Gooed, William Taylor the younger.
Wardsmen: Richard Elyot, William Beane, Nicholas Gonne, Robert Saly, Robert Muckle.
Cloth searchers: William Vawes, William Petoo.
Leather searchers: John Berell, Oliver Ball.
Ale tasters: William Beane, John Cannyng.
Cardenars: Nicholas Major, John Warren.
Tipplers with their sureties: Thomas Stagg and for him John Lawrens and Nicholas Hill; Thomas Hurst and for him Harry Jones and Nicholas Hill; Randell Margeryes and for him Thomas Hanckes and William Malen; Thomas Barnard and for him Anthony Larden and [Rich. *crossed out*]; Annes Fathers and for her Richard Umfrey and Philip Box; Eme Gyles and for her Thomas Hanckes and William Elmar; Katherine Legg and for her

---

[33] A well known Banbury clothier and wool dealer. He also offered cloth for sale in Blackwell Hall in the 1560s: E 159/350, Recorda, Hilary 1 Eliz.m.331. See above, p.lxxvi.

Roger Rydley and Richard Wever; Leonard Ranckell and for him . . .; Annes Shawe, widow, and for her Anthony Larden and Nicholas Major; John Coke and for him Giles Jones; Robert Carter and for him Edward Gooed and Robert Mukell.

f.95r   Orders: Wardsmen to attend every court day except with reasonable excuse on pain 12d. for default.

Brewers and tipplers to sell ale according to the order in the court on 15 Sept. 1564, on pain of 3s. 4d. for default. *Cancelled.*

Court held 26 Oct. 1565 by the bailiffs with others.

Agreed: Anthony Larden to pay Thomas Foord 6d. a week until 4s. 6d. is fully satisfied. Paid in hand 6d.

Court held 7 Dec. [1565] by the bailiffs.

Actions of debt : Thomas Rychards of Asthall against Harry Gyllet of Chimney for 11s. 3d. (3) Crippes is bound to pay it if the debt be proved above the 7s. already paid.

Richard Savery against John Purnel for 2s. 10d. (3) Paid.

Same against Edward Dowdswell for 15d. Paid.

Richard Umfrey against Richard Reynolds for 5s. 3d. (3) Ordered and Paid.

f.95v   Thomas Clemson against John Taylor for 19s. 9d. (3) Agreed.

Anthony Larden against William Penye for 13s. 4d. (3) Awarded to pay 12d. *Cancelled* [*A non suit crossed out.*]

Chamberlains' accounts by Thomas Clemson and Peter Ranckell. Remaining in the hands of Thomas Clemson 11s. 8d. More to receive in debts 9s. 2d. More in the hands of William Brygfyld 30s. 0d. More in the hands of Richard Reynolds 3s. 4d.

Orders: tipplers to sell indoors one quart of ale or beer for 1d. and a thirdendell outdoors on pain of 3s. 4d. for default.

Butchers not to open shop windows or doors on Sundays and other Holy Days to sell any flesh from the third peal to morning and evening prayer until the service be fully ended on pain of 3s. 4d. for default.

f.96r   Court held 4 Jan. 1566 by the bailiffs with others.

Md. whereas Philip Box distrained two pots of Anthony Larden for an amercement, valued at 13s. 4d., at this present court the said pots were priced by William Beane, Richard Elyot, Nicholas Gonne, Robert Mukell, Robert Saly, wardsmen at 11s.

Action of trespass: John Colyar against Anne Shaw, widow, for 12s. Agreed and paid.

Court held 25 Jan. 1566 by Richard Hyet, bailiff, with others.

Actions of debt : Richard Tymmes of Cassington against Katherine Legg for 39s. (3) Agreed.

Richard Umfrey the elder against Gregory Meryman for 18s. 11d. (2) To be paid two weeks after next Easter or else to distrain.

Action of trespass: Richard Reynolds against Richard Umfrey the elder for

13s. 7d . Agreed that Reynolds to receive one and a half bushels of malt to amend. Paid 29 March.

f.96v   Court held 15 Feb. [1566] by the bailiffs with the constables and others.
Actions of debt : John Wheley against Thomas Hyct, tailor, for 11s. 7d. (1).
        Ellys Saly, by his deputy Robert Saly, against Nicholas Huckwell for 8s. 9d. (3) Agreed.

Court held 8 March 1566 by the bailiffs with the constables and others.
Actions of debt : William Ryng against William Denye for 10s. 3d. (3) Paid.
        Same against Anne Shawe, widow, for 13s. 7d. (2) Agreed 26 April that Anne Shawe to pay William Ryng 5s. on 1 Aug., and 5s. on 23 Nov. next; surety Edward Gooed.
        Margery Harrys of Ducklington, widow, against Anthony Larden for 11s. 2d. (2); Philip Box surety. Agreed 29 March to pay 4d. a week until 10s. to paid. Edward Gooed surety, beginning next week.

f.97r   Md. a possession: taken 28 Feb. 1566 by the bailiffs of William Shawle and Mary his wife of Wenford, Newchurch, Isle of Wight, of one tenement with curtilage and garden ground, lying beyond the bridge in the West End of Witney between the tenement of Roger Wheler on the east side and the tenement of William Jonson on the west side, to the use of the same Roger Wheler of Witney, carpenter. Witnesses: the constables and Robert Mukell, Robert Carter, Nicholas Goonee, William Jonson and others.

Court held 29 March 1566 by the bailiffs.
Actions of debt : Richard Ockley against Anthony Larden for 7s. 9d. (3) Agreed.
        Same against the same for 38s. 3d. (3) Agreed.
f.97v   Md. 10 April 1566. Guy Humfrey of Witney against Harry Fyssher of Stanton Harcourt for 18s. 7d. (2)

Court held 26 April 1566 by the bailiffs.
Action of debt : Md. 30 April 1566 John Barnabe against Thomas Bartlet of the Field [Leafield] for 10s. 7d. (3) Condemned for not answering.
Covenanted servant: in court John Lyvyngston, servant with William Hychyns, confessed himself to stand bound to the same for seven years from Easter 1564 from year to year to be instructed in the occupation he now uses in the best manner he can be; to be given at the end of the seven years 26s. 8d. wages and double apparel as is usual for such a servant.
f.98r   Actions of debt : Md. 11 May 1566 Philip Boxe against . . . Golding of Asthall for 3s. 7d. Paid.
        Md. 6 May 1566 same against Richard Ryder for 4s. 4d. (3) Paid.

Court held 17 May 1566 by the bailiffs with others.
Action of debt : Edward Gooed against Harry Fyssher of Staunton [i.e. Stanton Harcourt] for 7s. 4d.
Complaint: made against Thomas Barnard for lodging evil disposed persons without the knowledge and advice of the officers; Barnard was discharged

by the bailiffs that not to occupy nor tipple from henceforth and from and after Pentecost next on pain of £5 for default to the use of the bailiffs and the lord of the franchise. [Signatures of] Humfrey Malyn and Richard Hyet, bailiffs, Edward Goode, Leonard Yate, Thomas Marten; [marks of] Thomas Taylor, William Ryng.

f.98v Action of debt : William Secoolle of Staunton [i.e. Stanton Harcourt] against Harry Busshop of Witney for 10s. 3d. (3)

Distress taken: two new canvas sheets and one bearing sheet of William Denye at the suit of William Ryng, priced by Robert Mukell, William Beane, Nicholas Gonne, Richard Elyot, wardsmen, at 10s. 6d; delivered to Ryng for his debt, awarded by order of the court.[34]

Action of debt : Md. 2 June [1566] Humfrey Malen of Witney against George Franklyn of North Leigh for 6s. 1d. (3) Condemned for not answering.

Court held 14 June 1566 by Humphrey Malen, bailiff, with others.
Action of debt : Thomas Busshop against John Coke for 8s. 3d. (2)

f.99r Court held 5 July 1566.
Actions of debt : Richard Lewes against Hew Sowtherne for 13s. 11d. (1) Agreed 12 July for all things in controversy between them.
            Md. 15 July [1566] Leonard Dalton against Harry Fyssher of Staunton [i.e. Stanton Harcourt] for 16s. 7d.

Court held 26 July 1566 by Richard Hyet, bailiff, with others.
Actions of debt : William Riche of Cogges against Anthony Larden for 19s. 9d. (3) Confessed.
            Richard Umfrey against Anne Shawe, widow, for 17s. 3d. (2) Agreed.
Action of detinue: Md. 15 Aug. [1566] Harry Hyet of Minster [i.e. Minster Lovell] against Richard Ockley for 10s. 3d. (2)

f.99v Court held 6 Sept. 1566 by the bailiffs.
Actions of debt : Edmund Massheroder, parson of Kencot, against Thomas Penne of Bourton [i.e. Black Bourton] for 5s. 7d. Cancelled. (1)
            William Smythe of Kencot against Richard Hawlle of Broadwell for 7s. 7d. Cancelled. (1) Thomas Colyer surety to answer for each of the above written.
Order: tipplers to sell ale and beer outdoors for 1d. the thirdendell and a quart of ale indoors for 1d. on pain of 3s. 4d. for default to the use of the lord of the franchise.

f.100r Court held 27 Sept. 1566 by the bailiffs.
Distress: Md. 20 September Robert Mukell, William Beane and Nicholas Goone, wardsmen, with others priced at 18s. one cart of Thomas Bartlettes of the Field [i.e. Leafield], taken by distress at the suit of John Barnabe for 10s. 7d.

[34] See also above, p.41.

Actions of debt : Richard Umfrey the elder against Robert Horne for 6s. 3d. (2)
        Thomas Toolle against William Vawsse for 36s. 3d. Non suit
for not presenting, 18 Oct.
        Fabian Payne against Thomas Stagg for 16s. 8d. Ordered in
the same court that Stagg to pay 3s. 4d. next 25 Dec.

f.100v   Md. 28 Sept. 1566 Thomas Clemson and Peter Rankell, then
chamberlains, against Richard Reynolds for 3s. 7d.
        Md. same day Thomas Taylor, deputy for William Beynord of
'Coolebrak' [i.e. Colwell brook in Witney?] against Richard Reynolds for
25s. 7d.

Court held 4 Oct. by John Lawrence and Thomas Clemson, bailiffs.
Constables: William Peny, Thomas Hickes.
Wardsmen: Richard Eliot, Thomas Hannes, James Beacham, John Powell,
    William Beane.
Cardenars: John Purnell, Nicholas Maior.
Ale tasters: Roger Harison, Robert More.
Leather Sealers: Jerome Hannes, Roger Wilshere.
Cloth searchers: William Vawse, William Peto.

f.101r Tipplers with their sureties: Eme Giles and for her William Elmer and Thomas
    Hanckes; Anne Shawe, widow, and for her Anthony Larden and Nicholas
    Hill; Thomas Barnard and for him Nicholas Hill and Anthony Larden;
    Thomas Stagg and for him John Lawrence and Nicholas Hill; Thomas
    Hurst and for him Roger Ridley and William Taylor the younger; John
    Coke . . .; Robert Carter and for him Edward Gooed and Robert Mukell;
    Annes Fathers and for her Richard Humfrey the elder and Philip Box;
    Katherine Legg and for her Giles Jones and Richard Weaver; Randell
    Margeries and for him Thomas Hanckes and William Malen; Peter Payne
    and for him Thomas Colyar and John Colyar; Richard Lewes and for him
    Roger Ridley and Robert Stevens; Richard Kellyng and for him Philip
    Cakebred and Davy Birt; Edward Good and for him Philip Box and Roger
    Ridley.
Actions of debt : William Peto against Randell Margeries for 6s. 11d.
        William Elmer against William Vawse for 32s. 4½d.
        Anthony Larden against William Riche of Cogges for 25s. 3d.
Order: ale and beer to be sold as was set at the last court held on 6 Sept.

f.101v Court held 18 Oct. 1566 by the bailiffs and others.
Actions of debt : John Toole of Charlbury, deputy of Thomas Toolee, against
    William Vawse for 36s. 3d. (3). Agreed 8 Nov. to abide by the order and
    arbitration of Richard Bryce and Anthony Watsun. Paid 31 Jan. 28s. *Agree-
    ment cancelled*.
        Thomas Clemson against John Rackley for 24s. 3d. Agreed
Rackley to pay the same at 6d. a week until all paid.
        Same against John Wall for 8s. 0½d. (3)

Court held 8 Nov. 1566 by the bailiffs.
Order: no pigs over a quarter of a year old to go in the streets unringed after
    next Wednesday, on pain of 3s. 4d. for each pig each time.

f.102r Actions of debt : John Coliar against Anthony Larden for 13s. 9d. (3)
Condemned for not answering.

　　　　　　　Richard Foord against Jerome Hannes for 4s. 3d. (1). Agreed
29 Nov. Hannes to pay 20d. Paid the bailiffs. *Cancelled.*

　　Court held 29 Nov. 1566 by the bailiffs.
　　Actions of debt : Luke Leysam against John Rackley for 2s. 11d. (3)
　　　　　　　Joan Yate, widow, against John Meysie for 5s. 3d. (3)
　　　　　　　William Vawes against Thomas Toole for 30s. 3d. Void.
　　　　　　　Md. order taken between William Secoole of Staunton [i.e.
Stanton Harcourt] and Harry Busshop touching a previous action, that
Busshop to pay 5s. 8d. to Secolle within a fortnight after 2 Feb.; surety
Philip Box.[35]

f.102v Order: after the first warning immediately after this court, tipplers allowing the
following to drink within their house to forfeit for every pot of drink
drunk 3s. 4d. to the use of the lord of the franchise: Nicholas Jackson, John
Godfree, Richard Rider, Walter the dyer.

　　Court held 20 Dec. 1566 by the bailiffs.
　　Actions of debt : Harry Jones against Thomas Toole for 39s. 11d. (1)
　　　　　　　Jerome Hannes against John Meysye for 17d. (3)

　　Court held 10 Jan. [1567] by the bailiffs.
f.103r Actions of debt : Roger Heryng of South Leigh against Randell Margeryes for
　　4s. 3d. (3)
　　　　　　　William Jenkyns, servant with Mr Kelwey, against Michael
Pebworthe for 4s. 3d. (3)
　　　　　　　Md. 20 Jan. [1567] Richard Shawe of Lew against John
Cryppes of Stanton Harcourt for 36s. 3d.

　　Court held 31 Jan, [1567] by the bailiffs.
　　Actions of debt : Thomas Clemson against Thomas Stagg for 19s. 8d.
　　　　　　　Same against Harry Alen for 8s. 9d.

f.103v Court held 28 Feb. [1567] by Thomas Clemson, bailiff, with others.
　　Action of debt : Richard Savery against John Meysy for 2s. 1d. Paid. (2)
　　Order: tipplers to sell ale and beer at two ale quarts for 1d. outdoors and a
　　thirdendell indoors for 1d. on pain of 3s. 4d. for default.
　　Md. a possession: given 18 Feb. 1567 by the bailiffs to John Shipton the younger
　　　　of Shaw, Berks., of one tenement in Witney on the north side of
　　　　Corndelstrete [i.e. Corn St.] between the tenement of Richard Newman on
　　　　the east side and the tenement of Leonard Yate on the west side, together
　　　　with the rest of the lands late belonging to Morris Smart deceased. In the
　　　　presence of the constables, the wardsmen and John Shipton the elder of
　　　　Shaw, John Grene of Newbury [Berks.], Thomas Hynd, Philip Boxford
　　　　and many others.

[35]　See above, p.42.

f.104r Court held 21 March [1567] by the bailiffs with others.

Court held 11 April 1567 by Thomas Clemson, bailiff, with others.
Actions of debt : Randell Margeryes against John Akyns for 2s. *Cancelled*.
William Peto against Alexander Harys for 11s. 8d. (2)

Court held 2 May 1567 by the bailiffs.
Actions of debt : Richard Myllward of Ducklington against Gregory Meryman
for 3s. (1)
William Elmer against John Meysye for 8s. 7d. (3)
Action of detinue: Thomas Hurst alias Smythe, servant of Mr Sherles, against
John Steven, servant of Philip Boxe, for 10s. 3d.
f.104v Action of trespass: Richard Reynoldes of Yardley, [Worcs.], by his deputy
Gregory Meryman, against Richard Ockley for 20s. 3d. (3)

Court held 23 May 1567 by the bailiffs.

Court held 13 June 1567 by the bailiffs.
Amerced: Joan Daulton, widow, for that her candles lacked weight, in the sum
of 3s. 4d. Forgiven.

Court held 4 July [1567] by the bailiffs.

Court held 1 Aug. 1567 by the bailiffs.
Actions of debt : John Whelley against Harry Alen for 4s. 5d. (1) Paid.
f.105r   John Cok against Harry Busshop for 3s. 3d. (1)
Katherine Bannyng against Edward Dowdeswell alias Wheler
for 7s. 4d. (3)

Court held 22 Aug. 1567.
Action of debt : John Jones of Brize Norton, by his deputy John Slowe, against
Randell Margeyes for 6s. 7d. (1) Agreed to be paid 20d. every quarter till
all paid.

Court held 12 Sept. 1567 by the bailiffs.
f.105v Md. a possession: taken 27 Aug. 1567 by the bailiffs of Lionel Ranckell of one
messuage and one acre of arable adjoining, in Witney on the south side of
Corndlestret [i.e. Corn St.] between the tenement of Harry Jones on the
east and the tenement where Alexander Towneshend dwells on the west, to
the use of Harry Jones forever.
given 3 April 1567 of a tenement with appurtenances in
Witney on the east side of the High St. between the tenement of Philip
Boxe, now in the tenure of John Swyfte, on the north and the tenement,
now in the tenure of Agnes Fathers, widow, on the south, to Peter
Humfrey by his father Richard Humfrey the elder of Witney, dyer. Said
Peter gave possession and seisin of the same to John Alldworth of Wantage,
Berks., a tanner, on the same date, and in the presence of the bailiffs, the
constables, James Beacham wardsman there, William Maior sergeant and
divers others.

f.106r Covenanted servants: 6 Oct. 1567 in court Nicholas Lawrence, son of John Lawrence of Witney, tucker, acknowledged himself bound to his father for seven years from 29 Sept. 1566; to be given at the end of seven years 40s. wages and double apparel.

6 Oct. in court John Padelfort, son of William Padelfort of Stow, Gloucs., was bound to John Lawrence of Witney, tucker for seven years from 29 Sept. 1567; to be given at the end of seven years wages [*sum not entered*] and double apparel.

f.106v Court held 10 Oct. 1567 by Thomas Taylor and Harry Jones, bailiffs.

Contstables: Richard Savery, Nicholas Gonne.

Wardsmen: Richard Elyot, William Hodson, Thomas Hannes, James Beacham, Robert Grynder.

Coth searchers: Leonard Dalton, sworn; John Wheley.

Leather searchers: Edward Hannes, Oliver Ball.

Ale tasters: Robert More, Roger Haryson.

Cardenars: John Purnell, Nicholas Major.

f.107r Orders: Wardsmen to be present and make presentments for their wards at each court on pain of 12d. for each default. To send a substitute if they have urgent excuse.

Tipplers not to allow unlawful games on pain of 3s. 4d. for default. Tipplers to sell indoors a quart of ale for 1d. and outdoors a thirdendell for 1d. on pain of 3s. 4d. for default.

Pigs not to go in the streets or to stay there unorderly on pain of 4d. for every pig taken.

Actions of debt : William Elmer against William Ryng for 19s. 7½d. (3)

Same against the same for 22s. 0½d. (3)

Court held 7 Nov. [1567] by the bailiffs.

Actions of debt : Hugh Pawlyngs against Harry Busshop for 10s. 9d. (3)

f.107v William Blew against John Skargill for 36s. 11d. (1) Agreed.

William Peto against Thomas Stagge for 12s. 7d. (2) Action discharged on agreement of the parties and committed to the ordering of Thomas Tayler and William Slype.

Md. Annes Shaw's sureties for honest government in her house for tippling: Anthony Larden and Nicholas Hill.

Court held 5 Dec. 1567 by the bailiffs.

Action of debt : George Hyde of Bengeworth, Worcs., by his deputy Thomas Hurst, against Harry Busshop for 11s. 3d.(3)

Amerced: Edward Hannes for refusing to take his oath, 5s. Day given to the same and Oliver Balle to be at the next court ready to take their oath on pain of 10s.

f.108r Court held 19 Dec. 1567 by the bailiffs.

Sworn to office: constable Nicholas Gonne, wardsman James Beacham, cloth searchers John Wheley, Leonard Dalton, leather searchers Oliver Ball, Edward Hannes.

Action of trespass: Roger Grene of Stow, Gloucs., against William Such of Witney, cooper, for 6s. 3d. Action let fall. Enquire.

Actions: Thomas Taylor, bailiff, testified that William Ryng confessed both actions that William Elmer had against him and promised payment on 6 Jan.[36]

John Scargell has day with his two hands to wage his law at the next court against William Blewe plaintiff. Paid.

William Hodson confessed to pay William Jenkyns the sum of 7s. 6d. i.e. 6d. a week until paid. Whereof he paid presently 12d. Richard Weaver to receive the sum weekly.

f.108v Amerced: Hew Pawling 6d. for not following his suit in the court against Harry Busshop.[37]

Court held 30 Jan. [1568] by the bailiffs.

Actions of debt : Robert James, servant with Edward Goed, against Mark Fathers for 3s. 11d.(1) Let fall 10 Mar. 1569.

William Ryng confessed to pay William Elmer 19s. 7d. this side of 25 March next, as demanded in the court on 10 Oct. 1567.

Surety: promised by Harry Busshop within one week of the present court for the payment to George Hide of Bengeworth, Worcs., or his deputy, i.e. 5s. 6d. on 14 Sept. next and 5s. 6d. on St. Peter's Day [i.e. 1 Aug.]

f.109r Court held 20 Feb. 1568 by Harry Jones, bailiff, and others.

Action of trespass: Davy Horne against John Horne for 10s. Let fall the same day.

Action of debt : Edward Chambers of Minster [i.e. Minster Lovell] against William Harys for 12s. 3d. Agreed. *Cancelled.*

Court held 12 March 1568 by Thomas Taylor, bailiff, with others.

Actions of debt : Edward Gooed against William Kyng of North Leigh for 4s. (2) Paid by Kyng 30 April.

Mark Fathers against William Blewe for 5s. 3d. Paid the same day in full consideration 3s. 4d.

Court held 9 April [1568] Roger Wilshere against William Lambart for 17s. 10d. (3) Md. Lambart condemned in the action 14 Jan. 1569.

f.109v Court held 30 April 1568 by the bailiffs.

Actions of debt : Hew Cock against John Taylor for 2s. 7d. (3) Paid.

Richard Savery against William Lambert for 29s. 1½d. (3)

Thomas Clemson against Nicholas Cowells for 9s. 4d. (2) Paid.

Same against Edward Dowedeswell alias Wheler for 5s. 5d.

Action of detinue: Thomas Clemson against William Ryng for 16s. 11d. (3)

---

[36] See above, p.46.
[37] See above, p.46.

Court held 21 May 1568 by Harry Jones, bailiff.

Actions of debt : Phillip Curtes of North Leigh against John Swyft for 39s. 11d. (3) Agreed 30 July 1568.

William Malen of Ducklington against Luke Leysham for 5s. 3d. (3) Agreed 9 July that Malen to pay within a fortnight or the plaintiff to have a distress. Paid.

f.110r   Thomas Breckspere against William Vawes for 34s. 7d.
Cancelled.

Md. 10 June [1568] Robert Hunnybourne of the Field [i.e. Leafield] against John Goldyng of Asthall Leigh for 17s. 7d. (3) Condemned 10 Sept. for not answering. Md. Humfrey Malen paid Honyborn 15s. 8d. in full contentment.

Court held 18 June 1568 by the bailiffs.

Court held 9 July 1568 by Thomas Taylor, bailiff.
Action of debt : Md. 28 July [1568] Thomas Colyar against Thomas Coke of South Leigh for 5s. 8½d.

Court held 30 July 1568 by Henry Jones, bailiff, with others.
Actions of debt : Thomas Colyar against Fabian Payne for 3s. 3d. (3)
                     Same against John Magood for 2s.
f.110v Distress: Thomas Hurst attorney for George Hyde of Bengeworth, Worcs., received in open court one little brass pot, one pewter platter, one pewter porringer, one wooden kever, taken from Harry Busshop at the suit of the said George Hyde. Priced by Thomas Hannes, William Hodson, Richard Eliot, James Beacham, Robert Grynder, wardsmen, at 7s. on 30 July 1568.
Action of debt : Md. 5 Aug. 1568 Thomas Wenman, gent., by his servant William Turner, against John Hillyard of Bampton for 13s. 11d.(2) Md. William Elmer and Thomas Clemson sureties that John Hillyard shall answer at the next court in Witney so to present. Md. court withdrawn 11 Sept. to be tried in Bampton.

Court held 20 Aug. 1568 by Thomas Taylor, bailiff, with others.

Court held 11 Sept. [1568] by Thomas Taylor and Harry Jones, bailiffs, with others.
Action of debt : Andrew Dottyn of Bampton against Richard Ockley for 16s. 11d. (3) Md. Dotten received of Giles Jones on 12 Nov. 7s. and was content to receive 7s. more on 2 Feb. next in full payment of the 16s. 11d. 22 Nov.

f.111r Court held 1 Oct. 1568 by Philip Box and Peter Ranckell, bailiffs.
Constables: Giles Jones, Richard Humfrey junior.
Wardsmen: Richard Wisdome, sworn; John Hannes, John Wylder alias Wyly, sworn; John Horne; John Stevens alias Chawney.
Cloth searchers: Leonard Dallton, John Wylder.
Leather searchers: Edward Hannes, Oliver Ball.

Ale tasters: Robert More, Richard Prior.

Cardenars: Anthony Larden, Luke Leysame.

Orders: wardsmen to attend and present at each court or send a substitute on pain of 12d. for default.

f.111v   tipplers to sell one quart of ale for 1d. indoors and one thirdendell at 1d. outdoors on pain of 3s. 4d. for default.

Actions of debt : Thomas Collier against Randell Margeris for 15s. 3d. (3) Look an order in court 22 Dec. next.

   Andrew Dotyn against Richard Ockley, by his attorney John Hyllarde, for remainder of payment for 11 cocks of hay, price 17s. bought 21 July 1568; 4d. already paid.

   Anthony Ashfyelde against Anthony Larden for 10s. 3d. (3) Paid etc.

Court held 22 Oct. 1568 by the bailiffs with the constables and others.

f.112r Court held 12 Nov. 1568 by Peter Ranckell, bailiff.

Action of debt : Richard Gooslyng of Bampton, by his deputy Andrew Dottyn of Bampton, against Harry Alen of Witney for 4s. 3d. Paid.

Court held 3 Dec. 1568 by the bailiffs and others.

Action of debt : William Richardes of Minster Lovell against Hew Croke of Charlton [i.e. either Charlton Abbots or Charlton Kings] Gloucs., for 36s. 7d.

Court held 24 Dec. 1568 by the bailiffs.

Action of debt : Roger Rydley against William Hodson for 5s. 3d. (3)

Order: Randell Margeryes to pay Thomas Colyar 15s. as demanded in his action, i.e. 5s. the same day to William Major for Thomas Colyar and 5s. on 2 Feb. and 25 March.

f.112v Md. a possession: given 24 Dec. 1568 by Humfrey Malen to Philip Boxe, bailiff, of one tenement with appurtenances on the west side of the High St. Witney, between Stephen Brice's tenement on the south and William Elmer's on the north, to the use of William Buckyngham and his heirs for ever. In the presence of the bailiffs, the constables, William Maior the sergeant, Richard Wysdom, wardsman of the same ward, and divers others.

Court held 14 Jan. 1569 by the bailiffs. All well.

Court held 4 Feb. 1569 by the bailiffs.

Actions of debt : James Whytley against William Harys for 12s. 3d. (3) 18 March condemned for not answering. Agreed.

   Edward Abreck of Burford against John Horne for 16s. 3d. (1) Agreed 18 March that Horne to pay the Sunday next before Whitsun or a distress to be taken.

f.113r Court held 25 Feb. [1569] by Philip Boxe, bailiff, with the constables and others.

Actions of debt : Annes Tomson against Randell Margerys for 3s. 11d. (3) Paid.
Edward Gooed against Nicholas Huckwell for 6s. 3d. (1) Paid.
Thomas Hanckes against John Taylor for 6s. 11d.(3) Agreed
Taylor to pay the Friday before Whitsun or a distress to be taken. Paid.

Court held 18 March 1569 by the bailiffs.
Action of debt : Richard Dytton against John Hannes for 5s. 3d. Paid.

Court held 29 April 1569 by Philip Boxe, bailiff, and others.
Actions of debt : William Lambert, gent., against Richard Eliot for 39s. 3d. Put
to the arbitration of Philip Box and Harry Jones.

f.113v   John Colyar against William Vawes for 7s. 10d.

Court held 20 May [1569] by Peter Ranckell, bailiff, with others.
Actions of debt : John Taylor against Robert Horne for 6s. 11d.(3)
Md. . . . May [1569] William Harrys against Robert Kene of
South Leigh for 3s. 7d.
Md. 26 May [1569] Anthony Robson of Abingdon, deputy for
Thomas Mate of Abingdon [Berks.], against Sylvester Viccars for 20s. 7d.

Court held 10 June [1569] by the bailiffs.
Action of debt : John Wheley against Mark Fathers for 8s. 1d.(3)

f.114r Court held 1 July 1569 by Peter Ranckell, bailiff, and others
Actions of debt : Ralph Tomson against William Peny of Witney for 3s. 7d. (1)
Same against Richard Buttler of Curbridge for 3s. 7d. (1)
Richard Shawe against William Hodson for 23d. Paid.
Md. 11 Aug. [1569] Richard Savery against John Webbe of
Burford for 9s. 7d. Paid.

Court held 12 Aug. 1569 by the bailiffs.
Action of debt : Md. 22 Sept. 1569 Peter Payne against John Golding of Asthall
Leigh for 2s. 7d.

f.114v Court held 21 Oct. 1569 by Giles Jones and Philip Boxe, bailiffs, with the
constables and others.
Constables: Robert Stevens, Roger Wheler.
Wardsmen: Richard Dytton, William Buckingham, Giles Pawmer, John
Swyfte, Harry Wright.
Cardenars: Luke Leysham, Anthony Larden.
Cloth searchers: Leonard Dalton, John Wheley.
Leather searchers: Edward Hannes, Oliver Ball.
Ale tasters: John Purnell, John Canyng.
Orders: tipplers and brewers to give notice of their brewing ale to be sold to the
ale tasters for tasting before sale on pain of 12d. for default. Tipplers to sell
outdoors one thirdendell of ale or beer for 1d. and one quart for 1d. indoors
in pain of 12d. for default.

f.115r Sureties for good rule according to the statute:[38] Anthony Larden and Richard
Elyot for John Purnell.
Actions of debt : Robert James against Richard Eliot for 11s. 9d. (3)
Thomas Clemson against John Skargyn for 11s. 8d. (3)
Same against John Jones for 6s. 9d. (2) Agreed to pay 2s. on
2 Feb., 2s. on 25 March, and the rest presently.
Same against John Rackley for 20s. (2) Agreed to pay 4d. a
week or to be distrained.

Court held 11 Nov. 1569 by the bailiffs.
Action of debt : Thomas Stagg, deputy for Robert Stagg, his son, against
Richard Kyllyng for 15s. (3)

Court held 2 Dec. [1569] by the bailiffs.
f.115v Court held 23 Dec. 1569 by the bailiffs.

Court held 14 Jan. [1570] by the bailiffs.
Actions of debt : William Elmer against William Vawes for 30s. 3d. (1)
Ordered.
Same against the same for 19s. 0½d. (1) Ordered.
Same against Thomas Smythe of Witney for 14s. 6d.

Court held 3 Feb. 1570 by the bailiffs.
Action of debt : Thomas Barnard against Richard Byrd, bear ward, for 3s. 7d.

Court held 3 March [1570] by the bailiffs.
Court held 24 March [1570] by the bailiffs.

f.116r Court held 14 April 1570 by the bailiffs.
Action of debt : John Steyntun of Standlake against Anne Shawe, widow, for
26s. 11d. (3) Cancelled.

Court held 5 May 1570 by the bailiffs.
Actions of debt : Edward Hannes against John Horne, carpenter, for 5s. 1d. (3)
Cancelled. Paid.
Jerome Hannes against John Racklife for 3s. 2d. (1) Cancelled.
Paid.
Same against William Hodson for 2s. 2d. (1) Cancelled. Paid.
Order: Brewers to sell ale under the hair sieve for 21d. the dozen and tipplers
one thirdendell indoors for 1d. and one quart of ale outdoors for ½d. and
so after the rate etc., on pain of 3s. 4d. for each default.

f.116v Court held 26 May 1570 by the bailiffs.
Actions of debt : Richard Savery against William Ryng for 14s. 3d. Cancelled.
Paid.
Roger Wilshere against George Dey for 3s. Cancelled. Paid.

[38] See above, p.xxix.

Court held 16 June 1570 by the bailiffs.
Action of debt : Md. 30 June 1570 William Wayte of Ducklington against John
Hayes, brazier, for 5s. 3d.

Court held 7 July 1570 by Giles Jones, bailiff.
Actions of debt : Richard Shawe against Richard Ockley for 24s. 3d. *Cancelled.*
Paid.

                    Md. 21 June [1570] Roger Ridley against John Hart of South
Leigh for 12s. 9d. One half paid presently; Thomas Hicks surety for 6s.

f.117r Court held 28 July 1570 by Giles Jones, bailiff, with others.
Action of debt : Katherine Freman, servant of Richard Mylward, against
William Burnell for 9s. Ordered to pay 6s. this side of 29 Sept. next in full
compensation for the demand.

Court held 18 Aug. 1570 by Giles Jones, bailiff, with others.

f.117v Court held 13 Oct. 1570 by Leonard Yate the elder and William Ryng, bailiffs.
Constables: Leonard Dalton, Roger Wilshere.
Wardsmen: William Boukyngham, Richard Dytton, Giles Pawmer, John
Swyft, Harry Wright.
Cardenars: Anthony Larden, Richard Shawe.
Cloth searchers: William Peto, William Vawes.
Leather sealers: Oliver Balle, George Lawson.
Ale tasters: Anthony Larden, John Canyng.
Actions of debt : John Smythe against Robert Cley for 6s. 1d. (1) Agreed.
               William Peto against Cuthbert Margeryes for 7s. 3d. (2) Paid.
etc.
               Sáme against Nicholas Huckwell for 2s. 7d. (3)
f.118r   Md. 23 Oct. 1570 Leonard Dalton against William Blackman
of Eynsham for 11s. 1d. *Cancelled.* Paid.
               Md. same day Humfrey Malen against the same for 39s. 11½d.
(3) Paid.
               Md. 2 Nov. 1570 William Horne of Standlake against Edmund
Huckwell for 20s. 7d. Md. 7 Dec. 1570 Huckwell entered an action for
trespass against Horne for 33s. 11d. Agreement made for all things from
the beginning of the world to that day.

Court held 3 Nov. [1570] by Leonard Yate the elder, bailiff, and others.
Tippler with his sureties: Thomas Bellewodde and for him Hew Rodes and
Robert Saly.
Amerced: William Peto for not presenting his action before entered against
Nicholas Huckwell, 2d.
f.118v Actions of debt : John Wright of Wilcote, deputy of Edward Lee of North
Aston, against John Horne of Witney, carpenter, for 39s. 9d. (3)
               Thomas Hanckes against Alexander Harris for 6s. 7d. (2)
Received 3s. and the rest to be answered on the next day ensuing[39] which is
by agreement.
[39]   i.e. next court day.

Jerome Hannes against Nicholas Hill for 8s. 5d. (2) *Cancelled.*
Paid.

Action of trespass: Md. 4 Nov. [1570] Leonard Dalton against Anthony Savery for 39s. 11½d. Agreed.

Actions of debt: Md. 8 Nov. [1570] Roger Wilshere against John Hadon of Curbridge for 6s. 1d. Paid.

Md. same day Thomas Clemson against William Vawes for 12s. 4d. Agreed.

Md. 16 Nov. [1570] Richard Shawe against Thomas Myssen of Oxford for 39s. 11½d. Agreed.

f.119r Court held 24 Nov. 1570 by the bailiffs with others.

Actions of debt : Leonard Yate the younger against William Hodson for 3s. 7d. Paid.

John Wryght of Wilcote, deputy of Edward Lee of North Aston, against John Horne of Witney, carpenter, for 10s. 3d.

Court held 15 Dec. [1570] by the bailiffs with the constables and others.
Actions of debt : Jerome Hannes against William Brigfyld for 26s. 11d. Agreed.
Same against the same for 31s. 4d. Agreed.

f.119v Court held 12 Jan. 1571 by the bailiffs with the constables and others.

Actions of debt : William Peto, woollen draper, came to demand a certain debt of Cuthbert Margeris for 7s. 3d. Which debt was called upon, according to the custom of the said court, three several court days before. And Margeris came into the same court and in the face thereof paid in part payment of the whole 4s. and then and there promised to pay 2s. 8d. within ten days next following upon a full agreement of and for the whole debt beforesaid. Paid etc.

Md. 8 Feb. 1571 Richard Savery, mercer, against John Trewman alias Trewepenny of Curbridge, yeoman, for 9s. 4½d. [16s. 7d. *crossed out*] Paid.

Court held 9 Feb. 1571 by the bailiffs with the constables and others.
Actions of debt : William Elmore against Leonard Dallton for 6s. 5d. for the debt of Margery Reade of Curbridge. (3)

Md. 21 Feb. [1571] Roger Horne of Eynsham against Nicholas Egerley of Hardwick for 35s. 6d. Agreed.

f.120r Md. 21 Feb. 1571 Robert Walker of Woodstock, shoemaker, against John Horne of Witney, carpenter, for 16s. 11d. (3) Md. in face of a court held on 11 May, Horne promised to pay on 22 July next and Walker was fully contented.

Md. 23 Feb. 1571 Edward Abrecke of Burford, carpenter, against John Horne of Witney, carpenter, for 6s. 11d. (3)

Md. 28 Feb. 1571 Peter Lockley of Chipping Norton, weaver, against John Gosson alias Pynner of Witney, mercer, for 6s. 7d. (3)

Court held 2 March 1571 by the bailiffs with the constables and others.

Actions of debt : Luke Leysam against James Meryman for 3s. 3d. (3)

William Ellmore of Witney, woollen draper, against John Gosson otherwise Pynner of Witney, mercer, for 23s. 9d. (3) Paid.

Md. John Horne of Witney, carpenter, delivered 20s. in court in part payment of the whole debt in the two actions with Edward Lee and promised to deliver the rest to the bailiffs.

f.120v

Action of debt : Md. 19 March 1571 Roger Rydley of Witney against Roger Wheeler of Witney, carpenter, for 5s. 3d. (3)

Court held 30 March 1571 by the bailiffs with the constables and others.

Actions of debt : Edward Goode against Nicholas Maior for 19s. 3d. Agreed.

Same against Harry Dey for 3s. 3d. (3) Agreed.

Same against Anthony Pebworthe for 2s. 7d. (3) Agreed at the court on 3 Aug. that Pebworthe to pay the same day 18d. and 6d. every week until paid.

f.121r

William Harrys of Witney, innholder, against William Brygfeelde of Witney, woollen draper, for 34s. 3d. (3) Md. at the request of the bailiffs on 8 June the case in respite for six weeks.

Nicholas Maior of Witney against Richard Leowce of Witney, broadweaver, for 10s. 3d. (3)

Cuthbert Margeris of Witney, tailor, against William Peto of Witney, tailor, for 3s. 2d. (3) Agreed to be ended by Thomas Taylor.

George Laws of Witney, shoemaker, against Nicholas Hucwell of Witney, mason, for 3s. 10d. (3) Paid.

Same against William Cordewell of Witney, baker, for 4s. (3)

William Ellmore of Witney, woollen draper, against William Brygfeelde of Witney, woollen draper, for 20s. 3d. Agreed.

Same against the same for 20s. 4d. Agreed.

f.121v

Md. 6 April 1571 Hugh Pollyn of Northmoor, labourer, against Thomas Jones of Standlake, butcher, for 12s. 3d.

Court held 20 April 1571 by the bailiffs with the constables and others more.

Actions of debt : James Cooke of Shipton, butcher, against John Gosson of Witney, mercer, for 12s. 3d. (3) Agreed.

Leonard Yate, son of Thomas Yate of Witney, clothier, against Alice Byngham of Witney, widow, for 13s. 9d. (3) Agreed.

Same against John Hannes of Witney broadweaver, for 6s. 3d. (2) Agreed.

f.122r

Thomas Clempson of Witney, woollen draper, against Anthony Pebwoorth of Witney, sawyer, for 8s. 1½d. (3) Granted at the court on 10 Aug. to pay 12d. every Sunday after until paid.

Same against John Hoorne of Witney, carpenter, for 8s. (3)

Same against Richard Ellyot of Witney, broadweaver, for 19s. 10d. (3)

William Ellmore of Witney, woollen draper, against John Byrrell of Witney for 4s. 1d. (3)

William Peto of Witney, woollen draper, against John Gosson,

alias Pynner, of Witney, mercer, for 6s. 3d. (3)
Thomas Taylor of Witney, clothier, against Anthony Larden of Witney, butcher, for 38s. 3d. (3)

f.122v Court held 11 May 1571 by William Ring, bailiff, and Roger Wilttshere, constable, with the sergeant and other townsmen.
Actions of debt : John Rimell of Witney, broadweaver, against John Gosson alias Pynner of Witney, mercer, for 8s. 2d. (3) Paid.
Robert James of Witney, butcher, against Richard Morris of Langford, husbandman, for 4s. 7d. Paid.
John Horne of Witney, carpenter, against Robert Walker of Woodstock, shoemaker, for 13s. 7d. (3)

f.123r Court held 8 June 1571 by the bailiffs and divers other inhabitants of Witney.
Action of debt : Richard Rowlande of Witney, miller, against John Warren of Witney, weaver, for 17d. (3) Paid.

Court held 6 July 1571 by the bailiffs with divers other inhabitants of Witney.
Action of debt : Richard Rickettes of Witney against John Swyfte of Witney, broadweaver, for 25s. 1d. (3) Agreed and Paid. Md. at the court on 3 Aug. Richard Bryce, attorney for the said John Swyfte, paid 5s. in part payment and promised that 5s. more should be paid the next time that Philip Boxe shall come from London after the said court day; further to pay the residue on this side of 29 Sept. next Rickettes contented.

f.123v Court held 3 Aug. 1571 by William Ring, bailiff, with Leonard Dallton, constable, with divers others.
Actions of debt : Edward Goode of Witney, butcher, against John Jones of Witney, broadweaver, for 20s. 3d. (2) It was agreed at the court on 5 Oct. that Goode to pay 5s. every quarter after the said court.
William Peto of Witney, tailor, on behalf of Robert Stagge, son of Thomas Stagge, against Richard Kyllyng, broadweaver, for 9s. 5d. (3)
Thomas Clempson against Harry Allen of Witney, sawyer, for 14s. 7d. (3) At the court on 2 Nov. Allen promised to pay before 6 Jan. next.
Same against William Cordewell of Witney, baker, for 5s. 7d. (3) At the court on 5 Oct. Cordewell granted to pay every Sunday following 12d. till paid.
Same against William Osmunde of Witney, dyer, for 12s. 5d. (3)
f.124r   William Browne of Witney, attorney for William Bryan of Cogges, against Cuthbert Margeris for 4s. 3d. (3) Agreed.
Md. 16 Aug. [1571] Richard Rignolls of Yardley, Worcs., shoemaker, against John Frenche of Aston, yeoman, for 13s. 7d. (1) Agreed.
Same against the same for 13s. 7d. (1)

f.124v Court held 7 Sept. 1571 by the bailiffs with the constables and others.

Action of trespass: John Swyfte of Witney, broadweaver, against Richard Rickettes of Witney, broadweaver, for 39s. 11½d. in damage (2) Agreed.

Actions of debt : Thomas Clemson of Witney, woollen draper, against Daniel Bulleniam alias Perryn broadweaver, for 5s. 11d. (3) Md. Leonard Penye agreed to pay Clempson on 25 July next 3s. and on 24 Aug. next 2s. 11d; and so commenced an action of debt for 22s. 8d. against Bulleniam for which he distrained a loom.

Md. 20 Sept. [1571] William Stokes of Bampton, yeoman, against William Keerce of Cogges, husbandman, for 27s. 3d. Discharged.

Md. 2 Oct. [1571] Nicholas Huckwell of Witney, mason, against Thomas Disling for 5s. 3d. (3)

f.125r   Md. 4 Oct. 1571 Hugh Pollyn of Northmoor, labourer, against Thomas Absten alias Austen of South Leigh for 4s. 5d. (3) Agreed.

f.125v Court held 10 Oct. 1571 by Thomas Bishoppe, bailiff, with the constables and others.

Constables: Leonard Yate, John Colliar.

Wardsmen: Nicholas Colls, Richard Shawe, William Vauce, William Goulde, William Johnson.

f.126r At this court Thomas Watson . . .

Order: wardsmen to attend every court day to make true presentment for their wards. To send a substitute if they have urgent let[40], on pain of 12d. for default.

Actions of debt : William Ellmore of Witney, woollen draper, against William Brygfeelde of Witney, draper, for 20s. 3d. due on 7 March last. (2) Agreed and paid.

Same against the same for 20s. 3d. due 7 June last. (2) Agreed and paid.

f.126v   Same against the same for 20s. 3d. due 7 Sept. last. (2) Agreed.

Thomas Wattson of Hertford, shoemaker, against John Horne of Witney, carpenter, for 6s. 5d; charges of entrance 3d. (2) Paid.

Same against Anthony Pebworthe of Witney, sawyer, for 2s. 3d. (2) At the court on 11 Jan. agreed to pay 6d. every Saturday till paid.

Same against Cuthbert Margeris, tailor, for 19d.; charges 3d. (2)

Same against Robert Wryght, smith, for 17d; charges 3d. (2) Henry Pecke.

f.127r Court held 2 Nov. 1571 by Thomas Bishoppe, bailiff, with the constables, the wardsmen and others more.

Actions of debt : William Browne of Witney, labourer, deputy of William Bryan of Cogges, against Alexander Harris, labourer, for 4s. 3d. (3)

William Hutchins against John Wylde, labourer, for 8s. 3d. (2) Agreed.

Agreed: between John Trewman alias Trewepennye of Curbridge, yeoman, and

---

[40]   i.e. excuse.

Humfrey Malen of Witney, woollen draper, that Malen is to enjoy quietly and peaceably two closes in Witney, which he holds of Trewman, for an annual rent from the above date to 29 Sept. next at the accustomed rent and then to give up the said closes without cause or delay. In the presence of the bailiffs, Philip Boxe and Richard Bryce.

f.127v Court held 16 Nov. 1571 by Thomas Bysshoppe, bailiff, with the wardsmen and divers chief inhabitants.
Order: pigs not allowed under the Tollsey [i.e. guildhall] on pain of 2d. for each pig and 2d. for each time.
Actions of debt : John Banister of Eynsham, husbandman, against Nicholas Hill of Witney, baker, for 33s. 7d. (3) Paid.
Same against the same for 30s. 3d. (3) Agreed at the court on 1 Feb. to pay £3 in full satisfaction of the two actions.
Leonard Yate the younger, mercer, against Thomas Suche of Swinbrook, husbandman, executor of the last will and testament of William Suche late of Witney, cooper, deceased, and for his debts, for 14s. 7d. (3)

f.128r Court held 14 Dec. 1571 by Thomas Yate and Thomas Bisshoppe, bailiffs, with the constables and others.
Tippler with his sureties: Humfrey Malen and for him William Ellmore and John Lawrence.
Actions of debt : John Collyar of Witney, tucker, against Nicholas Clempson of Witney for 34s. 1d. (2) Agreed to be paid on the Friday before Psalm Sunday.
Ellen Eve, daughter of Ralph Eve of Burford, late servant with John Horne of Witney, carpenter, against the same John for 9s. 3d., besides half a coffer which he promised her. (3)
Thomas Rickettes of Long Combe against Nicholas Hill of Witney, baker, for 15s. 3d. (3) Discharged and paid 14 March 1572.
Thomas Lawrence of Witney, tucker, against Gregory Meryman for 10s. 3d. (3) Paid.
Md. John Slowe became surety with Richard Keelyng that Robert Stagg, servant with Richard Wisedome, at the coming forth of his years shall be truly paid all such things as were promised to him by Keelyng at his first entering into service with Wisdome according to the agreement made for the same specified in the Weaver's Court Book, i.e. 9s. 5d. By me [signature of] Richard Keling. [Mark of] John Slowe.
f.128v Md. a possession: given 24 Nov. 1571 by Nicholas Hill of Witney, baker, to Thomas Bishoppe alias Marten then bailiff, of a house which the said Hill dwelt in with appurtenances on the east side of the High St. between the tenement of Joan Yate, widow, on the north, then in the tenure of Richard Horsall, broadweaver, and the tenement of Thomas Hanckes, then in the tenure of Giles Pallmer, on the south; to the use of Avis, then wife of Nicholas Hill, and her assigns for the term of her natural life after his decease. Delivered immediately after to the said Avis according to the tenor and effect of a deed made by said Nicholas to the said Avis on 24 Nov.

1571. Possession given in the presence of Thirstone Standish, clerk[41], Philip Boxe, Richard Horne, Anthony Pebworth and Richard Bryce with others.

f.129r Md. a possession: taken 17 Dec. 1571 by the bailiffs of two tenements then in the tenure of Robert Gryffth alias Bodye, broadweaver, with appurtenances on the west side of the High St. between the tenement then in the tenure of Hew Rodes on the south and the tenement then in the tenure of Robert Saly on the north. Delivered by the bailiffs, on behalf of Roger Willsheere, shoemaker, to Richard Hyat of Hull alias Hill, Gloucs., slater, according to a deed made by Willsheere to Hyat and to a letter of attorney in the same deed made to the bailiffs dated 10 Nov. 1571, in the presence of John Colliar, constable, William Vawce, wardsman of the same ward, Robert Bodye, Nicholas Maior, John Godfrey and many others more.

f.129v Court held 11 Jan. 1572 by the bailiffs with the constables, the wardsmen and others.

Actions of debt : Richard Bryce, attorney of Dorothy Poore of Fyfield, Berks., against William Osmunde, dyer [Gregory Meryman *crossed out*], for 13s. 3d. (3) On 12 April 1572 paid to Bisshoppe 4s. in part payment of the said action and the bailiffs ordered the other 4s. to be paid on 24 June next and 5s. 3d. on 25 July next. For which the payment remains with the sergeant.

Humfrey Malen against Robert Clay of Witney, smith, for 23s. Agreed.

Same against Cuthbert Margeris of Witney, tailor, for 18s. 10d. Agreed.

Same against Alexander Harris, labourer, for 8s. 3d. (3)

Richard Goulde of Witney, labourer, against Gregory Meryman of Witney, weaver, for 6s. 3d. (3) Order taken by the bailiffs on 12 April to be paid the week after Whitsun.

f.130r   William Ellmore, woollen draper, against George Dey of Witney, broadweaver, for 3s. 11d. (3)

Annys Fathers, widow, against John Rackley, tailor, for 6s. 8d. Agreed.

Court held 1 Feb. 1572 by Thomas Bysshoppe, bailiff, with the constables and others.

Actions of debt : Leonard Morwyn of North Leigh, mason, against Gregory Meryman, broadweaver, for 3s. 4d. At the court on 22 Feb. Richard Bryce promised to see the 3s. above written the same day three weeks following. Paid 14 March.

William Ellmore, woollen draper, against William Hodson of Witney, broadweaver, for 2s. 11d. (3)

Leonard Dallton of Witney, woollen draper, against George Dey of Witney, broadweaver, for 18s. 4d. (3)

[41]   Rector of Tadmarton 1546-96: *V.C.H. Oxon.* ix.157.

f.130v Court held 22 Feb. 1572 by the bailiffs with the constables and others.
Amerced: Nicholas Colls, William Goulde and William Johnson, wardsmen,
12d. apiece for neglecting their duties at the same court, 3s.

Court held 14 March 1572.
Action of debt : Md. 11 April 1572 Robert Wyllett of Long Hanborough against
Thomas Askall of Witney, glover, for 5s. 7d. (3) Agreed and paid 30 May
4s. 5d.

Court held 12 April 1572 by the bailiffs with the constables and others.
Actions of debt : Mark Fathers against William Osmunde, dyer, for 6s. 3d. (3)
Paid and discharged.
            John Collyar against Randell Margeris for 8s. 3d. (3) Distrained
and satisfied.

f.131r Court held 9 May 1572 by Thomas Yate, bailiff, with one constable, the
wardsmen with others.

Court held 30 May 1572 by the bailiffs with one constable and others more.
Action of debt : Richard Bryce of Witney, attorney for Richard Hyett of Hull
alias Hyll [i.e. Hill], Gloucs., yeoman, against Richard Wysedome of
Witney, broadweaver, for 15s. 3d. Md. 26 June William Brooke,
Wysedome's father-in-law promised Hyatt to pay one half on 25 July next
and the rest on 29 Sept. next. Agreed.

Court held 20 June 1572 by the bailiffs with one constable and the sergeant with
others more.
Action of debt : Edward Handes of Witney against Davy Byrte for 11s. 3d. At
the court on 11 July Byrte promised before the said bailiffs to pay 12d. the
Thursday following and so every Thursday until paid. Agreed.

f.131v Court held 11 July 1572 by the bailiffs with other officers.
Actions of debt : Leonard Penye of Witney, broadweaver, against Daniel
Bulleniam for 22s. 8d. For which debt Penye, by an agreement made the
same day with Thomas Clemson of Witney, woollen draper, has a loom
which Clemson had distrained by order of the Witney court for a debt of
5s. 11d. due to him from Bulleniam. Penye promised to pay Clemson 3s.,
on 25 July and 24 Aug. next.
            Md. 22 July [1572] Mark Fathers of Witney, tailor, against
Richard Reinolles of Yardley, Warws., shoemaker, for 4s. 9d.
            Md. 24 July [1572] Thomas Dawson of Moore [i.e. The
Moors, Ducklington?], husbandman, against William Clarcke of Clanfield,
husbandman, for 15s. 7d.

f.132r Court held 8 Aug. 1572 by Thomas Bysshoppe, bailiff, with the clerk, the
sergeant, the crier and three others.

Court held 12 Sept. 1572 by the bailiffs with others more.

Covenanted servants: Nicholas Hyll, son of Nicholas Hyll of Witney, baker in
consideration of seven pence delivered in court confessed himself to be
bound to Edward Hannes of Witney, shoemaker, for seven years from 10
Aug. last past to be taught the occupation of a shoemaker in all points; to be
given at the end of seven years 13s. 4d. wages and double apparel, i.e. one
suit for Holy Days and one for working days, meet and decent for a servant
of such occupation to wear.

f.132v   Nicholas Androse, son-in-law [i.e. stepson] of Thomas
Mattkyns of Witney, sawyer, in consideration of seven pence paid in court
to be bound to . . . Carter of Ascott, rough mason, for seven years from 24
June last past to be taught the occupation of rough mason with due order of
correction and all manner of necessary things belonging to such a servant as
well in sickness as in health. To have in the first year 1d. a quarter to spend
at his pleasure and in the other six years 4d. a quarter; to be given at the end
of the seven years 10s. wages and double apparel, one suit for Holy Days
and one suit for working days and a trowel, a stone hammer and a plumb
rule.

f.133r Court held 17 Oct. 1572 by William Hutchyns and Nicholas Ifeelde, bailiffs,
with others.
Constables: William Peto, Leonard Ranckyll.
Wardsmen: William Gunne, Thomas Smarte, Mark Fathers, Richard Horsall,
Thomas Barnarde.
Ale tasters: Anthony Larden, Richard Fyckett.
Cardenars: [not named]
Leather sealers: Jerome Hannes, George Lawson.
Cloth searchers: John Wylye, Robert Salye.
Actions of debt: Thomas Hanckes of Witney, baker, against Richard Wallwen
of Witney, broadweaver, for 4s. 3d. (3)
f.133v   Edward Goode of Witney, baker, against Anthony Larden for
6s. 3d. (3)
Jerome Weerig of Hailey against Richard Okeley of Witney,
dyer, for 8s. 3d. (1)

f.134r Court held 20 Oct. 1572 by William Hutchyns, bailiff, the constables and
William Maior the sergeant, with Thomas Yate and Thomas Bysshoppe,
late bailiffs, the wardsmen and many others.
Tipplers with their sureties: In the fisrt ward called Paternoster Row:[42] Agnes
Shaw and for her Anthony Larden and Thomas Hanckes. In the second
ward called the West Ward: Richard Dytton and for him Thomas Foorde
and John Sowtherne; William Cordewell and for him John Sloowe and
William Tayler junior; Thomas Hurste and for him Roger Rydley and
William Tayler; Thomas Hanckes and for him . . . ; at the court on 27 Feb.
1573 Humfrey Malen admitted as a tippler, sureties Leonard Yate, son of
Thomas Yate, and William Ring. Bound himself by subscribing his name
to this present book to discharge and save harmless his sureties concerning

[42]   The wards are named for the first time; see above, p.xxxiii.

f.134v   this suretyship. By me [signature of] Humfrey Malyn. In the Middle
             Ward: Mark Fathers and for him Philip Boxe and Nicholas Ifeelde. In the
             East Ward: Nicholas Hyll and for him . . . ; Robert Carter and for him
             Henry Jones and Philip Boxe; Edward Goode and for him Philip Boxe and
             Roger Rydley; Randell Margeris and for him Thomas Byshoppe and
             Thomas Hannes; Jerome Hannes and for him Thomas Byshoppe and John
             Collyar. In the ward beyond the bridge: Thomas Barnarde and for him . . .
             Humfrey Malen admitted as a common brewer to serve the town and
             especially the poor of small drink.[43]

f.135r Court held 7 Nov. 1572 by William Hutchins, bailiff, the constables and
             William Maior the sergeant with the wardsmen and others.
        Actions of debt : John Barnabye of Witney against Randell Margeris for 10s. 3d.
             Lost by the death of Margeris. (1)
                           John Banister of Eynsham against Richard Leowel for 9s. 7d.
             (2) Agreed.
                           Mark Fathers against Thomas Smith of Witney, tucker, for
             6s. 1d. (2) Discharged.
                           Thomas Yate of Witney, clothier, against Nicholas Hyll of
             Witney, baker, for 20s. 3d. (2) Agreed.
                           William Barnes of Witney, labourer, against William
             Osmunde of Witney, dyer, for 3s. 7d. (3)
f.135v Order: victuallers to attend every court from henceforth on pain of 4d. for
             default, unless lawful cause shown to the contrary.
        Amerced: tipplers for lack of appearance at the court held on 28 Nov.: Randell
             Margeris 4d; Edward Goode 4d.
                           the like for the court held on 19 Dec.: Thomas Shawe, Thomas
             Hurste, Thomas Hanckes, Nicholas Hyll, Robert Carter, all at 4d.

f.136r Court held 28 Nov. 1572 by the bailiffs with the constables and others.
        Actions of debt : William Hyll, deputy for Thomas Hyll of Fulbrook, against
             Roger Atkyns of Witney for 7s. Dicharged.
                           Robert Stevens, deputy for Ralph Jordan of Eynsham, against
             Gregory Meryman for 8s. 4d. (3) Paid 3s. to Robert Stevens on 6 Feb. 1573;
             the rest to be paid before Easter next. Paid.
                           Elizabeth Halve, servant to William Peto of Witney, against
             William Goulde of Witney, weaver, for 4s. 3d. Agreed in the next court
             that Goulde to pay 4s. 3d. on 2 Feb. next. 2s. paid to her by Bailiff
             Hutchyns at the court held on 27 Feb. 1573.

f.136v Court held 19 Dec. 1572 by the bailiffs with the constables and many others.
        Action of debt : William Trewe, deputy for Harry Cowborne, against Michael
             Pebworth of Witney for 3s. 3d. (2) Agreed.
        Settlement: Richard Wryte of Gylde Mill [i.e. Gill Mill, Ducklington] on receipt
             of 4s. from Richard Rider promised that Ryder shall quietly receive the
             next crop of a little ham at the said mill and in the meantime he will save it

43   See above, p.xxvii.

harmless. Ryder to receive from the said mill a pail and all his clay now lying at the said mill and if those who have spent of his clay since 29 Sept. will not allow the said Ryder for it, Wryte will satisfy him for it. Discharged at the court on 8 Oct. 1574 in the face of the court.

f.137r Court held 16 Jan. 1573 by Nicholas Ifeelde, bailiff, and the constables, the sergeant and others.

Action of trespass : Md. 5 Feb. [1573] James Whyttley of Witney, broadweaver, against Geoge Boxe of Crawley for killing a pig with his cart; damage with costs of action and arrest 3s. 11d.

Court held 6 Feb. 1573 by the bailiffs with the constables, the sergeant and the most part of the householders of the town.

Actions of debt : Robert Wattes of Witney, mason, against William Burnell, carpenter, for 3s. 3d. (3)

          William Cordewell against Thomas Turtle of Witney, tailor, for 4s. 5d. (3)

f.137v Amerced: Henry Tackley 5s. that his tenant the tanner was taken with breaking a hedge.

      . . . Bramley 3s. 4d. for his tenant Steven Roftincate a common breaker of hedges.[44]

Court held 27 Feb. 1573 by William Hutchyns, bailiff, with the constables and others.

Amerced: Thomas Hanckes 12d. for making his bread too light.

Actions of debt : William Maior, deputy for Thomas Snofall of Langford, against . . . Vernam for 2s. 9d. (2) Agreed.

          Richard Savery, deputy for Christopher Stokes, against George Sagar of Witney, broadweaver, for 5s. 11d. (2) Agreed.

Distraint: the bailiff distrained five blocks of Anthony Larden's[45], lying before his door in the street, appraised at 6s. by Henry Jones, Philip Boxe, Thomas Bysshoppe, William Ellmore, Thomas Clempson, William Wyat and John Rackley, carpenters.

f.138r Court held 3 April 1573 by Nicholas Ifeelde, bailiff, with the constables, the sergeant and others.

Actions of debt : Anne Campden, servant with Thomas Hycks of Witney, broadweaver, against John Horne of Witney, carpenter, for 10s. 9d. (3) Whereof for a kerchief 18d., a pair of shoes 12d. Distress taken: one christening sheet of holland and one locram sheet 14s., appraised by Edward Goode, Thomas Hurste, Jerome Hannes, William Maior and Mark Fathers with others.

          Richard Savery of Witney, mercer, against Gregory Meryman of Witney, broadweaver, for 6s. 3d. (2) Agreed on 22 May that Meryman to pay 2s. 6d. on 22 July next and 2s. 6d. on 29 Sept. next.

---

[44]   See above, pp.xxviii, liii.

[45]   Perhaps chopping blocks or supports for a stall outside Larden's butcher's shop.

Robert Hande of Newland against Nicholas Hyll of Witney, baker, for 4s. 3d. (3)

Md. 14 April [1573] William Hodson of Witney, broadweaver, against . . . Vernam of Witney, surgeon, for 10s. 9d. Lost.

f.138v Court held 24 April 1573 by William Hutchins, bailiff, with the constables, the sergeant and others.

Tippler with his sureties: Jerome Hannes admitted and for him Thomas Bysshoppe and John Colliar. The sureties not to permit any evil rule or gaming contrary to the statute.

Court held 22 May 1573 by the bailiffs, with the constables etc.

Actions of debt : Leonard Yate junior against Richard Wallwen of Witney, broadweaver, for 2s. 7d. (3)

Harry Gryffen of Witney, sawyer, against Anthony Pebworth of Witney, sawyer, for 20s. (3)

f.139r Chamberlain's account: Md. reckoning 22 May 1573 with Thomas Clempson, chamberlain of Witney: In his hands clear, all other reckonings discharged: 18s. 11d. Paid to William Ellmore and Richard Humfrey, bailiffs, 11 Dec. 1573, 11s. 4d. Allowed to him by the bailiffs last before for a pair of harness lost at a muster, 6s. 8d.

Action of debt : John Collier [?] of Witney against Robert Saly [?] for 5s. 7d. Agreed and paid. *Cancelled.*

Md. money received: 2s. of Robert Stevens by William Huttchyns, bailiff, in part payment of 4s. due to Roger Rydley which he gave to the great bell of Witney.[46] Delivered to Philip Boxe to the use aforesaid on 25 Sept. 1573.

2s. 10d. by William Ellmore, bailiff, of William Maior for use of the poor in Jan. 1573. Discharged as in the particulars in a paper annexed to the present leaf.[47]

11s. 4d. paid to the bailiffs by Thomas Clempson was likewise discharged as in the said paper annexed, which paper was brought and showed in the court on 18 June 1574. Witnesses: Thomas Bisshoppe, Thomas Clempson, Humfrey Malen, William Harris, Edward Goode, Richard Bryce with divers others more.

f.139v Court held 12 June 1573 by the bailiffs with the constables and divers others.

Action of debt : Thomas Brygfeelde of Cogges against William Burnell alias Purnell of Witney, carpenter, for 4s. 3d. (2) Received 2s. on 29 June and 2s. on 24 July.

Action of trespass: Philip Boxe of Witney against John Lawrence of Witney for 20s. (3)

Amerced: William Harris, innholder, 3s. 4d. for baking cakes in his house.

[46] In 1573 the churchwardens' accts. recorded the balance owed for costs of new-casting the great bell and the third bell of Witney. These bells were predecessors of the 18th century ones noted in F. Sharpe, *The Church Bells of Oxfordshire*, O.R.S.xxxiv (1953), 444-5.
[47] No longer annexed.

Amerced: The same on 3 July 5s. for baking against St. Peter's Day [29 June] being aforewarned by the officers.[48]

Humfrey Malen 3s. 4d. for baking cakes in his house.

f.140r Court held 3 July 1573 by the bailiffs with the constables, the sergeants and others.

Actions of debt : Richard Rowley of Witney, miller against Harry Dey of Witney, broadweaver, upon demand of payment promised by Nicholas Ifyelde 4s. 11d. (3)

Same against Richard Mukell of Witney, tucker, for 2s. 9d. Received 6d. on 24 July. Paid in the face of the third court before he was proclaimed the third time. (3)

Same against Richard Wallwen of Witney, broadweaver, for 2s. (2) Lost by reason that he went forth of the town.

Court held 24 July [1573] by Nicholas Ifyelde, bailiff, with one constable, the sergeant and others.

Actions of debt : Richard Savery of Witney, mercer, against Leonard Dallton for 7s. 3d. (3)

Md. 5 Aug. [1573] Henry Smyth junior of Hailey, yeoman, against Robert Becke alias of Hawkesbury, Gloucs., husbandman, for 13s. 3d. Paid in part payment the same day 6s. 8d. Agreed. Nicholas Ifeelde gave word to see the rest paid at 29 Sept. next, 6s. 4d. [sic]

f.140v   Md. 11 Aug. 1573 Henry Tackley of Witney against Ellis Brabonde of Witney, labourer, for 11s. 6d. Distress taken.

Court held 12 Aug. 1573 by William Hutchyns, bailiff, with others.

Actions of debt : Richard Harris of Witney, cooper, against Richard Okeley of Witney, dyer, for 5s. 5d. (2) Agreed and paid.

Hew Pollyn against Harry Dey of Witney, weaver, for 19d. (3)

Same against William Burnell of Witney, carpenter, for 19d.(3)

Robert James of Witney, butcher, against William Brygfeelde of Witney, woollen draper, for 33s. 7d. (3) At the first court held by the new bailiffs William Ellmore and Richard Humfray, they promised the debt to be paid before the next court or a distress to be levied at the same court.[49]

f.141r Court held 3 Sept. 1573 by the bailiffs with the constables and others.

Action of debt : Mark Fathers of Witney, tailor, against Robert Carter, mason, for 13d. Paid and quit 25 Sept.

Court held 25 Sept. 1573 by the bailiffs with the constables and others.

f.141v Court held 9 Oct. 1573 by the persons hereafter nominated then bearing office.

[48] Presumably the day before St Peter's Day. Only licensed victuallers could bake to sell: see below, p.70.

[49] i.e. 9 Oct. 1573.

Bailiffs: William Ellmore, Richard Humfrey.

Constables: Robert Saley, William Harris, glover.

Wardsmen: George Lawson, Robert Miller, William Hunte, William Hodson, Davy Horne.

Ale tasters: Alexander Townesende, Oliver Ball.

Cardenars: Anthony Larden, Mark Fathers.

Cloth searchers: John Wylye, Robert Steevens.

Leather sealers: Edward Hannes, Morris Tayler.

f.142r Action of debt : John Wylye of Witney, tailor, against Gregory Meriman of Witney, broadweaver, for 9s. 1d. (2)

Orders: no person keeping a tippling house to bake any penny bread, halfpenny bread or cakes or horse bread to be sold or uttered to guests in their houses, on pain of 3s. 4d. for default.

by the bailiffs that at every court day held within the borough during the time of their office ten persons inhabiting within the borough, who have at any time been bailiff, shall accompany the said bailiffs in the 'yelde' [i.e. guild] hall while the court endure, on due notice each evening before the court. On pain of 12d. for each default, not having lawful excuse.

Chamberlain: William Hutchins of Witney, clothier, appointed for one year from 29 Sept. last past.

f.142v Court held 30 Oct. 1573 by the bailiffs with the constables, the sergeant and others.

Action of debt : Gregory Gunnes, parson of Yelford, against Davy Horne for 2s. 9d. Paid 2s. 6d. on 1 Nov. Paid.

Tipplers with their sureties: Agnes Shawe bound by recognizance and for her Thomas Hanckes and Anthony Larden; Thomas Hurste and for him William Tayler and John Wyly; Nicholas Huckwell and for him Nicholas Ifeelde and . . . ; Jerome Hannes and for him Thomas Bysshope and John

f.143r Collyer; Richard Dytton and for him John Sowtherne and Thomas Foorde; John Margeris and for him Thomas Hanckes and Thomas Hannes; Mark Fathers and for him Philip Boxe and Nicholas Ifeelde; Robert Carter and for him William Jonson and John Tymmes; Edward Goode and for him Philip Boxe and Thomas Bisshoppe; Nicholas Hyll and for him Hew Rodes and Peter Payne; Humfrey Malen and for him . . . ; William Cordewell and for him William Tayler and John Sloowe.

f.143v Actions of debt : Richard Dytton of Witney, broadweaver, against William Peerson, broadweaver, for 2s. 6d. Agreed at the next court that William Tayler and John Sowtherne, broadweavers, shall end the matter for this action.

Md. 9 Nov. [1573] William Wryght of Crawley, husbandman, against Michael Egerley of Hardwick, husbandman, for 11s. 7d.

Order: by the bailiffs with the consent of the constables and many other inhabitants of Witney, that wardsman are to attend every court and make true presentment of such defaults in their wards worthy of presentment, on pain of 12d. for each absence, not having lawful excuse.

f.144r Court held 20 Nov. 1573 by Richard Humfrey, bailiff, with the constables and others.

Order: tipplers to sell ale outdoors at 1d. a quart and indoors at 1d. the wine quart on pain of 12d.

Action of debt : Thomas Peersone of Lew, labourer, against Anthony Pebworth of Witney, sawyer, for 5s. 3d. (2)

Court held 11 Dec. 1573 by the bailiffs with the constables, the sergeant and others.

Action of debt : Nicholas Gunne against Thomas Barnarde of Witney, weaver, for 6s. 8d. (1) Agreed at the next court that 12d. to be paid every court day, the first payment to be made at the next court on the other side of the leaf or distress to be taken by the bailiffs. Md. 18 June last payment made. Paid and quit.

f.144v Court held 15 Jan. 1574 by the bailiffs with the constables and others.

Actions of debt : Geoffrey Wested of Hanborough, yeoman, against John Collsburne of Witney, labourer, for 2s. 7d. (3)

Roger Bramley of Witney, labourer, on behalf of Maud Owtfeelde his daughter-in-law, against Peter Payne of Witney, broadweaver, for 3s. 6d. At the court on 5 March the bailiffs agreed that Payne to pay Bramley 18d. in full satisfaction. Agreed and paid.

Edward Goode of Witney, butcher, against Gregory Meryman, broadweaver, for 10s. 3d. (3)

Same against Nicholas Horne, broadweaver, for 6s. 3d. (3)

f.145r Court held 5 Feb. 1574 by the bailiffs with the constables, the sergeant and others.

Court held 5 March 1574 by the bailiffs with the constables and others more.

Actions of debt : Mark Fathers of Witney, tailor, against Nicholas Horne of Witney, broadweaver, fugitive, for 14s. 6d. (2)

George Kempe of Witney, yeoman, against Giles Jones, clothier, for 15s. 3d. (3). At the court on 6 May Jones promised to pay within ten days. Paid 28 May in face of the court 15s.

Md. 11 March [1574] Humfrey Weaver of Ramsden, husbandman, against Ellis Kyngcome, husbandman, of the same for 4s. 3d. (1) Put in the hands of Thomas Taylor and John Barnabye to end it before the April court next after the above date.

f.145v Court held 26 March 1574 by the bailiffs with the constables and others.

Actions of debt : Martin Jonson of Ducklington, miller, against Nicholas Hyll of Witney, baker, for 19s. 7d. (3)

Alexander Townesende of Witney, cobbler, against Richard Lewis of Witney, broadweaver, for 4s. (2) At the court on 28 May 1574 agreed to pay 22d. in full satisfaction before 22 July next.

Ewen Jacson of Ambleside, Westmoreland, clothier, by William Harris of Witney, innholder, his lawful attorney, against Humfrey Malen of Witney, woollen draper, for 25s. 3d. (3)

Apprentice: Md. Rafe Pyckmere, tailor, confessed in the face of this court that he served seven years apprentice with one Joan Warberton, a woman tailor dwelling in St. Thomas Apostles in the city of London.[50]

f.146r Order: by the bailiffs with the consent of Thomas Yate, Thomas Taylor, Henry Jones, Peter Ranckell, John Barnabye, Thomas Hanckes, William Harris, glover, Edward Goode and William Hutchyns and with the counsell of the inhabitants, that no tenant or inhabitant of Witney take any undertenant into his house or tenement on pain of 40s. for such offence. Any such undertenant that has not been within the borough for one whole year past the date above to be dismissed before 29 Sept. next, other than those born in the borough or having dwelt there for three years last past before the above date. On pain of 10s. for each person not dismissing such undertenants.

Covenanted servant: Thomas Shawe, son of Agnes Shawe, bound himself to his mother, with her to dwell and serve from the above date for one year, to buy, kill and dress and sell flesh meat to the use and behoof of his said mother; to be given 40s. for wages and to be found meat in the said time.

f.146v Action of debt : William Wayght of Ducklington, husbandman, against George Kempe of Witney, yeoman, administrator of the goods and chattels of Margery Reade, late of Curbridge, widow, deceased, for two bushels of barley due to Wayght by the award of William Neweman, Richard Barber alias Buttler, deceased, and of Adam Greeneway of Curbridge, wheelwright, for certain harm done to Wayght's corn in the lifetime of John Reade, late husband of the aforesaid Margery Reade, deceased. On 6 May paid 3s. in full contentment.

Court held 16 April 1574 by the bailiffs with the constables and others.
Action of assumpsit: Humfrey Malen against William Harris of Witney, innholder, for 16s. 11d. (3)
Actions of debt : Same against Robert Clay of Witney, blacksmith, for 23s. 3d. (2) At the court on 18 June agreed to pay 6s. 8d. in the first week after 1 Aug. next and the rest before 29 Sept. next.

f.147r   Thomas Hurste of Witney, attorney for Richard Jonson of Gloucester, fishmonger, against Thomas Barnarde of Witney, weaver, for 2s. 9d. (3)

        Nicholas Gunne against Richard Okeley of Witney, dyer, for 37s. 3d. (3)

Agreed: before the bailiffs, that whereas Luke Leysam of Witney confessed to owe 20s. to Richard Pryar, servant of William Bryan of Cogges, if he does not pay 5s. the Sunday before St. Peter the Apostle [29 June] for the next four years, then the said Richard Pryar and assigns, paying to Leysam or his executors 7s., are to have the lattermath of College Close of Witney in every year that default is made. But if the said 5s. be paid, then it shall be lawful for Leysam to sell the lattermath in that year to his most advantage. *Cancelled.*

f.147v Richard Ryder of Witney, tucker, brought into the face of the court 13 yards of white plain cloth, priced at 18d. the yard which amounted to the sum of

[50] Presumably to establish that he was a fully qualified tailor.

19s. 6d., praised by Mark Fathers and William Hunte, wardsmen, Nicholas Ifeelde, Thomas Barnarde and William Hodson with divers others. Which cloth Ryder has remaining in his own hands and has promised to answer to one . . . Millington late dwelling in the 'Armentage' [i.e. The Hermitage] of Standlake the said sum of 19s. 6d.

Actions of debt : Richard Fawkner, servant to Thomas Byshoppe of Witney, against Giles Jones, clothier, of Witney for 20s. 3d. (3) Assigned.

Thomas Bysshoppe of Witney, clothier, against Joan Margeris of Witney, widow, for 39s. 11d. (3)

James Fisher of Abingdon, [Berks.,] mercer, against Giles Jones of Witney, clothier, for 39s. 11d. (3) Assigned.

f.148r   Thomas Hawkyns, servant to William Wickes of Witney, shepherd, against Giles Jones of Witney, clothier, for 19s. 7d. (3) Assigned.

Court held 6 May 1574 by the bailiffs with the constables and others.

Actions of debt : Bailiff Ellmore against Richard Whytyng of Witney, labourer, for 6s. 9d. (3)

William Woodwale of Witney Park, clerk, against Cuthbert Scott, vicar of Witney, for 8s. 3d. Agreed. Fully satisfied on 27 May.

William Peto of Witney, tailor, against Richard Wysdome, broadweaver, for 27s. 11d. (3) Agreed 30 July. To pay 25s. 11d. before the next court. Paid 20s. on 10 Sept; promised to pay the rest next Tuesday following.

Action of trespass: Humfrey Malen of Witney, woollen draper, against George Lawson of Witney, shoemaker, for 10s. (3)

f.148v Court held 28 May 1574 by the bailiffs with the constables and others.

Court held 18 June 1574 by the bailiffs with the constables and others.

Actions of debt : William Ellmore, bailiff, against Thomas Bellwood of Witney, fuller, for 5s. 9d. (3) Md. order taken at the court on 30 July that the action to be paid on 23 Nov. next. Agreed.

William Harris of Witney, innholder, against Humfrey Malen, woollen draper, for 15s. 7d. (3)

Md. the bailiffs took and made stray two mares, one a roan mare with a brand mark on the near hip much like to this mark [drawing of brand mark] and being whole eared, which was delivered into the hands of Humfrey Malen to be kept, appraised at 20s. The other was a grey mare, marked on both buttocks with an R.B. and slit on the near ear and spade marked on the far ear, and was delivered to the hands of Thomas Byshoppe to be kept. Appraised at 6s. 8d. by George Lawson, William Hunte, Humfrey Malen, and William Hodson. *Cancelled.*

Both strays were challenged the same day by the servant of Mr Doctor Barber of Hanborough and set away the morrow after.

f.149r Court held 9 July 1574 by the bailiffs with the constables and others more.

Actions of debt : John Haddon of Curbridge, husbandman, against Robert Clay of Witney, blacksmith, for 10s. 3d. (1) Agreed and paid 19 Aug.

Richard Shawe of Witney, butcher, against Alexander Townesende of Witney, cobbler, for 3s. 11d. (3) Agreed and paid 10d. in court on 1 Oct., at the request of the bailiffs in full contentment of the whole.

Md. 20 July [1574] Thomas Bysshoppe of Witney, clothier, against Henry Fyssher of Stanton Harcourt, husbandman, for 5s. 7d. Md. one horse of Fyssher was arrested on 20 July by Richard Bryce, deputy for William Maior then sergeant, whereupon the said debt of 5s. was paid.

f.149v Court held 30 July 1574 by the bailiffs with the constables and others.
Action of trespass upon the case: William Peto and Nicholas Gunne of Witney against William Wryght of Crawley, carter for . . .

Court held 20 Aug. 1574 by the bailiffs with the constables and others.
Actions of debt : Leonard Yate of Witney, mercer, against Robert Horne of Witney, broadweaver, for 5s. 7d. (3)
Same against William Burnell of Witney, carpenter, for 6s. 3d. (3)
Alexander Townsend of Witney, cobbler, by consent of the bailiffs, against Richard Shawe of Witney, butcher, for 5s. 9d. (1) Agreed and discharged at the court on 1 Oct. Paid.

f.150r Court held 10 Sept. 1574 by the bailiffs with the constables and others.
Actions of debt : John Wylye against Robert Claye of Witney, blacksmith, for 5s. 3d. (3) At the court on 19 Nov. John Wylye gave day for the said debt until 6 Jan. next at the request of William Harris, innholder, [bailiff crossed out] who promised to see payment on condition of respite given.
Md. 16 Sept. 1574 William Gamble alias Bowyere of Standlake, tucker, against . . . Smyth of Witney, shoemaker, for 8s. 1d. Lost.

f.150v Court held 1 Oct. 1574 by the bailiffs with the constables and others.
Chamberlain's account: William Hutchins, then chamberlain of Witney, made his account before the said bailiffs. In his hand all reckonings discharged: 5s. 6d.
Actions of debt : Thomas Hannes of Witney, tucker, against Thomas Barnarde, weaver, for 2s. 1d. (2) Paid and quit.
William Ryng of Witney against Richard Okeley, dyer, for 33s. 7d. (3)

f.151r Court held 8 Oct. 1574 by Thomas Hanckes and William Harris, bailiffs, with the constables, the sergeant and many of the substantials of the town.
Constables: John Sloowe, Edward Hannes.
Wardsmen: John Grangier, Richard Pebworth, Hew Jackson, John Bolte, Richard Peesley.
Ale tasters: Robert Claye, Richard Hewys.
Cardenars: Anthony Larden, Mark Fathers.
Cloth searchers: John Wylye, Robert Steevens.
Leather sealers: George Lawson, Morris Taylor.

f.151v Court held 29 Oct. 1574 by the bailiffs with the constables, the sergeant and others.

Tipplers with their sureties appointed at this court by the bailiffs to keep tippling houses during the present year to come: Agnes Shawe, widow, and for her Thomas Hanckes and Thomas Bysshoppe; Thomas Hurste and for him John Wyly and William Tayler; Jerome Hannes and for him Thomas Bishoppe and John Collyer; Joan Margeris and for her Robert Steevens and ...; Edward Goode and for him Philip Boxe and Thomas Bisshoppe; Richard Dytton and for him John Sowtherne and William Peto; Mark Fathers and for him Philip Boxe and Nicholas Ifeelde; Thomas Bellwood
f.152r and for him William Peto and Robert Saley; Robert Carter and for him John Tymmes and William Johnson; William Corduell and for him John Slowe and William Tayler; Thomas Barnarde and for him John Barnaby and William Hutchyns; Humfrey Malen and for him George Dey and Nicholas Hill. Malen in these presents bound himself, his executors and administrators to save and keep harmless his said sureties concerning their said suretieship. In testimony whereof Malen subscribed his name. By me Humfrey Malen [signature].

Orders: tipplers to sell ale and beer indoors at one quart of ale for 1d. and outdoors likewise on pain of 12d. for default.

persons other than the common bakers of the town or those who have been apprenticed to the baker's craft not to bake any manner of bread or cakes to be sold on pain of 10s. for each default.

Action of debt : Md. Thursday 4 Nov. [1574] Leonard Yate the younger of Witney, mercer, against John Shealer of Charlbury, chapman, for 5s. 8d. Distrained and paid.

f.152v Covenanted servant: at the court on 29 Oct. 1574 Thomas Rydley, aged 14 years, son of John Rydley of Witney, broadweaver, in the face of the court as well of his own free assent and consent and by the advice and consent of his father, in consideration of eight covenant pence bound himself to William Hutchyns of Witney, clothier and broadweaver, for eight years from 1 Nov. next ensuing; to be taught the occupation of a broadweaver; to be given at the end of the term 26s. 8d. and double apparel, one suit for Holy Days and one for working days such as be meet for a servant of such science or occupation to wear. R.B. [Initials of Richard Bryce]

Action of debt : Md 13 Nov. [1574] Henry Browne, servant to the Right Worshipful Sir Edward Unton, against . . . Grevell of North Leigh for the debt of Alice, now his wife, for 27s. 3d., whereof 26s. 8d. was due to Browne on the day of her marriage.

f.153r Md. a possession: taken 16 Nov. 1574 by the bailiffs of William Brygfelde of Witney, woollen draper, of a certain piece of ground containing east to west 26½ feet in breadth and 96 feet in length, lying in Witney on the south side of Crondell St. [i.e. Corn St.] next between the town house, now in the tenure of Richard Fyckett, pearmonger, on the east and the ground of William Brigfeelde on the west, extending from the street to the ground called the West Croft towards the south; to the use of Roger Wheeler of Witney, carpenter, and his heirs and assigns for ever, according to a certain writing thereof made by Brygfelde to Wheeler on 5 Nov. 1574. Delivered to Wheeler after the custom of the borough and in the presence of the constables, the sergeant and Richard Pebworth then wardsman of the same ward, John Sowtherne, John Smyth, Thomas Smarte and William Blewe, broadweavers, and Richard Bryce the writer of these presents with divers others.

f.153v Court held 19 Nov. 1574 by the bailiffs with the constables, the sergeant, the wardsmen and many others.

Actions of debt : William Hyckes of Charlbury, husbandman, against John Robertes of Witney, woolwinder, for 20s. 3d. Agreed and clearly discharged by Robertes. Assigned.

Thomas Allen of Eynsham, by Richard Horsall his attorney, against the same for 16s. 3d. (2) Assigned. Discharged.

Laurence Goode of Cogges, yeoman, against Giles Jones of Witney, clothier, for 37s. 7d. (3) Paid and quit.

Covenanted servant: Thursday 25 Nov. 1574 . . . Cleaver, son of William Cleaver of . . . Oxon., husbandman, bound himself to William Hutchins of Witney, clothier, for ten years from 29 Sept. last past to be instructed in all points of broadweaving; to be found sufficient food and raiment and to be given at the end of the terms 26s. 8d. and double apparel meet for a journeyman of such occupation.

f.154r Court held 10 Dec. 1574 by the bailiffs with the constables, the sergeant and others.

Action of debt : Thomas Sill, alias Tayler, of Shipton-under-Wychwood, by his attorney, William Maior of Witney, against William Corduell of Witney, baker, for 5s. 11d. Award in the court on 18 Feb. Cordewell to pay 3s. of action. (3) Paid.

Action of assumpsit: William Harris, the bailiff, against John Streete, of Witney, surgeon, for 7s. 6d. (3)

Action of debt : Md. Thursday 16 Dec. 1574 John Fisher of Abingdon, Berks., mercer, by his servant and deputy Abraham Walker, against Anthony Hunter of . . . for 14s. 7d. Lost by non suit.

f.154v Court held 7 Jan. 1575 by the bailiffs with the constables and others.

Action of debt : Alice Rose, servant to William Ellmore of Witney, woollen draper, against John Street of Witney, surgeon, for 9s. 3d. Paid 9s. in court 28 Jan.

Court held 28. Jan. 1575 by the bailiffs with the constables, the sergeant and others.

Action of debt : William Ellmore of Witney, woollen draper, against William Penye of Witney, broadweaver, for 6s. 7½d. (1) Paid and discharged by Robert Bowman of Hailey.

Order: tipplers to sell ale and beer indoors at a quart of ale for 1d. and outdoors a thirdendell for 1d., on pain of 12d. for default.

Tippler with his sureties: Richard Savery of Witney, mercer, admitted by the bailiffs, and for him William Gillmer and William Huttchyns.

f.155r Court held 18 Feb. 1575 by the bailiffs with the constables, the sergeant and others.

Covenanted servant: in court John Boxe, son-in-law [i.e. stepson] of Edmund Townsende of Witney, cobbler, aged 15 years, bound himself to William Gunne of Witney, tailor, for seven years from Easter next to be instructed in the art of a tailor; to be found etc. [as on p.83; no correction clause]; at end of term double apparel. In witness whereof the said William Gunne here subscribed his name with his own hand in the face of the said court. By me[signature of] Wyllyam Gunne. J.B. [Initials of John Box]

Action of debt : Thomas Clempson of Witney, woollen draper, against Harry Allen of Witney, sawyer, for 8s. 2d. (2)

f.155v Md. a possession: taken 8 March 1575 by the bailiffs of Richard Adeane of Horton, yeoman, of a certain messuage or tenement, now in the tenure and occupation of Giles Pallmer of Witney, broadweaver, with all the houses, shops, cellars, solars and gardens [etc.] thereto belonging together with one court and one close adjoining [etc.], in Witney on the east side of the High St. next between the tenement of Peter Ranckell, clothier, on the south and that of Nicholas Hyll, baker, on the north. To the use of the said Giles Pallmer [etc.] according to a deed made by the said Adeane to Pallmer, 2 March 1575. Possession delivered to Pallmer after the custom of the borough and in the presence of the constables, the sergeant and John Bollte, wardsman of that ward, Peter Ranckell, Thomas Clemson, Leonard Yate junior, Thomas Hyckes, John Sharpe, Christopher Foorde, Abraham Daunter and Richard Bryce, then town clerk, writer of these presents with many other more whose names are written on the backside of the said deed.[51]

f.156r Court held 11 March 1575 by the bailiffs with the constables, the sergeant and others more.

Court held 16 April 1575 by the bailiffs with the constables, the sergeant and others.

Actions of debt : John Gollde of Asthall Leigh, husbandman, against William Burnell of Witney, carpenter, for 2s. 11d. (3)

John Barnabey of Witney against Richard Ryder, of Witney, fuller, for 16s. 11d. (3)

Richard Okeley of Witney, dyer, against Robert Clay of Witney, blacksmith, for 30s. 3d. (3)

f.156v Hew Pollyn of Witney, loader, against Richard Leowis of Witney, broadweaver, for 5s. 1d.

Same against Harry Dey of Witney, broadweaver, for 2s. 3d. Agreed 12d. to be paid on Whitsun Eve next.

Same against John Ellyat of Witney, labourer, for 15d. Agreed and paid.

Thomas Wilshere of Ducklington, yeoman, against Robert Gryffeth alias Bodye of Witney, broadweaver, for 13s. 7d. (2) Paid to

[51] For the final concord about this transaction see CP 25(2) 196 Mich. 17 & 18 Eliz.

Wilshere by the hands of Gryffeth 14s. 7d. Which action was drawn by Humfrey Malen.

f.157r Court held 6 May 1575 by the bailiffs with the constables and the sergeant.
Actions of debt : Richard Delfe of Stanton Harcourt, tailor, against Cuthbert Margeris of Witney, tailor, for 8s. 1d. Confessed by Margeris in the face of the court. Paid 4s. on 27 May. The rest promised to be paid on 24 June next.
　　　　　Richard Rider against William Pursser of Witney, fuller, his late servant, for 16s. 11d. (2)
　　　　　William Purcer, late servant to Richard Rider, against his said master for wages owed 13s. 4d.; for a pair of fuller's shears which he esteems worth 13s. 4d.; for two dozen fuller's handles esteemed worth 16d. [4s. *crossed out*]. (2)
Tippler with his sureties: Thomas Hannes of Witney, fuller, admitted. Sureties for good order in his house for the whole year: Nicholas Gunne and Robert Saley.

f.157v Court held 3 June 1575 by the bailiffs with Thomas Taylor, William Hutchyns, Richard Humfrey and the wardsmen.
Covenanted servant: in court William Hutchyns, son of William Hutchyns of Witney, clothier, aged 14 years, bound himself to his father for eight years from Easter last past; to be taught the occupation of a broadweaver; to be given at the end of the term 26s. 8d. wages and double apparel. In witness whereof both parties have set their hands to this present writing in the face of the court.
f.158r Tippler with his sureties: Alexander Townsende of Witney, cobbler, admitted. Sureties for good order in his house for the whole year: Leonard Yate the younger, mercer, and John Sloowe of Witney, broadweaver.
Actions of debt : William Harris, bailiff, against Thomas Hyxe of Witney, broadweaver, for 8s. 3d. (1)
　　　　　Md. 30 June [1575] Leonard Yate the younger of Witney, mercer, against Thomas Sparcheforde of the 'Feelde' [i.e. Leafield], gent., for 8s. 1d. (1)

Court held 1 July 1575 by the bailiffs with the constables, the sergeant and others.
Actions of debt : John Sloowe of Witney, broadweaver, attorney for . . . Tawney of Stow, Gloucs., against Nicholas Hyll of Witney, baker, for 39s. 11½d. (1)
　　　　　Thomas Pemerton of Standlake, husbandman, against the same for 20s. 3d. Agreed at the court on 29 June that Hyll to pay this action at the end of . . .
f.158v Action of trespass: Alice Hannes of Witney, widow, against Philip Boxe of Witney, clothier, for . . . Agreed.
Action of debt : Md. 28 July 1575 Robert Pytt of Charlbury, butcher, against Thomas Snell of Spelsbury, baker, for 20s. 1d. Agreed.

f.159r Court held 29 July 1575 by the bailiffs with the constables, Thomas Yate, Harry
Jones, Philip Boxe, Thomas Taylor and many others.
  Covenanted servant: in court Nicholas Pemerton, brother of Thomas
  Pemerton of Standlake, husbandman, aged about 13 years, bound himself
  to Nicholas Hyll of Witney, baker, for six years from 29 Sept. next to make
  up the full complement of nine years with the three years already served
  with the said master; to be found etc. [as on p.83; no correction clause]; at
  end of the term 6s. 8d. wages and double apparel. In witness whereof both
  have set hands to the present writing. [Marks]

f.159v Court held 30 Sept. 1575 by the bailiffs with the constables and Thomas Yate,
  Philip Boxe, Leonard Yate, William Hutchyns, Richard Humfrey,
  Nicholas Gunne and many others.
  Chamberlain's account: William Hutchyns, then chamberlain, made his account
  before the said bailiffs and others above nominated. Town money in hand,
  clear of all reckonings then discharged with 6s. 6d. from the last account:
  19s. 10d.

f.160v Court held 7 Oct. 1575 by Thomas Taylor and Nicholas Gunne, bailiffs, with
  the constables after nominated, the sergeant, the wardsmen, Thomas Yate,
  Henry Jones, Philip Boxe, Thomas Hanckes, William Harris, William
  Hutchins, Thomas Clempson and many others more.
  Constables: William Hunt, Richard Shawe.
  Wardsmen: Alexander Townesend, Nicholas Maior, John Wylye, Richard
  Jonson, William Dunforde.
  Cardenars: Luke Leysam, Thomas Hurste.
  Ale tasters: Alexander Harris, Richard Hoane.
  Leather sealers: Jerome Hannes Oliver Ball.
  Cloth searchers: Leonard Dallton, William Gunne.

f.161r Tipplers with their sureties: appointed by the bailiffs at this court for the next
  year. Annys Shawe and for her Thomas Hanckes and Thomas Bishoppe;
  Humfrey Malen and for him Nicholas Hill and George Deye; Jerome
  Hannes and for him Thomas Bisshoppe and John Colliar; Alexander
  Townesende and for him Philip Boxe and John Slowe; Richard Dytton and
  for him John Sowtherne and William Peto; Edward Goode and for him
f.161v Philip Boxe and Thomas Bisshoppe; Richard Savery and for him William
  Ellmore and William Hutchins; Thomas Hannes and for him Nicholas
  Gunne and Robert Saley; Thomas Bellwood and for him William Peto and
  Robert Saley; Mark Fathers and for him Philip Boxe and Nicholas Ifeelde;
  Robert Carter and for him John Tymmes and William Jonson; William
  Cardewell and for him William Taylor and John Slowe; John Margeris and
  for him William Tayler and Robert Saley; Leonard Ranckell and for him
  William Peto and Robert Saleye; Thomas Hurste and for him William
  Tayler and John Wylye; Thomas Barnarde and for him . . .
  Action of debt : Edward Gunne of Eynsham, yeoman, against John Streete of
  Witney, surgeon, for 20s. (2)
  Action of trespass: Same against the same, for default of doing reparations in the
  house of the said Gunne wherein Streete has dwelled, for 39s. (2) Agreed
  and discharged.

f.162r Action of debt : Md. 31 Oct. 1575 Nicholas Saunders of Stanton Harcourt, husbandman, against Henry Fishar of Witney, husbandman, for 13s. 11d.

Court held 4 Nov. 1575 by Thomas Taylor, bailiff, and Henry Jones, deputy of Nicholas Gunne the other bailiff, with the constables, the sergeant and others.

Court held 25 Nov. 1575 by the bailiffs, with the constables, the sergeant, Thomas Hanckes, Thomas Bisshoppe, William Hutchyns and divers others.

Actions of debt : William Peto against Gregory Meryman for 2s. 11d. (3)
William Ellmore of Witney, woollen draper, against Thomas Sheppard of Witney, carpenter, for 16s. 8d. (3) Agreed at the court on 3 Feb. 1576 to pay one half of this action on 3 May next and the other half a fortnight before 25 July following.

f.162v   John Boothe of Chipping Norton, weaver, against Thomas Barnarde of Witney, weaver, for a brass pot, which Boothe had of Barnarde as a pawn for 16d., valued by Boothe at 7s. 6d. besides the entrance of this action, i.e. 7s. 9d. The pot delivered at the next court and weighed 11½lb. *Cancelled.* Discharged.

Assize of bread: Humfrey Malen baked bread to sell to contrary to the order of the last lawday. Likewise Richard Savery of Witney, mercer, baked cakes and sold them.

Covenanted servant: . . . Oliflex, son of Giles Olyflex of . . . Oxon., husbandman, in consideration of ten covenant pence . . . bound to William Wiltshire, shoemaker [?] . . . 26s. 8d. wages and double apparel. 28 Nov. 1575. [A cancelled covenant, mostly illegible. Entry in margin:] This was discharged and released.

f.163r Md. a possession: taken 8 Dec. 1575 by the bailiffs, of Leonard Ranckell of Witney, broadweaver, of a certain messuage and tenement with garden and certain plot of ground adjoining, now in the tenure of William Cordewell, baker, containing in breadth on the street side east to west 50 feet, in breadth on the north end of the said plot 39 feet; in length from the street side to the farthest end to the north six score and six feet [126 feet]; being on the north side of Crondell St. most commonly called Corne St., next between the tenement of Leonard Ranckell on the west and the tenement of John Barnarde now in the tenure and occupation of William Tayler, broadweaver, on the east part; for the use of Robert Harris of Chillstone, alias Chilson, yeoman, his heirs and assigns. Immediately after Harris gave possession to Nicholas Gunne, one of the bailiffs, to the use of the said William Cordewell and his assigns. In the presence of the bailiffs, the constables, the sergeant and Richard Jonson wardsman of the same ward, Richard Bryce, then keeper of the present town book, Leonard Ranckell and Alexander Townsende with others more. By me Richard Bryce.

f.163v Court held 15 Dec. 1575 by the bailiffs with the constables, the sergeant and Henry Jones, William Ellmore, Thomas Bisshoppe and others.

Action of debt : Henry Tackley of Witney against William Boothe of Chipping

Norton, weaver, for 13s. 4½d. Agreed and discharged at the present court. *Cancelled.*

Action of debt : John Collyar of Witney, clothmaker, against Thomas Hannes of Witney, fuller, for 32s. 3d. (3) Paid and quit.

f.164r Court held 13 Jan. 1576 by Nicholas Gunne, bailiff, and Thomas Hanckes, deputy for Thomas Taylor the elder, the other bailiff, with the constables, the sergeant and others.

Amerced: Nicholas Maior, Richard Jonson, William Forde, wardsmen, by the bailiffs, 6d. apiece for being absent from the present court.

Actions of debt : Agnes Shawe of Witney, widow, against Jerome Hannes of Witney, shoemaker, for 15s. 11d. (2) Agreed.

   Thomas Willshere of Ducklington against Robert Gryffeth alias Bodye of Witney, broadweaver, for 8s. 3d. (2) Paid and quit.

f.164v Court held 3 Feb. 1576 by the bailiffs with the constables, the sergeant and Henry Jones, Leonard Yate senior, William Ellmore, Thomas Clempson, Richard Humfrey and others.

Md. a possession: taken 16 Feb. 1576 by Thomas Taylor, bailiff, of William Brygfeelde of Witney, woollen draper, of a certain messuage or tenement with a shop, garden and certain plot of ground adjoining ; containing in the whole on the street side in breadth from the south side to the north 29 feet 8 inches, in length from the street side into the farthest part of the premises on the north three score and six feet; in length from the street side into the farthest part towards the west on the south side five score feet; in breadth at the west end 14 feet; all on the west side of the High St. between the tenement of William Brygfeelde on the north and of Roger Willsheere on the south; to the use of William Hunte of Witney, cardmaker, his heirs and assigns. Possession given by Thomas Taylor after the ancient custom of the borough in the presence of Nicholas Gunne the bailiff, Richard Shawe the constable, the sergeant and William Ellmore, Thomas Clemson, William Gunne, Edward Bradforde, Richard Bryce.[52]

f.165r Court held 24 Feb. 1576 by the bailiffs with the constables, the sergeant and others.

Order: by the bailiffs with the consent of the rest of their company that persons letting their pigs go into the market place on market day to forfeit for each default 12d.

Court held 23 March 1576 by Thomas Taylor, bailiff, with the constables and others.

Actions of debt : William Wickes of Witney, gent., against Richard Okeley of Witney, dyer, for 33s. 7d. (2) To pay 20s. part payment on the fourth Sunday after Trinity and the rest at such time as the parties shall agree upon hereafter. (2) Agreed.

[52] For the final concord about this transaction see CP 25(2) 197 Hilary 21 Eliz.

Richard Humfrey of Witney, dyer, against Giles Jones of Witney, clothier, for 27s. 3d. Agreed.

Md. 5 April 1576 John Colls of Long Hanborough, yeoman, against Richard Caswell alias Wayght of Shifford, husbandman for 30s., 'due rest' for a heriot. 30s. 3d.

f.165v Court held 13 April 1576 by the bailiffs with the constables, the sergeant and Henry Jones and others.

Action of trespass: Robert Horne of Witney, broadweaver, against Richard Okeley for 20s. 3d. At the next court Richard Bryce, attorney for Okeley, called a non suit, for that none came to the court to prosecute.

Action of debt : John Magood of Witney, glover, against Henry Allen of Witney, fugitive, for 2s. 9d. Agreed and paid.

Court held 4 May 1576 by the bailiffs with the constables, the sergeant and others.

Actions of debt : Md. 10 May 1576 Leonard Yate, son of Thomas Yate, mercer, against John Lydall of Charlbury, chapman, for 21s. 9d. Agreed.

Md. 17 May 1576 John Collyar of Witney, clothmaker, against Robert Keene of South Leigh, husbandman, for 13s. 7d. Agreed.

f.166r Md. a possession: taken 17 May 1576 by Thomas Taylor, bailiff, of Robert Yeman of Witney, broadweaver, of a certain messuage or tenement with a shop, court, garden and orchard ajoining with all appurtenances, lying on the north side of Crondell St. [i.e. Corn St.] between the tenement of Leonard Yate the elder of Witney, clothier, on the east and of Philip Cakebred on the west, extending from the street to the ground of Leonard Yate, now in the tenure of Ralph Tackett of Witney, shepherd. Possession given to Tackett by Taylor after the ancient custom of the borough in the presence of the constables, the sergeant, Richard Jonson then wardsman of that ward, Richard Bryce then keeper of the present court book, Philip Cakebred, George Sagar, Richard Dytton, Alexander Townsende, William Playce, William Blewe, Richard Pebworth.

f.166v Court held 25 May 1576 by the bailiffs with the constables, the sergeant and divers others.

Court held 22 June 1576 by the bailiffs.

Actions of debt : James Tasker of Hook Norton, chapman, by his attorney Roger Deacon, carpenter, against John Collsburne of Witney for 3s. 3d. (2) Paid.

Peter P . . . of Hailey [?] against . . . of Witney[?] for 19s. (2) Paid and quit. [names blotted out]

Same against Mark Fathers of Witney, tailor, for 10s. 3d. (2) Agreed.

Edward Goode against William Byrde the younger of Cogges for 6s. 11d. (2) Paid and quit.

f.167r Md. a possession: taken 5 July 1576 by Thomas Taylor, bailiff, of Francis Dustling of Allciter [i.e. Alcester, Warws.] tailor, by his attornies Robert

Mukell and Richard Bryce, of three messuages with appurtenances on the south side of West End St. next between the tenements of Mukell on the east and of John Colles alias Barnes on the west; to the use of Philip Boxe and his heirs according to a certain deed made by Dustling to Boxe 4 July 1576. Witnesses to the possession: Richard Shaw and the constable, the sergeant and William Dunforde wardsman of that ward, Moses Mukell, Robert Browne, son of Arther Browne, William Smyth, son of James Smyth, with others. Written by the abovenamed Richard Bryce, then keeper of this present book.

f.167v Court held 3 Aug. 1576 by the bailiffs with the constables, the sergeant, the wardsmen and others.

Actions of debt : Richard Harris of Oxford, by Thomas Harris his attorney, against Edward Bradfeelde of Witney, hatter, for 5s. 3d. (1) Discharged by a non suit.

John Wylye against William Hodson of Witney, broadweaver, for 10s. 3d. Agreed 6d. to be paid every week till paid.

Henry Brooke of Witney against the same for 13s. 7d. To be paid every week until the whole be paid.

John Haddon of Curbridge, husbandman, against Thomas Sheppard of Witney, carpenter for 2s. 2d. (3) Paid and quit.

Richard Bisshoppe of Hailey, tucker, against Gregory Meryman of Witney, broadweaver, for 11s. 3d. (3)

f.168r   Md. 24 Aug. 1576 Leonard Morwen of North Leigh, rough layer, against Lawrence Stutter of Newland, fugitive, for 10s. 1d.

Md. 30 Aug. 1576 Marmaduke Fletcher of Aylesbury, Bucks., chapman, by his deputy William Maior, against Richard Pen, chapman, for 38s. 1d.

Same against the same for 38s. 1d.

f.168v Court held 7 Sept. 1576 by the bailiffs, with the constables and the sergeant.

Actions of debt : Richard Bryan of Cogges, yeoman, against Richard Okeley of Witney, dyer, for 30s. (3)

Same against Richard Leowys of Witney, broadweaver, for 8s. 3d. Discharged by free gift. (3)

Ralph Tackett of Witney, shepherd, against Thomas Pebworthe of Witney, sawyer, for 5s. 3d. (3) Forgiven.

Actions of debt : William Birde of Witney, butcher, against Edward Goode of Witney, butcher, for 6s. 3d. Action discharged 25 Sept. by a non suit.

f.169r Court held 28 Sept. 1576 by the bailiffs with the constables, the sergeant, the wardsmen and others.

f.169v Court held 5 Oct. 1576 by Henry Jones and Peter Ranckell, bailiffs, with all the underwritten officers and Thomas Yate, Thomas Taylor, Nicholas Gunne, William Hutchins, Thomas Hanckes, Edward Goode and many others.
Constables: George Lawson, William Penye: sworn.
Wardsmen: Robert Claye, Thomas Breakspeare, Thomas Ranckell, Robert

James, Roger Wheler junior: sworn.

Cardenars: Edward Wheler alias Dodeswell, William Peerson: sworn.

Ale tasters: Nicholas Maior, William Hearne: sworn.

Leather sealers: Oliver Ball, William Wall: sworn.

Cloth searchers: John Wylye, William Gunne: sworn.

Chamberlain's account: Md. William Hutchyns, then chamberlain of Witney, made his account before the bailiffs above named. The town remained in the chamberlain's debt clear, all rents then due to the chamber of Witney received and all receipts reckoned: 3s 1d.

f.170r Order: wardsmen to come to each court held and make presentments pertaining to their charge, on pain of 12d. for each default.

Court held 26 Oct. 1576 by the bailiffs with the constables.

Actions of debt : Ralph Tackett of Witney, shepherd, against Robert Claye of Witney, blacksmith, for 10s. 3d. (3) Agreed.

         John Haddon of Curbridge, husbandman, against Richard Okeley of Witney, dyer, for 20s. 3d. (2) Agreed.

f.170v   John Collyar of Witney against William Gonne of Witney, tailor, for the debt of Robert Keene of South Leigh for 12s. 3d.

Order: by the bailiffs. Tipplers to sell beer and ale at 1d. a quart indoors and outdoors on pain of 12d. for each default.

Agreed: at the same court between John Trewman of Curbridge, yeoman, of the one part and Humfrey Malen of Witney, woollen draper, of the other. For 20s. to be paid to Trewman at the two most usual feasts or terms of the year by equal parts. Malen to hold and enjoy Combar Close in Witney borough now in the said Malen's tenure for two years from 29 Sept. last past; to have in the same close one reasonable cart load of shroud by the assignment of the said Trewman and not to plie nor plough up the said close nor any part thereof during the said term; to leave the close and mounds tenantable at the end of the term, and not to shred the trees there. Made in the presence of Peter Ranckell, Thomas Yate, Thomas Taylor, William Peny, Robert Stevens, Richard Bryce. [Signatures of] Thomas Yate, Thomas Taylor, William Peny.

f.171r Court held 7 Dec. 1576 by the bailiffs with the constables and others.

Actions of debt : Richard Humfrey of Witney, dyer, against Nicholas Hill, baker, for 10s. 3d. (1) Discharged and paid.

         Simon Jonson, clerk, deputy for Richard Pore of Wilcote, gent., against Robert Saley of Witney, clothmaker, for 6s. 2d. (3)

         Thomas Bryan, citizen and grocer of London, against William Harris of Witney, innholder, for 5s. 1d. (3)

         William Harris of Witney, innholder, against Humfrey Malen of Witney, woollen draper, for 4s. 6d. (3)

         William Bolton of Standlake, glover, against William Jonson of Witney, broadweaver, for 16s. 11d. (3)

f.171v Court held 18 Jan. 1577 by the bailiffs, with one constable, William Ellmore, Richard Humfrey and others.

Actions of debt : Thomas Bisshoppe of Witney, yeoman, against Roger Legge of Witney, baker, for 9s. 3d. (3)

William Wickes of Witney, yeoman, against the same for 39s. 11d. (3)

Philip Boxe of Witney, yeoman, against the same for 26s. 11d. (3) Agreed.

Richard Pore of Wilcote, gent., against Gregory Meryman of Witney, broadweaver, for 3s. 11d. (3) Paid 12d. on 8 Mar., and 12d. more another time by Richard Bryce.

Richard Rollyns of Ducklington, husbandman, against Richard Brice [*name heavily deleted*] of Witney for 20s. (3) Agreed to be paid day next after Low Sunday [i.e. first Sunday after Easter]. *Cancelled*. Paid and quit.

f.172r Court held 8 Feb. 1577 by Henry Jones, bailiff.

Actions of debt : Richard Humfrey of Witney, dyer, against Richard Shawe of Witney, butcher, for 10s. 3d. (1) Discharged.

Leonard Yate, son of Thomas Yate of Witney, clothier, against Robert Saley of Witney, fuller, for 27s. (3) Agreed. To be paid 6s. 8d. in hand and 5s. every quarter next following until the whole debt be satisfied, beginning 24 June next.

Same against Richard Ryder of Witney, fuller, for 8s. 9d. (3)

Richard Saverye of Witney, mercer, against John Slowe of Witney, broadweaver, for 3s. 5d.

Robert Wryght of Witney, blacksmith, against John Collsburne of Witney, labourer, for 3s. 5d. (3) Agreed.

f.172v Action of trespass upon the case: Adam Greeneway of Curbridge, wheelwright against John Townes of Witney, yeoman, for 16s. (3)

Actions of debt : Roger Legge of Witney, baker, against Edward Goode for 30s. *Cancelled*.

f.173r Court held 1 March 1577 by the bailiffs with the constables, the sergeant and others.

Actions of debt : Margaret Ridley of Witney, widow, against Roger Legge of Witney, baker, for 12s. Paid and quit.

Thomas Hannes of Witney, tucker, against Edward Prydye for 20s. 6d. Agreed.

f.173v Court held 29 March 1577 by the bailiffs with the constables, the sergeant and others.

Action of debt upon the case: Md. 18 April [1577] John Croftes of Sutton [i.e. Stanton Harcourt], yeoman, against James Shreeve of North Leigh, husbandman, for 20s. 7d. (1) Dismissed by the bailiffs.

Court held 19 April 1577 by Henry Jones, bailiff.

Actions of debt : Richard Bryan of Cogges, yeoman, against William Harris, innholder, for 18s. 3d. (1) Agreed.

Nicholas Colls of Witney, broadweaver, against Edward

Dodeswell of Witney, weaver, for 13s. 1d. (1)

> Md. 6 May [1577] Robert Turner of Eynsham, sawyer, against Harry Allen, sawyer, fugitive, for 2s. 7d.

f.174r
> Md. at the last court Annys Taylor, wife of John Taylor, sleymaker, against John Scargyll of Witney, tailor, for 3s. 3d. (1) Agreed to be paid 20d. next Whit Sunday, and 4d. every Saturday next following until satisfied.

Court held 17 May 1577 by the bailiffs with the constable, Philip Boxe and others.

Actions of debt : John Quyll of South Leigh, yeoman, against Robert Saleye of Witney, fuller, for 14s. 3d. Paid 5s. by the hands of Harry Jones above at the court on the other side of the leaf; and 3s. to be paid on 24 Aug. next in full contentment of the whole debt.

> Henry Jones above named against Robert Saley for 26s. 3d. Md. at the court held on the other side of this leaf it was agreed between the said Henry Jones and Robert Saley that whereas Richard Weaver now holds a shop and a broad loom with certain implements belonging to the said loom for the yearly rent of 6s. 8d., Saley, in consideration that Jones of his own goodness granted Saley four years day of payment, promised that Weaver should pay Jones the said yearly rent of 6s. 8d. for four years next ensuing after the date above written, in full contentment of the said debt, and further that Weaver should hold, occupy and enjoy the said shop and loom during the said four years, and thereupon Weaver promised to pay the said debt in manner aforesaid and so agreed this action.

f.174v Court held 14 June 1577 by the bailiffs with the constables, the sergeant and others.

Court held 26 July 1577 by the bailiffs.

Actions of debt : Anthony Ashefeelde of Shipton-under-Wychwood, gent., by his deputy Richard Bryce, against John Horne of Witney, carpenter, for 26s. 11d. (3)

> Same against the same by the said deputy for 20s. 3d. (3) Both actions paid and quit by the hands of Philip Boxe.

f.175r Court held 20 Sept. 1577 by the bailiffs.

Actions of debt : Henry Jones against John Horne of Witney, carpenter, for 20s. 3d. (3)

> Same against Robert Saley for 3s. (3)
> Thomas Boxe of Witney, tucker, against Robert Saley of Witney, fuller, for 8s. 3d. (3)
> Richard Harris of Witney, miller, against Thomas Taylor of Witney, mason, for 21d.

f.175v Court held 4 Oct. 1577 by Philip Boxe and William Ring, bailiffs, with the constables and Thomas Yate, Henry Jones, Peter Ranckell, Thomas Bisshoppe, John Barnaby, Richard Savery.

Constables: William Taylor, Thomas Ranckell: sworn.

Wardsmen: Richard Clempson, William Cordewell, John Bollt, Roger Legge, Richard Bisshoppe: sworn.

Cardenars: Nicholas Maior, Henry Wryght: sworn.

Ale tasters: Henry Gryffyn, William Tommes: sworn.

Leather sealers: Oliver Ball, William Wall.

Cloth searchers: John Wylye, William Gunne.

f.176r Actions of debt : Richard Okley of Witney, dyer, against Walter Kinges of Cogges, yeoman, for 8s. 3d.

William Austen of Witney, loader, against Richard Wysedome of Witney, weaver, for 3s. 3d. (1)

Md. grant: the bailiffs with the consent of all whose names are hereunto subscribed have granted to John Ifeelde of Witney, broadweaver, all that house or cottage which Ifeelde has begun to build in the Quarry in Crondell St. [i.e. Corn St.]; to have and to hold for ever and to his heirs lawfully begotten of his body in as ample a manner and wise as the same may be let by the said bailiffs and townsmen. Ifeelde and his heirs to pay yearly to the bailiffs 12d. on 29 Sept. at one entire payment.

Witnesses: [signatures of] William Ryng, Thomas Yate, Henry Jones, Peter Rankell, John Barnaby, William Elmer, William Maior, Richaard Savery, Richard Bryce, Thomas Ranckell; [mark of] Philip Boxe.[53]

f.176v Court held 25 Oct. 1577 by the bailiffs with the constables, the sergeant, Thomas Yate, Peter Ranckell, Nicholas Gunne and many others.

Actions of debt : William Peto of Witney, woollen draper, against Mark Fathers of Witney, tailor, for 5s. 3d. (3) Paid to the bailiffs at the court on 3 Jan. 1578 in part payment 2s. 6d. and promised to pay rest before Easter next.

Md. 7 Nov. 1577 John Pyddell of Wilcote, carpenter, against Ambrose Lardener of Ramsden, husbandman, for 13s. 7d. Paid.

At the same court William Ring against Nicholas Colles of Witney, broadweaver, for 11s. 3d. (3) Paid and quit.

Mark Fathers of Witney, tailor, against John Rackley of Witney, tailor, for 5s. 11d. (3) Paid to the bailiffs at the court held on 3 Jan. 1578.

f.177r Court held 15 Nov. 1577 by the bailiffs with the constables, Henry Jones, William Ellmore and divers others.

Actions of debt : John Warren of Witney, weaver, against William Osmunde late of Witney, dyer, for 30s. (3)

John Baker of Witney parish, labourer, against Richard Okeley, dyer, for 3s. 3d. (3)

Md. 21 Nov. 1577 Thomas Ryman of Charlbury, glover, against Robert Pytt of Charlbury, butcher, for 3s. 0½d., with the entrance and arrest.

John Beeseley of Witney, carpenter and joiner, against John Boollocke of Hardwick for 4s. 3d. (3)

[53]   Town property; see above, p.00.

f.177v Court held 3 Jan. 1578 by William Ring, bailiff with the constables and others.
  Action of debt : John Hunte of Fawler Mill, miller, against Nicholas Hill of
  Witney, baker, for 36s. 7d. (3) Discharged and paid 21 March 1578.

  Court held 24 Jan. 1578 by the bailiffs.
  Actions of debt : William Austen of Witney, loader, against Thomas Sheppard
  of Witney, carpenter, for 23d. (2) Paid and discharged.
          William Peto of Winey, tailor, against Richard Dytton of
  Witney, weaver, for 10s. (2) Agreed.

f.178r Covenanted servant: at the court on 24 Jan. 1578 John Tompson, son of Richard
  Tompson late of South Leigh, husbandman, deceased, as well by the advice
  and counsel of his dear friends Thomas Collyns, William Bylbye and
  Andrew Drewatt, overseers of the last will and testament of the said
  Richard Tompson, as also of his own free assent and consent and in
  consideration of eight covenant pence received in earnest of William
  Harrison, of Witney, tailor, the said John Tompson being then examined
  by William Ring, bailiff, did confess himself covenanted servant to and
  with William Harrison to be learned in the art, science, faculty or occupation of a tailor . . . and with him to dwell and serve from 25 March next
  ensuing for eight years. John Tompson covenanted by these present to
  serve the said master in such manner and form and in all respects as
  becomes a servant of such science to do. In consideration whereof and in
  further consideration of 40s. which the said Harrison received to his own
  use at the hands of the parties abovenominated before, and at the sealing
  and subscribing of these present, the said William Harrison promised and
  covenanted by this present writing to teach and instruct the said John
  Tompson in the art, science or occupation of a tailor after the best manner
  that he can or knoweth and in all points thereof to the uttermost of his
  power and also to find to the said servant* sufficient and wholesome bread,
  meat, and drink, linen, and woollen hose, shoes and bedding and all things
  necessary as well in sickness as in health, with due order of correction. And
  in the end and expiration of the said term to give and deliver to his said
  servant* double apparel, i.e. one suit for holy days and another for working
  days such as shall be meet and decent for a servant of such science or
f.178v occupation to wear.[54] [The section of this covenant on f.178r is crossed through]
  Further covenant for repayment of 20s., if the said Harrison dies within one
  year or next ensuing after the date of the court last held before the writing
  of these present, to and for the use of the said John Tompson. In witness
  whereof Harrison and Tompson have to the present set their hands 24 Jan.
  [Their marks]

[54] This covenant has been given in detail to show the terms of an apprentice's maintenance;
for a discussion see above, pp.xxxii–iv. Similar maintenance clauses occur (with variations) in
later indentures, where their content is indicated by reference to this example: see the sections
between asterisks. (The variation seem to be of form rather than intent: e.g., the correction
clause may be omitted, the words 'in sickness and health' may be left out, bread may be
described as 'good and lawful' or not.) Such clauses are found elsewhere in both contemporary and later indentures. For additional clauses at Witney, see below, pp.158, 165, 186.

Action of debt : Md. 20 Feb. 1578 Anne Butler, daughter-in-law of Robert Foster of South Leigh, husbandman, against John Streete of Malmesbury, Wilts.,[55] surgeon, for 5s. 7d. (2) Md. William Penny of Witney, broadweaver, in the face of the next court mentioned on the other side of this book, gave his word to see the court answered and the debt paid upon due proof. Md. at the court on 11 April 1578 William Peny granted to pay the debt above expressed upon 1 May next following. Paid, discharged and quit.

f.179r Court held 21 Feb. 1578 by the bailiffs with the constables, the sergeant, Henry Jones, John Barnabye, William Ellmore, Thomas Bishoppe, Richard Savery, John Colliar and many others more.

Actions of debt : Henry Jones of Witney, clothier, against Roger Legge of Witney, baker, for 10s. 3d. (2)

Thomas Woodwarde of Brize Norton, yeoman, against Cuthbert Margeris of Witney, tailor, for 11s. 1d. (1)

Order: by the bailiffs. Tipplers to sell outdoors a thirdendell of beer and ale for 1d., indoors a quart of ale and beer for 1d. on pain of 12d. for default.

f.179v Court held 21 March 1578 by the bailiffs with Henry Jones, Thomas Bishop, Peter Ranckell and divers others.

Action of debt : John Maygood of Witney, glover, against William Hunte of Witney, cardmaker, for 15d. Action respited at the court on 23 May 1578 until the next court for Hunte to bring in his hands for due proof of the matter.

Court held 11 April 1578 by the bailiffs.

Action of debt : Richard Bryce of Witney against Joan Dallton of Witney, widow, for 8s. 4d. (2) Received in the face of the court on 13 June 1578 in full satisfaction, 6s. 8d.

Action of detinue: William Bradshawe of Curbridge against George Deye of Witney, broadweaver, for the detaining of a calf from him and certain money whereby Bradshawe is indemnified to the value of 13s. 4d. Agreed and discharged.

f.180r Court held 2 May 1578 by William Ring, bailiff.

Court held 23 May 1578 by the bailiffs with the constables and the sergeant.

Actions of debt : William Ellmore of Witney, woollen draper, against John Horne of Witney, carpenter, for 3s. 4d. (3) Paid and quit.

Same against Richard Wisedome of Witney, weaver, for 17s. 11d. (3) At the court on 1 Aug. 1578 Wisedome promised to pay half at or before 17 Aug. and the rest before 23 Nov. next.

f.180v Court held 13 June 1578 by Philip Boxe, bailiff, William Taylor, constable, the sergeant, William Ellmore, Richard Savery and others.

[55] Formerly of Witney; see pp.71, 74.

Actions of debt : Alexander Townesende of Witney, cobbler, against Richard Rider of Witney, tucker, for 20s. 2d. (3) Distress made. At the court on 31 Oct. 1578 agreed to pay 9s. in full satisfaction, i.e. 4s. 6d. on 2 Feb. and 3 May following.

John Collier of Witney, mercer, against Thomas Hickes of Witney, broadweaver, for 2s. 5d. (2) Discharged, paid.

Robert Harris of Northmoor, husbandman, against Robert Saley of Witney, tucker, for 39s. 10d. (3) At the court on 26 Sept. 1578 Henry Jones to pay 20s. on 23 Nov. next in full satisfaction to Harris and to have the close behind Saley's house from 2 Feb. next for one whole year.

Order: by the bailiffs. Inhabitants next to the Market Place to rid their blocks[56] from the street before St Peter's Day [29 June] next on pain of 3s. 4d. for default.

f.181r Court held 4 July 1578 by the bailiffs with the constables, the sergeant and others.

Actions of debt : Richard Bryce, attorney for William George of South Leigh, husbandman, against John Collsburne of Witney, labourer, for 17d. (3) Distress made. 29 Oct. 1578 received of Stephen Bryce in full satisfaction 14d.

William Tayler of Witney, weaver, against Richard Leowis of Witney, broadweaver, for 4s. 3d. (3) Discharged, paid.

Philip Boxe against Anthony Larden, butcher, for 10s. 3d. that Boxe paid for Larden by suretyship. (3)

Action of trespass: Thomas Hanckes of Witney, baker, against Thomas Pebworth of Witney, sawyer, for 10s. 3d. (3) Distress awarded against the defendant. To appear at the next court.

f.181v Court held 1 Aug. 1578 by the bailiffs.

Actions of debt : John Robyns of Witney, labourer, against John Collsbourne of Witney, labourer, for 17d. Paid.

Thomas Bellwood of Witney, fuller, against John Scargyn of Witney, tailor, for 6s. 3d. (3) At the court on 26 Sept. the defendant confessed he owed 4s.; given day to wage law for the rest with himself and two hands against the next court. Md. 31 Oct. promised to pay before 25 Dec. next. Costs 4d.

Md. 16 Aug. [1578] George Maye of Witney, glover, against George Harding, late of Witney, butcher, now fugitive, for 14s. 4d.

f.182r Court held 29 Aug. 1578 by the bailiffs with the constables, the sergeant, Henry Jones, William Ellmore and others.

Action of debt : Richard Bryan of Cogges, yeoman, against John Scargyll for 4s. 3d (3) Distress to be made against the defendant. At the court on 31 Oct. the defendant confessed this action and given day to bring surety for the debt before Sunday next after the said court.

[56] Perhaps for stalls.

Court held 26 Sept. 1578 by William Ring, bailiff, with the constables, the sergeant and others.

Actions of debt : Henry Jonson of Witney, mason, against George Sagar of Witney, broadweaver, for 19d. (3) Paid at the court on 31 Oct.

Nicholas Hill of Witney, baker, against William Phillippes of Witney, tucker, for 10s. 3d. (3) Distress to be made.

Gratian Colles of South Leigh, husbandman, against Richard Wisedome of Witney, weaver, for 20s. 5d. (3) Distress to be made.

f.182v Covenanted servants: in court Thomas Croftes, son and heir of Thomas Croftes late of Witney, rough mason, deceased, aged about 18 years in consideration of seven covenant pence bound himself to William Hutchyns of Witney, clothier and broadweaver, for seven years from 24 June last past to be taught the occupation of a broadweaver; to be found etc. [as on p.83]; and at the end of the seven years to receive 26s. 8d. wages and double apparel. R.B. [Initials of Richard Brice]

f.183r   in court Richard Norton, son of John Norton of Burford, shepherd, aged 11 years, in consideration of ten covenant pence bound himself to the same William Hutchyns for ten years from 29 Sept. last past. Terms as above. R.B. [Initials of Richard Brice]

f.183v Court held 10 Oct. 1578 by Leonard Yate bailiff, with William Sleepe, then steward of the said court, with the constables and other inferior officers hereunder nominated with many the substantial of the said town and commoners of the same, John Barnaby senior being then the other bailiff elected and nominated.

Constables: Roger Coxe, Richard Jonson: sworn.

Wardsmen: William Cordewell, Lancelot Lawson, Thomas Warde, all sworn; Thomas Shawe, Robert Grynder.

Cardenars: Nicholas Maior, Henry Wryght: sworn.

Ale tasters: Henry Gryffyn, William Tommes: sworn.

Leather sealers: Oliver Ball, William Wall: sworn.

Cloth searchers: John Wylyes, William Gunne: sworn.

Actions of debt : John London the younger of Long Combe, tallow chandler, against Robert Clay of Witney, blacksmith, for 10s. 3d. (1) Dismissed by the bailiffs for default, non appearance.

Actions of debt : John Collyar of Witney, mercer, against Thomas Sheppard, carpenter, for 13s. 3d. (3)

f.184r Court held 31 Oct. 1578 by the bailiffs with the constables, the sergeant and many others.

Actions of debt : John Butt of Bampton against John Collsburne of Witney, labourer, for 3s. 3d. (3) Paid and discharged at the court on 15 Jan. 1579.

Robert Harris of Chilson against the same for 2s. 11d. Agreed.

Order: by the bailiffs. Tipplers to sell beer and ale outdoors at 1d. a thirdendell of sealed measure and indoors an ale quart of sealed measure at 1d.; and small drink 1d. a gallon and ½d. a half gallon, on pain for default according to the statute.[57]

f.184v Actions of debt : James Shreeve of North Leigh, husbandman, against Richard Okeley of Witney, dyer, for 4s. 3d. (3) Paid and quit.

Md. 13 Nov. 1578 Nicholas Dennye of Witney, weaver, against Evans Geffrye, late of Islip, chapman, for 12s. 9d. Agreed and discharged.

Court held 28 Nov. 1578 by the bailiffs.
Action of debt : John Jones of Witney, broadweaver, against Edward Hannes of Witney, shoemaker, for 4s. 11d. (1) Dismissed by non suit.
Order: by the bailiffs. No inhabitant to sell tallow candles above 3d. a pound until further permission, on pain of 3s. 4d. for each default.

f.185r Covenanted servant: in court George Bruce, son of John Bruce of Woodstock, shoemaker, on being examined by the bailiffs confessed himself bound to Thomas Warde of Witney, shoemaker, for four years from 24 June last past to make up the term of seven years with the three years last past that he served his father in the art aforesaid; to be found etc. [as on p.83]; at the end of four years 26s. 8d. wages and double apparel. In witness whereof both parties have to these present set their hands. [No marks or signatures]

f.185v Md. a possession: taken 28 Nov. 1578 by the bailiffs of John Horne of Witney, carpenter, of a messuage or tenement wherein he then dwelt with all courts, houses, rooms, chambers, solars, trees, casements, all being on the west side of the High St. next between the tenements of Richard Shawe on the north and one late of Thomas Cawcott and now of Thomas Woodwarde on the south; the said tenement being in breadth on the east 39½ feet; at the west 39½ feet and in length from the street to the further end of the premises to the west seven score and five feet; to the only proper use of Robert Abraham, late of Cheltenham, Gloucs., and his heirs for ever. Delivered by the said bailiffs to Abraham in the presence of Roger Coxe constable, Robert Steevens the sergeant, Peter Ranckell, Thomas Boxe, John Collyar, Thomas Duffyn, Thomas Wirgge, Esau Warren and Richard Bryce, the writer of the deed thereof and of the present also. R.B. [Initials of Richard Brice.][58]

f.186r Actions of debt : Md. 4 Dec. 1578 Richard Fletcher of Charlbury, broadweaver, against Robert Pytt of Charlbury, butcher, for 37s. 3d.

Md. 18 Dec. 1578 Richard Bryce of Witney, scrivener, against Robert Egicare of Hanborough, tailor, for 4s. (1) Discharged, paid and quit 19 Dec. by Henry Fletcher of Hanborough.

---

[57]   By law local officials were responsible for maintaining weights and measures stamped with the king's seal as conforming to the standards in the Exchequer. They were authorized to examine measures in their jurisdiction and impose fines for infractions: Act 11 Hen. VII c.4; and see Zupko, Br. Weights and Measures, p.81.
[58]   For the final concord about this transaction see CP 25(2) 197 Hilary 21 Eliz.

f.186v Court held 19 Dec. 1578 by the bailiffs with the constables, the sergeant and many other commoners.

Amerced: every baker within the borough for not coming into court, 12d.

Court held 15 Jan. 1579 by the bailiffs with the constables, the sergeant and others.

Action of debt : Md. 22 Jan. 1579 William Gunne of Witney, tailor, against John Gollding of Crawley for 33s. 11d. (2)

f.187r Court held 6 Feb. 1579 by the bailiffs with the constables, the sergeant and others.

Actions of debt : Mark Fathers of Witney, tailor, against Hew Rodes of Witney, weaver, for 15s. 3d. (3) At the court on 29 May respited until 29 Sept. next so that Rodes in the meantime should go to Humfrey Berrye in Worcestershire, for whom he was surety, to receive the said debt. Otherwise Rodes to pay the debt on 29 Sept. next.

Edward Stafforde of North Leigh against Richard Okeley of Witney, dyer, for 16s. 3d. (3) Paid and quit.

f.187v   William Ellmore of Witney, woollen draper, against John Scargyll of Witney, tailor, for 2s. 7d. (3) Distraint to be made.

John Gybson of Long Hanborough, weaver, against William Peny of Witney, broadweaver, for 10s. 3d. (3)

Md. 20 Feb. [1579] John Croftes of Sutton in Stanton Harcourt, yeoman, against Walter Sexton of South Leigh, husbandman, for 39s. 11d. (2)

f.188r Court held 6 March 1579 by the bailiffs with the constables, the sergeant and others.

Action of debt : William Taylor of Witney, broadweaver, against Gregory Meryman of Witney, weaver, for 3s. 9d. (3)

Amerced: by the bailiffs. Thomas Hanckes, Edward Goode, Nicholas Hill and Roger Legge, 12d. apiece for absence from the court and not having any bread to be weighed at the same court.

f.188v Court held 27 March 1579 by the bailiffs with the constables and the sergeant and others.

Actions of debt : Edward Goode against Thomas Bellwood of Witney, tucker, for 11s. 3d. (3) At the court on 14 Aug. Bellwood agreed to pay 8s. in full satisfaction at the rate of 12d. every Sunday till paid.

Philip Boxe of Witney, clothier, against Thomas Barnarde of Witney, weaver, for 8s. 7d. (3) Distress to be made.

Md. 8 April 1579 Robert James of Witney, butcher, against John Boollocke of Hardwick, husbandman, for 3s. 2d; charges of arrest and entrance of the action 7d.

Md. 9 April [1579] Richard Savery of Witney, mercer, against Elizabeth Webbe of Witney, widow, fugitive, for 11s. 1d; charges 7d.

f.189r   Md. Saturday 2 May 1579 Robert Harcourt, esq., of Stanton Harcourt, by his deputy Thomas Eliot of South Leigh, against William

Wynter of . . . Oxon., yeoman, for 6s; charges 7d. Paid and quit.

Court held 8 May 1579 by the bailiffs with the constables and others.
Actions of debt : Thomas Willsheere of Ducklington against Robert Gryffeth
alias Bodye of Witney, broadweaver, for 12s. 4d.; charges 3d. (3)

   Edward Goode of Witney, baker, against Richard Ryder of
Witney, tucker, for 20s. 3d. (3)

   Md. Thursday 21 May 1579 Richard Bryan of Cogges,
yeoman, against John West of Swinbrook, husbandman, for 6s. 8d; charges
7d. (3) At the court on 14 Aug. West was taken in his default for not
answering and so condemned by this court.

f.189v Court held 29 May 1579 by the bailiffs with the constables and the sergeant.
Action of debt : Md. Tuesday 2 June 1579 Thomas Yate of Witney, clothier, by
his deputy Richard Steevens, against John Cossen of North Leigh,
husbandman, for 3s; charges 7d. Paid and quit.

Court held 26 June 1579 by the bailiffs with the constables and Thomas Yate,
Thomas Taylor, Henry Jones, Philip Boxe, William Ellmore, Thomas
Bisshoppe, Thomas Hanckes, Thomas Boxe, Edward Goode with others.
Actions of debt : Md. 30 June 1579 John Maygood of Witney, glover, against
John Scargill late of Witney, tailor, for 5s; charges 7d.

   Md. 9 July 1579 Dorothy and Adam Greenewaye of Curbridge
wheelwright, against Philip Parsons of Shilton, Berks., husbandman, late
master of the said Dorothy, for 16s, for one year's wages and for four yards
of red cloth at 2s. 8d. the yard and more for an apron cloth of linen valued
at 8d; 27s. 4d; charges 7d. (3)

f.190r   Md. same day Richard Okeley of Witney, dyer, against
William Winter late of Wilcote, yeoman, for 39s. 11d. Declaration to the
court on 15 April 1580: Okeley, by his attorney Richard Bryce, complained
and declared that whereas he bought of Winter certain wood at Ramsden
and gave 4d. in earnest and paid for the spoiling and making of the same
wood into faggots 16s. 10d., the said Winter forcibly took and conveyed
away the same to the damage of Okeley to the value of 39s. 11d. and
therefore he brings this action.

Judgement: at the court held on 10 June 1580 by Thomas Yate, bailiff,
Winter defaulted by not answering. Thomas Taylor of Witney, tanner, by
pledge for Winter confessed the action. The bailiffs gave judgement that
Okeley should be satisfied for the said action at or before the next court to
be held without any further delay.

f.190v Court held 14 Aug. 1579 by the bailiffs with the constables and the sergeant.
Actions of debt : Richard Bryan of Cogges, yeoman, against Roger Legge of
Witney, baker, for 30s. (3)

   Same against Mark Fathers of Witney, tailor, for 13s. 7d. (3)

   John Peacocke of Shilton, Berks., quarrier, against William
Maynarde of Witney, slater, for 20s. 7d. (3) Action agreed as by and in the
paper to this leaf annexed more plainly appears. Which agreement being

not performed, Peacocke set away the said paper of agreement on Sunday
30 July 1581, intending to sue the said Maynarde in the higher court.[59]
Action of debt : Walter Jones of Lincoln's Inn, London, gent., by his deputy
Nicholas Gunne of Witney, against Richard Bryce of Witney for 10s. Paid
8s. to Gunne at the court on 30 Oct. 1579 in full satisfaction.

f.191r Court held 18 Sept. 1579 by the bailiffs with the constables and the sergeant.

f.191v Court held 9 Oct. 1579 by Thomas Yate and Peter Ranckell, bailiffs, with
William Sleepe, steward, Leonard Yate and John Barnaby, late bailiffs,
Philip Boxe, Richard Humfrey, Richard Savery, Nicholas Gunne and
many commoners of the said borough.
Constables: Richard Clempson, Thomas Hyckes.
Wardsmen: Richard Maior, Edward Dodeswell, Hew Jackson, Nicholas
Stratton, John Maygood.
Cardenars: Nicholas Maior, Robert Claye.
Ale tasters: Henry Gryffeth, William Tommes.
Leather sealers: Oliver Ball, William Wall.
Cloth searchers: John Wylye, William Gunne.
Actions of debt : Thomas Willsheere of Ducklington, by his attorney William
Gunne of Witney, tailor, against Robert Gryffeth of Witney, broadweaver,
for 13s. 6d. (3) Discharged.
f.192r   Robert Griffeth of Witney, broadweaver, against William
Harrison of Witney, tailor, for 10s. 1d. Agreed and set over to be paid to
Willsheere before Easter next towards the discharge of the action
commenced in the last leaf before this.[60]

Court held 30 Oct. 1579 by the bailiffs with the constables, the sergeant and
Henry Jones, Philip Boxe, Thomas Bisshoppe, Richard Savery with divers
others.
Chamberlain of Witney: the bailiffs with the consent of the benchers and
commoners then present chose William Hutchyns. In the hands of Richard
Fyckett one year's rent due from the town house wherein he dwells on 29
Sept. last: 6s. 8d. Also the same to answer for another year's rent due on 29
Sept 1578, which he paid to William Ring : 6s. 8d.
Action of debt : William Ellmore of Witney, woollen draper, against Robert
Steevens of Witney, broadweaver, for 9s. 2d; charges 3d. (2) Agreed.
f.192v Tipplers within the borough 30 Oct. 1579: In the first ward:[61] Humfrey Malen,
Agnes Shawe, Jerome Hannes, Alexander Townesende, Robert Clay [all
licensed]. In the second ward: William Cordewell, Thomas Hurste,
Richard Savery [all licensed]; Richard Lewis, John Collyar, Thomas
Hanckes. In the Middle Ward: Mark Fathers, Edward Goode. In the East
Ward: Nicholas Hill, Edward Hannes, Roger Legge, William Harris, Joan

[59] There is now no annexed paper. The higher court might be Quarter Sessions or a central
royal court such as Requests.
[60] See above, p.89.
[61] The first and second wards were Paternoster Row and West Ward; see above, p.60.

Margeris. In the ward beneath the bridge: Thomas Barnarde, Robert Carter.

f.193r Action of trespass: Md. Thursday 5 Nov. 1579 Edith Wysdome of Witney, widow, against George Hilliarde late of Bampton, mercer, to the value of 13s. 4d; charges 7d. Paid and quit.

Actions of debt : Md. 12 Nov. 1579 John Taylar, servant of William Wickes of Witney, against William Fisher of Kencot, clerk, for 11s; charges 7d. (1) Action discharged 15 Jan. 1580 by reason that Mr Fissher brought proof that he had satisfied the debt long before.

Md. same day Alexander Smyth of Charlbury, horse gelder, against Charles Gryffeth of South Leigh, joiner, for 13s. 3d; charges 7d.

f.193v Court held 4 Dec. 1579 by Thomas Yate, bailiff, with the constables, Leonard Yate senior and Leonard Yate junior with others more.

Actions of debt : James Streete of Witney, currier, against Hugh Walker of Witney, labourer, for 2s. 8d; charges 3d. Discharged and quit.

George Maye of Witney, glover, against Edward Dodeswell, broadweaver for 18s. 10d; charges 3d. (3) At the court on 15 Jan. 1580 put unto the bailiffs' hands to determine, who awarded Dodeswell to pay 15s. in full satisfaction, 7s. 6d. to be paid five weeks after this court and 7s. 6d. at Easter next.

f.194r Court held 18 Dec. 1579 by the bailiffs with Thomas Bishoppe and Leonard Yate junior, William Ellmor, Henry Jones, Richard Saverye.

Md. all actions commenced before in this book between Thomas [Roger *crossed out*] Willsheere of Ducklington, yeoman, against Robert Gryffeth of Witney, broadweaver, and all other reckonings discharged.[62] Gryffeth to give Willsheere the close of his house until the said Roger [*sic*] has forgiven the 13s. 4d. on 25 Mar. next and the lord's chief rent from the said house and Willsheere to give Gryffeth and his wife 2s. yearly for their natural lives on 29 Sept. and 25 Mar.

f.194v Court held 15 Jan. 1580 by the bailiffs with the constables, the sergeant, Philip Boxe, Leonard Yate junior, Edward Goode with divers commoners.

Action of detinue: John Hodges of South Leigh, yeoman, one of the overseers of last will and testament of . . . of South Leigh, and in the name of the other overseers, against William Harrison of Witney, tailor, for 39s. 11d. for the behoof of the children of the said . . ., which money was delivered to the said Harryson with one of the children. *Cancelled.* (3) Discharged and quit.

Action of debt : Md. 6 Feb. 1580 Leonard Ranckell of Witney, broadweaver, against John Snape of Standlake, gent., for 10s.; charges 7d. Agreed and discharged.

f.195r Court held 14 Feb. 1580 by the bailiffs with the constables and the sergeant. Names of all the common bakers within the borough: Thomas Hanckes, Edward Goode, Roger Legge, William Cordewell.

[62] See above, pp.89, 90.

Order: by the bailiffs. Innholders or tipplers in the borough not to bake in their houses for sale any manner of halfpenny bread, penny bread, twopenny bread nor cakes of any price, on pain of 10s. for default.

Presentments: at the court on 6 May 1580 Thomas Hanckes of Witney, baker, presented William Harris of Witney, innholder, for baking both bread and cakes contrary to the said order, affirmed by Joan Harris and confessed to Edward Dodeswell, wardsman, being sent thither for some of her bread. The same presented Richard Savery, mercer, for baking cakes in his house contrary to the order.

f.195v Court held 4 March 1580 by the bailiffs with the constables, the sergeant and others.

Action of debt : John Peacocke of Shilton, Berks., quarrier, against Richard Okeley of Witney, dyer, for 6s. 8d; charges 3d. (3)

Order: inhabitants not to keep their shop doors nor shop windows open on the Sabbath Day after the last peal has rung to service until the service be quite closed, on pain of 12d. to the poor men's box.

Covenant money: ordered by the bailiffs that John Lynley of Witney, broad-weaver, to pay Frances Hobbes his late servant, for the rest of his covenant money 6s. 8d.; or distress to be levied. Agreed and paid by Leonard Yate junior.

f.196r Court held 15 April 1580 by the bailiffs with the constables, the sergeant and others.

Amerced: Roger Legge 12d. for not coming to court, being sent for and for his bread being too light by one and a half ounces.

Action of debt : Md. 22 April 1580 John Caning of Witney, blacksmith, against William Keerse of Cogges, husbandman, for 6s.; charges 7d. Paid and quit.

f.196v Court held 6 May 1580 by the bailiffs with the constables, the sergeant and Henry Jones, Thomas Taylor, Richard Humfrey, William Ring, Richard Jonson, Thomas Hanckes, William Taylor and many others.

Action of debt : John Hyarne of Burford, dyer, by his attorney Richard Bryce, against Richard Okeley of Witney, dyer, for 30s.; charges 3d. (3) Paid and quit.

Court held 10 June 1580 by Thomas Yate with the constables, the sergeant and others.

Action of debt : John Rider of Witney, tucker, against Robert Yeman of Witney, broadweaver, for 10s.; charges 3d. Agreed by order.

Action of assumpsit: John Williams of Great Faringdon, Berks., clerk, and William Shaw of the same, draper, by their attorney Richard Bryce, against Richard Okeley of Witney, dyer, for 13s. 10d; charges of entering this action and attorney's fees 6d. (3) Agreed at the court on 9 Sept. 1580 by Richard Bryce and William Ellmore, with the consent of the bailiffs, Okeley finding sufficient surety to pay 4s. next 25 Dec. and on every quarter day.

f.197r Action of debt ; Richard Bryan of Cogges, yeoman, against Nicholas Hill of

Witney, baker, for 7s.; charge 3d. (2) Discharged and paid.

Covenanted servant: in court Edward Goode, son of Thomas Goode late of Witney, deceased, with the consent of his uncle Edward Goode of Witney, butcher, and of his own free assent and in consideration of seven covenant pence received in earnest in court, confessed himself bound to John Sloowe of Witney, broadweaver, for seven years from Whitsun last past to be taught the occupation of a broadweaver; to be found etc. [as on p.83]; at the end of the term 26s. 8d. and double apparel. In witness whereof the parties set their marks to the present writing. [*No marks or signatures*]

f.197v Court held 8 July 1580 by the bailiffs with the constables, the wardsmen and the sergeant.

Actions of debt : Elizabeth Claye, wife of Robert Claye of Witney, blacksmith, against Robert Hutchins of Witney, chapman, for 7s.; charges 7d. At the present court 18d. paid in part payment; order by the bailiffs to pay 2s. more in full satisfaction, viz. 4d. every Thursday.

Richard Sewell of Witney, mercer, against Henry Gryffeth of Witney, cobbler, for 3s. 4d; charges 3d. (2) Agreed.

f.198r Court held 29 July 1580 by the bailiffs with the constables, the wardsmen and the sergeant.

Action of assumpsit: Thomas Taylor of Witney, tanner, against William Winter late of Wilcote, yeoman, for 39s. 9d., for that Taylor, being pledge for Winter for the like sum to be paid to Richard Okeley of Witney, dyer, was distrained for the debt which was awarded to Okeley by order of the court.

Action of debt : Robert Saley of Witney, tucker, against William Peny of Witney, broadweaver, for 39s. 11d. (3) At the court on 25 Nov. it was agreed that the action be satisfied by payments of 13s. 2d. on 2 Feb. next and 13s. 2d. on 24 June following. Saley to come by the residue of the said debt as he may by order come by the same.

f.198v Court held 9 Sept. 1580 by the bailiffs with the constables, the wardsmen and others.

Action of trespass: William Abraham of Woodstock against Thomas Hurst of Witney, tailor, for 8s. 8d.; charges 3d. Paid to the bailiffs in full satisfaction 5s. 3d.

Action of debt : Md. 13 Sept. 1580 Peter Ranckell by his attorney Robert Steevens, against . . . Bearde of Brize Norton, husbandman, for 8s.; charges of 7d. *Cancelled.*

f.199v Court held 7 Oct. 1580 by Thomas Bysshoppe and Richard Jonson, bailiffs, with the constables, the sergeant, the wardsmen and with Mr Thomas Yate and Peter Ranckell, late bailiffs, with many other commoners of the same.

Constables: Thomas Boxe, Robert James: sworn.

Wardsmen: Nicholas Denye, Thomas Colliar, Roger Lane, James Hodson, Richard Puisley: sworn.

Cardenars: Nicholas Maior, Alexander Townsende: sworn.

Ale tasters: Harry Benned, Edward Carter: sworn.

Leather sealers: Oliver Ball, William Wall.

Cloth searchers: John Wyleye, William Gunne, to whom the town seal was delivered at this court: sworn.

Order: by the bailiffs. Tipplers who defaulted of their appearance at this court to appear at the next court with names of sureties or be dismissed of their tippling.

f.200r Tipplers who showed their licences[63] to the bailiff at the same court: Agnes Shawe, widow, and surety for her Thomas Bisshope and Thomas Hanckes; Jerome Hannes and for him Thomas Bishoppe and Nicholas Hill; Alexander Townesend and for him [Thomas Hanckes *crossed out*]; Robert Claye and for him John Slowe and Nicholas Colles; Margaret Carter, widow, and for her . . .; Alice Hurst and for her John Wyly and William Tayler; Richard Savery; William Cordewell and for him John Slowe and William Tayler; Edward Dodeswell; Edward Goode and for him Thomas Bisshoppe.

Actions of debt : William Allen of Ducklington, blacksmith, against John Rackley of Witney, tailor, for 2s.; charges 3d. (3) Discharged and paid.

f.200v   Richard Sparcke of Eynsham, miller, against Nicholas Hill of Witney, baker, for 16s.; charges 3d. Agreed.

Md. 17 Oct. 1580 George Wattkyns of Eynsham, yeoman, against George Francklyn of North Leigh, husbandman, for 26s. 8d; charges 7d.; pledge Leonard Ranckell of Witney, broadweaver. Non suited at the court on 16 Dec. 1580. Plaintiff to pay 2s. 6d. towards the defendant's trouble and expense within seven days.

Md. 20 Oct. 1580 William Marten, servant to Stephen Bryce of Witney, yeoman, against George Franklen of North Leigh, husbandman, for 21s. 10d.; charges 7d. *Cancelled.*

Md. 21 Oct. [1580] Richard Wenman, son and heir of Thomas Wenman of Witney Park, esq., by his deputy Thomas Whyght, labourer, against Thomas Webbe of Drayton [near Banbury], yeoman,[64] for 36s. 8d.; charges 7d. Discharged by a non suit at the court on 16 Dec. 1580 by Nicholas Gunne, deputy for the said Thomas.

f.201r Court held 4 Nov. 1580 by the bailiffs with Mr Yate, Henry Jones, William Ellmore, Giles Jones and many other commoners.

Md. Richard Fyckett paid to the bailiffs for three years rent of his house ended on 29 Sept. 1580 in ready money, 18s. 4d. The same paid for the chief rent and knowledge of the guild hall 20d. which made up his whole three years rent.[65]

[63] From the Justices.

[64] For Webbe see *VC.H. Oxon.* ix. 106, 107. He held the manor of Drayton and in 1579 had dealings with his tenant there, a woolgrower, and with a Bath clothier: P.J. Bowden, 'The Home Market in Wool 1500–1700', *Yorks. Bulletin of Economic and Social Research*, viii (1956), 138.

[65] A town house. The payment for the acknowledgement of the guild hall presumably was made to the town as against the 'chief' rent, which was a rent paid to the chief lord, i.e. the bishop. On the other hand there was 'knowledge money' paid when the bishop first came: see customs in Giles, *Witney*, p.ix.

Court held 25 Nov. 1580 by the bailiffs with the constables.

Action of detinue: John Townes of Penley Park in 'Awberrye' [i.e. Pendley Park in Aldbury], Herts., yeoman, by his attorney Robert Steevens of Witney, broadweaver, against George Poell of Witney, gent., and Joan, now his wife, for certain pieces of pewter particularly expressed in a letter of attorney made by Townes to Steevens dated 15 Oct. last to the value of 26s.; charges 3d.

f.201v Court held 16 Dec. 1580 by Thomas Bisshoppe, bailiff, with John Barnaby, Thomas Clemson, Nicholas Gunne, William Ring with divers other commoners.

Order: by the bailiffs with the consent of the parties above. Pigs above one quarter old abroad in the street to be ringed, on pain of 4d. for every hog or pig taken. One half to remain to the poor men's box and the other to him that shall take them.

Covenanted servant: Andrew Marlow of Witney, son of Thomas Marlowe of Witney, tailor, of his own free assent and with the consent of his father and in consideration of eight covenant pence received in earnest in the face of the court, confessed himself bound to John Slowe of Witney, broadweaver, to be taught the art of a broadweaver for eight years from 1 Jan. next; to be found etc. [as on p.83]; at end of term 20s. wages and double apparel.

f.202r Court held 13 Jan. 1580 by the bailiffs with the constables and the sergeant.

Order: against pigs or hogs seen or taken unringed in Langdale[66] after 20 Jan. on pain of 6d. for each time, one half to the poor men's box, the other to him that takes them.

Action of debt : Md. Thursday 26 Jan. 1581 Robert Starre of Burford, baker, against William Grynder, late of Fairford, Gloucs., for 6s.; charges 7d.; pledge Robert Grynder of Witney, broadweaver, for his brother, to answer the action on his behalf. *Cancelled.*

f.202v Court held 3 Feb. 1581 by Thomas Bisshoppe, bailiff.

Actions of debt : Peter Ranckell of Witney against William Hodson of Witney, broadweaver, for 20s.; charges 3d. At the court on 21 Apr. Bailiff Jonson gave his word to pay the same on 24 Aug. next. Agreed.

William Brygfeelde of Witney, woollen draper, against Henry Tackley of Witney, fishmonger, for 5s; charges 3d. (3) Paid in full satisfaction by judgement of the court 2s. 6d.

William Barnes of Hailey, labourer, against Thomas Shepparde of Witney, carpenter, for 5s., charges 3d. (2)

Agreed to pay 12d. a week.

f.203r Court held 3 March 1581 by Thomas Bishoppe, bailiff, with the constables and Mr Thomas Yate, Richard Humfrey, William Brygfeelde and divers other commoners.

[66] Langdale Common. For regulations about fences on it see Top. Oxon.d 211, p.75. It lies near the river Windrush east of Witney High Street.

Court held 31 March 1581 by the bailiffs with the constables, the sergeant and Henry Jones.

Action of debt : Md. Friday 14 April 1581 William Harris of Witney, glover, against John Scargyn of Witney, tailor, fugitive, for 33s. 4d.; charges 7d.

f.203v Court held 21 April 1581 by the bailiffs with the constables, the sergeant, Peter Ranckell, William Brygfeelde, Nicholas Gunne with many others.

Action of debt : Elizabeth Arnollde, servant to William Ring of Witney, against Mark Fathers of Witney, tailor [*no sum stated*]. Paid and quit.

Court held 12 May 1581 by Thomas Bishoppe, bailiff, with the constables and the sergeant.

Action of debt : Md. Saturday 20 May [1581] Henry Jones of Witney, clothier, against John Frenche of Aston, yeoman, fugitive, for 33s. 4d. Charges 7d. *Cancelled.*

f.204r Court held 2 June 1581 by Thomas Bisshoppe, bailiff, with the constables, the sergeant and others.

Action of debt : Richard Shewell of Witney, mercer, against . . .

Court held 23 June 1581 by the bailiffs with the constables, the sergeant, William Brygfeelde, Nicholas Gunne with many other commoners.

Covenanted servants: in court Thomas Smyth, son of Robert Smyth of Eynsham, tailor, of his father's and his own free assent, on examination by the bailiffs and in consideration of seven covenant pence confessed himself bound to James Streete of Witney, currier, for seven years from 25 July last

f.204v past to be taught the occupation of a currier of leather; to be found etc. [as on p.83]; at the end of the term 26s. 8d. wages and double apparel, i.e. a jerkin and a pair of venetians [i.e. breeches] of grey frieze for working days, to be made in the very last year of the said term, two shirts of 15d. the ell to be made in the same year and one new shirt of locram to wear on Holy Days with a meet and seemly band to each of the three shirts; also a jerkin and a pair of venetians of medley russet at 2s. 8d. the yard to wear on Holy Days with like nether stockings, good shoes, a seemly fair doublet and a felt hat, meet and decent for a journeyman of such an art. In witness whereof both parties set their hands 23 June 1581. [*No marks or signatures*]

f.205r   Robert Smythe, son of Robert Smythe of Eynsham, tailor, of his father's and his own free assent and in consideration of eight covenant pence received in court and being examined by Richard Jonson, bailiff, confessed himself bound to Nicholas Taylor of Witney, shoemaker,

f. 205v for seven years from 25 March last past to be taught the occupation of a shoemaker; to be found etc. [as on p.83]; at the end of the term 18s. wages and double apparel as in the covenant above. Witnesses: [marks of] Nicholas Taylor, Robert Smythe junior.

Actions of debt : Md. Thursday 29 June 1581 Thomas Lawrence of Cassington Mill, fuller, against William Phillippes, late of Witney, fuller, for 38s.; charges 7d.

f.206r   Md. Thursday 20 July 1581 Anthony Machyn of Charlbury, weaver, against Robert Weatherhead, alias Leake, of Charlbury, butcher, for 25s.; charges 7d. Agreed.

Court held 28 July 1581 by Thomas Bisshoppe, bailiff.

Actions of debt : John Hunt of Burford, mercer, by his servant and deputy, William Tayler, against Leonard Yate, son of Thomas Yate, clothier, for 19s.; charges 3d. (3)

f.206v   John Hiarne of Burford, dyer, by his attorney Richard Bryce, against Mistress Anne Dormar of Farthinghoe, Northants., widow, for 30s.; charges 3d. (3)

Same against the same, by virtue of a letter of attorney from Robert Steevens of Witney, broadweaver, and by the above named attorney and in the name of the said Robert Steevens, for 9s.; charges 3d. (3) Attachment made by Richard Bryce, the said attorney, of three coverlets of coloured lyst yard, appraised by the wardsmen of Witney at . . ., being the goods of the said Mistress Anne Dormer and attached only for the discharge of the said two actions and for the charges of the court.

Md. Friday 4 Aug. 1581 Thomas Jonnes of Norton in the town liberties of Gloucester, husbandman, against Walter Cysemoore of Down Hatherley within the aforesaid liberties for 20s. 3d. [39s. 11d. *crossed out*]. Sureties Davye Byrte and James Smythe. Agreed.

f.207r Court held 18 Aug. 1581 by the bailiffs with the constables, the sergeant and many other commoners.

Actions of debt : John Haddon of Curbridge, husbandman, against Giles Jones of Witney, clothmaker, for 20s.; charges 3d. (3)

John Wylye of Witney, woollen draper, against John Fawle of Witney, broadweaver, for 8s.; charges 3d. Agreed.

Action of detinue: Anthony Boosshe of Witney, broadweaver, against William Huntt of Witney, cardmaker, for a dagger delivered to him to dress for 3s. 4d.; charges 3d. (3)

f.207v Court held 8 Sept. 1581 by the bailiffs with the constables, the sergeant, Thomas Yate, Leonard Yate his son, Nicholas Gunne with divers commoners.

Action of assumpsit: Md. Thursday 12 Oct. [1581] Nicholas Launce of Eynsham, tanner, against . . . Clynche of Cote, husbandman, for 6s.; charges 7d. Agreed.

f.208v Court held 13 Oct. 1581 by Philip Boxe and Leonard Yate, son of Mr Thomas Yate, town bailiffs, with the constables, the sergeant, the wardsmen, Thomas Bishoppe and Richard Jonson, late bailiffs, Thomas Clempson, Richard Humfrey, Nicholas Gunne, Richard Savery with many other commoners.

Constables: Thomas Taylor junior, John Lynley: sworn.

Wardsmen: Thomas Heires, William Harrison, John Horsell, Cuthbert Harris, Humfrey Yorcke: sworn.

Cardeners: Thomas Colliar, Roger Legge: sworn.

Ale tasters: Anthony Larden, Alexander Harris [Robert Yeman *and* Anthony Brown *crossed out*]: sworn.

Leather sealers: Oliver Ball, William Wall.

Cloth searchers: John Wylye, William Gunne, in whose hands remained the town seal.

f.209r Action of debt : Thomas Pemerton of Standlake, husbandman, by his deputy Leonard Yate, fuller, against Nicholas Hill of Witney, baker, for 20s.; charges 3d. On 5 Jan. paid to Leonard Yate, bailiff, in court by Richard Bryce 5s.

Covenanted servant: in court William Bingham, son of Alice Bingham of Witney, widow, in consideration of eight covenant pence received in court bound himself to Robert Steevens of Witney, broadweaver, for eight years from 24 June last past to be taught the occupation of a broadweaver; to be found etc. [as on p.83; no correction clause] at the end of the term 26s. 8d. wages and double apparel. In witness whereof the parties have set their hands. 13 Oct. 1581. [No marks or signatures]

f.209v Court held 3 Nov. 1581 by the bailiffs with the constables, the sergeant, Henry Jones, Richard Saverye, Nicholas Gunne with many other commoners.

Court held 24 Nov. 1581 by Leonard Yate junior, bailiff, with the constables, the sergeant, Henry Jones, Peter Ranckell, William Ellmore, Nicholas Gunne with John Barnaby junior and many other commoners.

Actions of debt : Peter Ranckell against Nicholas Hill of Witney, baker, for 23s. 3d. On 5 Jan. paid 10s.

John Croftes of Sutton [i.e. Stanton Harcourt], yeoman, against George Dey of Witney, broadweaver, for 10s.; charges 3d. (1) The bailiffs ordered that if Croftes at the first court held after 25 Dec. next does not put into the court sufficient declaration in writing re this action he shall be taken upon his default and this action dismissed. Agreed.

f.210r   Md. 24 Nov. 1581 Henry Brooke of Witney, broadweaver, against William Goudge of South Leigh, husbandman, for two new silver spoons delivered to his own hands which cost 14s.; charges 7d.

Court held 15 Dec. 1581 by the bailiffs with the constables, the sergeant and Henry Jones.

The bailiffs delivered to Richard Jonson of Witney, clothier 27s. 10d. of the town money toward the buying of a black corslet with his furniture.

Orders: by the bailiffs that 18s. debt owed by William Harrison of Witney, tailor, to John Hodges of South Leigh and other to be paid to Thomas Taylor the elder of Witney at the rate of 4s. on 25 Dec. next, 4s. on Easter Day next, 4s. on Whit Sunday next and 6s. on 29 Sept. next. Paid to John Hodges 26 Dec. by the hands of Thomas Taylor senior of Witney, 4s. 6d. Paid and quit.

f.210v Wardsmen to attend every court and during the whole time on pain of 12d. for default.

Brewers and tipplers to sell ale and beer indoors at 1d. a quart and outdoors 1d. a thirdendell and to call the ale tasters to taste of every their brewing on pain of 6d. for every default.

Action of debt : Thomas Bisshoppe of Witney, yeoman, against Thomas Ivyee of Witney, labourer, for 3s. 2d.; charges 3d. Agreed.

f.211r Order: inhabitants having hogs in the market place on market day to forfeit 4d. for every hog.

A stray: on Friday 24 Nov. last past a stray dun-coloured colt with a grey mane and cloudy face was brought to Leonard Yate, now bailiff, by William Brygfeelde of Witney, which colt was appraised at 13s. 4d. by Peter Ranckell, Thomas Bisshoppe and Henry Brooke on 15 Dec. 1581. Paid for crying of the said colt 3d; and for drink to the appraisers 3d.

f.211v Court held 5 Jan. 1582 by the bailiffs with the constables, the sergeant, Henry Jones, Richard Savery and others.

Actions of debt : Henry Jones of Witney, clothier, against William Hoane of Witney, slater, for 5s.; charges 3d. Agreed.

Richard Savery of Witney, mercer, against Leonard Yate senior, clothier, for 15s. 6d.; charges 3d.

f.213r Court held 8 Feb. 1582 by the bailiffs, the constables, the sergeant and Thomas Bisshoppe.

Court held 6 April 1582 by the bailiffs with the constables, the sergeant, the wardsmen, Mr Thomas Yate, Henry Jones, Leonard Yate senior and many others.

Actions of debt : Md. Friday 8 June 1582 Richard Savery of Witney, mercer, against William Wickes of Curbridge, yeoman, for 8s.; charges 7d. (3) Paid and quit.

Md. same against the same for 6s. (3) Leonard Yate, bailiff, promised that the two actions be answered or the cart arrested for the same be brought in place again at the next court day, if the said debt be not satisfied in the meantime. Respite given on distress on 3 Aug. until the next court when Leonard Yate gave his word for payment. Actions paid 28 Sept.

f.213v Court held 15 June 1582 by the bailiffs with the constables and the sergeant and with Henry Jones.

Actions of debt : John Stampe of Witney, gent., against Edward Meysye of Witney, labourer, for 3s. 3d. (3)

John Hutchins of Burford, broadweaver, against Robert Yeman of Witney, broadweaver, for 10s.; charges 3d. (2) Paid in part payment 6s. and Richard Pebworth gave his word to pay the rest on 29 Sept. next.

Robert Saley of Witney, tucker, against Roger Larden of Witney, broadweaver, for 7s.; charges 3d. (3)

John Peacock of Shilton, Berks., quarrier, by his attorney Richard Bryce, against William Maynarde of Witney, slater, for 29s. 6d.; charges 3d. (3)

f.214r Same against the same for 17s. 11d.; charges 3d.

Order: by the bailiffs that every householder in Witney to have standing or set without his street door on every night from this court day until 29 Sept. next one tub, cowl, barrel, pail, pan, or cauldron with water in readiness for necessity against fire on pain of 6d. for every default to the contrary.

f.214v Court held 6 July 1582 by the bailiffs with the sergeant, the wardsmen and others.

Court held 3 Aug. 1582 by the bailiffs with the constables, the sergeant, the wardsmen and others.

Action of debt : Margaret Ryddley of Witney, widow, against Thomas Taylor of Witney, mason, for 18d.; charges 3d. Discharged and quit.

f.215r Covenanted servant: in court John Horne, son of John Horne late of Witney, carpenter, deceased, in consideration of ten covenant pence received in court bound himself to Thomas Puckforde of Witney, broadweaver, for ten years from 24 Aug. next to be taught the occupation of a broadweaver; to be found etc. [as on p.83; no correction clause]; at the end of the term 26s. 8d. wages and double apparel. In witness whereof the said Puckforde and Horne have set their hands 2 Aug. 1582. [*No marks or signatures*]

f.215v Court held 28 Sept. 1582 by the bailiffs with constables, the sergeant and others.

Court held 5 Oct. 1582 by John Stampe and Nicholas Gunne, bailiffs, with the constables, the sergeant, the wardsmen and with Mr Thomas Yate, Leonard Yate, son of the said Thomas, John Barnaby, Thomas Taylor junior with many commoners of the said town.

Constables: Andrew Byrde, Humfrey Yorcke: sworn.

Wardsmen: William Peereson, Richard Shewll, William Purcer, Nicholas Tayler, Moses Muckwell: sworn.

Cardenars: Thomas Colliar, Oliver Ball: sworn

Ale tasters: Oliver Ball, William Thoms: sworn.

Leather sealers: Oliver Ball, William Wall: sworn.

Cloth searchers: John Wylye, William Gunne: sworn.

f.216r Court held 26 Oct. 1582 by . . .

Actions of debt : Md. Thursday 18 Oct. [1582] Richard Clempson of Witney, woollen draper, against Henry Cooke of Upton, husbandman, for 9s. 6d.; charges for entering and drawing of the action and for the bailiffs' fees 8d. (2) Surety John Lawrence of Witney. Defendant impleaded to the next court. At the court on 7 Dec. 1582 the bailiffs gave judgement that the defendant should pay. Paid and quit.

Edward Dodeswell of Witney, tippler, against William Hodson of Witney, broadweaver for 16s. 8d.; charges 8d. (3) At the court on 11 Jan. agreed to pay half next Shrove Sunday and half on Whit Sunday next or a distress to be levied.

f.216v Henry Tackley of Witney, fishmonger, against Roger Wheeler senior of Witney, carpenter, for 14s.; charged 7d. (3)

Same against John Collisburne, labourer, for 3s. 4d.; charges 3d. (3) To be paid on 2 Feb. next or a distraint. Agreed.

Same against Edward Meysye of Witney, labourer, for 2s. 10d.; charges 7d. Paid and quit.

f.217r Henry Jones of Witney, clothier, against John Rackley of Witney, tailor, for 7s. 7d.; charges 7d. (3) Agreed.

Same against Oliver Ball, pearmonger, for 7s.; charges 7d. (3)
Agreed.
Order: by the bailiffs. Wardsmen to come to every three weeks court and
accompany the bailiffs and their officers during the time of every court, on
pain of 3d. for default.

f.217v Actions of debt : Md. Thursday 15 Nov. 1582 Henry Brygfeelde of Witney,
broadweaver, against . . . Gryffeth of South Leigh, widow, for 22s.;
charges of arrest, bailiffs' fee and entrance 11d. (1)

Md. same day William Gunne of Witney, tailor, against
Thomas Gorram of Great Barrington, Gloucs., yeoman, fugitive, for 3s.
9d.; charges 11d. Agreed, discharged and quit.

f.218r Court held 16 Nov. 1582 by the bailiffs with the constables, the wardsmen and
Mr Thomas Yate, Thomas Bysshoppe, William Brygfeelde, Thomas
Clempson with many other commoners.
Action of debt : Thomas Hanckes of Witney, baker, against Robert Yeoman of
Witney, broadweaver, for 10s.; charges 7d. (3)
Tippler with his sureties: William Peto licenced by the bailiffs; and for him
Nicholas Stratton and Robert Wryght of Witney, on pain of £5 apiece if
default made, to be paid to the bailiffs for the use of the Queen.

f.218v Court held 7 Dec. 1582 by the bailiffs with the constables, the sergeant, Mr
Thomas Yate, Henry Jones with divers commoners.
Covenanted servant: John James, son of Thomas James of Brize Norton,
husbandman, in consideration of . . . covenant pence received in earnest in
the sight of the bailiffs and being examined confessed himself bound to
John Lynley of Witney, broadweaver, for . . . from 1 Nov. last past to be
taught the occupation of a broadweaver; to be found etc. [as on p.83; no
correction clause]; at the end of the term . . . wages and double apparel. In
witness.

f.219r Court held 11 Jan. 1583 by the bailiffs with the constables, the sergeant, Henry
Jones and many others.
Action of detinue: Md. Thursday last past Nicholas Lawnce of Eynsham,
tanner, against [William Perkyns, tailor crossed out] James Hixe, of Witney,
butcher, for wrongful detaining of a hide which Lawnce late bought of
Hixe to the value of 5s.; charges 11d. At the court on 1 Feb. Perkins [sic]
brought into court William Bollters of Eynsham, husbandman, and John
Rose of Eynsham, shoemaker, who testified that Perkins bought the cow
and had right to the hide. Adjudged to Perkins with costs and damages.
Actions of debt : William Austen of Witney, loader, against John Rackley of
Witney, tailor, for 2s. 4d.; charges 7d.
Henry Jones of Witney, clothier, against William Hodson of
Witney, broadweaver, for 39s. 11d.

f.219v Court held . . . Feb. 1583 by the bailiffs with Mr Thomas Yate, Philip Boxe,
Thomas Bisshoppe with divers other commoners.
Action of debt : John Colliar of Witney, vintner, against Robert Mukell of

Witney, fuller, for 26s. 8d.; charges 7d. (3)

Action of debt : Md. 14 Feb. 1583 John Croftes of Sutton [i.e. Stanton Harcourt], yeoman, against Leonard Orpwood of Sandford, Berks., yeoman, against Leonard Orpwood of Sandford, Berks., yeoman, for 6s. 8d.; charges 11d. (3) Paid and quit.

f.220r Md. a possession: taken 30 Jan. 1583 by Marian Tylcocke of Oxford, widow, by her attorney Robert Sampson of Oxford, gent., of a messuage or tenement with a court, garden or close on the backside of the same now in the tenure or occupation of Hew Rodes, broadweaver, situated on the west side of the High St. between the tenement of Mary Butterworth alias Miller on the south and the tenement of Thomas Willshere on the north. Possession presently given to John Stampe, gent., bailiff, for the use of Roger Wheeler the elder of Witney, carpenter, his heirs and assigns for ever. The bailiff delivered possession to Wheeler according to the ancient custom of the borough and according to a certain deed made by Tylcock to Wheeler on 29 Jan. 1583, and in the sight and presence of Nicholas Gunne, bailiff, Hew Rodes, Robert Stagge, Henry Wryght, George Allen, Robert Allen, John Godfrey, Richard Bryce the elder, the recorder of this possession, Humfrey Yorck, constable, Robert Steevens, sergeant. By me Richard Bryce. R.B.[67]

f.220v Court held 1 March 1583 by Nicholas Gunne, bailiff, with the constables, the sergeant and Thomas Bisshoppe, Leonard Yate, junior, with many commoners.

Actions of debt : Richard Cakebread of Witney, broadweaver, against Nicholas Denny late of Witney now of Circencester, Gloucs., weaver, for 20s.; charges 7d. (1) *Cancelled*.

Nicholas Denny against Richard Cakebread for 23s.; charges 7d. (1)

Richard Sheweell of Witney, mercer, against Richard Okeley of Witney, dyer, for 4s.; charges 7d. (1) Paid and quit.

f.221r   William Cordewell against Simon Peerson of Witney, broadweaver, for 2s. 6d.; charges 7d. Paid and quit.

Covenanted servant: Edward Busbye, son of William Busbye of Yarnton, husbandman, by the counsel of his father and with own assent and in consideration of seven covenant pence received in court bound himself to Robert Steevens of Witney, broadweaver, for seven years from 25 March next to be taught the occupation of a broadweaver, to be found etc. [as on p.83; no correction clause]; at end of term 26s. 8d. wages and double apparel. In witness whereof both parties have set their mark: [marks of] Edward Busby, William Busbye.

f.221v Court held 22 March 1583 by John Stampe, bailiff, with Mr Thomas Yate, Thomas Taylor and divers others.

---

[67] For the final concord about this transaction see CP 25(2) 197 Easter 26 Eliz.

Court held 18 April by the bailiffs with Henry Jones and one constable.

Amerced: William Peereson, William Purcer and Moyses Muckewell, wards-men, 6d. apiece for being absent from court this day.

Acknowledged: John Rackley of Witney, tailor, that he owed John Stampe 4s. 2d. to be paid on or before St. Peter's Day [1 Aug.] next or distraint to be lawful for any officer within the borough.

Actions of debt : Bailiff Stampe against John Collsburne of Witney, labourer, for 20d.; and 12d. more for an iron wedge which he wrongfully detains; charges 7d. (3)

f.222r   Md. Monday 22 April 1583 William Ellmore of Witney, woollen draper, against Nicholas Huckwell, late of Witney, mason, fugitive, for 11s. 2d.; charges 7d.

f.222v Court held 11 May 1583 by the bailiffs with the constables, the sergeant and others.

Action of debt : Richard Saverye, mercer, against Thomas Lugge of Witney, labourer, for 2s. 4s.; charges 7d. (3) Action respited 14 days by the bailiffs and if not paid to be presently distrained for the same. Paid and quit.

Court held 31 May 1583 by the bailiffs with the constables and the sergeant.

Court held 22 June 1583 by the bailiffs with the sergeant, Mr Thomas Yate, Thomas Taylor senior, Leonard Yate senior, John Lawrence with divers other commoners.

Action of debt : Md. Tuesday 2 July 1583 Thomas Collyar of Witney, chandler, against John Frenche of Aston, gent., fugitive, for 20s.; charges 11d. Paid and quit.

f.223r Court held 12 July 1583 by the bailiffs with the constables and the sergeant.

Actions of debt : Richard Shewell of Witney, merecer, against George Maye of Witney, glover, for 4s.; charges 8d. *Cancelled.*

                    John Cannyng of Witney, blacksmith, against Richard Okeley of Witney, dyer, for 5s. 8d.; charges 7d. (3)

                    Md. Tuesday 16 July 1583 Thomas Dallton against William Keerce of Cogges, fugitive, for 39s. 11d.

f.223v Court held 9 Aug. 1583 by John Stampe, bailiff, with Mr Thomas Yate, Thomas Taylor senior, Andrew Byrde, constable, with the sergeant and divers others.

Actions of debt : Richard Fissher of Witney, broadweaver, against William Goullde of Witney, broadweaver, for 10s. 4d.; charges 7d. Agreed.

                    Md. Wednesday 20 Aug. 1583 Robert Wryght of Witney, blacksmith, against William Ryng of Cogges, yeoman, for 4s.; charges 11d.

f.224r Court held 13 Sept. 1583 by the bailiffs with the constables, the sergeant, the wardsmen, Thomas Taylor, Thomas Bisshoppe, William Ellmore, and many other commoners.

f.224v Court held 4 Oct. 1583 by Henry Jones and Thomas Taylor the younger, bailiffs, with the constables, the sergeant, John Barnabey, Thomas Bisshoppe, Thomas Clempson, John Lawrence, William Brygfeelde, John Collyar with many other commoners.

Constables: William Gunne, Henry Brooke.

Wardsmen: Christopher Cotes, Edward Cakebread, Richard Haskyns, Richard Maior, William Bryan.

Cardenars: Robert Chapman, Thomas Smarte.

Ale tasters: Alexander Harris, William Tommes.

Leather sealers and searchers: William Wall, Walter Turner.

Cloth searchers: John Wylye, William Gunne.

f.225r Covenanted servant: in court Michael Lucas, son of James Lucas late of Chipping Norton, weaver, being examined by the bailiffs and in consideration of ten covenant pence delivered in court, confessed himself bound to William Bryan of Witney, broadweaver and linen weaver, for ten years from 29 Sept. last past to be taught the occupation of a broadweaver; to be found etc [as on p.83]; at end of term 33s. 4d. wages and double apparel.

f.226r Court held 15 Nov. 1583 by the bailiffs.

Actions of debt : Richard Wallcrofte of Eynsham, weaver, against John Skargill of Witney, tailor, for 9s. 3d.; charges 7d. (2) Md. Skargill died; action cut off.

William Allen of Ducklington against Mark Fathers of Witney, tailor, for 13s. 4d.; charges 7d. (2) Agreed at the court on 10 Jan. that Fathers to pay 6s. 8d. on Black Monday [i.e. Easter Monday], and 6s. 8d. on Whit Monday; Henry Jones gave his word for payment.

Amerced: Thomas Colliar of Witney, chandler, 3s. 4d. for absenting himself from court, having warning of the same.

f.226v Action of debt : Md. Thursday 5 Dec. [1583] Henry Bewe of Hailey, husbandman, against Richard Burgyn of Eynsham, butcher, for 9s.; charges 11d. Agreed.

Court held 6 Dec. 1583 by the bailiffs with the constables, the sergeant and others.

Collectors for the poor: elected and nominated by the bailiffs for one year to come, Richard Maior and William Cordewell.

Actions of debt : Richard Bryan of Cogges against Nicholas Maior of Witney, broadweaver, for 3s. 2d.; charges 7d. (2) Paid and quit.

Same against Robert Hutchyns of Witney, tinker, for 7s. 6d.; charges 7d. (1) Paid.

f.227r Court held 10 Jan. 1584 by the bailiffs with the constables and the sergeant.

Action of debt : Henry Jones, bailiff, against William Hodson of Witney, broadweaver, for 39s. 11d. (2) Agreed.

Court held 31 Jan. 1584 by Thomas Taylor, bailiff, with the constables, the sergeant, Thomas Bisshoppe, Nicholas Gunne and others.

Action of debt : Md. Thursday 27 Feb. [1584] Richard Sparcke of Eynsham,

miller, against Peerce Woollyn of Eynsham, butcher for 14s.; charges 11d.
Agreed.

f.227v Court held 6 March 1584 by the bailiffs with the constables, the sergeant
and certain commoners.

Court held 27 March 1584 by the bailiffs with the sergeant, Richard Jonson and
others.
Action of debt : Richard Shewell of Witney, mercer, deputy for John Sharpe of
South Leigh, husbandman, against Richard Lewis of Witney, broadweaver,
for 4s.; charges 7d. (3) Distraint for the satisfying of this action on Friday 29
May 1584.

f.228r Court held 17 April 1584 by the bailiffs with the constables, the sergeant and the
wardsmen.
Action of debt : Henry Jones against Cuthbert Margeris of Witney, tailor, for
18s.; charges 7d. Agreed.

Court held 8 May 1584 by the bailiffs with the constables, the sergeant and
divers others.
Action of debt : Hew Rodes against Mark Fathers of Witney . . .

f.228v Court held 29 May 1584 by the bailiffs with the constables, the sergeant, Mr
Thomas Yate and divers commoners.
Actions of debt : Md. Wednesday 3 June 1584 John Willyams of Burford, tailor,
against Thomas Packstafe of . . . Gloucs., fuller, fugitive, for 5s. 8d.;
charges 11d. Discharged and paid.
          Md. Thursday 18 June 1584 Roger Hearing of South Leigh,
husbandman, against Henry Buntin of Northmoor, tanner, fugitive, for
9s.; charges 11d.

f.229r Court held 26 June 1584 by the bailiffs with the constables and the sergeant.
Court held 31 July 1584 by the same.
Court held 28 Aug. 1584 by Thomas Taylor, bailiff, with the constables, the
sergeant, Giles Jones with diver commoners.
Court held 18 Sept. 1584 by Henry Jones, bailiff, with the constables, the
sergeant and others.

f.229v Court held 6 Oct. 1584 by Leonard Yate the elder and Richard Clempson,
bailiffs, with the constables, the wardsmen and other inferior officers
hereunder nominated and with Thomas Clempson, Thomas Bishoppe
and other commoners.
Constables: Leonard Yate, fuller, Robert Chapman.
Wardsmen: John Bryce, Bartholemew Cordewell, Edward Ashfeelde, William
Cannyng, Thomas Townesende.
Cardenars: William Maior, Thomas Stone.
Ale tasters: Lancelot Lawson, Nicholas Maior.
Leather searchers: William Wall, Walter Turner.
Cloth searchers and sealers: William Gunne, John Wylye.

THE WITNEY COURT BOOKS, 1584

f.230r Court held 29 Oct. 1584 by the bailiffs with the constables, the sergeant, Mr
Thomas Yate, Philip Boxe, Thomas Bishoppe and divers other
commoners.

Tipplers with their sureties: Robert Claye and for him John Sloowe and
Nicholas Colles, 2d. received; Margaret Carter, widow, and for her
Richard Humfris and Nicholas Hill, 2d.; Jerome Hannes and for him
Thomas Bisshoppe and Nicholas Hill, 2d.; Thomas Hurste and for him
John Wylye and William Tayler, weaver, 2d.; William Cordewell and for
him John Sloowe and William Tayler, 2d., Richard Lewis and for him John
Hannes and Richard Dytton, 2d., *cancelled*; Alexander Townsend and for
him Thomas Hanckes and Richard Jonson, 2d.; Edward Hannes and for
him George Maye and Robert Saley, 2d.; Thomas Shawe and for him
Thomas Bisshoppe and Humfrey Yorcke, 2d., Edmund Dodeswell and for
him William Taylor and John Wylye [*no sum stated*].

f.230v Orders: brewers and tipplers to sell indoors a quart of ale and beer for 1d. and a
thirdendell outdoors for 1d., and to send for the ale tasters to taste every of
their brewing on pain of 12d. for each default.

wardsmen to attend every three week court on pain of 6d. for default.

f.231r Actions of debt : Thomas Howse of Minster Lovell, yeoman, deputy and
attorney for the Right Worshipful Sir John Harrington, kt., against Richard
Maior of Witney, broadweaver, for 20s.; charges 7d. (3) Paid and quit.

Same against Thomas Shepparde of Witney, carpenter, for
10s. 8d.; charges 7d. (3)

Same against Richard Lewis of Witney, broadweaver, for
26s. 10d.; charges 7d. (3)

Same against Cuthbert Margeris of Witney, tailor, for
17s. 4d.; charges 7d. (3) Paid upon this action 11s. 7d.; so rests 6s. 4d.

f.231v   Same against George Warde of Witney, tinker, for 11s.;
charges 7d. (3)

against Richard Lewis of Witney, broadweaver, for
21s.; charges 7d. (3)

f.232r Court held 20 Nov. 1584 by the bailiffs with the constables, the sergeant, Philip
Boxe, Thomas Bisshoppe and divers commoners.

Court held 11 Dec. 1584 by the bailiffs with the constables, the sergeant, the
wardsmen, Thomas Bysshoppe.

Collectors for the poor: Humfrey Yorcke and Thomas Shawe elected for the
year to come.

Presented: by the ale tasters Lancelot Lawson and Nicholas Maior for not
calling to taste their brewing: Edward Goode, Nicholas Hill, Ellen
Barnarde, Andrew Byrde, Edward Dodeswell, Robert Claye, Leonard
Ranckell, William Cordewell, John Collyar, Richard Saverye.

Order: by the bailiffs. Tipplers not licenced by the Justices to sell ale or beer in
their houses are to cease to victual or sell ale in their houses unless they
purchase licence of the Queen's Majesty's Justices and put in their sureties
according to the order of the statute at or before the next court in Witney.

f.232v Court held 22 Jan. 1585 by the bailiffs with the constables, the sergeant, the wardsmen, Henry Jones, Thomas Bisshopp.

Actions of debt : John Craftes of Sutton [in Stanton Harcourt], yeoman, against Davy Horne of Witney, carpenter, for 12s.; charges 7d. (3)

Nicholas Gunne of Witney, clothier, against Thomas Packesforde of Witney, broadweaver, for 20s.; charges 7d. (3) At the court on 16 April agreed to pay 5s. on 1 Aug. next and 5s. every quarter day following or distraint to be made.

Md. Thursday . . . 1585 Richard Spencer of Woodstock, cuttler, against Robert Winter of Woodstock, saddler, for 8s.; charges 11d. (3)

f.233r Court held . . . Feb. 1585 by the bailiffs with the constables, the sergeant, Thomas Bisshoppe, Nicholas Gunne, Richard Humfrey and divers other commoners.

Actions of debt : William Lardner of Witney, broadweaver, against Gregory Meriman of Witney, broadweaver, for 12s. 9d.; charges 7d. (3)

Margery Harris of Newland, widow, against Thomas Taylor of Witney, mason, for 6s.; charges 7d. (3)

Henry Jones of Witney, clothier, against Richard Lewis of Witney, fugitive, for 26s.; charges 7d. (3)

Nicholas Gunne of Witney, clothier, against Richard Lewis, fugitive, for 12s.; charges 7d. (3)

f.233v Court held 19 March 1585 by the bailiffs with the constables, the sergeant, Henry Jones, Thomas Hanckes, Nicholas Gunne and divers commoners.

Actions of debt : Edmund Dodeswell of Witney against Clement Pemerton of Witney, sawyer, for 10s.; charges 7d. (3) 8s. paid on the action by Henry Jones.

Henry Jones of Witney, clothier, against John Cooke of Witney, sawyer, for 6s.; charges 7d. (3)

William Steevens of . . . weaver, against Robert Eeman of Witney, broadweaver, for 8s.; charges 7d. (3) Paid and quit.

Alice Croker of Witney, servant of John Pytt of Witney, cobbler, against Henry Eysham of Witney, broadweaver, for 5s. 4d.; charges 7d. (3) Paid 4s.; Eysham promised to pay the rest before 25 July next.

f.234r Court held 16 April 1585 by the bailiffs with the constables, the sergeant, the wardsmen, Peter Ranckell and divers other.

Action of debt : Richard Bryan, farmer of Cogges, against James the saddler of Witney for . . .; charges 7d. (3)

Court held 7 May 1585 by the bailiffs with the constables, the sergeant and the wardsmen.

Actions of debt : John Nickason of Eynsham against Thomas Taylor of Witney, mason for 5s. 6d.; charges 7d. (3)

Robert Grynder [John crossed out] of Witney, broadweaver,

against Giles Jones for 11s. 6d.; charges 7d. (3) Received 9s. on 30 June in part payment.

Actions of debt : Action against Giles Jones of Witney [*crossed out*].

f.234v   Same against Richard Rydley of Witney, broadweaver, for 14s.; charges 7d. (3) To pay 12d. a week; surety John Horsall.

Richard Clempson, bailiff, against Richard Maior of Witney, broadweaver, for 16s. 10d.; charges 7d. Agreed.

f.235r Court held 28 May 1585 by Richard Clempson, bailiff, with the constables, the sergeant and others.

Court held 18 June 1585 by the bailiffs with the constables, the sergeant, Henry Jones, Thomas Bisshoppe, Nicholas Gunne, Thomas Waters and others.

Actions of debt : Robert Grynder of Witney, broadweaver, against Clement Pemerton of Witney, sawyer, fugitive, for 11s.; charges 11d. (2) Received 4s. in part payment; the rest promised before 25 July next.

Thomas Ranckell of Witney, broadweaver, against Richard Shawe of Witney, butcher, for 3s. 4d.; charges 7d. (2)

William Gunne of Witney, woollen draper, against Cicely Lugg, wife of Thomas Lugg, fugitive, for 21s. 6d.; charges 11d. (2)

f.235v Court held 16 July 1585 by Richard Clempson, bailiff, with the constables, the sergeant, Thomas Bisshoppe, William Ellmore and divers other commoners.

Actions of debt : Richard Clempson against Thomas Taylor of Witney, mason, for 4s. 11d.; charges 4d. (2)

Henry Unton of Bruern, esq., by his deputies Edward Colles and Richard Saverye, against Thomas Taylor of Witney, mason, for 17s.; charges 4d. (2)

Same by the same deputies against Mark Fathers of Witney, tailor, for 8s.; charges 4d. (2)

Md. Monday 19 July 1585 Robert James of Witney, butcher, against William George of South Leigh, husbandman, for 30s.; charges 8d. Agreed and discharged.

f.236r Court held 6 Aug. 1585 by the bailiffs with the constables, the sergeant and others.

Md. grant: the bailiffs and the underwritten inhabitants at the humble suit of James Rowlande of Witney, labourer, granted their good will to Rowlande for his having a certain plot of ground towards the west end of Corndell St. alias Corne St. containing in length 27 feet and in breadth 14 feet, whereupon he has built a house and inhabits therein; which house is set at the south side of the street near the house of James Foster, now in the occupation of Edmund Haynes, labourer, on the west side and nigh the way leading to pasture close called Well Close now in the tenure of William Ellmore. Which ground and house the inhabitants of Witney, in consideration that the house was built at Rowlande's only cost and charge, have given, granted and by the present confirmed to Rowlande and his heirs to

have and to hold for ever, for 12d. a year to the chamberlain of Witney for
the use of the town to be paid always on 29 Sept. In witness whereof we
have caused this present writing to be recorded in the court book in the day
and year above written, and have hereunto subscribed our names.
[Signatures of] Francis Wenman, Leonard Yate, son of Mr Thomas Yate,
William Brygfeelde, William Ryng, Leonard Yate, John Barnabye senior,
Stephen Bryce, Thomas Boxe senior, Richard Clemson, William Elmore,
Nicholas Gunne, Roger Wheeler, Thomas Hanckes, Richard Jonson,
William Bukkingame, Thomas Taylor, Philip Boxe, Richard Humfrey,
Thomas Bisshoppe, Richard Bryce, the town clerk of Witney and recorder
of these present.[68]

f.236v   Court held 17 Sept. 1585 by the bailiffs with the constables, the sergeant, Peter
Rankell, Thomas Bisshoppe, Humfrey Yorcke with other commoners.
Action of debt ; William Cordewell of Witney, baker, against Nicholas Colles
of Witney, broadweaver, for 7s.; charges 3d. (1) At the court on 8 Oct.
time granted for payment at the request of the bailiffs and other of the
bench until 7 Jan. next, at which time Richard Jonson of Witney, clothier,
gave his word to pay 7s. 3d. to Cordewell.

f.237r   Md. grant: we, Leonard Yate and Richard Clempson, bailiffs, and all other
inhabitants whose names are underwritten before and at the last court
mentioned in this present book have granted our goodwill to Cuthbert
Margeris of Witney, a tailor, for the having of a certain plot of ground
towards the west end of Corndell St. alias Corne St. in length north and
south 30 feet and in breadth east and west 20 feet. To create and build a
messuage and house thereupon for him and the heirs of his body lawfully
begotten to inhabit and dwell therein. Which said plot is lying on the south
side of the street between the way to Well Close now in the tenure of
William Ellmore on the west side and the ground granted by us to John
Rackley, tailor, on the east part for the like purpose; adjoining towards the
north to the highway and extending itself to the way towards Well Close to
the south. Granted together with the housing to be built there, in as large
and ample a manner as we the said bailiffs [etc.] may. For 12d. a year to the
chamberlains of Witney to the use of the town, always to be paid on 29
Sept. at one entire payment.[69] Witnesses: the bailiffs and other of the chief
inhabitants. [Signatures of] Leonard Yate, Richard Clempson.

f.237v   Like grant to John Rackley, tailor, of land towards the west side of Corndell St.
[i.e. Corn St.] 30 feet in length from the highway southwards and 24 feet
east to west, lying between the ground mentioned on the other side of the
present leaf on the west and the dwelling house of John Faule, broadweaver, on the east. To create and build a messuage and house thereon on
conditions as above. Witnesses and signatures as above.[70]

[68]   Town property; see above, p.xxvii.
[69]   Town property; see above, p.xxvii.
[70]   Town property; see above, p.xxvii.

f.238v Court held 8 Oct. 1585 by Richard Humfrey and Thomas Boxe, bailiffs, with
William Sleepe, gent., then steward, Leonard Yate senior, gent., and
Richard Clempson, late bailiffs, and all other officers here under nominated
and Henry Jones, Thomas Bisshoppe, William Ellmore, Nicholas Gunne,
Richard Jonson and many other commoners.

Constables: Thomas Smarte, Thomas Collyar.

Wardsmen: William Allen, Robert Baker, Thomas Saley, George May, William
Bisshoppe.

Cardenars: Roger Clarcke, Nicholas Colles.

Ale tasters: Alexander Harris, Henry Bennett.

Leather sealers and searchers: Walter Turner, William Wall.

Cloth sealers[71] and searchers: William Gunne, John Wyly.

Md. victuallers and alesellers licenced and allowed to use victualling are
nominated at the court on 29 Oct. 1585 and all those bound as sureties for
every such victualler.

f.239r Actions of debt : John Wylye of Witney, tailor, against Thomas Packesford of
Witney, broadweaver, for 3s. 9d.; charges 3d. (3)

Robert Baker of Witney, baker, against Walter Turner of
Witney, shoemaker, for 5s.; for 5s.; charges 4d. (3)

John Bryce of Witney, broadweaver, against Richard Hodson
of Witney, broadweaver, for 10s. (2) At the court on 10 Dec. Richard
Jonson gave word to pay 10s. to Bryce within sevennight after 6 Jan. next.
Agreed. Paid.

Action of assumpsit: Robert James of Witney, butcher, against Nicholas Ifeelde
of Witney, clothier, for the debt of William George of South Leigh,
husbandman, for 20s. 8d.; charges 4d. (3)

Chamberlain's reckoning: by Nicholas Gunne, chamberlain. The town indebted
to Gunne at this court 2s.

f.239v Covenanted servant: in court Thomas Ifeelde, son of John Ifeelde late of
Witney, broadweaver deceased, being examined by the bailiffs confessed
that in consideration of seven covenant pence he bound himself to Richard
Undrell of Witney, broadweaver, for seven years from 24 June last past to
be taught the occupation of a broadweaver; to be found etc [as on p.83]; at
the end of the term 20s. wages and double apparel. Witnesses: all those
persons nominated to accompany the bailiffs at the said court.

f.240r Court held 29 Oct. 1585 by the bailiffs with the constables, the sergeant, the
wardsmen, Leonard Yate senior and Richard Clempson, late bailiffs, with
Thomas Bishoppe, Nicholas Gunne, Thomas Taylor, William Ellmore,
Humfrey Yorcke and many other commoners.

Covenanted servant: in court being then and there examined Anthony Cope,
son of Robert Cope of Ansley, Warws., minister, confessed himself bound
to Henry Jones of Witney, clothier, for eight years from 25 July last past to
be taught the occupation of a broadweaver; to be found etc. [as on p.83]; at
the end of the term 26s. 8d. wages and double apparel. Witnesses: all those
nominated to accompany the bailiffs at the said court.

---

[71]   This is the first time they are called cloth sealers as well.

f.240v Action of debt : Md. Thursday 11 Nov. 1585 Roger Wilsheere of Witney, shoemaker, against John Fyttchett of Hailey, husbandman, for 5s.; charges 8d.

Court held 19 Nov. 1585 by the bailiffs with the constables, the sergeant, Thomas Yate, Thomas Bishoppe with some others.

f.241r Court held 10 Dec. 1585 by Richard Humfrey, bailiff, with the constables, the sergeant, Mr Thomas Yate, Philip Boxe, Richard Jonson, Leonard Yate senior, Richard Clempson, Henry Jones.

Actions of debt : William Maior, deputy for Robert Foster of Ducklington, against Nicholas Hill of Witney, baker, for 5s.; charges 7d.

Nicholas Ifeelde of Witney, clothier, against William George of South Leigh, husbandman, for 20s.; for which Ifeelde gave his word to Robert James, to whom George owed so much debt and who had George in suit of law in Witney. With the cost of three several actions the whole debt was 21s. 4d.

Collectors for the poor: Thomas Hurst and John Hannes elected, nominated and chosen.

f.241v Court held 31 Dec. 1585 by the bailiffs with the constables, the sergeant and others.

Action of debt : Md. Wednesday 19 Jan. 1586 Richard Saverye of Witney, mercer, against Robert Vicaryes alias Boweare of Witney, fencer, fugitive, for 28s.; charges 8d. (1) Paid and quit.

Court held 21 Jan. 1586 by the bailiffs with the sergeant, William Bisshoppe, then wardsman, the clerk, the crier and no other person.

Actions of debt : Richard Bannyng of Witney, broadweaver, against George Warde of Witney, tinker, for 6s.; entrance 3d. (3)

Edward Goode of Witney, butcher, against Thomas Packesforde of Witney, broadweaver, for 24s.; charges 3d. (3)

f.242r   John Croftes of Sutton in Stanton Harcourt, yeoman, against William Jonson of Witney, wheelwright, for 20s.; charges 3d. (3)

Court held 11 Feb. 1586 by the bailiffs with the constables, Mr Thomas Yate, Thomas Bisshoppe and divers other commoners.

Actions of debt : Henry Jones of Witney, clothier, against Eleanor Peto of Witney for 20s. (3)

John Wilye of Witney, tailor, against Robert Yeman of Witney, broadweaver, for 3s. 3d.; charges 3d. (3) Paid 13 May.

Edward Goode of Witney, butcher, against George Lawson of Witney, shoemaker, for 7d.; charges 3d. Paid and quit.

f.242v   Md. Thursday 24 Feb. 1586 William Bowbyee of Hailey, husbandman, against Andrew Parratt of Milton, fugitive, for 10s.; charges 7d. Distraint of a sack, three bushels of vetches, appraised at 5s. Paid and quit.

Court held 4 March 1586 by the bailiffs with the constables, the sergeant and Richard Jonson.

Actions of debt : Leonard Harte of South Leigh, husbandman, against Edmund Dodeswell of Witney, broadweaver, for 15s.; charges 3d. (1) Paid and quit.

    Md. Monday 11 April 1586 John Honyburne of Witney, carpenter, against John Tommes of the Field [i.e. Leafield], husbandman, for 5s.; charges 7d.

    Md. Thursday 14 April 1586 Henry Jones of Witney, clothier, against one . . . Savage of Eynsham, glover, fugitive, for 39s. 11d.; charges . . .

f.243r Court held 15 April 1586 by the bailiffs with the constables, the sergeant, the wardsmen, Thomas Yate, Henry Jones, Leonard Yate senior, Thomas Taylor and many other commoners.

Action of assumpsit: George Lake of Bristol, joiner, against William Gunne of Witney, tailor, for the debt of Morris Lewis late of Witney, joiner, for 5s.; charges 3d. (3) Paid and quit 28 Oct. 1591.

Awarded: the case between John Croftes and William Jonson was committed into the hands of Richard Clempson and Humfrey Yorcke to be determined; agreed by both parties; award to be made and pronounced at or before Pentecost next. In witness whereof the said bailiffs and defendant have set their hands. Paid and quit. [Mark of] John Croftes. Md. at the court on 15 July 1586 Jonson paid 10s. to Richard Clemson in court for the use of Croftes.

    the action between Richard Bannyng and George Warde judged by the bailiffs to be paid; order to the sergeant for distraint on the goods of Warde to satisfy the said debt.

Action of debt : Humfrey . . . of Crawley, loader, against Thomas Taylor of Witney, mason, for 3s. 10d.; charges 3d. (3)

f.243v Court held 13 May 1586 by the bailiffs with the constables, the sergeant, Thomas Bisshoppe, John Lawrence.

Actions of debt : Robert Austen of Witney, miller, against William Gerratt of Witney, broadweaver, for 2s. 8d.; charges 7d. (3) He fled.

    Elizabeth Hedges of Milton in Shipton-under-Wychwood against Davy Horne of Witney, carpenter, for 2s. 8d.; charges 3d. (3) Paid and quit.

    Mr Jeinckyns of Minster Lovell, gent., deputy for the Rt. Worshipful Sir John Harrington, kt., against William Harrison of Witney, tailor, for 5s.; charges 3d. (3)

    Mr Francis Wenman of Caswell, gent., by his servant Robert Ballarde, against Richard Gardnar of South Leigh, husbandman, for 6s.; charges 3d. (3)

f.244r Covenanted servant: Henry Watkyns, shoemaker, son of Henry Wattkyns of Gloucester, being examined in court confessed that he put himself a covenanted servant with William Clempson of Witney, shoemaker, from 29 Sept. next for one year; in every working day of the year to make for his master four pair of childrens' shoes and three pair of big shoes having sufficient stuff delivered to him therefore; to be given sufficient and wholesome bread, meat and drink during the year aforesaid and two new shirts, two seemly shirt bands, two pairs of new shoes, a pair of stockings, a frieze jerkin, a pair of frieze venetians and a felt hat, over and besides all such working tools as he has already received of his said master and 6d. which Clempson has promised to pay to Mr Thomas Hallam, now vicar of Witney, for his offerings and other duties due for the year.

f.244v Court held 2 June 1586 by the bailiffs with the sergeant, one constable, Mr Thomas Yate, Humfrey Yorcke and certain other commoners.

Covenanted servant: Robert Baggatt, son of Humfrey Baggatt of Preston, Gloucs., shoemaker, being examined in court confessed that he put himself a covenanted servant with William Clempson of Witney, shoemaker, from the date above to 25 Dec. next; to be found sufficient and wholesome bread, meat and drink in this time and on 25 Dec. next 8s. wages.

f.245r Court held 15 July 1586 by the bailiffs with the constables, the sergeant, Richard Clempson, Roger Willsheere, John Colliar and others more.

Action of debt : Richard Hundrell of Witney, broadweaver, against Simon Peereson of Witney, broadweaver, for 3s.8d.; charges 3d. (2)

Covenanted servant: John Hill, son of John Hill late of Gillingham, Dorset, minister, by the advice and consent of Walter Barbar, minister, uncle to the said John the younger, being examined in court confessed that in consideration of nine covenant pence he bound himself to Richard Shewell of Witney, mercer and bone-lace maker, for nine years from 24 June last past to be taught the occupation of a broadweaver; to be found etc. [as on p.83; no correction clause]; at the end of the term 20s. wages and double apparel. Witnesses: all persons above nominated and Richard Bryce the writer hereof, then town clerk of Witney.

f.245v Actions of debt : Ralph Tuckatt of Witney, shepherd, against William Blewe of Witney, broadweaver, for 5s. 4d.; charges 3d. (3)

James Blewe of Witney, labourer, against William Hodson of Witney, broadweaver, for 5s. 6d.; charges 3d. (3)

Alexander Townsende of Witney, victualler, against Thomas Shawe of Witney, butcher, for 10s.; charges 3d. (3) Agreed.

Md. Thursday 11 Aug. [1586] Thomas Collyar of Witney, chandler, against William Vesye of Burford, 'pereman', for 26s.; charges 7d.

f.246r Court held 19 Aug. 1586 by the bailiffs with the sergeant, William Bisshoppe, wardsman, and certain commoners.

Court held 9 Sept. 1586 by the bailiffs with the constables, the sergeant, Thomas Yate, Roger Willshire.

f.246v Court held 7 Oct. 1586 by John Clarcke and Peter Ranckell, new elected bailiffs, with the steward and officers hereunder nominated and with Mr Thomas Yate, Henry Jones, Thomas Boxe, William Ellmore, Richard Jonson, Roger Willsheere, Thomas Hancks.

Constables: Hugh Jackson, Christopher Cotes.
Wardsmen: Richard Fisher, John Shawe, John Smythe, James Hodson, Nicholas Ifeelde junior.
Cardenars: Ralph Tackett, Richard Fickett.
Ale tasters: Alexander Harris, Henry Bennett.
Leather searchers and sealers: Nicholas Stratton, William Wall.

f.247r Actions of assumpsit: Richard Merywether of Burford, grocer, against Giles Pallmer of Witney, broadweaver, for 13s. 4d.; charges 3d. (3) Agreed.

Same against Edmund Dodeswell of Witney, victualler, for 13s. 4d; charges 3d. (3) Agreed.

Same against Thomas Heires of Witney, broadweaver, for 13s. 4d.; charges 3d. (3) Agreed.

Action of debt : George Adams of [Little] Faringdon, upholder, against Thomas Whyte of Witney, labourer, for 11s.; charges 3d. (3)

f.247v Court held 11 Nov. 1586 by Peter Ranckell, bailiff, with Henry Jones, Philip Boxe, Richard Humfrey, Nicholas Ifeelde.

Actions of debt : Robert Austen of Witney, miller, against Gregory Meryman of Witney, broadweaver, for 4s. 8d.; charges 3d. (3)

Martin Jonson of Ducklington, yeoman, against Nicholas Hill of Witney, baker, for 36s.; charges 3d. (3) Agreed at the court on 10 March 1587 James Hodson, at the request of Hill to pay 30s. at the rate of 10s. on 25 March and 29 Sept. 1587 and 25 March 1588, all which payments are granted by Hill to be paid from the rents due to be paid for the house wherein Hodson now dwells.

William Bowy of Hailey, yeoman, against Edmund Dodeswell of Witney, broadweaver, for 10s.; charges 3d. (3)

Roger Willsheere against Gregory Meryman, broadweaver, for 12s.; charges 3d. (3)

f.248r Court held 2 Dec. 1586 by Peter Ranckell, bailiff, with Henry Jones, deputy for John Clarcke the other bailiff, with the constables, the sergeant, Philip Boxe, Richard Humfrey, Thomas Bisshoppe, Thomas Taylar, John Barnabye and divers commoners.

Order: by the bailiffs with the consent of all the other magistrates above named that brewers and tipplers to sell indoors ale and beer at 1d. a quart and outdoors a thirdendell at 1d. on pain of 6d.

Collectors for the poor: Walter Dallton and Robert Baker chosen for the year following.

f.248v Court held 13 Jan. 1587 by the bailiffs with Philip Boxe, Thomas Bisshoppe, Thomas Boxe beside the constables and divers commoners.

Action of debt : John Smythe of Oxford, chandler, by his attorney William Maior, now sergeant of Witney, against Thomas Colliar of Witney, chandler, for 14s.; entrance 3d. (3)

Court held 3 Feb. 1587 by John Clarcke, bailiff, with Philip Boxe, Thomas Bisshoppe, Richard Humfreye with others.

Actions of debt : Robert Hood of North Leigh, cooper, against William Peto of Witney, fugitive, for 10s.; charges 3d. (3)

        Md. Thursday 9 day of 1586 [*sic*] John Hunt of Burford, mercer, by his servant William Taylor, against Thomas Yate of Norton Bruyn alias Brize Norton, gent., for 38s. 2d.; charges 7d. (3) John Collyar bound by his word for answering this action.

f.249r Court held 10 March 1587 by Peter Rankell, bailiff, with Henry Jones, Thomas Bisshoppe, Humfrey Yorcke and some other commoners.

Actions of debt : Robert Austen of Witney, miller, by his deputy and master, Thomas Bisshoppe, against William Cordewell of Witney, baker, for 9s. 5d.; charges 3d. (3)

        Robert Claye of Witney, blacksmith, against George Burds of Witney, wiredrawer, for 3s. 3½d.; charges 3d. (3)

        Richard Shawe of Witney, butcher, against Nicholas Colls of Witney, broadweaver, for 3s.; entrance 3d. (3)

f.249v Court held 7 April 1587 by Peter Rankell, bailiff, and Nicholas Gunne, then deputy for Bailiff Clarcke, with the constables, the sergeant and some other commoners.

Actions of debt : William Bryce of Curbridge, husbandman, against Roger Willsheere of Witney, shoemaker, for 30s.; charges 4d. (3) Paid and quit and clearly discharged for ever.

        Richard Shepparde of Clappun Leasowes in Mickleton, Gloucs., 'byson man', by his attorney Richard Bryce of Witney, keeper of this book, against Annys Lyvingstone, daughter of Christian Lyvingstone late of Witney, widow, deceased, for 11s.; charges 3d. (3) Paid and quit.

f.250r Court held 5 May 1587 by the bailiffs with Mr Thomas Yate, Henry Jones, Thomas Bisshoppe and divers commoners.

Action of debt : Md. Thursday 8 June 1587 Anthony Leache of Finstock, rough mason, against John Hill of Fawler, badger and labourer, for 5s. 8d.; charges 7d.

Court held 16 June 1587 by John Clarcke, bailiff, with Philip Boxe, Thomas Bisshoppe, Leonard Yate and divers commoners.

f.250v Court held 14 July 1587 by Peter Ranckell, bailiff, and Henry Jones, deputy for Bailiff Clarcke, with Christopher Cotes, constable, Thomas Clempson, Roger Willsheere and John Collyer with other commoners.

Actions of debt : John Colliar of Witney, vintner, [Thomas *crossed out*] against his tenant Thomas Webster of Witney, sawyer, for 15s. which is three quarters rent due on 24 June last; charges 3d. (3)

        Thomas Belson of Long Hanborough, husbandman, against Richard Shewell of Witney, mercer, for 17s. owed to Elizabeth, now wife of Thomas Belson, for service when she was his covenanted servant and for money which she lent him of her purse; charges 3d. (3)

f.251r Court held 11 Aug. 1587 by Peter Ranckell, bailiff, with the constables, the sergeant and some other commoners.

Action of debt : Christopher Buttler of Witney, husbandman, against Thomas Shepparde of Witney, carpenter, for 21d.; charges 3d. Paid and quit.

Court held . . . Sept. 1587 by Peter Ranckell, bailiff, with Henry Jones, deputy for Bailiff Clarcke, Christopher Cotes, constable, Richard Jonson.

Actions of debt : Thomas Hawkyns, now servant to Mr Richard Bryan of Cogges, against Gregory Meryman of Witney, broadweaver, for 28s.; charges 3d. (3) Paid and quit.

Same against the same for 20s.; charges 3d. (3) Paid.

f.251v Court held 6 Oct. 1587 by Thomas Bisshoppe and Roger Willsheere, bailiffs, with the constables, the wardsmen, the sergeant and Peter Ranckell, late bailiff, Henry Jones, Thomas Clempson, John Colliar and many other commoners.

Constables: Humfrey Yorcke, Walter Dallton.

Wardsmen: Andrew Hodson, Rowland Lacon, Thomas Bramley, John Pytt, Richard Puisley.

Cardenars: Ralph Tackett, Richard Fickett.

Leather sealers and searchers: Nicholas Stratton, William Wall.

Cloth searchers and sealers: William Gunne, John Wylye.

f.252r Actions of debt : Md. Monday 23 Oct. [1587] Agnes Maior, wife of Nicholas Maior of Witney, against William Broocke of Lew in Bampton, yeoman, for 15s.; charges 8d.

Md. same against John Bowell of South Leigh, husbandman, for 6s.; charges 8d.

Md. of purchase: Thursday 12 May 1597 Mr William Godard of Brize Norton, gent., bought in the borough of Witney 12 oxen whereof five of them black to follow, three brown and two black 'taggyd' of Mr William Harmane, esq., of Shipton, price £40. Item sold to Thomas Hannds of Witney by the parties aforesaid one pied cow cropped on both ears, price 20s.

f.252v Court held 27 Oct. 1587 by the bailiffs with William Sleepe, gent., steward, the constables, Henry Jones, Philip Boxe, Leonard Yate senior, John Clarcke, Richard Johnson, Thomas Taylor, Nicholas Gunne with divers other commoners.

Action of debt : Richard Saverye of Witney, mercer, against Richard Okeley of Witney, dyer, for 10s.; charges 3d. Agreed to be paid at 12d. a week.

Orders: by the bailiffs and magistrates above. Ale sellers to sell beer and ale outdoors at 1d. a thirdendell and 1d. a quart indoors, on pain of 2d.

Tipplers to attend every court and answer such matters as shall be presented for disorder in their houses.

Action of debt : Md. Tuesday 7 Nov. [1587] Thomas Shawe of Witney, butcher, against Robert Birde late of Cogges, fugitive, for 7s.; charges 8d.; pledge Andrew Byrde.

f.253r Covenanted servant: Mathew Hallton, son of Richard Hallton of Chipping Norton, shoemaker, being examined in court confessed himself bound to

William Clempson of Witney, shoemaker, for three years from 24 Aug. last
past; to be found etc. [as on p.83]; at the end of the term 30s. wages and
double apparel and also all kind of working tools belonging to a journeyman of that occupation. In witness whereof the parties have subscribed
their hands to the present writing. R.B. [Initials of Richard Brice. *No
signatures or marks*]

f.253v Court held 17 Nov. 1587 by the bailiffs with the constables and the sergeant.
Order: wardsmen to attend at every and during the time of the same courts on
pain of 6d. for default.
Actions of debt : Alexander Townesende of Witney, victualler, against John
Harris of Burford, millwright, for 8s.; charges 8d. (3)
Thomas Clempson of Witney, woollen draper, against
Edmund Dodeswell, victualler and baker, for 22d.; charges 3d. (3)
Nicholas Gunne of Witney, clothier, against Edward
Dodeswell for 36s. 8d.; charges 3d. (3) Agreed to be paid within three years
next.
Same against William Taylor of Witney, broadweaver, for
36s. 8d.; charges 3d. (3) Agreed to pay within three years next.
f.254r   Thomas Waters, fuller, now servant to Thomas Boxe of
Witney, against William Purcer of Witney, fuller, for 3s.; charges 3d. (2)
Paid and quit.

Court held 8 Dec. 1587 by the bailiffs with the constables, the sergeant and with
Mr Thomas Yate, Henry Jones, Thomas Clempson, Richard Humfrey,
Richard Jonson and many commoners.
Actions of debt : John [Good *inserted above line*] Barne of Witney, brazier,
against George Warde of Witney, tinker, for 9s. 4d.; charges 3d. (3)
Henry Tackley of Witney against Mary Shale of Witney,
widow, for 20s.; charges 3d. (3)
Same against Richard Okely the elder of Witney, dyer,
for 19s. 3d.; charges 3d. (3)
f.254v   Henry Tackley of Witney, cobbler, against Thomas Taylor
of Witney, mason, for 3s. 9d.; charges 3d. (3) Md. a kettle of Taylor's
distrained and priced by William Hunte, Alexander Townsende, Richard
Shawe and Richard Shewell at 5s., which 5s. was paid upon the kettle by
Roger Willsheere at the first court held by Mr Thomas Yate and Thomas
Walles.
Md. Thursday 12 Dec. 1587 Peter Ranckell of Witney,
clothier, against one . . . Dycks sometime of Witney, flockman, fugitive,
for 34s. ; charges 8d. Agreed.
Md. Thursday 11 Jan. 1588 William Bisshoppe of Witney
broadweaver, against Thomas Willyams of Hailey, fugitive, for 3s. 4d.;
charges 8d.
Md. same day Awdwen Willyams of Asthall Leigh,
yeoman, against Thomas Collyar of Witney, fishmonger, for 13s. 4d.;
charges 3d. (3)

f.255r Court held 12 Jan. 1588 by the bailiffs with the constables and the sergeant.

Court held 9 Feb. 1588 by Thomas Bisshoppe, bailiff, with the constables, Philip Boxe, John Clarcke.

Actions of debt : William Gunne of Witney, tailor, against Nicholas Hill of Witney, baker, for 20s. 8d.; charges 3d. (3)

Richard Puysley of Witney, broadweaver, against Gregory Maryman of Witney, broadweaver, for 13s. (3)

Edward Colles of Shipton–under–Wychwood against John Maygood of Witney, glover, for 12d.; charges 3d. (1) Paid and quit.

f.255v   Same against Henry Brygfeelde of Witney, broadweaver, for 16d.; charges 3d. (2) Paid.

Same against Thomas Taylor of Witney, mason, for 3s. 4d.; charges 4d. (3) At the court on 20 Sept. 1588 a cauldron was distrained for this action priced at 4s. 6d., whereof this action is to be discharged on 30 Sept. 1588. Debt paid at the court on 8 Nov. 1588 to Thomas Walter, bailiff.

Same against John Asshett of Witney, weaver, for 5s. 8d.; charges 3d. (3)

Same against Nicholas Colles of Witney, broadweaver, for 3s. 4d.; charges 4d. (3) Paid to Bailiff Willsheere to the use of Edward Colls 3s. 8d.

f.256r   Leonard Yate of Witney, fuller, attorney for Mrs Margaret Yate, wife of Thomas Yate of Witney, gent., against Edmund Dodeswell of Witney, broadweaver, for 20s.; charges 3d. Agreed to be paid in the first week after Low Sunday [i.e. first Sunday after Easter] next.

Same against Edmund Dodeswell for 20s.; charges 3d. Agreed to be paid upon 25 July next.

Same against the same for 20s.; charges 4d. Agreed to be paid the morrow after 23 Nov. next.

Same against the same for 20s.; charges 3d. Agreed to be paid on Whitsun Day 1589.

f.256v Court held 1 March 1588 by the bailiffs with the constables, the sergeant, Henry Jones, Philip Boxe, Thomas Taylor, Thomas Wallter and many other commoners.

Action of debt : . . . Hannes of Ramsden, husbandman, against Richard Okeley the elder of Witney, dyer, for 4s.; charges 3d. Paid at the next court.

Court held 29 March 1588 by the bailiffs with Mr Thomas Yate, Henry Jones, Peter Ranckell, Nicholas Gunne, Richard Jonson, Richard Humfrey.

Actions of debt : Elizabeth Francklen of Westhall Hill [in Fulbrook], widow, by her attorney William Maior, against John Asshatt of Witney, coverlet maker, for 20s.; charges 3d. (3)

Roger Wheeler of Witney, carpenter, against George Dey of Witney, broadweaver, for 4s. 7d.; charges 3d. (3)

f.257r Court held 19 April 1588 by the bailiffs with one constable, the sergeant and
many commoners.
Actions of debt : Alexander Townesende against Davy Horne of Witney,
carpenter, for 23d.; charges 3d. (3)
Richard Jurden of Burford against Richard Savery of Witney
for 22d.; charges 3d. (3)
Md. Monday 22 April 1588 William Hanckes of Witney,
parish clerk,[72] against . . . Boollocke of Hardwick for 10s.; charges 8d.
Md. Thursday 9 May 1588 John Haddon of Curbridge,
husbandman, against John Bowell of South Leigh, husbandman, for 10s.;
charges 8d.

f.257v Court held 17 May 1588 by Thomas Bysshoppe, bailiff, with the constables,
Mr Hallam, Mr Thomas Yate, Henry Jones, Philip Boxe, Peter Rankell,
Giles Jones, Humfrey Yorcke with the churchwardens and many
commoners.
Action of debt ; John Humfrys of Ducklington, miller, against Thomas Smarte
of Witney, broadweaver, for 4s. 4d.; charges 3d. (3) Paid and quit.

Court held 7 June 1588 by the bailiffs with the constables and the sergeant.
Agreed: by the bailiffs and other of the magistrates of Witney, namely Henry
Jones, Philip Boxe, Peter Rankell and Nicholas Gunne, that on 29 Sept.
next John Tymmes junior shall pay 5s. to Henry Tackley for the debt of
Mary Shale of Witney, widow, in part payment of 7s. which she has agreed
to pay Tackley, and to pay 2s. out of the half year's rent at 17 March next,
which shall then be due to said Mary, which two payments she has agreed
in court John Tymmes shall pay without any danger of forfeiture of his
lease. Paid 4 Oct. 5s. to Dorothy, now wife of Henry Tackley, and 2s. on
11 April 1589.
f.258r Actions of debt : Mr Richard Bryan of Cogges against Davy Horne of Witney,
carpenter, for 14s.; charges 3d. (2)
Same against John Smythe of Witney, broadweaver, for 9s.;
charges 3d. (3)
Same against Roger Rydge of Witney, broadweaver, for
11s. 6d.; charges 3d. Paid and quit. (3)
Same against Thomas Wall of Witney, broadweaver, for
3s. 4d.; charges 3d. (3)
Same against Thomas Shepparde of Witney, carpenter, for
4s.; charges 3d. (3) Paid and quit.

f.258v Court held 28 June 1588 by the bailiffs with Thomas Yate, Henry Jones,
Thomas Taylor, William Ellmore with the inferior officers and many of the
chiefest commoners.
Action of debt : Nicholas Ifeelde of Burford, broadweaver, by his deputy
Richard Bryce the writer hereof, against Roger Larden of Witney, broad-
weaver, for 8s.; charges 3d. (3) *Cancelled.*

[72] See the churchwardens' accts. for his activities. He was later their scribe.

Court held 9 Aug. 1588 by the bailiffs with the constables and the sergeant.
Action of debt : Bartholomew Harris of Ducklington, yeoman, against George
Maye of Witney, glover, for 30s.; charges 3d. (3) At the court on 11 Oct.
the action respited to be paid at the next court.

f.259r Court held 30 Aug. 1588 by the bailiffs with Peter Ranckell.

Court held 20 Sept. 1588 by the bailiffs with Mr Sleepe, John Clarcke, Thomas
Walter, with the constables, the sergeant, the wardsmen, and divers
commoners.
Action of debt ; Md. Saturday 27 Sept. 1588 William Browne of Witney, miller,
against Richard Bisshoppe of Cassington Mill, fuller, for 4s. 6d.;
charges 8d.

f.259v Court held 11 Oct. 1588 by Mr Thomas Yate and Thomas Waters with Thomas
Bisshoppe and Roger Willsheere, late bailiffs, and Henry Jones with the
constables, the sergeant and divers commoners.
Constables: John Colliar, William Bryan.
Wardsmen: Michael Sclatter, Thomas Breakespeare, John Birkett, John Bollt,
John Tymmes junior.
Cardenars: Nicholas Maior, Richard Fyckett.
Leather sealers and searchers: Nicholas Stratton, William Wall.
Cloth sealers and searchers: William Gunne, John Wylye.

f.260r Court held 8 Nov. 1588 by the bailiffs with Mr Sleepe, then steward, Mr
Leonard Yate senior with the sergeant and divers commoners.
Agreed: in settlement of the debt between William Buckinggame of Crawley
and William Cordewell of Witney. Cordewell to pay the sum of 18s. 8d.
at the following terms or to be distrained: 8s. 8d. on or before 21 Dec. next,
5s. 0d. on or before 2 Feb. next and 5s. 0d. at or before 31 May next.
Actions of debt : Humfrey . . . of Crawley, loader, against John Collesbourne
of Witney, labourer, for 2s. 6d.; charges 3d.
　　　　William Taylor of Witney, broadweaver, against James Harte
of Witney, mason, for 6s. 6d.; charges 3d.

f.260v Court held 29 Nov. [1588] by the bailiffs with Henry Jones, John Clarke,
Roger Willsheere, the inferior officers and divers commoners.
Actions of debt : Nicholas Huckwell of Witney, mason, against Edward Hannes
of Witney, shoemaker, for 9s.; charges 3d. (3)
　　　　Md. Thursday . . . Nov. [1588] last Nicholas Harte of
South Leigh. husbandman, against Richard Smyth of Ven End [i.e. Venney
End] in Hailey for 20s.; charges 8d. Distraint made of two sacks, six
bushels of barley; pledge Philip Boxe.
　　　　Robert Carter, servant to Leonard Yate of Witney, fuller,
against William Purcer of Witney, fuller, for 27s.; charges 3d. (3) Paid and
quit.
　　　　Henry Egglestone of Eynsham, yeoman, against John Smyth
of Corn St., broadweaver, for 4s. 8d.; charges 3d. (3)

f.261r Court held 20 Dec. 1588 by Mr Thomas Yate and Thomas Wallter (alias
Walters), bailiffs, with the constables, the sergeant and divers commoners.
Action of debt : Md. Saturday 21 Dec. 1588 Richard Savery of Witney against
William Brygfeelde of Cogges, fugitive, for 5s.; charges 8d. Paid and quit.

Court held 17 Jan. 1589 by the bailiffs with the constables, Philip Boxe, Thomas
Bisshoppe and divers commoners.
Agreed: between Walter Dallton and Richard Shewell that whereas Shewell
bought from Dallton the slated penthouse which stands on the street side of
Shewell's dwelling house and adjoining the house, Walter Dallton
promised to repay the 20s. received if Shewell or his heirs cannot enjoy the
penthouse at the end of his lease of the house. [Signature of] Walter
Dallton.

f.261v Court held 7 Feb. 1589 by the bailiffs with Leonard Yate senior, Thomas
Bisshoppe, John Lynley with divers other commoners.
Actions of debt : Mr Richard Bryan of Cogges against Thomas Goullde of
Witney, broadweaver, for 6s. 4d.; charges 3d. (3) Paid and quit.
         Same against Anthony Greeneway of Witney, carpenter, for
7s. 4d.; charges 3d. (3)
         Nicholas Ifeelde of Burford, broadweaver, against Roger
Larden of Witney, broadweaver, for 8s.; charges 3d. (3)
         Same against Roger Larden for 6s. 8d.; charges 3d. (2) Action
not allowed because Larden never received the loom which he took to hire
for a noble [i.e. 6s. 8d.] a year.
         Edward Tommes of Witney, yeoman, against William Maior
of Witney, broadweaver, for 10s.; charges 3d. (2) Paid and quit.

f.262r Court held 28 Feb. 1589 by the bailiffs with Philip Boxe, Thomas Bisshoppe,
Humfrey Yorcke, Peter Ranckell and certain of the commoners.
Action of debt : William Maior, attorney for William Harris of Burford,
carpenter, against Davy Horne of Witney, carpenter, for 16s. 6d.; charges
3d. (3) Paid and quit.

Court held 21 March 1589 by the bailiffs with Mr William Sleepe, then steward,
Henry Jones, Leonard Yate senior, Thomas Bisshoppe.
Constable: Rowland Lacon of Witney, haberdasher, elected and chosen instead
of John Colliar late constable of Witney until such time as new constables
shall be chosen; sworn to execute the office by William Sleepe, gent., then
steward. Which election was made by the bailiffs and the other magistrates
above nominated with the consent and agreement of the said Rowland
Lacon and divers commoners then present at this court, namely William
Hunte, John Lynlye, Leonard Yate, fuller, William Maior, John Bollte,
Michael Slatter, John Tymmes junior, Thomas Breakspeare and Richard
Bryce, recorder of this present.

f.262v Court held 11 April 1589 by the bailiffs with Mr Sleepe, steward, Rowland
Lacon, constable, John Clarke, Thomas Bysshoppe, Richard Savery with
divers commoners of the town.

Actions of debt : Henry Cockrell of Asthall, yeoman, by his deputy Richard Bryce, against John Colliar of Witney, clothmaker, for 13s. 4d.; charges 3d. (3) On 11 July discharged by Rowland Lacon.

Md. Wednesday 23 April [1589] John Taylor of Witney, sleymaker, by his deputy William Maior, now sergeant of Witney, against Walter Cowell of Fifield, Shipton-under-Wychwood, broadweaver, for 4s. 4d.; charges 8d. Paid and quit.

f.263r Court held 27 May 1589 by Mr Thomas Yate, bailiff, with the constable, the sergeant, Thomas Bisshoppe, Richard Jonson.

Actions of debt : Ferdinando Smyth of Fyfield, Berks., fuller, by his attorney William Maior, against Richard Tussell of Witney, broadweaver, for 5s.; charges 3d. (3)

Md. Saturday 7 June [1589] William Gunne of Witney, tailor, against William Brooke of Lew, husbandman, fugitive, for 22s. 10d.; charges 8d. Agreed.

f.263v Court held 13 June 1589 by Mr Thomas Yate, the only bailiff, with Henry Jones, John Clarcke, one constable and certain commoners of the town.

Action of debt : James Burde of Witney, wiredrawer, by his wife, against John Willyams of Witney, wiredrawer, for 7s.; charges 3d. Agreed in court that Williams to pay Henry Jones 6d. for the use of Burd's wife until the action discharged; first payment on Saturday 21 June.

Court held 11 July 1589 by Mr Thomas Yate, bailiff, with the constables, Philip Boxe, John Clarcke, Thomas Bisshoppe and certain commoners.

Action of debt : William Ball of Witney, broadweaver, against George Deye of Witney, broadweaver, for 8s.; charges 3d. (3) Paid and quit.

f.264r Court held 1 Aug. 1589 by Mr Thomas Yate, bailiff, with the constables, Henry Jones, Peter Ranckell, Nicholas Gunne and certain commoners.

Md. debt paid: Richard Maior of Witney, broadweaver, paid 10s. to Richard Wright of Curbridge for the use of John Owtefeelde, late servant to Maior, in part payment of 20s. which Maior received with Outefeelde at his first going to him.

Court held 22 Aug. 1589 by Mr Thomas Yate, bailiff, with the constables, the sergeant, Thomas Bisshoppe.

Actions of debt : John Ricardes of Weald, husbandman, against George Warde of Witney, tinker, for 4s. 6d.; charges 3d. (3)

William Harris of Hanborough, weaver, against Richard Maior of Witney, broadweaver, for 18s.; charges 3d. (3)

Md. Monday 8 Sept. 1589 William Slaymaker, now covenanted servant to Richard Smyth the younger of Hailey, yeoman, against John Fytchett of Hailey, husbandman, for 6s. 8d.; charges 8d. 11 Sept. paid 6s. 8d. to Richard Maior for the use of Slaymaker.

f.264v   Md. Thursday 11 Sept. 1589 Cuthbert Harrys of Abingdon, Berks., fishmonger, against William Veysye of Burford, chandler, for 35s.; charges 8d.

Court held 12 Sept. 1589 by Mr Thomas Yate, bailiff, with one constable, the sergeant, Thomas Bysshoppe.

Agreed: between William Goulde and Thomas Shepparde at the request of Mr Bailiff; Shepparde to pay 2s. by a groat [i.e. 4d.] weekly.

Action of debt : Md. Wednesday 24 Sept. 1589 John Smyth of Witney, broad-weaver, against William Browne, miller, fugitive, for 4s.; charges 8d.

f.265r Court held 3 Oct. 1589 by Mr Thomas Yate, bailiff, with Rowland Lacon, constable, the sergeant, the wardsmen and other commoners.

Action of debt ; Md. 4 Oct. [1589] Robert Fostare of Ducklington, yeoman, against Michael Egerlye for 39s. 11d.; charges 8d. A grey mare arrested for this action; pledge Nicholas Gunne.

Md. of purchase: Monday 31 Jan. 1596 Richard Knowlles of Lew, Bampton, bought three ewes and one teg, two of them spade marked on the further ear and the horn there cropped on the near ear and the further, the teg two notches on the further ear marked with a J and an S on the near side, of Symon Hybbard of Witney, servant to William Dallbe, butcher, priced 16s. 6d. [73]

f.266r Md. a possession: taken 7 Oct. 1589 by Thomas Yate, gent., bailiff, of Nicholas Hill of Witney, baker, of one messuage or tenement wherein Hill dwelled and of one other little house to the same adjoining and belonging then in the tenure of Edward Ayshefeelde, glover, with all appurtenances, being on the east side of the High St. between the tenement late of one Richard Adeane, now in the tenure of Giles Pallmer, broadweaver, on the south part and the tenement late of one Leonard Yate on the north part; to the only use of one Richard King, citizen and grocer of London, and of his heirs and assigns. Possession delivered according to the form of a deed hereof made by Nicholas Hill under his hand and seal and delivered to King after the ancient custom of the said town. In the sight and presence of Rowland Lacon, constable, William Maior, the sergeant, John Bollte, wardsman of that ward, Edward Byrde of Cogges, Robert Slaughter, citizen of London, and Richard Bryce, the recorder of this possession. R.B.

f.266v Court held 10 Oct. 1589 by Philip Boxe, bailiff, with the constables, the wardsmen, the sergeant and other inferior officers hereunder nominated, and with Mr Thomas Yate, late the only bailiff, Mr Sleepe, then steward, Thomas Bisshoppe, Nicholas Gunne, Richard Humfrey, and many commoners of the said town.

Constables: John Lynley, Rowland Lacon.

Wardsmen: Christopher Foorde, Edward Cakebread, John Horsall, William Dawbye, Philip Boxe, weaver.

Cardenars: Nicholas Maior, Richard Fickett.

Leather sealers and searchers: Nicholas Stratton, William Wall.

Cloth sealers and searchers: William Gunne, John Wylye.

Ale and bread tasters: William Purcer, Nicholas Maior.

---

[73]   This entry was evidently added later in a different hand and at the bottom of the page.

f.267r Court held 31 Oct. 1589 by the bailiffs with the constables, Mr Thomas Yate,
Mr William Sleepe, John Clarcke and Thomas Taylor, then churchwardens
of Witney, and many commoners.

Action of debt : William Gunne of Witney, tailor, against Thomas Smarte of
Witney, broadweaver, for 39s. 11d. Agreed to be paid by Mr John Clarcke.

Md. George Warde of Witney, tinker, promised and agreed in court to deliver
on 23 Nov. next to John Rickardes of Weald, husbandman, and to his
assigns the new brass pot which shall weigh at least 18lb for a pot which
Warde a long time past received of Rickardes. Or else to pay 4s. 6d.

f.267v Court held 21 Dec. 1589 by Richard Jonson, bailiff, with the constables, the
sergeant and very few commoners.

Actions of debt : John Stampe of Witney, gent., against Edward Etkyns of
Witney, broadweaver, for 3s.; charges 4d. (3) To be paid by Hew Rodes by
6d. a cloth.

    Same against John Ryder of Witney, fuller, for 4s. 8d. (2)
Paid and quit.

    Richard Ayshecombe of Curbridge, gent., against John
Willyams of Witney, wiredrawer, for 8s. 3d. (3)

    Md. Thursday 8 Jan. 1590 Robert Foster of Ducklington,
yeoman, against John Bowell of Eynsham, husbandman, for 39s. 10d.

f.268r Court held 9 Jan. 1590 by the bailiffs with the constables and the sergeant.

 Court held 6 Feb. 1590 by Richard Jonson, bailiff, with the constables and the
sergeant.

Actions of debt : John Stampe of Witney, gent., against Gregory Meryman of
Witney, broadweaver, for 18s. 8d.; charges 4d. (3) Agreed at the court on
10 April to be paid at the next court. Paid 18s. by the hands of William
Brygfeelde at the court on 29 May.

    Nicholas Huckwell of Witney, mason, against James Harte of
Witney, rough layer, for 4s. 8d.; charges 4d. (3)

f.268v Court held 27 Feb. 1590 by Philip Boxe, bailiff, with the constables, the
sergeant, some of the wardsmen and other commoners.

Actions of debt : Richard Ayshecombe of Curbridge, gent., against Gregory
Meryman of Witney, broadweaver, for 12s.; charges 4d. (3) Paid 12s. at the
court on 29 May by the hands of William Brygfeelde.

    Same against Henry Eysham of Witney, broadweaver, for
12s.; charges 4d. (3) Paid 12s. at the court on 29 May by the hands of
William Brygfeelde.

    Same against Henry Eysham of Witney, broadweaver, for 9s.;
charges 4d. (3) At the court on 10 April Bailiff Jonson gave his word to see
this action discharged as follows, viz. 4s. 8d. on 24 June and the same on 29
Sept.

    Same against Richard Burnell of Witney, broadweaver, for
6s.; charges 3d. (3) Paid and quit.

    Same against William Blewe of Witney, broadweaver, for 6s.;
charges 4d. (3)

Same against John Rackley of Witney, tailor, for 8s. 8d.;
charges 4d. (3) Paid at the court on 8 May 12d.

Same against Thomas Marle of Witney, tailor, for 6s.; charges
3d. (3)

f.269r   Same against William Purcer of Witney, fuller, for 7s.;
charges 4d. (3)

Same against Henry Wryght of Witney, broadweaver, for 5s.;
charges 4d. (3) Henry Jones gave his word to see this paid.

Same against Thomas Raynolles of Witney, warper, for
3s. 4d.; charges 3d. (2) Paid at the next court 3s. 4d.

Davy Horne of Witney, carpenter, against Thomas Webster
of Witney, sawyer, for 8s.; charges 4d. (3)

John Sharpe of South Leigh against Richard Shewell of
Witney, victualler, for 17s.; charges 3s. (3) Paid.

f.269v Court held 20 March 1590 by Philip Boxe, bailiff, with Mr Thomas Yate and
with . . .

Action of debt : Christopher Cotes of Witney, broadweaver, against Thomas
Burnell of Witney, broadweaver, for 4s. 3d.; charges 3d. (3)

Action of assumpsit: Henry Egastone of Eynsham, yeoman, against William
Maior, broadweaver, now sergeant of the Mace in Witney, for 4s. 8d.;
charges 3d. (2) Discharged at the court on 19 June by payment to Bailiff
Jonson.

f.270r Court held 10 April 1590 by the bailiffs with the constables, the sergeant, Mr
John Clarcke and divers commoners.

Action of debt : Thomas Penrys of Burford, broadweaver, by his attorney
William Maior, now sergeant of Witney, against Thomas Greene of
Witney, broadweaver, for 23s. 5d.; charges of arrest, entrance, drawing of
the action, attorney's fees 10d. (3) Greene and Richard Cooke the creditor
put the action into the hands of the bailiffs to end the matter at the court on
10 July and were contented to stand to their judgement concerning the
whole matter. [Signature of] Thomas Greene: [mark of] Richard Cooke.

Md. Mr Bailiff Jonson gave word to Mr Ayshecombe that he would see him
paid 11s. on 24 June next for the debt of Nicholas Colls.

Action of debt : Md. 31 May 1590 Thomas Gryme, late of Broad Rissington
[i.e. Great Rissington] Gloucs., and now of Bledington, Gloucs., butcher,
against Thomas Haynes of Burford, butcher, for 20s.; charges 8d. A sorrel
coloured mare distrained but proved to be another man's so the action was
lost.

f.270v Court held 8 May 1590 by the bailiffs with the constables, the sergeant and
Henry Jones.

Court held 29 May 1590 by the bailiffs with the constables and Mr John
Clarcke.

Action of debt : John Steevens alias Chawney of Witney, broadweaver, against
John Moore of Witney, broadweaver, for 4s.; charges 4d. (1) At the court

on 19 June Bailiff Jonson gave word to pay in the week before 24 Aug. next.

Action of debt : John Wyly against Esau Warren of Witney, tailor, for 2s. 10d.; charges 4d. (3) Agreed.

Court held 19 June 1590 by Richard Jonson, bailiff, and Henry Jones, then deputy for Bailiff Boxe, with John Clate [i.e. Clarke] clothier, Richard Clempson and divers commoners.

Action of debt : Thomas Fowler of Witney, husbandman, against Gregory Meryman for 5s. 1d.; charges 4d. Paid and quit.

f.271r Court held 10 July 1590 by the bailiffs with the constables and divers commoners.

Court held 11 Sept. 1590 by the bailiffs with the constables, Mr Thomas Yate, Mr Stephen Bryce, Mr Henry Jones, John Clarcke, Thomas Taylor, Richard Humfrey.

Actions of debt : Richard Blake of Shipton-under-Wychwood, by his attorney Richard Bryce, keeper of this book, against John Willyams of Witney, wiredrawer, for 8s. 6d.; charges 4d. (3)

    Same by the same attorney against Henry Lewis of Witney, broadweaver, for 6s.; charges 4d. (3)

    Thomas Bennett of Burford, 'seevegar', against Thomas Pebworthe of Witney, sawyer, for 3s. 8d.; charges 4d. (3)

    Damyan Ryvar of Witney, carpenter, against Thomas Pebworth of Witney, sawyer, for 4s. 4d.; charges 4d. (3)

f.271v   Md. Thursday 1 Oct. 1590 William Dawbye of Witney, butcher, against William Byrde of Bampton. butcher, for 2s. 6d.; charges 8d.

f.272r Md. a possession: taken 7 Oct. 1590 by the bailiffs of Thomas Boxe of Witney, yeoman, of a capital messuage and tenement wherein Boxe dwells with all appurtenances, lying on the east side of Bridge St. next between the water at the bridge there called Wynryshe [i.e. Windrush] water on the north side and the ground of Richard Humfrey, dyer, on the south side, and extending itself to the water aforesaid towards the east, late the lands of Walter Harecourte, esq.; to the use of Crescent Warner of Witney, broad weaver, and his heirs. Delivered to him in the sight and presence of Robert Baker, then constable, William Maior, sergeant, William Meryman wardsman of that ward, Richard Maior, wardsman of the East Ward, Henry Rankell and Richard Bryce, the writer of this record.

f.272v Court held 9 Oct. 1590 by Thomas Taylor and Nicholas Gunne, bailiffs, with the constables and other inferior officers hereunder nominated.

Constables: William Clempson, Robert Baker.

Wardsmen: Richard Shewell, Robert Cakebread, William Meriman, Richard Maior, John Bisshoppe.

Cardenars: Thomas Stone, William Cordewell.

Leather sealers and searchers: Nicholas Stratton, William Wall.

Ale tasters: William Purcer, Nicholas Maior.

Received by John Clarcke, one of the churchwardens of Witney, from Richard Fyckett for one whole year's rent of the house which he holds of the town, due 29 Sept. last, 6s. 8d.

f.273r A true copy verbatim of the declaration and confession of William Ellmar of Witney, made to Francis Serle, now steward of the manor of Witney, concerning the house wherein Joane Gyles of Witney now dwells. Recorded in this court book at the earnest suit and entreaty of the same Joane Gyles, made to the bailiffs of Witney and other the chief magistrates of Witney, whose names are hereunto subscribed, at the court last before mentioned in this book and hereafter immediately followeth. Viz. Md. 5 Oct. 1590 one William Aylmer of Witney, tailor, being required by Francis Serle, gent., then steward of the manor of Witney, to speak and declare his knowledge concerning the last will and testament of one William Giles late of Witney, deceased, says as followeth. First he says, being with the aforesaid William Giles in his sickness, Giles then said to Aylmer that his substance was very simple and that for making of any will in writing or for giving any thing by such means was not his purpose. But he had a little house and a backside which he held freely he would give unto his daughter Elizabeth Giles and so after her decease to remain unto her heirs. And further he gave unto his son John Giles 4s. All which Giles did utter and deliver in speech unto one Walter Jones, now deceased, as the aforesaid William Aylmer did affirm. And also one Thomas Hanckes and Henry Jones did affirm that the aforesaid Walter Jones uttered the speeches before rehearsed in the presence of us: [signatures of] Thomas Taylor, Thomas Yate, Nicholas Gunne, Henry Jones; [mark of] Philip Boxe[74]

f.274r Court held 30 Oct. 1590 by the bailiffs with Mr Thomas Yate, Mr Henry Jones, Philip Boxe, John Clarcke, John Lawrence, Roger Willsheere with the constables, the sergeant and divers commoners.

Actions of debt : William Gunne of Witney, tailor, against Thomas Juyce of Witney, sawyer, for 20s.; charges 4d. (3) Agreed at the court on 4 Feb. 1591 to be paid S... next 12d. and 6d. every Sunday after.

Md. Friday 11 Dec. [1590] Elizabeth Meryman, now servant to Edward Kyng of Witney, broadweaver, against Thomas German of Witney, labourer, fugitive, for 5s. 3d. wages; charges 4d. Lost by conveying away his goods by night.

f.274v Md. a possession: taken Thursday 5 Nov. 1590 by Peter Ranckell of Witney, clothier, attorney of Walter Harecourte of Stanton Harcourt, esq., of a messuage or tenement wherein one Arthur Brown late dwelled, and wherein one Awdwyn Williams now dwells, with a yard and garden, one orchard and a close of ground adjoining, being in Witney on the west side of the street there beneath the bridge extending to a tenement of Philip Boxe, now in the tenure of William Bryan, on the south part and to a tenement of

[74] A nuncupative will, i.e. one delivered orally, and indeed some thirty years before this entry: Jones died in 1560. See above, p.lxv.

James Foster, now in the tenure of Henry Tackley, on the north, abutting on Hailey mead on the west and the said street on the east. Possession delivered after to Nicholas Gunne, bailiff, for the use of the said Awdwyn Williams and of his heirs for ever according to a certain deed made by Harcourte to Willyams on 6 July 1589, and in the sight and presence of the constables, William Maior, sergeant, Robert Cakebread, wardsman and me, Richard Bryce, the recorder of this possession with divers children. Witnesses also: Christopher Geffrey, blacksmith, Robert Geffrey, William Geffrey and John Geffrey, sons of the said Christopher, Richard Lawrence, Nicholas Peereson.

f.275v Court held 20 Nov. 1590 by the bailiffs with Mr Henry Jones, John Clarcke with one constable and certain commoners.

Court held 18 Dec. 1590 by Nicholas Gunne, bailiff, with Philip Boxe, John Clarcke, Richard Jonson, Robert Baker, constable, with certain commoners.
Collectors for the poor: Christopher Foorde and Richard Fyssher of Witney, broadweavers, elected and nominated by the bailiffs and other magistrates above named for the year to come.
Actions of debt : Md. 17 Dec. 1590 Edmund Surell of Burford, haberdasher, against John Greene of Holly Court, North Leigh, and his wife for 10s.; charges 8d. Paid and quit.
      Margery Saley of Witney, widow, against Moses Muckwell alias Muckell of Witney, fuller, for 20s.; charges 4d. (3)

f.276r Court held . . . Jan. 1591 by the bailiffs with the constables, the sergeant, Mr Henry Jones and certain commoners.
Actions of debt : John Towley now servant to Mr Stephen Bryce of Witney Farm against Richard Harris of Witney, wheeler, for 3s. 4d.; charges 4d. Paid and quit.
      Henry Bennett of Witney, 'seevegar', against William Munmowth, 'seevegar', for 9s. 4d.
Order: tipplers to sell ale and beer indoors and outdoors at 1d. an ale quart of lawful measure on pain of 12d. for default.

f.276v Court held 29 Jan. 1591 by the bailiffs with the constables, Mr Thomas Yate, Mr Henry Jones, Philip Boxe, John Clarcke, Richard Clempson.
Actions of debt : Henry Jones of Witney, clothier, against Jerome Westley of Witney, saddler, for 4s.; charges 4d. (2) Paid and quit.
      Richard Clempson of Witney, woollen draper, against George Maye of Witney, glover, for 22s. 4d.; charges 4d. (3)
      Robert Baker of Witney, baker, against the same for 10s.; charges 4d. (3)
      Henry Lardner of Ramsden, lime burner, against the same for 4s. 6d.; charges 4d. (3)
      John Sharpe of South Leigh, husbandman, against Richard Shewell of Witney, victualler, for 20s.; charges 4d. (3)

f.277r Court held 18 Feb. 1591 by the bailiffs with Mr Henry Jones, John Clarcke,
Richard Clempson and divers commoners.
Actions of debt : Thomas Brygfeelde of Newland, husbandman, against
Richard Lewis of Witney, broadweaver, for 4s.; charges 4d. (3)
    Same against John Rider of Witney, fuller, for 3s. 4d.;
charges 4d. (3) Agreed to be wrought out.
    Same against Thomas Secoll of Witney, broadweaver, for . . .
Cancelled.
    William Gunne of Witney against Henry Brooke of Witney,
broadweaver, for 12s. 10d.; charges 4d. (3) Agreed to be paid upon 25 April
next.
    Henry Lardner of Ramsden, husbandman, against Richard
Okeley the elder of Witney for 31s. 8d.; charges 4d. (3)
f.277v   Richard Clempson of Witney, woollen draper, against Michael
Sclatter of Witney, broadweaver, for 34s. 3d.; charges 4d. (3)
    Md. 11 March 1591 Roger Cooper of Burford, miller, against
Abraham Hill of Bampton, millwright, for 4s. 11d.; charges 8d., total
5s. 6d. Paid 7 May 1591. (3)

Court held 26 March 1591 by the bailiffs with the constables and the sergeant.
Actions of debt : Roger Willsheere of Witney, yeoman, against John Smyth of
Witney, broadweaver, for 4s.; charges 4d. Paid. (3)
    Henry Bettes of Bampton, shoemaker, by suretyship against
John Willis of Witney for 9s. 2d.; charges of suit in the hundred court of
Bampton[75] and charges of entrance and for arresting and distraining a pan
for the said debt and for drawing this action 8d. (1) Agreed.

f.278r Court held 16 April 1591 by the bailiffs with Mr Henry Jones, John Clarcke,
Richard Jonson, Roger Willsheere, Richard Clempson with divers
commoners.

Court held 7 May 1591 by Thomas Taylor, bailiff, with Philip Boxe, John
Clarcke besides the constable, the sergeant and some others.
Action of debt : Thomas Newman of Chipping Norton, by his deputy Richard
Fickett, against Richard Sutton of Curbridge for . . . *Cancelled.*

Court held 28 May 1591 by the bailiffs with the constables, Mr Henry Jones,
Peter Ranckell, with the wardsmen and many commoners.
Actions of debt : Mr Richard Pore of Wilcote, by his deputy Nicholas Marriatt,
against Roger Larden of Witney, broadweaver, for 5s.; charges 4d. (3)
    Md. Thursday 10 June 1591 Edward Arnollde of Standlake,
shoemaker, against William Geffes of Beard Mill in Stanton Harcourt,
miller, for 5s.; charges 8d. A grey nag arrested for the debt. Richard
Shewell surety for answering the said debt. Paid 29 July 1591.

[75] See above, p.xxxvi.

f.278v Actions of debt : Md. Thursday 17 June 1591 John Boys of Finstock, sieve-maker, attorney for John Carter of Swinbrook, husbandman, against William Rydsdale of Cornbury Mill for 38s.; charges 8d. *Cancelled*.
      Md. same day, the same against William Rydsdale of Cornbury Park, miller, for 38s.; charges 8d. Md. pledge Mr Thomas Preedye; part paid at the next court, 4s., which will be due upon 24 June next by agreement.

  Court held 18 June 1591 by the bailiffs with Mr Henry Jones, John Clarcke, the constable, the sergeant and divers commoners.
  Action of debt : Robert Carles alias Dawes of North Leigh, yeoman, against Edward Harris of Witney, wheeler, for 30s.; charges 4d.

  Court held 9 July 1591 by the bailiffs with the constables, the sergeant and some commoners.
  Action of debt : Thomas Androse of Newland, broadweaver, against Michael Sclatter of Witney, broadweaver, for 9s. 10d.; charges 4d. (3) Agreed before Bailiff Gunne at the next court to be discharged within five weeks or to be distrained for the same.

f.279r Court held 30 July 1591 by Nicholas Gunne, bailiff, with the constables, the sergeant, Henry Jones with other commoners.
  Actions of debt : Mr Richard Ashecombe, by his servant John Bryce, against Nicholas Colles of Witney, broadweaver, for 4s. 4d.; charges 4d.
      Richard Blake of Wadley, Berks., yeoman, against Giles Gollding of Witney, broadweaver, for 3s. 6d.; charges 4d. Paid
      Same against Nicholas Colles of Witney, broadweaver, for 20s.; charges 4d. (3)
      Md. Thursday 5 Aug. 1591 Joan Smarte, wife of Robert Smarte of Stanton Harcourt, carpenter, against William Monmowth, late of Witney, 'seevegar', for 17s. Which is for nursing and keeping of his child; charges 4d.

f.279v Court held 27 Aug. 1591 by Thomas Taylor, bailiff.
  Actions of debt : Mrs Margaret Yate of Witney, widow, against George Maye of Witney, glover, for 8s., charges 4d. (3) Paid.
      Same against Davy Horne of Witney, carpenter, for 7s. 6d.; charges 4d. Paid and quit.
      Md. Wednesday 1 Sept. 1591 James Foster of Ducklington, yeoman, against Thomas Egerley of Hardwick, husbandman, for 33s. 4d.; charges 8d.
      Same against the same for 30s.; charges 8d.

f.280r Court held 24 Sept. 1591 by the bailiffs with the constables and Henry Jones, Philip Boxe, Richard Jonson, Thomas Clempson with divers commoners.
  Actions of debt : Edward Sleepe of South Leigh, yeoman, against John Rider of Witney, tucker, for 11s.; charges 4d. (3) Paid and quit.
      Mr Henry Jones of Witney, clothier, against Richard Shawe of

Witney, butcher, for 25s.; charges 4d. (3) Received in part payment of this action at the court on 29 Oct., 20s.

f.280v Court held 8 Oct. 1591 by Henry Jones and Wallter Dallton, bailiffs, with all the others under nominated and with Mr John Clarcke, Leonard Yate senior, Nicholas Gunne, Richard Humfreye, William Brygfeelde, Thomas Taylor with many other of the commoners of the town.

Constables: Richard Ranckell, Roger Clarcke.

Wardsmen: Thomas Hannes, Richard Harris, Richard Okeley, Nicholas Stratton, William Harrys.

Cardenars: Nicholas Maior, Thomas Stone.

Leather sealers and searchers: Nicholas Stratton, William Wall.

Ale tasters: William Harrisson, John Ryder.

Clother sealers and searchers: William Gunne, John Wylye.

Agreed: between William Jones of Witney, bedder, and Richard Bannying, for recompense of the money for which he was troubled by the said Jones, to repay 20s., 10s. at the next court day, 10s. on 29 Sept. next and so to be clearly discharged.

f.281r Court held 29 Oct. 1591 by the bailiffs with Philip Boxe, John Clarcke, Richard Clempson, the constables, the sergeant and others.

Md. a possession: taken 27 Nov. 1591 by Henry Jones, bailiff, of Leonard Yate of Witney, tucker, of a messuage and tenement wherein Thomas Shawe, butcher, now dwells with a court, garden and half acre of ground on the west side of the same tenement adjoining, being on the west side of Witney between the tenement of Francis Wenman, gent., now in the tenure of Henry Jones, clothier, on the south part and the tenement of Roger Willsheere and of Marett his wife now in the tenure of John Humfris alias Maior, shoemaker, on the north part and extending itself from the street aforesaid on the east to a ground called Crofts to the west. To the use of Thomas Marten the younger, son of Thomas Marten the elder of Witney, yeoman and barber, and his heirs. And likewise by the said bailiffs to the said Thomas Marten the elder to the use of his said son, according to the form of a deed poll hereof made under the hand and seal of the above named Leonard Yate, dated the day of this possession, and after the ancient custom of the borough of Witney, in the sight and presence of the bailiffs above nominated and of Richard Ranckell, constable, William Maior, sergeant, Nicholas Gunne, Richard Jonson, and of me Richard Bryce, recorder of this possession and writer of the said deed, with some other of the said town of Witney as upon the backside of the deed poll more plainly it appears.

f.281v Court held 3 Dec. 1591 by the bailiffs with the constables, the sergeant and John Clarke, Nicholas Gunne, Thomas Taylor, with others more.

Actions of debt : Robert Baker of Witney, baker, and John Dey of Witney, broadweaver, against . . . Mabbatt, late of Witney, fugitive, for 3s. 10d.; charges 8d.

William Parsons of Witney, broadweaver, against John

Smythe, broadweaver, now servant to Peter Ranckell, for 7s.; charges 4d. Agreed and discharged.

Court held 24 Dec. 1591 by the bailiffs with the constables, the sergeant, John Clarcke and other commoners.
Action of debt : Leonard Morwen of North Leigh, maltman, against Nicholas Colles of Witney, broadweaver, for 2s. 4d.; charges 4d. (3)
Collectors for the poor: Robert Cakebred and Richard Shewell chosen for the year following.

f.282r Court held 14 Jan. 1592 by the bailiffs with the constables, Philip Boxe, John Clarcke and certain commoners.
Action of debt : Md. Thursday 20 Jan. [1592] John Snape junior of Standlake, gent., against Edward Arnolde of Standlake, shoemaker, for 20s.; charges 8d. Paid and quit on the day of entrance.

Court held 4 [sic] Jan. 1592 by Henry Jones, bailiff, Richard Ranckell, constable, John Clarke, the sergeant and others.

f.282v Court held 3 March 1592 by the bailiffs with Philip Boxe, John Clarke.
Action of assumpsit: Nicholas Launce of Eynsham, tanner, against Thomas Smythe of Witney, currier, for 8s.; charges 4d. (3) Agreed.
Actions of debt : Roger Willsheere of Ducklington against Widow Cordewell of Witney for 9s. 6d.; charges 4d. (3)
        Same against Michael Sclatter for 13s. 4d.; charges 4d. (3) Agreed.
        Same against John Collsburne of Witney, labourer, for 13s. 7d.; charges 4d. (3) Agreed.
        Thomas Shawe of Witney, butcher, against his brother Richard Shawe of Witney, butcher, for 36s. 8d.; charges 4d. (3)
        Md. Thursday 13 April [1592]Thomas Taylor of Witney, tanner, against Thomas Pryckyvaunce of Burford, shoemaker, for 26s.; charges 8d. Paid and quit.

f.283r Court held 24 March 1592 by the bailiffs with Nicholas Gunne.
Order: wardsmen to attend every court and make presentments according to their charge, on pain of 6d. apiece.

Court held 14 April 1592 by the bailiffs with Constable Clarcke, the sergeant, John Clarcke, Thomas Taylor, Richard Clempson and divers commoners.
Leonard Huck [sic].
Action of debt : Md. Thursday 4 May 1592 William Okeley of Witney, broadweaver, against Thomas Egerley of Hardwick, husbandman, for 25s.; charges 4d.

f.283v Court held 5 May 1592 by Walter Dallton with John Clarcke, then deputy for Mr Bailiff Jones, with the constables, Nicholas Gunne, Richard Humfris and divers others.

Action of detinue: Richard Shewell of Witney, victualler, against Richard Bannyng of Witney, labourer, and against John Willyams of Witney, wiredrawer, for two iron wedges of the value of 2s.; charges 4d. (3)

Action of debt : Bartholomew Harris of Ducklington, yeoman, against Thomas Shawe of Witney, butcher, for 20s.; charges 4d. (3) Agreed.

Court held 26 May 1592 by the bailiffs with John Clarcke.
Actions of debt : Edward Sleepe of Cogges, yeoman, against Anthony Greenewaye of Witney, carpenter, for 3s. 8d.; charges 4d. At the next court Greenewaye promised to pay 20d. at the next following court and 20d. three weeks after. Agreed.

        Md. Monday 5 June 1592 Anthony Wattson of Witney, clerk, against Jane Allen of Witney, wife of George Allen late of Witney, broadweaver, fugitive, for 3s. 6d.; charges 8d.

f.284r Court held 16 June 1592 by Henry Jones, bailiff, with the constables, Philip Boxe, John Clarcke, Nicholas Gunne.
Amerced: Leonard Goode of Witney, baker, 3s. 4d. because his bread lacked two ounces weight in the halfpenny loaf.

Court held 14 June 1592 by Henry Jones, bailiff, with Richard Ranckell, one of the constables and certain commoners of the town.

f.284v Court held 18 Aug. 1592 by the bailiffs with the constables, the sergeant and others.
Actions of debt : Thomas Weste of Witney, mercer, against Nicholas Maior of Witney for 3s. 1d.; charges 4d. (2) Paid and quit.
        Same against Gregory Meryman, broadweaver, for 8s. 6d.; charges 4d. (2) Paid and quit.
        Same against Robert Horne of Witney, pearmonger, for 3s. 4d.; charges 4d. (3)
        Same against Mathew Norgrove of Witney, broadweaver, for 2s.; charges 4d. (3)

f.285r Court held 8 Sept. 1592 by Henry Jones, bailiff, with Mr Stephen Bryce, Mr Cullyn, Mr Leonard Yate, the constables, Nicholas Gunne.
Actions of debt : John Sea of Witney, joiner, against Roger Rackley of Witney, glover, for 6s. 8d.; charges 4d. Paid.
        Md. Thursday 12 Sept. [1592] Elizabeth Buttler of Longworth, Berks., now servant to Thomas Hobbs of Longworth, against Davy Poell of Barley Park [in Ducklington], yeoman, for 7s.; charges 8d.
        Md. Thursday 28 Sept. [1592] Ralph Cooke of Asthall, husbandman, against William Hitcheman of Asthall, husbandman, for 13s. 4d. And for not fallowing five acres of land for Cooke, 5s.; charges 8d.

f.285v Court held 6 Oct. 1592 by Leonard Yate, clothier, and Richard Clempson, woollen draper, bailiffs, with the officers hereunder nominated and Leonard Yate senior, John Clarcke, Nicholas Gunne, Thomas Clempson and many commoners of the town.

Constables: Henry Ranckle, Robert James.

Wardsmen: Richard Hodson, Charles Aliphexe, William Purcer, John Willyams, Ellis Hannes.

Cardenars: Thomas Lyvingstone, Nicholas Maior.

Ale tasters: John Smyth, John Moore.

Leather sealers: Nicholas Stratten, William Wall.

Cloth searchers: John Collyar, John Bollte.

f.286r Tipplers allowed to sell beer and ale in their houses, according to the tenor of their licences and sureties brought: Edward Hannes, Alexander Townsende, Robert Claye, John Thomas, licenced by Sir Edward Unton, kt., Edmund Bray and Lawrence Tanfeelde esq., 4 March 1587; Robert Tayler alias Cakebred by Bray and Samuel Coxe, 4 March 1591; Richard Dytton, Margaret Carter, widow, by Bray and Tanfeelde, 8 Feb. 1591; Richard Fissher the like 4 March 1587. Henry Harper by Bray 17 Oct. 1588. William Dawby given to the next court to bring in his licence.

f.286v Action of debt : Md. Saturday 7 Oct. [1592] Leonard Yate of Witney, clothier, against Andrew Williams of Witney, yeoman, for 4s. 4d.; charges 8d.; pledge Thomas Boxe. (2) Paid and quit.

Orders: tipplers and alesellers to sell beer and ale indoors a full quart for 1d. and a thirdendell for 1d. outdoors on pain of 6d.

wardsmen to attend every court and make their presentments according to their charge, on pain of 6d.

four of the freeholders of Witney borough to attend the three week court being warned thereto by the wardsmen or bellman, on pain of 12d., one half to the use of the bailiffs and the other to the poor.

f.287r Court held 3 Nov. 1592 by the bailiffs with Mr William Sleepe, Henry Jones, Thomas Taylor, Richard Humfreys, Thomas Clempson, Walter Dallton, Richard Boxe with the Justices' Officers.

Actions of debt : Robert Saverye, servant to the Rt. Worshipful Sir Henry Unton, kt., against Henry Lewis of Witney, broadweaver, for 3s.; charges 4d. (1) Paid 18d. by Henry Jones at the court on 15 Dec. to Richard Clempson for the use of Saverye.

Same against Michael Sclatter of Witney, broadweaver, for 3s.; charges 4d. (2)

Same against Thomas Smarte of Witney, broadweaver, for 3s. 4d. (2)

Thomas Smythe of Eynsham, tanner, against Michael Slatter of Witney for 2s.; charges 4d. (3)

f.287v Court held 24 Nov. 1592 by the bailiffs with Richard Jonson.

Action of debt : Martin Craftes of North Leigh, husbandman, against Henry Wryght of Witney, broadweaver, for 5s. 6d.; charges 4d. (3) Paid 4s. at the court on 16 Feb. to Leonard Yate, bailiff.

Court held 15 Dec. 1592 by the bailiffs with the constables, the sergeant, Mr Jones, the wardsmen and certain commoners.

Collectors for the poor: William Bisshoppe and Robert Chapman chosen for the year following.

Action of debt : Md. Wednesday 3 Jan. 1593 Thomas Turtlle of Witney, tailor, against Anthony Richardson of Oxford, chapman, for 2s. 6d.; charges 8d; pledge William Dalbye. (3) Agreed to be paid to John Browne of Newland within two days, viz. by 11 March.

f.288r Court held 12 Jan. 1593 by the bailiffs with Mr Jones, Mr Clarcke.

Actions of debt : Henry Jones of Witney, clothier, against Ellis Welles of Witney, broadweaver, for 10s.; charges 4d. (3)

Richard Shewell against William Penye of Witney, broadweaver, for 4s.; charges 4d. Paid and quit.

Court held 16 [Feb. 1593] by the bailiffs with Robert James, constable, the sergeant and some others.

Actions of debt : Sebastian Walker of Witney, smith, against George Warde of Witney, tinker, for 2s. 6d.; charges 4d. (3)

John Browne of Newland, tailor, against Thomas Turtle of Witney, tailor, for 2s. 6d.; charges 4d. (1)

f.288v Court held 9 March by the bailiffs with one of the constables, the sergeant and with some of the commoners of the town.

Court held 30 March 1593 by Leonard Yate, bailiff, with Thomas Clempson, deputy for Bailiff Clempson, Mr Henry Jones, Mr Clarck.

Action of debt : William Dalbye of Witney, butcher, against John Asshett of Witney, weaver, for 4s. 3d.; charges 4d. (3) 3s. paid at the court on 13 July in part payment.

Court held 2 April 1593 by Richard Clempson, bailiff, with the constable, the sergeant, Nicholas Gunne, Richard Humfrey and some others.

Action of detinue: Md. Tuesday 1 May [1593] John Williams of Witney, wiredrawer, against William Towlye of the 'Fallde' [i.e. Leafield], far carter, for 31s. 4d.; charges 8d. Andrew Byrde has given his word for the answering. Agreed.

f.289r Court held 11 May 1593 by Leonard Yate, bailiff, with Mr Thomas Hallam, Mr John Clarke, Richard Humfreye, Walter Dallton, Thomas Clempson and many other commoners.

Covenanted servant: Richard Stanforde, being examined by the bailiffs, confessed himself bound to Richard Bryce, broadweaver, from Whit Sunday next for seven years; to be given at the end of the term 26s. 8d. wages and double apparel.

Court held 1 June 1593 by the bailiffs.

Actions of debt : Md. Friday 15 June 1593 Leonard Yate, bailiff, against William Brooke of Lew, Bampton, yeoman, for 39s. 11½d.

Same against the same for 39s. 11d.

Actions of debt: Md. Thursday 7 June [1593] Robert Loovestie of Long Combe, labourer, against Christopher Hill of Long Combe, husbandman, for 20s. 6d.; charges 8d.; pledge Thomas West. (2) Paid and quit.

Md. same day Christopher Bancrofte late of Asthall, gent., by his son John Bancrofte, against William Towlye, carrier, for 21s.; charges 8d. Edward Hannes [Andrew Byrde *crossed out*] of Witney has given word for the answering of the action. (2) At the court on 5 Oct. Bancroft received 20s. of Hannes in satisfaction and withdrew the action.

f.289v Court held 20 June 1593 by Leonard Yate, bailiff, and Thomas Clempson, deputy for Bailiff Clempson, with Henry Jones, Robert James, constable, the sergeant, one wardsman, the wiredrawer[76] and a few commoners of the town.

Action of debt : Md. Thursday 28 June 1593 Agnes Launce of Eynsham, widow, by her deputy Nicholas Launce of Eynsham, tanner, against Thomas Gatefeelde of North Leigh, blacksmith, for 2s.; charges 8d.

Court held 13 July 1593 by the bailiffs with Mr Henry Jones, John Clarcke, Thomas Clempson, the constables and certain commoners.

Action of debt : Md. Saturday 28 July 1593 Martin Jonson of Ducklington, yeoman, and Edward Dodeswell of Ducklington, wheeler, against Edward Harris late of Witney, wheeler, for 28s.; charges 8d.

f.290r Court held 10 Aug. 1593 by the bailiffs with the constables, Henry Jones, John Clarcke, Richard Jonson.

Court held 31 Aug. 1593 by Richard Clempson, bailiff, and John Clarcke, deputy for Mr Bailiff Yate with Mr Henry Jones, Richard Humfreye and some other commoners.

Court held 28 Sept. [1593] by the bailiffs.

f.290v Court held 5 Oct. 1593 by John Clarcke and Thomas Boxe, bailiffs with the following:

Constables: Richard Sheowell, Edward Ayshefeelde.

Wardsmen: Robert Raybone, William Yeman, Richard Budde, Henry Brygfeelde, Gyles Brown.

Cardenars: John Ryder, John Bircott.

Ale tasters: Arthur Browne, Roger Rudge.

Leather sealers: Edward Hannes, Ellis Hannes.

Cloth searchers and sealers: John Bollte, William Purcer.

f.291r Order: no innholder or victualler in Witney at any time henceforth to receive into any of their houses or lodge any person coming from any house or houses of infection as from Burford, Eynsham, Abingdon, [Berks.,] or any other infected place whatsoever to their knowledge, upon pain of 5s. for each default. If any such person or persons suspected shall come to this town the victualler to whom the said suspected person or persons shall come shall make the bailiffs or constables privy thereto, on pain aforesaid.

[76]   i.e. John Williams; see above, pp.133, 134.

Actions of debt : George Byrdseye of Crawley against Widow Okeley of Witney for 8s.; charges 4d. (2)

Md. Thursday 25 Oct. 1593 John Drinckwater of Eynsham, husbandman, against John Shingleton of Witney, chandler, for 5s.; charges 4d.

f.291v Court held 26 Oct. 1593 by John Clarcke, bailiff, with Mr Leonard Yate, Richard Humfrey, Walter Dallton and Thomas Clempson with the constables and divers commoners.

Amerced: Henry Brygfeelde for his absence at court today, 12d., by the bailiffs.

Actions of debt : Richard Shewell of Witney against Richard Okeley, dyer, for 16s.; charges 4d. (1)

Thomas Cossam of Eynsham, carrier, against the same for 12s.; charges 4d. (3) Paid to Busbye, servant to Cossam, for the use of his master, in the sight of Andrew Byrde and his wife, 12s.

f.292r Tipplers and their licences shown in court: Edward Hannes, Henry Brooke, Richard Shewell, Richard Dytton, Margaret Carter, widow, John Thomas, Alexander Townesende licenced by Mr Bray and Mr Tanfeelde; Roger Cakebred alias Tayler by Mr Bray and Mr Samuel Coxe; John Collyar, William Yeman, Roger Coxe, William Perye, Henry Harper, Richard Fysaher by Mr Bray; Robert Claye by . . .

f.292v Court held 16 Nov. 1593 by the bailiffs with the constables, the sergeant, Leonard Yate, late bailiff, Richard Jonson, Richard Humfrey, Richard Clempson, Walter Dallton, John Collyar, Humfrey Yorcke, the wardsmen and many commoners.

Actions of debt : Thomas Bryan against Arthur Browne for 7s. 4d.; charges 4d. (2) Agreed to be paid weekly.

Same against Thomas Smyth of Witney, currier, for 10s.; charges 4d. (3)

Same against Roger Larden of Witney, broadweaver, for 3s.; charges 4d. (3)

Same against Edward Etkkyns and Esau Warren for 7s.; charges 4d. (3)

f.293r Court held 21 Dec. 1593 by the bailiffs with the constables, the sergeant, Nicholas Gunne, Walter Dallton, Thomas Taylor, William Clempson and some others.

Action of debt : John Lane of Warwick, tanner, against John Humfris alias Maior of Witney, shoemaker, for 32s.; charges 4d. (3)

Collectors for the poor: the bailiffs with the consent of the rest of the bench elected John Spooner and Thomas Hannes for the year following.

f.293v Court held 11 Jan. 1594 by the bailiffs with Constable Ayshefeelde and Leonard Yate.

Action of debt : Richard Goullde of Woodgreen against John Lawrence of Witney, glover, for 13s. 4d.; charges 4d. (2)

Court held 1 Feb. 1594 by the bailiffs with Nicholas Gunne, constable, and some commoners.

Actions of debt : Richard Lorde of Ascott, tailor, against Thomas Beddall senior of Witney for 28s.; charges 4d. (3)

Mr Walter Jones of Worcester, gent., against Margery Whight of Witney, widow, for 39s. 11d. (3)

f.294r   Same by his deputy Richard Boxe against Henry Leowis of Witney, broadweaver, for 20s.; charges 4d. (3)

John Wylye against John Lawrence of Witney, glover, for 3s.; charges 4d. (3)

Md. Friday 3 May 1594 Ursula Ranckell, wife of Peter Ranckell of Witney, clothier, against Widow Shingleton for 10s.; charges 4d. Md. John Shingleton and his wife were both departed and buried before this last action above written was entered.

f.294v Court held 22 Feb. 1594 by the bailiffs with the constables, Thomas Taylor, Walter Dallton, John Collyar, Humfrey Yorcke with certain commoners.

Actions of debt : John Wylye of Witney, tailor, against Giles Browne of Witney, saddler, for 2s. 11d.; charges 4d. (3) Paid.

John Horsall against John Shingleton of Witney, chandler, for 6s.; charges 4d. (2) Md. Shingleton died before this action was recorded by order of the court.

Court held 15 March 1594 by the bailiffs with the constables, Nicholas Gunne, Richard Clempson and divers commoners.

f.295r Court held 5 April 1594 by the bailiffs with Leonard Yate senior, Richard Humfreye, Walter Dallton.

Action of debt : Bailiff Clarcke against Alexander Townesende of Witney, victualler, for 20s.; charges 4d. (3)

Court held 10 May 1594 by Thomas Box, bailiff, and Nicholas Gunne, deputy for Bailiff Clarcke, with Mr Leonard Yate, Richard Jonson, the constables, Richard Clempson, Thomas Taylor, Walter Dallton and divers commoners.

Action of debt : Md. Monday 13 May 1594 Robert Foster of Ducklington, husbandman, against Thomas Egerley of Hardwick, husbandman, for 29s. 11d.; charges 8d.

f.295v Court held 31 May 1594 by the bailiffs with the constables, Richard Clempson, John Colliar, Christopher Cotes and many commoners.

Action of debt ; John Wylye of Witney, tailor, against Thomas Burnell of Witney, tailor, for 2s. 2d.; charges 4d. (2) Burnell paid 8d. for his part of the action; agreed at the next court that William Burnell to pay the other 20d. by a groat [i.e. 4d.] a cloth.

Md. John Tymes delivered to John Clarcke towards the maintenance of Michael Hedgeman 20s. of the stock or goods of the said Hedgeman; which 20s. was delivered to Giles Pallmer presently.

Actions of debt : Robert Baker of Witney against William Greene of Witney, sawyer, for two and one half years' baking, 6s. 8d.; charges 4d. (3)

    Same against Thomas Knight of Witney, broadweaver, for three quarters baking and for baking by the bushel, 6s. 8d.; charges 4d. (3)[77]

f.296r   Same against Thomas Taylor of Witney, mason, for baking by the bushel, 8s.; charges 4d. (3)

    Same against John Lawrence of Witney, glover, for baking, 3s.; charges 4d. (3)

    Same against Thomas Shawe of Witney, butcher, for 15s.; charges 4d. (3)

f.296v Court held 21 June 1594 by John Clarcke, bailiff, with the constables, Leonard Yate, clothier, Nicholas Gunne.

Actions of debt : Walter Jones of Worcester, esq., by his deputy Richard Boxe of Witney, clothier, against John Thomas of Witney, tinker, for 26s.; charges 4d. (3)

    Md. Saturday 29 June 1594 Thomas Townsende of Calcutt [in Cricklade], Wilts., husbandman, against Richard Burguyn of Eynsham, butcher, for 23s. 4d., being the rest of a debt of £4.5s. which Burguyn yet wrongfully detains; charges 8d.

    Md. 5 Sept. [1594] Lawrence Taylor of Abingdon, Berks., innholder, against William Towley of Witney, far carter, for 39s. 11d. (3) By licence of the bailiff he arrested the overplus of a wagon now in the custody of William Jonson, wheeler.[78]

f.297r Court held 12 July 1594 by the bailiffs with the constables, the sergeant, Richard Clempson and divers commoners.

Actions of debt : Robert James of Witney, butcher, against Robert Moore of Witney, rough layer, for 8s. 2d.; charges 4d. (3)

    Md. Thursday 22 Aug. 1594 John Alldwoorth of Aston, yeoman, against Thomas Haynes of Burford, butcher, for 18s.; charges 8d. (3)

    Md. Friday 30 Aug. 1594 John Barnabye senior of Witney against William Toowley of Witney, far carter, for 23s. 4d.; charges 8d. (3) This action upon agreement made between Barnabye and William Jonson was released by Barnabye to Jonson, who had the said wagon from the said Barnabye, by reason that Jonson gave Barnabye a bill of his hand for the payment of the said 23s. 4d.

f.297v Court held 13 Sept. 1594 by the bailiffs with the constables, Richard Clempson, Walter Dallton, William Hunte and divers commoners.

Action of debt : Md. 18 Sept. 1594 William Hunt of Witney, cardmaker,

---

[77]   Presumably he baked for three quarters of the year and in large quantities, and was not licensed to do so.

[78]   The overplus must mean in this case the load of the wagon.

against William Toowley of Witney, far carter, fugitive, for 28s.; charges 8d. (1)

Actions of debt : Md. 24 Sept. 1594 Nicholas Gunne of Witney, clothier, against Robert Foster of Ducklington, husbandman, for 39s. 11d.; pledge Roger Willsheere. (3) Agreed.

                       Same against the same for 13s. 6d.; charges 8d; same pledge. (3)

f.298r Court held 4 Oct. 1594 by Leonard Yate senior of Witney, gent., and Richard Humfrey, bailiffs, with Leonard Yate junior, gent., then steward, the constables, the sergeant and the following:

Constables: Thomas Cave, John Spooner.

Wardsmen: Thomas Peesleye, Nicholas Huttchins, Henry Mayle, Thomas Webley, Andrew Williams.

Ale tasters: Arthur Browne, Henry Eysham.

Cardenars: John Ryder, John Bircott.

Leather sealers: Nicholas Stratten, Morris Taylor.

Cloth searchers: John Bolte, John Shawe.

Action of debt : Robert Baker of Witney against . . . Morris of Witney, bowyer, for 6s. 9d.; charges 4d.

f.298v Tipplers licenced by the Justices: Roger Cox, Edward Hannes by Mr Tanfeelde and Mr Bryce Jenkins; Richard Sheowell, John Colliar, William Yeman by Mr Bray; John Thomas by Mr Bray and Mr Tanfeelde; Robert Claye by Sir Henry Unton, Mr Bray and Mr Tanfeelde; Henry Harper, Henry Brooke, Thomas Townesende, Alexander Townesende by . . .

Md. at the court held on Tuesday 11 Feb. 1595 those present named were all discharged from using any more tippling or selling of ale in their houses or outdoors by virtue of a warrant to the said bailiffs directed from Sir Anthony Cope for the same purpose: Roger Cockes, Thomas Heynes, Richard Dytton, Robert Cakebred, Thomas Allain, Richard Fissher, John Thomas, William Cakebred, Bartholomew Cordewell.

Action of debt : Md. . . . Dec. [1594] Edward Harris of Witney, wheeler, against William Woodwarde of Brize Norton for a bushel of wheat; paid at the court on 14 March.

f.299r Court held 25 Oct. 1594 by the bailiffs with Mr Clarcke, Nicholas Gunne, Richard Clempson.

Court held 15 Nov. 1594 by the bailiffs with Constable Spooner, Roger Wilsheere, Thomas Peeseley.

Actions of debt : Annes Heires of Witney, seamster, against William Hoane of Witney, slater, her father-in-law, for 17s. 8d.; charges 4d. (3)

                       Leonard Morwell of North Leigh, maltman, against Roger Larden of Witney, broadweaver, for 5s.; charges 4d. (3)

                       Md. Saturday 16 Nov. 1594 Edward Dodeswell of Ducklington, wheeler, against Robert Foster of Ducklington, husbandman, for 32s. 8d.; charges 8d.

f.299v Court held 6 Dec. 1594 by the bailiffs.

Actions of debt : Nicholas Lawnce of Eynsham, tanner, against Nicholas Stratton of Witney, shoemaker, for 24s.; charges 4d. (2) Agreed. To be paid weekly.

Roger Willsheere of Witney, shoemaker, against Joan Cordewell of Witney, widow, for . . . (2)

Thomas Taylor of Witney, tanner, against Thomas Smyth of Witney, currier, for 9s.; charges 4d. (3)

Margaret Ridley of Witney, widow, against Richard Budde of Witney, broadweaver, for 8s. 6d.; charges 4d. (2) Md. Margaret died before the third court.

Collectors for the poor: the bailiffs with the consent of the Bench elected Thomas West and Richard Box for the year following.

f.300r Action of detinue: Md. Thursday 19 Dec. 1594 George May of Witney, glover, against Roger Hopkyns of Eynsham, butcher, for a certain number of sheepskins and calfskins which Maye long since bought and paid for from Hopkyns and yet Hopkyns wrongfully detains the same, to the value of 39s. 11d.

Court held 10 Dec. 1594 by the bailiffs with Richard Jonson and some commoners.

Actions of debt : Mr John Clarcke of Witney, clothier, against Richard Shawe of Witney, butcher, for 20s.; charges 4d. (3)

Md. Thursday 30 Jan. 1595 William Brocke of Eynsham, husbandman, against one Humfrey . . ., miller of Eynsham Mill, for 21s.; charges 8d. Agreed.

f.300v Court held 31 Jan. 1595 by the bailiffs with Mr John Clarcke, Thomas Taylor.

Covenanted servant: Richard Makepeace, son of William Makepeace of Chipping Warden, Northants., being examined by the bailiffs in court confessed himself very willing to serve John Clarcke of Witney, clothier and broadweaver, faithfully and truly as an apprentice from 25 Dec. last past; to be taught the occupation of a broadweaver; to be found etc. [as on p.83; no correction clause]; at the end of the term 40s. wages and double apparel.

f.301r Action of debt : Md. Thursday 20 Feb. 1595 William Clempson of Witney, mercer, against Nicholas Lawnce of Eynsham, tanner, for 38s. 2d.; charges 8d.; pledge George Lawson.

Court held 14 March 1595 by the bailiffs with Mr John Clarcke, Richard Clempson and other officers and commoners of Witney.

Action of trespass: Sebastian Walker of Witney, blacksmith, against Leonard Barnabye of Witney, broadweaver, for 2s. 6d.; charges 4d. (3)

Actions of debt : Mary Gunne of Witney, widow, against John Burnell of Witney, broadweaver, for 4s. 2d.; charges 4d. (2) Paid and quit.

Same against Michael Slatter of Witney, broadweaver, for 3s. 2d.; charges 4d. (3) Agreed at the court on 12 Sept. To be paid weekly from 18 Sept.

Action of debt : William Brigfeelde of Witney, maltmaker, against John Thomas of Witney, metalman, for 3s. 4d.; charges 4d. (1) Paid and quit.
Md. Richard Fickett paid the bailiffs for a pottel which was Shingleton's 3s.

f.301v Action of debt : Md. Friday 14 March 1595 Richard Clempson of Witney, mercer, against Edward Weekes of Yedson [i.e. Idstone?] Berks., gent., for 31s. 10d.; charges 8d.; pledge Mr Thomas Hallam. (3)

Court held 4 April 1595 by the bailiffs with Mr John Clarcke, Richard Clempson, Thomas Webley, William Brigfeelde and others.
Actions of debt : Richard Berrye of Chipping Norton, mercer, against John [Richard *crossed out*] Heires of Witney, glover, and Agnes his wife for 6s. 8d.; charges 4d. (3) To be paid to the sergeant by 6d. a week.
Md. 7 April 1595 Humfrey Yorcke of Witney, innholder, against William Towley of Witney, far carter, for 10s. 6d.; charges 8d. Agreed.

f.302r   Md. Thursday 24 April 1595 George Rudlande of Oxford, plumber, against Hugh Jonson alias Hollton of Aston in Bampton, butcher, for 22s.; charges 8d.; pledge William Clempson. (3) Action non suited because the plaintiff was not present at the court on 23 Jan. 1596.
Md. same day Leonard Goode against Robert Horne of Witney, broadweaver, for 18s. 4d.; charges 8d. Humfrey Yorcke to be paid 12d. a week until 10s. paid; the rest forgiven. First payment Thursday after Whitsun.
Md. Friday 25 April 1595 William Towley of Witney, far carter, against Martin Jonson of Ducklington, yeoman, for 30s. 4d.; charges 8d.; pledges William Maior and Nicholas Maior. (3)
Md. Thursday 8 May [1595] Thomas Tunckes of Burford, saddler, against Hugh Jonson alias Hollton of Aston in Bampton, butcher, for 10s.; charges 8d.

f.302v Court held 16 May 1595 by the bailffs with Richard Clempson, Thomas Peeseleye, Richard Jonson, Thomas Taylor, Mr Clarcke.
Actions of debt : Richard Yate of Witney, clothier, against Elizabeth Saley of Witney, widow, for 17s. 5d.; charges 4d. (3)
George Kempe of Witney, yeoman, against Giles Juorye of Witney, cobbler, for 12s.; charges 4d. (3)

f.303r Court held 6 June 1595 by the bailiffs with Richard Clempson, the sergeant and few others.
Court held 27 June 1595 by the bailiffs with Richard Clempson, Nicholas Gunne, the sergeant and few others.

Court held 18 July 1595 by the bailiffs with the sergeant and very few of the commoners of Witney.
Action of debt : Md. Wednesday 30 July 1595 James Foster of Hailey, yeoman, against Richard Gardner of South Leigh, husbandman, for 36s. 8d.; charges 8d.

f.303v Court held 12 Sept. 1595 by the bailiffs with John Clarcke, Richard Jonson, Nicholas Gunne, John Barnabye, certain wardsmen and a few commoners.

Actions of debt : Md. Tuesday 2 Oct. [1595] Richard Shawe of Witney, butcher, by his wife, against Richard Golldsmyth of Witney, fugitive, for 10s.; charges 8d.; pledge Richard Okeley, dyer. (3)

      Md. Monday 27 Oct. 1595 Humfrey Yorcke of Witney, innholder, against Thomas Jonson, yeoman, servant to Thomas Chester, esq., of Royston, Cambs., for 30s.; charges 8d. (3) A brown bay gelding distrained for this debt, left in the custody of Yorcke; appraised at the court on 12 Dec. by George Kempe, Robert Steevens, Andrew Hodson and Nicholas Harris at 11s. Appraisers paid 8d.; and to me Richard Bryce for recording thereof 2d.

f.304r Court held 10 Oct. 1595 by Richard Jonson and Henry Ranckell, new-chosen bailiffs, and Leonard Yate junior, gent., then steward, with Mr John Clarcke, Leonard Yate senior, Richard Humfrey, Thomas Clempson, John Barnabye and many other commoners.

Constables: Richard Box, Thomas West.

Wardsmen: Andrew Hodson, Nicholas Harris, Leonard Goode, George Kempe, John Tymmes junior.

Ale tasters: Peter Ryder, Henry Eysham.

Cardenars: William Maior, John Burcott.

Cloth sealers and searchers: John Bollte, John Richardson.

Leather sealers: Morris Tayler, Edward Hannes.

f.304v Tipplers with their licences: Roger Cox, Edward Hannes licenced by Mr Tanfeelde and Mr Bray, justices; Richard Shewell, William Yeoman by Mr Bray; Robert Claye by Sir Henry Unton, Mr Bray and Mr Tanfeelde; Henry Harper by Sir Henry Unton and Mr Bray; Alexander Townsend, Henry Brooke, Thomas Townesende by . . .

Actions of debt : Bartholomew Harris of Ducklington against Thomas Shawe, butcher, for 8s.; charges 4d. (3) Agreed 4d. paid to Richard Bryce for the use of Harris at the court held on 27 Nov.

      Thomas Beddall of Witney, baker, against Simon Peerson of Witney, broadweaver, for 3s.; charges 4d. (1) Agreed.

f.305r   Bailiff Ranckell against Arthur Browne of Witney, broadweaver, for 20s.; charges 4d. (3)

      Same against John Honyburne, carpenter, for 12s. 10d.; and 3s. 6d. more owing by his wife; charges 4d. Total 16s. 8d. (3)

      Same against Thomas Taylor, mason, for 13s.; charges 4d. (3)

      William Maior, now sergeant of the mace in Witney, against Leonard Barnabye, broadweaver, for 7s.; charges 4d. (3)

Paid 4s. to Widow Joanes on 12 July by the hands of Andrew Hodsonne for keeping a poor child.

f.305v Court held 30 Oct. 1595 by Henry Ranckell, bailiff, with the sergeant, John Barnabye senior, Richard Clempson.

Action of debt : John Colliar of Witney, clothmaker, against Giles Juorye of Witney, cobbler, for 2s.; charges 4d. (3)

Actions of debt : Md. Tuesday 4 Nov. 1595 William Clempson of Witney, mercer, against John Tymson of Witney for 3s. 9d.; charges 8d.

Md. Thursday 30 Sept. 1596 Richard Rathry of Witney, miller, against William Grene of Witney, labourer, for 8s.; charges 4d.[79]

f.306r Court held 7 Nov. 1595 by Richard Jonson, bailiff, with Mr John Clarcke, Thomas Taylor, Richard Clempson, Nicholas Gunne, two constables and many commoners.

Actions of debt : Md. Monday 10 Nov. 1595 William Towley of Asthall, far carter, against Richard Okeley of Witney, dyer, for 10s.; charges 8d.

Md. Thursday 13 Nov. 1595 John Brooke of Eynsham, yeoman, against Nicholas Harte of South Leigh, husbandman, for 20s.; charges 8d.; Henry Brooke of Witney surety. (3) Paid 10s. 8d. to Bailiff Jonson upon this action at the court on 2 June. Paid 10s. to Brooke himself by Bailiff Ranckell at the court on 23 Jan.

f.306v Court held 27 Nov. 1595 by Richard Jonson, bailiff, with Thomas Taylor, Nicholas Gunne, Richard Clempson, John Barnabye, Thomas Cave and divers commoners.

Action of debt : Augustine Hyatt of Witney, labourer, against John Honiburne of Witney, carpenter, for 5s. 4d.; charges 4d. (3)

Court held 12 Dec. 1595 by Richard Jonson, bailiff, with Thomas Taylor, Richard Clempson, Nicholas Gunne, George Kempe and certain commoners.

Actions of debt : Md. Thursday 18 Dec. [1595] Geoffrey Dickes, now servant to Richard Frame of Aston in Bampton, husbandman, against John Cottsmoore the younger of Brize Norton, husbandman, for 4s. 11d.; charges 8d.; pledge Robert Cakebradg of Witney. Agreed.

Md. Sunday 27 Dec. 1596 Anthony Charman of Witney, miller, against . . . Borvill of Eynsham [widow *crossed out*] for 16s.; charges 8d.; pledge George Lawson (3). Drawn 26 Mar. 1596 by Charman.

f.307r Court held 2 Jan. 1596 by the bailiffs with Mr John Clarcke, Leonard Yate, clothier, Richard Clempson, Walter Dallton and divers commoners.

Collectors for the poor: the bailiffs elected Thomas Webley and James Hodson.

Poor children part of the town charge: paid to Widow Jones by the hands of Leonard Yate, clothier, 2s. 6d., towards the keeping of the child which she has to keep at the charge of the town.

Actions of debt : Giles Juory of Witney, shoemaker, against John Colliar of Witney, clothmaker, for 6s. 6d.; charges 4d. (2)

Md. Thursday 6 Aug. 1596 Leonard Yate of Witney, clothier, against Robert Sparrowe of Come [Combe], yeoman, for 20s.; charges 8d.[80]

[79] Added later at the bottom of the page in a different hand.
[80] Added later at the bottom of the page in a different hand.

f.307v   Md. Thursday 8 Jan. 1596 Thomas Dudson of Stanton
Harcourt, deputy of Oliver Dudson of Stanton Harcourt, husbandman,
against Martin Radburne of Standlake, yeoman, for 5s., which debt is due
to Dudson; charges 8d. (1) Agreed.
                    Md. Thursday 15 Jan. 1596 George Kempe of Witney,
yeoman, against Richard Gardiar of South Leigh, husbandman, for
39s. 11d.; charges 8d.; surety and pledge Robert Wryght of Witney, smith.
(3) Paid and quit.
                    Md. same day Robert Payne of Cassington, yeoman, against
Mr Willyams of New Woodstock, baker, for 39s. 11d. (1) Agreed.
Md. agreed by Richard Johnsone, bailiff, that Thomas Suryile of Cirencester,
Gloucs., haberdasher, to have the stall ground that Rowland Leyghton had
before any other man, except that Leyghton or any other shall choose to
inhabit in the town of Witney.[81]

f.308r Court held 30 Jan. 1596 by the bailiffs with the constables, the sergeant, and
        Mr John Clarke, Nicholas Gunne, Thomas Taylor, Richard Clempson and
        divers commoners.
        Covenanted servant: Richard Foster, son of Robert Foster of Ducklington,
        husbandman, by the advice and counsel of his father and of his grandfather,
        James Foster of Hailey, yeoman, and being examined confessed himself
        bound in consideration of seven covenant pence to Hugh Rodes of Witney,
        broadweaver, for seven years from 25 March next, to be taught the
        occupation of broadweaver; to be found etc. [as on p.83; no correction
        clause]; at the end of the term 20s. wages and double apparel. In witness
        whereof the said parties have put their marks. [No marks.]
f.308v Action of debt : Md. Thursday 5 Feb. 1596 Henry Lyfe Holye of Minster
        Lovell, husbandman, against Alice Cove of Leafield, housewife, for 5s. in
        money and a short cloth of canvas, being two ells; charges 8d.

        Court held 26 Feb. 1596 by Richard Jonson, bailiff.
        Actions of debt : Walter Bennet of Clanfield, yeoman, against George May of
                Witney, glover, for 30s.; charges 4d. (3)
                    Robert Walkelatt of Eynsham, baker, against Roger Rackley
                of Witney, glover, for 9s.; charges 4d. (1) Agreed.
                    Md. Tuesday 9 March 1596 William Towley of the Field in
        Asthall, far carter, against William Busby of Eynsham, far carter, for
        39s. 11d.; charges 8d. Agreed.

f.309r Court held 26 March 1596 by the bailiffs with Thomas Taylor, Nicholas Gunne,
        Richard Clempson, Walter Dallton and divers commoners.

        Court held 12 April 1596 by the bailiffs with John Clarcke, Richard Boxe,
        Roger Wyllksheare, Richard Clempsonne and commoners.
        Action of debt : Roger Wyllksheare of Witney, shoemaker, against Joan
        Cordywell for 5s.; charges 4d. (3)

        [81]   Added later at the bottom of the page, in a different hand.

Action of debt : Md. Thursday 3 Sept. 1596 Robert Sealbe of Cassington, husbandman, against William Saxtone of South Leigh, husbandman, for 26s.; charges 8d. (3)[82]

f.309v Court held 21 May 1596 by Richard Johnson, bailiff, with Mr Leonard Yate senior, Thomas Taylare, Thomas Cave, Richard Humfrey and others.
Actions of debt : Md. Friday 21 May [1596] Giles Browne of Witney, saddler, against William Saxton of South Leigh, husbandman, for 20s.; charges 8d. Agreed.

Edward Bennat of Abingdon, Berks., woollen draper, against William Pennye of Witney, broadweaver, for 5s.; charges 4d. (3)

Court held 11 June 1596 with Mr Bryce and Mr Clarcke.

f.310r Court held 11 June 1596 by the bailiffs with Mr Bryse, Mr Clarke, Mr Leonard Yate junior, Richard Clempsonne, Mr Leonard Yate senior and others.
Amerced: Leonard Goode 12d. for default of appearance being lawfully summoned by the sergeant who was thereunto sworn.

Court held 2 July 1596 by Richard Johnson, bailiff, with Mr Clarcke, Nicholas Gunne, Thomas Cave, Thomas West, constable, and others.
Action of debt : Thomas White of Cogges against Sherman in Gloucs., thrum gatherer, upon 13s. 4d. and charges. Agreed.

f.310v Court held 23 July 1596 by the bailiffs with Mr Leonard Yate, [Roger] Wyllksheare, Richard Boxe, Thomas Weste, constable, and others.
Actions of debt : Henry Newmane of Curbridge, yeoman, against Christopher Cotes of Witney, clothman, for . . .; charges 4d. (3)

John Coke of Bladon, husbandman, against William Dallbe of Witney, butcher, for 13s.; charges 4d. (3)

Md. Wednesday 28 July [1596] William Maior of Witney, broadweaver, against William Broke of Lew, yeoman, for 26s. 8d.; charges 8d. (3); pledge Richard Shewell. Agreed by two arbitrators, Roger Wylksher and Robert Claye, at the court on 29 Oct., 39s. apiece for the agreement.

f.311r Md. a possession: taken 3 July 1596 by Richard Johnson, bailiff, of Roger Coxe of Witney, broadweaver, of a house on the north side of Corn St. towards the south [end] between the tenement of Leonard Yate junior on the west and the tenement of Ralph Take on the east; for the use of William Cakebred and Mary, his wife, and their heirs lawfully begotten. Delivered in the presence of Mr Clark, Thomas West, constable, William Maior the sergeant, George Kempe, Andrew Hodson, Nicholas Harys, John Tymes and others.

f.311v Actions of debt : Richard Byrye of Chipping Norton, linen draper, against William Clennard of Witney, tucker, for 2s. 2d.; charges 4d.

---

[82] Added later at the bottom of the page in a different hand.

Same against Thomas Atkynes of Witney, glover, for 2s. 2d.; charges 4d.

f.312r Court held 10 Sept. 1596 by the bailiffs with John Clarcke, Richard Boxe and others.

Order: the Right Worshipful Sir William Spensar, Sir Anthony Cope and Mr Laurence Tanfeld, Justices of Her Majesty's Peace, have commanded and straightly charged that the bailiffs of Witney shall not maintain nor uphold any alehouses but those that shall be allowed by the bailiffs aforesaid and that they shall sell two quarts for 1d. of good and wholesome drink outdoors and a thirdendell indoors, on pain of forfeiting their acognizances [i.e. recognizances], and further punishment as the bailiffs shall appoint, and that they shall not use no means of unlawful games within their houses and those are their names that are underwritten: Roger Coxe, Richard Showell, Alexander Townsend, Robert Claye, Richard Duttone, William Emanes, John Collyar, Robert Baker, Leonard Goode, Edward Handes, Henry Harpar, William Pennye, Robert Cakebred, Thomas Townsend, John Thomas, Richard Fyshar, and all others that will or can.

f.312v Actions of debt : Md. Tuesday 19 Oct. 1596 Richard Johnsones of Witney, clothier, against Richard Smote of Oxford, carrier, for 39s. 11½d.; charges 8d. (1)

Md. same against the same for 39s. 11½d.; charges 8d.

Md. Thursday 2 Dec. [1596] Henry Rankyll of Witney, clothier, against John Coke of Hanborough, yeoman, for 6s.; charges 8d.

f.313r Court held 8 Oct. 1596 by Thomas Taylor and Thomas Cave, bailiffs, with Mr Leonard Yate junior, Mr Clarke, Leonard Yate senior, Richard Humfrys, Henry Rankyll, Roger Willsheare and others.

Constables: Thomas Handes, Richard Haskynes: sworn.

Wardsmen: John Enstone for the Paternoster Row, John Workhouse, John Bakare, Thomas Personn: sworn. John Boullte.

Cardenars: John Byrkat, Arthur Browne: sworn.

Ale tasters: Peter Rydar, Henry Eysame: sworn.

Cloth searchers: John Richardsonn, John Wyllye junior: sworn.

Leather sealers: Morris Tayllar, Edward Handes: sworn.

f.313v Actions of debt : George Kempe of Witney against Richard Waynwryght alias Fyshar, broadweaver, for 28s.; charges 4d. (3)

Clement Rose of New Yatt against Anthony Watsonne of Witney for 10s.; charges 4d. (3) To pay 10s. in two payments.

Thomas West of Witney, clothier, against William Cakebred of Witney, broadweaver, for 7s; charges 4d. Agreed.

Robert Hodde of North Leigh, cooper, against Nicholas Cotes of Witney, brewer, for 9s.; charges 4d. (3)

f.314r Covenanted servant: John Bannyng, son of Richard Bannyng of Witney, broad-weaver, by consent of father and in consideration of eight covenant pence confessed himself bound to Thomas Smarte of Witney, broadweaver, for eight years from Easter last past to be taught the occupation of a broad-weaver; to be found etc. [as on p.83; no correction clause]; at the end of the term 10s. wages and double apparel. In witness whereof the parties have put their marks the day and year above written. [No marks.]

f.314v Action of debt : Md. Saturday 24 Dec. 1596 Mr Clarke of Witney, clothier, against Edward Chrese of North Leigh, husbandman, for 26s.; charges 8d. Agreed.

f.315r Court held 29 Oct. 1596 by Thomas Taylare, bailiff, with Mr Clarke, Mr Leonard Yate senior, Nicholas Gunne, Roger Wylksher, the constables and others.

Actions of debt : Md. Friday 5 Nov. 1596 William Toyle of the Field [i.e. Leafield], labourer, against Martin Johnson of Ducklington, yeoman, for 30s. 4d.; pledge William Clempsone, mercer. (3)

Md. Tuesday 9 Nov. 1596 John Stampe of Witney, gent., against William Saxtene of South Leigh, husbandman, for 26s.; charges 8d. Agreed.

Md. Thursday 2 Dec. 1596 Margery Maior, wife of John Maior of Burford, shoemaker, late deceased, against Henry Bates of Bampton, shoemaker, for 29s. 11d.; charges 8d. (2)

f.315v Court held 3 Dec. 1596 by the bailiffs with Richard Haskynes, Walter Doulton, Roger Wylkshear and others.

Actions of debt : George Kempe of Witney, yeoman, against John Thomas of Witney, tinker, for 12s.; charges 4d. (1)

Nicholas Cotes of Witney, brewer, against Giles Yenarye, cobbler, for 13s. 1d.; charges 4d. (3)

Same against Richard Waynwryte alias Fyshar, broadweaver, for 6s. 8d.; charges 4d. (3)

f.316r   Richard Haskynes of Witney, tucker, against William Pursare of Witney, tucker, for 33s.; charges 4d. (2)

Thomas Rankylle of Witney, broadweaver, . . .

Widow Gune of Witney, woollen draper, against Thomas Rankyle of Witney, broadweaver, for 27s.; charges 4d. (3)

Same against John Ashate, coverlet weaver, for 5s. 4d.; charges 4d. (3)

Thomas Brygfeld of Newland in Cogges, yeoman, against William Saxtone of South Leigh, husbandman, for 30s.; charges 8d. (3)

f.316v Court held 7 Jan. 1597 by the bailiffs with Thomas Handes, constable, Roger Wylkshear, William Hunte and others.

Actions of debt : Richard Nuberye of Burford, clothier, against Richard Hodson of Witney, broadweaver, for 12s. 8d.; charges 4d. (3) Agreed on 30 Sept. that Hodson to pay 7s. 6d. in part payment before Bailiff Gonne, Mr Clark and the constables, with charges upon further agreement.

John Workhouse of Witney, tucker, against Richard Horne, broadweaver, for 3s. 10d.; charges 4d. (3)

Richard Okley of Witney, dyer, against the same for 13s. 4d.; charges 4d. (3)

Md. Thursday 13 Jan. [1597] Richard Clempson of Witney,

draper, against Goodwife Pottar of Thrupp for 6s. 11d.; charges 8d. Agreed and paid.

f.317r   Md. Thursday 27 Jan. 1597 Thomas Bedowlle of Witney, baker, against John Sponar of Witney, dyer, for 29s., entrance upon this action being granted upon fugitive; charges 12d. Agreed that Mr Thomas Babyngton should pay Beddowll 5s. a quarter till the debt be paid.

        Md. Thursday 3 Feb. 1597 Thomas Weblye, clothier in the county of Oxford, against Edward Wyne of Wootton-under-Edge, Gloucs., end man, for 13s. 5d.; charges 12d. Agreed.

Action of fugitive: Md. Thursday 27 Jan. 1597 John Craftes of Hailey, yeoman, against John Bowell of Eynsham, baker, for 39s. 11½d.; charges 12d. Agreed.

f.317v Court held 18 Jan. 1597 by the bailiffs with Mr Clarke, Thomas Handes, constable, William Hunte and others.

Actions of debt : Widow Gune of Witney, draper, against Ellys Welles of Witney, broadweaver, for 10s. 6d.; charges 8d. (3)

        Same against John More of Witney, broadweaver, for 13s. 9d.; charges 8d. (2)

Agreed: John Craftes of Hailey, yeoman, received 23s. 4d. in part payment of 39s. 11½d. of John Bowell, the which was agreed and paid before the bailiffs, Mr Clarke and divers others.

f.318r Court held 19 Feb. 1597 by the bailiffs with Mr Clarke, Roger Wylksher, William Hunte, Thomas Hanndes, constable, and others.

Actions of debt : George Kempe of Witney, yeoman, against Robert Stevenes of Witney, broadweaver, for 5s. 8d.; charges 8d. Agreed and paid.

        Martin Johnson of Ducklington, yeoman, against Roger Wryte of Witney, broadweaver, for 8s.; charges 8d. (2)

        Edward Cowlles of the Field [i.e. Leafield], yeoman, against John Thomas of Witney, tinker, for 6s. 8d.; charges 8d. (3)

        Richard Boxe of Witney, clothier, against Thomas Shawe of Witney, butcher, for 6s. 8d.; charges 8d. (1) The peel ['pela'] and chafer of Shaw were appraised at 5s. and the appraising 3d.; appraisers William Maior, John Boullt, Giles Juory.

f.318v   Md. Thursday 12 March [1597] Richard Young of Fyfield, Berks., yeoman, against Simon Downe of Fyfield Wick, Berks., husbandman, for 39s. 11d.; charges 12d. Agreed before the bailiffs in the court on 13 May that Alexander Townsend should pay to Gyllan Cartar 4d. weekly until the whole paid, beginning 20th of this month.

        Richard Boshope of Witney, tucker, against Davy Horne of Witney, carpenter, and Domity Darpondare for 10s.; charges 8d. (3)

        Same against William Haynes of Witney, victualler, and Domity Darpondare for 10s.; charges 8d. (3)

f.319r Covenanted servant: in court Thomas Ayares, son of Thomas Ayares of Witney, broadweaver, late deceased, confessed himself bound to Roger Wylkshear of Witney, shoemaker, for 11 years from 25 March next to be taught the occupation of a shoemaker and received in earnest 11 pence; well and truly to keep his master's secrets lawful and honest everywhere and to fulfil all points of the covenant as thoroughly as though he were bound by indenture;[83] to be found etc. [as on p.83; no correction clause]; at the end of the term 40s. wages and double apparel.

f.319v Md. the goods of Thomas Ayares, late deceased, were leased at £9, of which goods Roger Wyllkshear of Witney, shoemaker, received £5 in value of goods in the behalf of the bringing up Thomas Ayres' son abovenamed, to train and bring up to the occupation of a shoemaker for 11 years; at the end of 11 years Ayares to have of Willkshear 30s. out of the said £5; and the daughter of Thomas Ayres, Joan, to have £4 of the aforesaid goods and whosoever shall have the said Joan to have the said goods for seven years and at the end of the terms of seven years the party what shall have the above named Joan is to deliver in money or goods to have again 40s. and if either of them decease within the term of their years that the whole part of the 40s. to remain to the longer living of them two. In witness whereof the above named Roger Wylkshear has caused this note to be recorded 12 March 1597.

Action of debt : Peter Johnson of Witney against Richard Okleye of Witney, dyer, for 4s.; charges 8d.

f.320r Covenanted servant: in court William Dussyne, son of William Dussyne of Cogges, labourer, confessed himself bound to Roger Wylksheare, shoemaker, to be taught shoemaking as a apprentice for eight years from 24 June next; well and truly to keep etc. and to be found etc. [as on pp.149-50]; at the end of the term 6s. 8d. wages and double apparel.

f.320v Court held 12 March 1597 by the bailiffs with Roger Wylkshear, William Hunte and others.

Actions of debt : Henry Bettes of Standlake, shoemaker, against Peter Rydare of Witney, tucker, for 6s. 8d.; charges 8d. (3)

John Enstone of Witney, butcher, against Thomas Walle of Witney, broadweaver, for 21s. 9d.; charges 8d. (3)

Md. Tuesday 22 March 1597 Thomas Townsend of North Leigh, labourer, against Edward Shrene of North Leigh, husbandman, for 39s. 11d.; charges 12d.; pledge Leonard Yate junior. (3)

f.321r   Md. Thursday 24 March 1597 Robert Fostar of Ducklington, yeoman, against Ellis Kenkam of Ramsden, husbandman, for 39s. 11d.; charges 12d.; pledge Robert Wryght. Agreed.

Md. Sunday 10 April 1597 John Gorge of South Leigh, husbandman, against Bennat of Winslow, Bucks., wooldraper, for 13s. 4d.; charges 12d. Agreed by the parties of North Leigh, Thomas Townsend and Edward Shrene, to bring in security for the satisfying of this action and other debts before Bailiff Gunne, Richard Johnson, Walter Daullton, Thomas Clempson with others. Agreed and paid.

---

[83] This is the first example in the court book of the common clause to keep secrets etc. The wording of the covenant implies that formal indentures had not been drawn up, perhaps in this case because the boy was young: see the following memorandum.

Richard Haskyns of Witney, clothier, against John Workhouse of Witney, tucker, for 28s.; charges 8d.

f.321v Court held 15 April 1597 by the bailiffs with Walter Dowllton, Thomas Handes and others.

Actions of debt : Robert Jhames of Witney, butcher, against Mary Myryeman of Witney, widow, for 6s, 7d,; charges 8d. (2) Her goods appraised, being a pot and kettle, for the debt of Jhames as above; appraisers William Maior, John Boullt, Giles Juory, Richard Maior.

Richard Haskyns of Witney, clothier, against Peter Rydar of Witney, tucker, for 30s.; charges 8d. (3)

Md. Thursday 12 May [1597] Syrake Okelye of Chipping Norton, tanner, against Henry Redgate of Woodstock, shoemaker, for 18s.; charges 12d.; pledge Roger Wylkshere. (3)

f.322r Covenanted servant: in court Anthony Yate, son of Bartholomew Yate of Standlake, yeoman, confessed himself bound to John Clarke of Witney, clothier and broadweaver, for four years from 25 Dec. next to be taught the occupation of a broadweaver and received four pence; to be found etc. [as on p.83]; at the end of the term 26s. 8d. wages and double apparel. In witness whereof we have caused this note to be recorded and put our hands thereto. [No marks or signatures.]

f.322v Court held 13 May 1597 by the bailiffs with Roger Wylkshear, Richard Haskynes and others.

Actions of debt : John Workhouse of Witney, tucker, against George Daye of Witney, broadweaver, for 12s.; charges 8d. (2)

Robert Jhames of Witney, butcher, against Thomas Walle of Witney, broadweaver, for 2s. 6d.; charges 8d. (1)

Md. Thursday 19 May 1597 George Day of Witney, broadweaver, against Robert Howttone of Brighthampton [in Standlake] for 15 bushels at 2s. 8d. the bushel; charges 12d.

f.323r Court held 4 June 1597 by the bailiffs with Richard Boxe and others.

Actions of debt : Humfrey Breyares, servant to Mr Fettyplace of Swinbrook, against John Thomas of Witney, tinker, for 23s.; charges 8d. (2)

Richard Boxe of Witney, yeoman, against Giles Juerye of Witney, cobbler, for 12s.; charges 12d. (3)

Md. Wednesday 8 June [1597] Robert Jhames of Witney, butcher, against Thomas Walle of Witney, fugitive, according to the orders of the bailiffs' court of the borough of Witney, for 4s. 10d. and all other charges so born.

Md. Monday 20 June 1597 William Prusar of Witney, tucker, against Mary Meryeman of Witney, widow, for 17s. 6d.; charges 12d.

f.323v Actions of fugitive: Md. Friday 24 June 1597 Roger Lanne of 'Rodsone' [i.e. Radstone, Northants.], yeoman, against Roger Horne for rent which he should have had of Horne or his deputies for 39s. 11d.; charges 12d.

Same against the same or his deputies for 26s. 9d.; charges 12d.

Action of debt : Md. Thursday 13 Sept. [1597] William Busbe of Eynsham, carrier, against Richard Poyntar of Eynsham, pargeter ['parrytar'], for 13s..; charges 12d. (3)

f.324r Md. 19 Oct. 1597 Walter Daulton of Witney, mercer, bought of Edward Lambard of Barton-on-the-Heath, [Warws.,] four calves, one black being an ox calf cropped on the further ear, one red calf with no mark, one black calf under hit on the near ear, one other black [calf] slit on the near ear, price 40s.

Md. Thursday 25 May 1598 Richard Sparkes of Eynsham, yeoman, bought four heifers, two brown, one brinded and one 'follow', [i.e. fallow?], tagged, cropped on the further ear, of Richard Stuttar of Hanborough, yeoman, priced at 25s. each, the sum £5.

f.324v Court held 7 July 1597 by the bailiffs with William Hunte, the wardsmen and others.

Action of debt : John Kinge of Filkins against Thomas Shawe of Witney for 20s.; charges 8d. (1) Agreed to be paid on 26 Dec. next.

Court held 5 Aug. 1597 by the bailiffs with Robert Jhames, the sergeant and others.

Action of debt : Mary Gonne of Witney, widow, against William Smythe late of Witney, broadweaver, for 23s. 10d.; charges 12d. Thomas Pearson, broadweaver, promised to pay the same 8s. a fortnight after, whereof Nicholas Gunne received in part payment 12d.; and the rest to be paid on 1 Nov. next.

f.325r Court held 30 Sept. 1597 by Nicholas Gonne, bailiff, with Mr Clarcke and others.

Actions of debt : Henry Humfrys of Witney, broadweaver, against Anthony Ebsworth, dyer, for 15s. 3d.; charges 8d. (3)

Davy Cove of Bourton [i.e. Black Bourton?], yeoman, against William Dalbe of Witney, butcher, for 10s.; charges 8d. (3)

Richard Geye of Nether Heyford [i.e. Lower Heyford], husbandman, against Simon Geye of Crawley for 20s.; charges 12d.; pledge Robert Cakbred. (3) Agreed and paid.

f.326r Md. grant Friday 4 Nov. 1597 Walter Dawlton and Richard Boxe, then bailiffs, and others in the presence of the masters of the same borough whose names are herein written, i.e. Thomas Tayllar, Nicholas Gonne and Humfrey Yorcke, then constable, with others then present, granted to Mary Gonne, widow, eight feet for hire of pageant ground to seat a pall from the quoin that butts towards the west of the High St. and forwards from the messuage or tenement of the aforesaid Mary towards the north and so adjoining to the 'Yelldarn' tree butting on the east.[84] The which Mary is to

[84]   A pall was perhaps a pale or fence and the Green in front of the Church seems the likely place for a pageant ground. The Gunnes had property near the town end of it; see above, p.xlix. Monk (Witney, pp.28, 30) speaks of an old jousting ground in the grounds of the bishop's palace, and quotes Lambarde's description (c.1570) of a pre-Reformation puppet show of the Resurrection held in Witney. Both of these may have taken place on or near the Green and on pageant ground.

have, hold, occupy and enjoy during the time of her former deed, i.e. for 999 years to her heirs, executors and assigns. In witness whereof the parties written have given and granted and full consented herein, paying to the bailiffs yearly for the same ground . . . *Cancelled*.

f.326v At the court on the other side came thither to take the oath for allegiance for the observing of the Queen's Majesty's Statute.[85] Henry Surbe, Anthony Yate, Richard Heallar, servants to Mr John Clarke, clothier; and William Burd, Thomas Handes, John Robynson, servants to Andrew Burd, butcher.

Action of debt : Md. Friday 25 Nov. [1597] Peter Powyll, petty chapman, against Robert Jenkyns, chapman, for 14s.; charges 12d. Md. Friday 20 Jan. 1598 Powyll received the goods from the bailiff because Jenkyns did not come to follow his suit.

f.327r Court held 7 Oct. 1597 by Walter Daullton and Richard Boxe, they being chosen for bailiffs, with the steward and divers and sundry masters of the town and others.

Constables: Humfrey Yorcke, Thomas Webley: sworn.

Wardsmen: Steven Collyar, Edmund Budd, Henry Tyrrye, Justinian Wellar, Edmund Busbe: sworn.

Ale tasters: Nicholas Maior, Richard Ficate: sworn.

Cardenars: John Byrcat, William Pursar: sworn.

Leather sealers: Edward Handes, Nicholas Stratton: sworn.

Cloth searchers: John Boulte, Robert Rawbone: sworn.

f.327v Actions of debt : Md. Thursday 30 Nov. 1597 Richard Bygnell of Filkins, traveller, against Robert Horne of Hailey, traveller, for 20s.; charges 12d. (1)

Md. Thursday 8 Dec. 1597 Thomas Redborne of Standlake, yeoman, against Andrew Steward, salter, for 6s. 8d.; charges 8d. Agreed for the same action.

Md. same day Richard Boshope of Witney against Robert Horne, traveller, for 20s.; charges 8d. Agreed.

f.328r Court held 4 Nov. 1597 by the bailiffs with Nicholas Gonne, Thomas Tayllar, Humfrey Yorcke and others.

Court held 18 Nov. 1597 by the bailiffs with Mr Clark, Mr Leonard Yate senior, Humfrey Yorke and others.

Actions of debt : Richard Martyne of Witney, tucker, against Thomas Suttone of North Leigh, husbandman, for 11s. 6d.; charges 12d.

Margaret Morryse, servant to John Tymes junior, against John Eyares upon fugitive for 8s. 9d.; charges 8d.

f.328v   Md. Monday 2 Jan. 1598 Giles Prate of Witney, collar maker, against Richard Barkar of Oxford, carrier, for 30s.; charges 8d. Agreed.

Agreed: Thomas Pearson, broadweaver, to pay Mary Gonne of Witney,

[85]   There was no statute which demanded an oath of allegiance from servants and this entry is unexplained, unless it concerns recusancy or the riots at Enslow Heath, which, however, do not appear in government records until December: see above, p.lvi.

widow, 3s., part payment of the debt on 21 Dec. next, 6s. 8d. on 25 Mar. and the same on 24 June and 29 Sept.

Essoined:[86] for want of appearance Justinian Wellar, Edmond Budde, Steven Collyar at 4s. 4d. apiece.

f.329r Court held 9 Dec. 1597 by Walter Daultone, bailiff, with Mr Clarke, Richard Johnson, Nicholas Gonne, Richard Humfrys and others.

Chamberlain: Thomas Webleye of Witney, clothier, elected and chosen. Received 40s. 4d. to his custody from Mr Clarke.

Collectors for the poor: Richard Bryce and Richard Haskynes chosen.

Action of fugitive: Md. Monday 21 Dec. 1597 John Heyes of Cirencester, Gloucs., brazier, against Nicholas Cotes of Witney, brewer, for 17s.; charges 8d.

f.329v Actions of debt : Md. Thursday 12 Jan. [1598] Moses Wybllyne of Bucklands in Marcham, Berks., yeoman, against John Enstone of Witney, butcher, for 33s. 4d.; charges 4d. (3)

Md. same against the same for 33s. 4d.; charges 4d. (3)

Md. same day Thomas Weste of Witney, mercer, against Thomas Bodeye of Hanborough, husbandman, for 30s.; charges 8d. (3) Agreed to be paid 3 March in part payment 5s. and 20s. on 1 May.

f.330r Court held 20 Jan. 1598 by the bailiffs with Mr Clarke, Richard Humfrys, Nicholas Gonne, Henry Rankyll and others.

Action of debt : Giles Prat of Witney, collar maker, against Richard Haskynes, clothier, for 13s. 4d.; charges 4d. (3)

Order: bakers not to bake white or wheaten bread other than 13 to the dozen on pain of 5s.

f.330v Actions of debt : Widow Wryte of Witney against Richard Maior of Witney, broadweaver, for 5s.; charges 6d. (2)

William Arndayll of Witney, salter, against John Thomas for 4s.; charges 8d. (2)

Thomas Lardyne of Witney, tailor, against Robert Rabone of Witney for 10s.; charges 8d. (3)

f.331v Agreed: 24 Jan. 1598 between Roger Whyllar senior of Witney, carpenter and Thomas Wyllar, son of the aforesaid Roger, that after Whyllar senior's decease the bailiffs of Witney shall have the rent of the messuage and tenement that Thomas Whyller dwells in on the south side of Crondaulle St. commonly called Corn St., between the tenement of Roger Wylkshear on the west and the tenement of Roger Whyllar on the east, now in the tenure and occupation of Thomas Jeffrys, cobbler, for the proper use and bringing up of Ursula Whyllar, the daughter of the aforesaid Thomas, until such time as the aforesaid Ursula shall be able to shift for herself by service, and after the decease of her father the within written Ursula to have the aforesaid messuage and tenement to her and her heirs for that time as the

---

[86]   Probably a mistake for 'amerced': this court did not use essoins or formal excuses for non-attendance. All the offenders were wardsmen who were supposed to attend, see pp.xx–xxi.

lease specifies paying the same rent as is in the same lease set down. In witness whereof the bailiffs have given and granted our consent.

f.332r Md. a possession: given 7 Sept. 1598 by William Clempsone of Witney, mercer, deputy for Thomas Daulltone of London, tailor, to the bailiffs for the use of Robert Cakebred of Witney, victualler, of one house on the west of the High St. between the tenement of Leonard Yate senior on the south and the tenement of the same Leonard on the north, now in the tenure and occupation of Robert Jhames, butcher, with the shops and others houses thereto adjoining and belonging with the backside, garden and orchard adjoining to the close and backside of the same Leonard Yate towards Witney. To have and hold from the heirs of Thomas Daullton by a special deed made from Daullton to Cakebread and his heirs for ever, so that Daullton or his heirs shall make no claim or challenge thereunto. Witnesses: the constables, William Maior the sergeant, Steven Collyar wardsman, William Clempson, Giles Pallmare, John Shawe, Giles Pratte and others.

f.332v Actions of debt : Md. Friday 2 June 1598 Hew Hollanes of Birmingham, Warws., against Anthony Gowllde, petty chapman, for 39s. 11d.; charges 12d. Paid.

> Same against the same for 12s. 1d.; charges 12d. Paid.

f.333r Court held 10 Feb. 1598 by the bailiffs with Nicholas Gunne, Humfrey Yorcke, Thomas Webley and others.

Actions of debt : Nicholas Gonne of Witney, clothier, against Bartholomew Cordywell of Witney, broadweaver, for 28s. 8d.; charges 8d. (3)

> John Hardwoke of Enstone, gent., against James Hykes of Witney, butcher, for 12s, 6d.; charges 8d. (3)

> Md. Thursday 16 Feb. 1598 Richard Beerye of Chipping Norton, linen draper, against Richard Faulknar of Ducklington, husbandman, for 11s.; charges 12d.; pledge for answering Christopher Cotes of Witney. Paid.

f.333v Court held 10 March 1598 by the bailiffs with Nicholas Gonne, William Hunte, Humfrey Yorke and others.

Actions of debt : Robert Bartlat of Asthall Leigh, husbandman, against Robert Surryll of Witney, haberdasher, for 7s.; charges 8d. (2)

> Richard Haskynes of Witney, clothier, against Leonard Goode of Witney, baker, for 20s.; charges 8d. (3) Ordered that Leonard Goode to come to the next court with his two hands to wage his law or else to be condemned. On 19 May received 40d.

> Widow Gonne of Witney against Henry Broke of Witney, broadweaver, for 21s.; charges 8d. (3)

f.334r Court held 24 March 1598 by the bailiffs with Mr Clarke and others.

Actions of debt : Richard Boxe, yeoman, against Richard Okleye of Witney, dyer, for 26s. 8d.; charges 8d. (3) Agreed.

> Md. Tuesday 25 April 1598 Nicholas Wykes of Oxford, yeoman, against Thomas Suttyn of North Leigh, husbandman, for 39s. 11½d.; charges 12d.; pledge Thomas Townesend of Witney. (2) 20s. paid by Thomas Townsend on 4 Aug. in full satisfaction.

f.334v Court held 28 April 1598 by the bailiffs with Nicholas Gonne, Humfrey Yorke, Thomas Webleye and others.

Actions of debt : Robert Harryse of Chilson, yeoman, against Robert Claye of Witney, blacksmith, for 6s. 6d.; charges 8d. (1) Agreed.

Md. Thursday 4 May 1598 Ann Hoytar of Burford, widow, against Edward Relye of Shipton-under-Wychwood, yeoman, for 4s. 8d.; charges 12d. (3) Agreed and paid.

Richard Brice of Witney, broadweaver, against James Hikes of Witney, butcher, for 12s.; charges 8d. (3)

f.335r Court held 19 May 1598 by the bailiffs with Mr Clarke, the wardsman and others.

Actions of debt : Roger Wyryng of Hailey, yeoman, against Peter Jonsone of Witney, wheeler, for 29s. 6d.; charges 8d. (3)

Henry Whyght of Witney, tucker, against Richard Horne of Witney, broadweaver, for 7s.; charges 8d. Agreed.

William Clempson of Witney against George Maye of Witney, glover, for 9s.; charges 8d.

f.335v   George Kempe of Witney against Thomas Shawe of Witney, butcher, for 10s.; charges 8d. (3)

Md. Thursday 27 July 1598 Edward Handes of Witney, broadweaver, against Simon Waulbe of Burford for 20s.; charges 12d. Agreed and paid.

f.336r Md. a possession: taken 20 May 1598 by Walter Daulton, bailiff, of Roger Willsheare of Witney, shoemaker, Margaret his wife and Thomas Wilsheare, their heir apparent, of one messuage or tenement situated on the west side of the High St. with the appurtenances and one half acre of arable ground in the crofts called West Crofts behind the tenement and arable ground of William Hunte, cardmaker, on the north side, then in the tenure of Robert Surell, haberdasher, and the tenement and ground of Thomas Marten, barber, on the south now in the tenure of Thomas Shawe, butcher; to the use of Thomas Handes, butcher, his heirs and assigns for ever, according to a deed made by the consent of the parties above to the within named Thomas Handes, his heirs or assigns, according to the ancient custom of the borough of Witney. In the presence of the constables, William Maior sergeant, Steven Collyar, Edmund Budd, Justinian Wellar, wardsmen.[87]

f.337r Court held 17 June 1598 by the bailiffs with Henry Rankyll, the sergeant and others.

Court held 15 July 1598 by the bailiffs with Thomas Tayllar, Humfrey Yorcke and others.

Actions of debt : Christian Clempsone of Witney, widow, against William Pursar of Witney, tucker, for 4s. 8d.; charges 8d. (3)

[87]   For the final concord on this transaction see CP 25(2) 197 Mich. 40 & 41 Eliz.

THE WITNEY COURT BOOKS, 1598

Henry Rawbone of Brize Norton against George Warde of
Witney, tinker, for 10s.; charges 8d. (3)

f.337v Covenanted servant: Henry Allyne of Witney bound himself to Robert More of
Witney to serve after the manner of an apprentice for five years from 25
March last past, to be taught the art of a rough layer; received in earnest five
pence and with him to serve after the manner of the Statute,[88] keeping his
master's lawful secrets; to be found etc. [as on p.83]; and to be given for
four years 30s. of lawful English money and a pair of shoes, to wit for the
first, second, third and fourth years and then the fifth, sixth and last years
£3 and a pair of shoes. In witness whereof the parties have set their hands
24 Aug. 1598. [No marks or signatures.]

f.338r Court held 4 Aug. 1598 by the bailiffs with Humfrey Yorke, constable, the
sergeant and others.
    Actions of debt : Md. Thursday 24 Aug. 1598 Thomas Cave against John Smith
    of Oxford, chandler, for 35s.; charges 12d.
                Md. [no date] Henry Adames of Farthinghoe, Northants.,
    upholsterer, against Josias Perse, 'paratar', for 13s. 4d.; charges 8d. (3)

f.338v Md. at the court on 17 June 1598 Richard Boshope alias Martyne brought into
court three lawful witnesses before the bailiffs, Mr John Clarke, Richard
Humfreys and Humfrey Yorcke, constable, upon an assumpsit between
himself and Richard Haskynes and thereupon paid certain money apiece
into the hands of the Bailiff Daulton. Witnesses: William Pursar, Peter
Ryder, John Pearsse.

f.339r Md. 25 Sept. 1598 Humfrey Yorcke of Witney, constable, took on suspicion of
felony one Nicholas Sparry for one sorrel gelding with four white feet and
a star on the forehead, being appraised at 33s. 4d. Appraisers: Richard
Humfrys, Richard Martyne, George Kempe, Nicholas Huchynes.
    Action of debt : Md. Sunday 15 Oct. 1598 Thomas Willkshear of Witney, shoe-
    maker, against . . . Sadlare of Weald, Bampton, yeoman, for 2s. 3d.;
    charges 12d.

f.339v Court held 28 Sept. 1598 by the bailiffs with Mr John Clarke, Richard Humfrys,
Richard Martyne, Humfrey Yorcke and others.
    Actions of debt : Thomas Yate, son of Mr Leonard Yate of Witney, clothier,
    against Josias Paratare[89] for 3s. 3d. with the charges. (2)
                Katrin Handes of Witney, servant to Mr John Clarke, against
    William Cakbred, broadweaver, for 4s. 10d.; charges 8d. Nicholas
    Huchynes gave his word for 4d. a week till paid. Agreed.
f.340r   Md. Thursday 16 Oct. 1598 Edward Younge, servant to
    Walter Dawlltone of Witney, shoemaker, against Widow Wastarne of
    South Leigh for 10s.; charges 12d. (1)
                Md. 4 Dec. 1598 Nicholas Gonne of Witney, yeoman, against
    Michael and Thomas Egleye of Hardwick for 20s. 8d.; charges 8d.; pledge
    Peter Rankyll of Witney. (2)

---

[88]   Presumably the Statute of Artificers, 5 Eliz. c.4.
[89]   Presumably Josias Perse above, f.338r.

f.340v Action of debt : Md. 24 Nov. 1598 George Lyffoley of Eastleach, Gloucs., husbandman, against Robert Smyth of Hardwick, broadweaver, for 6s. 6d.; charges 8d. (3)

Item received 9 Feb. 1599 by Mr Geyttynes from Thomas Webley, clothier and chamberlain of Witney, 10s. for the town of Tiverton, Devon, towards their loss by fire, 1598.

f.341r Court held 6 Oct. 1598 by John Clarke and Richard Boshope, bailiffs, with George Kempe, James Hoddson, with the officers being chosen and others.
Constables: George Kempe, James Hoddsonne: sworn.
Wardsmen: Henry Whighte, Henry Goylles, Giles Pratte, Thomas Bedwell, William Tyrke: sworn.
Cloth searchers: John Boulte, Peter Ridar: sworn.
Leather sealers: Edward Handes, Nicholas Stratton: sworn.
Cardenars: Nicholas Maior, John Robynson: sworn.
Ale tasters: Giles Pallmer, [Richard Budde crossed out] Andrew Hodsonn: sworn.

f.341v Court held 3 Nov. 1598 by the bailiffs.
Covenanted servant: in court William Jheffryse, son of Christopher Jeffryse of Witney, blacksmith, in consideration of eight covenant pence, confessed himself bound to Henry Whight of Witney, broadweaver, with him to dwell and serve in the manner of an apprentice for eight years from 29 Sept. last past, to be taught the occupation of a broadweaver;* to keep his master's secrets lawful and honest everywhere, not to marry, not to absent himself nor prolong himself from his master's service by day or night but behave towards him as a true and faithful servant, not to frequent taverns or alehouses nor haunt there save on his master's business, not to play his master's goods at any unlawful games. To be found good fit and lawful bread, meat and drink, and bedding, hose, shoes and all things necessary for an apprentice of that craft. And to be given* at the end of the term 13s. 4d. wages and double apparel. In witness whereof we have set our
f.342r   hands: [marks of] William Jeffryse, Henry Humfrey, Robert Payne.[90]

f.342v Court held 3 Nov. 1598 by the bailiffs with George Kempe, the sergeant, the wardsmen and others.
Actions of debt : Richard Take of . . ., Berks., husbandman, against John Hartley of Witney, ironmonger, for 20s.; charges 8d. (3)
        Richard Haskyns of Witney, clothier, against William Pursare of Witney, tucker, for 17s. 6d.; charges 4d. (3)
        Joan Patryke, servant to Bartholomew Cordywell of Witney, against John Pyte of Witney for 3s. 6d.; charges 8d. (3)
f.343r Order: tipplers and victuallers to sell indoors a full wine quart of ale and

[90] This covenant departs from the model hitherto used on p.83 and is therefore given in detail. The content of similar later clauses is indicated by reference to this example: see the section between asterisks.

outdoors one full ale quart on pain of forfeiture of their acognizances [i.e.
recognizances].

Tipplers bound by the Justices: Roger Coxe, Reynold Whitton, Elizabeth
Lovyll, Thomas Townseyend, Richard Dytton before Mr Edmund Braye
and Mr Laurence Tanfelde; Edward Handes before Sir Henry Unton and
Mr Braye; William Heynes, William Emanes before Sir Anthony Coppe
and Mr Braye; Thomas Hankes, William Cakbred, John Thomas, John
Seaye, Thomas Bedwell the younger, Robert Cakbred, John Trindall,
Thomas Bedwell the elder, Leonard Goode, Robert Bakar . . .

f.343v Court held 16 Dec. 1598 by John Clarke, bailiff, with James Hoddson,
constable, the sergeant and others.

Agreed: at this court on 19 Jan. [1599] by Mr John Clarke, bailiff that Michael
Slatare, broadweaver, should pay Mary Gonne, widow, on Shrove
Tuesday, Feb. 1599., 4d. a week till the debt of 2s. 4d. be paid.

Distraint: same day the sergeant distrained the goods of Ellis Welles whereof
there remains in the house three bolsters or pillows, two chaffers, one
cradle, one truckle bed, one table board above and a pair of trestles on top
to bolt in and a pair of trestles and one form, one plater, one candlestick, a
kettle and a little postnet and two barrels.

f.344v Md. a possession: taken 19 Dec. 1598 by Mr John Clarke, bailiff, of Richard
Boshope alias Martyne, bailiff, tucker, of one house with appurtenances, a
shop, garden and backside in the West End of Witney between the
tenement of Richard Bokes on the east, now in the occupation of Thomas
Syrye, and the tenement of Richard Boshope, in the tenure and occupation
of John Boshope alias Martyne, broadweaver, on the west side with the
backside, shop and garden lying on the close of Roger Whillare towards the
south; to the use of John Bakkar of Witney, broadweaver, and his heirs.
Witnesses: George Kempe constable, Richard Maior deputy for the
sergeant of the mace, William Tyrke wardsman of the same ward.

f.345r Actions of debt : Md. Thursday 22 Feb. 1598 Edward Young of Witney, servant
to Walter Daulton, against Henry Egylls . . . of Eynsham, yeoman, for 4s.;
charges 12d.

John Gaskyne of Caswell, keeper, against John Ashat, coverlet
weaver, for 5s. 2d.; charges 8d. (3)

f.345v Court held 19 Jan. 1599 by Mr John Clarke, the only bailiff, with George
Kempe constable.

Actions of debt : Peter Rankyll of Witney, clothier, against Richard Hodsone of
Witney, blanket maker, for 11s. 8d.; charges 8d. (3)

William Fostare of South Leigh, husbandman, against James
Hikes of Witney, butcher, for 16s.; charges 8d. (1)

Md. 28 Jan. 1599 Peter Johnson of Witney, wheeler, against
Antony Webbe of Hailey, husbandman, for 14s.; charges 12d. Paid.

f.346r Court held 9 Feb. 1599 by John Clarke, bailiff, with Mr Tayllar, Walter
Daullton and others.

Action of debt : Richard Raynowlles of Brize Norton, husbandman, against

Richard Waynwryte alias Fysharde, broadweaver, for 15s; charges 8d.

Action of debt : Widow Styrte of Bampton against George Warde for 10s.; charges 8d. (2).

Agreed: John Harllye of Witney to pay Richard Take of Buckland, Berks., 5s. on 25 Mar., 24 June, 29 Sept. and 21 Dec.for the sum of 20s., the debt of Robert Cleye.

f.346v Court held 2 March 1599 by Mr John Clarke with the sergeant and John Lynley.

Action of debt : Thomas Hemeyng of Burford, surgeon, against George Kempe of Witney, yeoman, for 10s.; charges 8d. Paid.

Court held 20 March 1599 by Mr John Clarke with Thomas Cave, William Hunte, Thomas Handes and others.

Actions of debt : Mary Gonne, widow, against Leonard Tayllare, shoemaker, for 4s.; charges 8d. (1)

f.347r   Nicholas Gonne junior against John Thomas, tinker, for 34s. 6d.; charges 8d. (2)

Collectors for the poor: John Bakar and Nicholas Harryse appointed for the year 1599.

Actions of debt : Md. Thursday 29 March 1599 Thomas Poole of Witney, chandler, against John Chawney of Asthall, yeoman, for 4s.; charges 12d.; pledge for answering Roger Wilksheare. (2)

                     Md. 12 April 1599 Henry Rankyll of Witney, clothier, against Edward Wynne of Wootton, Gloucs., for 13s. [?]; charges 12d. Agreed.

f.347v Md. 1 June Peter Yate, son of Leonard Yate senior, came into court and confessed or offered to be sworn before the bailiffs and others being there to answer for such certain cloths as he was demanded of his dressing, that was for two fine cloths of 35 and one broad list of 32.[91]

f.348r Ale sellers licenced and bound by recognizances: Robert Claye, Margaret Carter, widow, Thomas Hurste, William Cordewell, Alexander Townsende, Edward Hannes, Thomas Shawe, Richard Shewell, Edmund Dodeswell.

f.348v Action of debt : . . . Meryman against . . . for 39s. 4d.

Lease: Robert Abraham demised to Robert . . . of Witney, sawyer, his chamber at . . . from 29 Sept. next until the end of nine years, yielding 6s. 8d. at the beginning of every year and repairing the . . . *Cancelled.*

Robert Hannes of Highworth, [Wilts.], shoemaker, son and heir of Henry Hannes late of Chipping Norton, yeoman . . .

[Symbols for the planets].

Thomas [*entry incomplete*].

Bond: Walter Clarcke of Willoughby, Warws., yeoman, and George

The entry is repeated on f.1r of the second volume, p.162 below. There the fine cloths are said to be '35 . . . long' which suggests that the offence was to have produced cloths of the wrong measurements. The Act 27 Eliz. c.17 provided double penalties if either narrow-listed or broadlisted whites were more than 28 yards in length at the most. The name of Richard Maior, possibly clerk of the court, appears after the entry on p.162.

Makepeace of Chipping Warden, Northants., bound 28 May by a bill to pay John Clarke of Witney £50 upon 29 Sept. next 1599.

John Russell

Raphe Moys

Actions of debt : John Hurt of Fawler, miller, against Nicholas Hill for 27s. 8d. with the entrance. Md. that at the court on 3 . . . Nicholas Hill promised the bailiffs in the face of the court to pay 33s. 4d. on the next Thursday after 2 Feb. according to the award of Mr Pore and John Barnaby.

Md. enter an action against Robert Bodye for Thomas Wilsheere for 12s. 4d.; charges 4d. [*Last two entries inside back cover of M.S.*]

CALENDAR
OF THE WITNEY COURT BOOKS
VOLUME II, 1599–1610

f.1r   [See entry on f.347v, p.160]

f.1v   'God bless . . . suckessor whomsoever he be and pene hime goe [?]of this book borrowed then have I.' [*folio torn*]

f.2r   Court held 20 April 1599 by Mr John Clarke with divers masters of the town and others.
Action of debt : Md. 23 April [1599] by . . . Pratte of Witney, collar maker, against Widow House of Minster Lovell for 33s.; charges 12d.

f.2v   Action of account: Md. Thursday 17 May 1599 Nicholas Launce of Eynsham, tanner, against William Kinge and Thomas Forde of Eynsham, shoemakers, for a certain reckoning between them; charges 12d.; pledge Roger Wylksheare.

f.3r   Court held 11 April 1599 by Mr John Clarke, bailiff, with Richard Hasskynes and others.
Action of debt : William Shelle, servant to Katherine Wright of Witney, against William Dallbe and Nicholas Gonne, surety for Dallbe, for 20s.; charges 8d. (3) Agreed before the bailiffs and other masters of the town there present that Nicholas Gonne junior should pay Shelle 20s. on 25 March next.
Amerced: for late appearance at the court Henry Goylles, Giles Pratte, Thomas Beddowlle, William Tyrke, 3s. 4d. apiece.
Order: tipplers and alemen to sell good and wholesome ale indoors at 1d. an ale quart and outdoors 1d. a thirdendell on pain of 3s. 4d. for each default.

f.3v   Actions of debt : Richard Hasskynes of Witney, clothier, against Widow Byshope for 12s.; charges 8d. (3)
                John Stampe of Witney against Margery Tollye, widow, for 3s. 4d.; charges 8d. (3)
Surveyors of the Queen's Highway: Henry Harppar and John Tymes elected and chosen.

f.4r   Court held 1 June 1599 by Mr John Clarke, bailiff, with Nicholas Gonne, James Hodsone constable, the sergeant and others.
Action of debt : Nicholas Gonne junior against John Workhouse of Witney, tucker, for 15s.; charges 6d. (1)
Action of account: Md. 14 June 1599 Thomas Raddborne of Standlake, yeoman, against Henry Whightsyde of Churchill for 36s. 8d.; charges 12d. (2); pledge Thomas Polle of Witney, chandler.

f.4v   Court held 6 July 1599 by Mr John Clarke, bailiff, with the sergeant and Mr Stampe, Thomas Hanndes.

Amerced: for non-appearance at the court, George Kempe constable, Giles Pratte, Henry Whight, William Tirke, Thomas Beddowlle, 3s. 4d. apiece.

f.5r   Court held 3 Aug. 1599 by Mr John Clarke, bailiff, with the sergeant and others.

Action of account: Md. 8 Aug. 1599 William Austyne alias Abstyne of South Leigh, husbandman, against John Simones of same, husbandman, for 14s. 4d.; charges 12d. Agreed.

f.5v   Court held 31 Aug. 1599 by Mr John Clarke, bailiff, with the sergeant, the wardsmen, Mr Leonard Yate, steward of the same court, Roger Wylksheare, Richard Haskines.

Action of debt : Widow Byshope of Witney against John Ashat of Witney, coverlet weaver, for 13s. 4d.; charges 8d.

f.6r   Md. a possession: taken 4 Oct. 1599 by William Clempson and Thoms Webley, bailiffs, of Humfrey Yorke of Witney, glover, of one messuage or tenement with the backside, shop, garden and close adjoining, lying on the east side of the High St. between the tenement of Henry Rankyll on the north side and the tenement of Richard Fostar on the south side; to the use of Thomas Luker of Winchcombe, Gloucs., yeoman, his heirs, executors and assigns. Witnesses: Leonard Yate junior, Thomas Wilkshear, constable, Richard Maior, deputy for the sergeant, William Heynes, wardsman for the same ward, Giles Pallmar, George Boxe.

f.6v   Tipplers licenced by the Justices: Roger Coxe, John Thomas, Edward Handes, licenced by Mr Edmund Bray and Laurence Tanfeld esqs.; Henry Harpar, Elizabeth Louyll, Richard Dytton, by Mr Edmund Bray and Walter Coullpepar esqs.; Richard Cabred, William Emanes, William Heynes, by Sir Anthony Cope and Mr Edmund Braye esq.; John Trindaull by Mr Laurence Tanfelld and Mr Walter Collpepar esqs.

f.7r   Court held 12 Oct. 1599 by Thomas Webley and William Clempsone, bailiffs, with Mr Clarke, Mr Leonard Yate, steward of the court, Thomas Clempson and others.

[Constables]: Leonard Goodde, Thomas Wylkshear: sworn.

Wardsmen: John Hunte for Paternoster Row; Robert Baysley for the West Ward; Thomas Polle for the Middle Ward; Anthony Ebseworth for the ward beneath the bridge; William Heynes for the East Ward: all sworn.

Ale tasters: John Tymes, Christopher Fordes: sworn.

Leather sealers: Edward Handes, Leonard Tayllar: sworn.

Cloth searchers: Robert Raybone, John Wyllye: sworn.

Cardenars: John Byrcat, John Robynson: sworn.

f.7v   At this court were put to their oath before the bailiffs and divers others, masters of the borough of Witney, with divers others for certain sheep which Thomas Radborn of Standlake bought of Henry Whitsyd of Churchill and these are the name of the men sworn: Robert Hareys, George Brawborn, Richard Dene, Richard Collynes for proof that the sheep were rotten sore, that he, Whitsyd, gave Radborn leave to sell the skins and that he should give those 'speches' that if that he sold the skins that there was the less to be paid, whereof he sold ten for which he can bring proof.[92]

Action of debt : Md. 10 Nov. 1599 William Jeffes of Witney Mill, miller against George Dorell, 'aqae vyte' man, for 6s.; charges 8d.

f.8r   Court held 2 Nov. 1599 and received seven covenant pence for the covenant following.

Covenanted servant: Richard Gowllde, son of Henry Goulld of Woodgreen, Witney, broadweaver, confessed before the bailiffs himself bound to Peter Rankyll of Witney, clothier and broadweaver, for seven years from 1 Nov. last past to be taught the occupation of a broadweaver after the manner of an apprentice; to keep etc. [as on p.158, with correction clause]; at end of

f.8v   term 20s. wages and double apparel. Witness: [mark of] Richard Goulld.

Collectors for the poor: Richard Budde and Steven Brise elected; to be paid quarterly.

f.9r   Court held 2 Nov. 1599 by the bailiffs with Mr Clarke, Thomas Taylar, Nicholas Gonne, William Brigfelld, Thomas Clempson, Richard Haskines and others.

Actions of debt : William Brigfelld senior of Witney against Thomas Shawe of Witney, butcher, for 24s; charges 4d. (1)

Peter Rankyll, clothier, against John Ashate of Witney, coverlet maker, for 21s.; charges 4d. (1)

Md. Thursday 16 Nov. [1599] Widow Wryte of Witney against Alexander Townesend junior for 39s. 11d.

f.9v   Md. Thursday 3 Jan. 1600 Robert Ballard of Caswell, yeoman. against William Coke of Oxon. [sic] for 6s.; charges 8d.

Md. Tuesday 22 Jan. [1600] William Tirke of Witney, broadweaver, against John Sherin of . . . Gloucs., for 21d.

f.10r   Court held 7 Dec. 1599 by the bailiffs with Mr Clarke, Thomas Wylkshear, constable, Mr Tayllar and others.

Actions of debt : Thomas Polle of Witney, chandler, against James Hikes of Witney, butcher, for 13s.; charges 4d. (10)

Md. 31 Dec. 1599 John Ashat of Witney, attorney for Mr Edmund Braye of Taynton, esq., executor of Robert Sylvestar late of Burford, deceased, against Edward Wyne of Wootton Bassett, Gloucs. [recte Wilts.] broadweaver, for 33s. 7d.; charges 8d.

f.11r   Court held 11 Jan. 1600 by the bailiffs with Richard Humfrey, Thomas Wylkshear and others.

Actions of debt : Thomas Daullton of Witney against Davy Yenanes of Witney, broadweaver, for 3s. 4d.; charges 4d. (2)

Richard Prate of Witney against John Thomas, tinker, for 10s.; charges 4d. (2) Assigned for the first court to me Richard Maior.

[92] Presumably Redbourn was suing for his purchase price, less the money for the 10 skins sold.

f.12r Covenanted servant: 20 Jan. 1600 William Gould, son of Henry Gould of
       Woodgreen, Witney, broadweaver, acknowledged the receipt of eight
       pence in earnest and bound himself to William Tirke of Witney, broad-
       weaver, for eight years from 2 Feb. next to be taught the occupation of a
       broadweaver as an apprentice; to keep etc. [as on p.158]; not to lend his
       master's goods to any man without leave and to be given at the end of the
       term 20s. wages and double apparel. Witnesses: [marks of] William Gould,
       Richard Irland. And of me Richard Maior [signature].[93]

f.14r Court held 8 Feb. 1600 by the bailiffs with Mr John Clarke, Thomas Wylksher,
       constable, and others.
       Actions of debt : Thomas Bedowll of Witney, baker, against John Thomas of
       Witney for 13s.; charges 4d. (3)
               Thomas Humfris of Witney against Ellis Welles of Witney,
       broadweaver, for 3s. 4d.; charges 4d. (3)
               Henry Egyllstone of Eynsham, yeoman, against John Thomas
       of Witney for 20s.; charges 4d. (3)

f.15r Court held 8 Feb. 1600 by the bailiffs.
       Covenanted servant: Richard Watsonne, son of Anthony Watsone of Witney,
       clerk, acknowledged the receipt of eight pence in earnest and by the advice
       of his father, confessed himself bound to John Clarke of Witney, clothier
       and broadweaver, for eight years from 21 Dec. last past to be taught the
       occupation of a broadweaver as an apprentice; to keep etc. and not to lend
       etc. [as on pp.158, 165]; at the end of the term double apparel. Witnesses:
       [signatures of] Richard Wattson, Anthony Watson, Richard Maior.

f.16r Court held 1 March 1600 by the bailiffs with Mr John Clarke, Roger
       Wylkshere, Thomas Wylksher, constable, and others.
       Actions of debt : Henry Egyllstone of Eynsham, yeoman, against Richard Okly
       of Witney, dyer, for 26s. 8d.; charges 4d. (3)
               Same against the same for 20s.; charges 4d. (3)
               Richard Hulles of Kelmscott, yeoman, against Henry Broke of
       Witney, broadweaver, for 26s.; charges 4d. (3)
f.16v   Md. 11 March [1600] Thomas Handes of Witney, butcher,
       against Humfrey Startup alias Barllate of Lew, husbandman, for 26s. 8d.;
       charges 8d. Agreed.
       Md. that before 29 Sept. last past [?1599, *year crossed out*] Edward Page servant to
       Richard Hulles of Kelmscott, yeoman, made his assumpsit on his oath that
       Henry Broke of Witney, broadweaver, received certain wool of the afore-
       said Hulles, whereof the remnant remains 26s.

f.17r Court held 4 April 1600 by the bailiffs with the sergeant and Robert Beysly and
       others.

[93] The 'not to lend' clause appears here for the first time, though it is common in contemporary indentures. Four later covenants employ it. For Maior, see above, p.xxi.

Actions of debt : John Thomas of Witney, tinker, against Thomas Bryan of Witney, broadweaver, for 23s.; charges 4d. (2)

Same against Widow Horne for 8s. 2d.; charges 4d. (2)

William Deane of South Leigh, gent., against William Daube and James Hikes of Witney, butchers, for 34s. 10d.; charges 4d. (2)

f.17v   John West of Swinbrook, gent., against Timothy Collier of Fulbrook, husbandman, for 30s.

Same against the same for 10s. Agreed.

John Fipes of South Leigh, yeoman, against Leonard Yate, son of Thomas Yate, gent., for 30s.; charges 4d. (2)

Richard Birey of Chipping Norton, mercer, against Richard Hodsone of Witney, broadweaver, for 4s. 3d.; charges 4d. (2)

Md. 14 April 1600 William Haddune of Burford, salter, against William Sanng of North Leigh for 2s. 10d.; charges 8d. (2)

f.18r   Court held 2 May 1600 by the bailiffs with Thomas Tayllar, Richard Clempson, Thomas Wylkshear, the sergeant and others.

Actions of debt : Richard Surell of Witney, haberdasher, against William Nicoulds of Witney, yeoman, for 17s.; charges 4d. (2)

John Thomas of Witney against Agnes Oklye for 4s.; charges 4d. (3)

Thomas Beddowll of Witney against James Hikes of Witney, butcher, for 8s.; charges 4d. (3)

f.18v   Thomas Wylkshear of Witney, shoemaker, against Christopher Coles of Witney, broadweaver, for 12s. 9d. (3)

George Kempe of Witney, yeoman, against John Knowles of Witney for 38s. 6d.; charges 4d. (3)

Nicholas Gune of Witney, draper alias tailor, against Peter Shepard of South Leigh, narrow weaver, for 10s. 6d. (1) For entrance of the action, drawing the court and other fees and further for the behoof of Josias Perse, being his annual debt which I the said Shepard have discharged.

f.19r   Court held 23 May 1600 by the bailiffs with Thomas Wilksher, constable, the sergeant and others.

Actions of debt : John Carye of Hailey, shepherd, against John Pyte of Witney, shepherd, for 2s. 1d.; charges 4d. (2)

Same against Thomas Fatharson, broadweaver, for 2s.; charges 4d. (2)

John Richardsonne late of Curbridge, yeoman, against Robert Surrell of Witney, haberdasher, for 10s.; charges 4d. (2)

f.19v   Md. of purchase: John Kete and William Millton of Curbridge bought of William Broke of Lew three kyne, one black under hit on both ears, one red under hit on the near ear and the third red under hit on the near ear and cropped on the further, price for all three £5, to the use of three children, Henry, Agnes and Mary Smith.

f.20r   Court held 6 June 1600 by the bailiffs with Thomas Wilksheare, constable, Humfrey Yorke, Roger Wylksheare and others.

Amerced: the wardsmen and the constable, Leonard Goode, Robert Beysly, William Heynes, Anthony Ebsworth, Thomas Poole, 3s. 4d. apiece for want of appearance at this court.

Action of debt : Md. 16 Aug. 1600 Edmund Surrell of Burford, haberdasher, against Thomas Brodwaye of Kingston Bagpuize, Berks., for 39s. 11d.; charges 8d.

f.20v   Covenanted servant: 16 June 1600 Albone Ridare, son of John Ridare of Witney, tucker, in consideration of eight covenant pence and with the consent of Joan Ridare his mother confessed himself bound to Robert Tayllar of Witney, broadweaver, for eight years from 29 Sept. next to be taught the occupation of a broadweaver as an apprentice and to cut, set and make all manner of sleys and to strike all manner of harnesses belonging to the trade or occupation of a broadweaver; to keep etc. [as on p.158; no correction clause]; at the end of the term 16s. wages and double apparel. Witnesses: [signatures of] Edmund Budd, Henry White, Richard Maior; [mark of] Albon Ridar.

f.21v   Court held 26 June 1600 by the bailiffs with Nicholas Gonne, Richard Boxe, Thomas Wylkshear and others.

Actions of debt : Richard Falknare of Ducklington, husbandman, against Christopher Forde of Witney, broadweaver, for 3s. 1d.; charges 4d. (3)
    George Meke of Oxon. [sic] against Simon Yemesworth of Witney, baker, for 3s.; charges 4d. (2) Agreed.
    Md. 17 July 1600 George Kempe of Witney, yeoman, against Thomas Boxe of North Leigh, yeoman, for 23s. 4d.; charges 8d.

f.22r   Court held 1 Aug. 1600 by the bailiffs with Thomas Clempsone, Thomas Wylksheare, constable, and others.

Actions of debt : George Kempe of Witney, yeoman, against John Birkate of Witney for 39s. 11d.; charges 4d. (1)
    Md. 4 Aug. 1600 Nicholas Gonne of Witney, yeoman, against Thomas Edgarly of Hardwick, far carter, for 20s.; charges 4d. Agreed.
    Same against Hew Harryse of Ducklington for 11s.; charges 8d.

f.22v   Covenanted servant: 1 Aug. 1600 William Dussyne, son of William Dussyne of Cogges, acknowledged the receipt of four pence and before the bailiffs confessed himself bound to Thomas Wylkshere of Witney, shoemaker, for four years from 29 Sept. next to be taught the occupation of a shoemaker; to keep etc. [as on p.158, with correction clause]; not to procure or cause to be procured hurt or damage to his master but with all speed he may let or hinder it and thereof warn him: to be given at the end of the term 6s. 8d. wages and double apparel.[94] Witnesses: [signatures] Henry Lewes, Simon Peason, Richard Maior; [mark of] William Dussyne.

f.23v   Distraint: at this court [1 Aug.] were appraised certain goods distrained for the fifteenth, being the fifth and sixth granted to Her Majesty in the 38th year

---

[94]   The 'not to . . . hurt' clause appears for the first time here, though again it is common in contemporary indentures. See also below, p.186.

of her reign,[95] the which goods are these: one kettle belonging to Thomas Shawe, appraised at 5s. 6d.; one pair of tucker's shears belonging to Peter Ridare, appraised at 3s. and out of the same house one cupboard cloth and a cradle cloth, appraised at 2s.; one brake belonging to Robert More, a 'trene' [i.e. wooden] platter, a salt of pewter, a saucer, appraised at 8d.

f.24r   Court held 22 Aug. 1600 by the bailiffs with Thomas Wylkshear, George Kempe, Leonard Goode, Robert Beysley, Anthony Ebsworth.

Action of debt : John Trewman alias Trewpeney of Minster Lovell against John Thomas of Witney for 14s.; charges 4d. (2)

Action of account: Md. 19 Sept. 1600 Thomas Townsend of Witney, broad-weaver, against William Wyse of Eynsham, carpenter, on further reckonings.

Actions of debt : Md. 23 Sept. 1600 Richard Smyth of Witney against Martin Johnson of Ducklington for 2s. 10d.; charges 8d.

f.24v   Md. at the court on 22 Aug. 1600 Nicholas Gunne senior against George Smythe, sawyer, for 16s.; charges 4d.

f.25r   Court held 19 Sept. 1600 by the bailiffs with Thomas Wylksher, constable, William Maior, sergeant, the wardsmen.

Actions of debt : Md. 25 Sept. 1600 Richard Cooke of Signet, Oxon., husband-man, against Simon Haulle of Burford, glover, for 4s. 4d.; charges 8d.

                      Andrew Chamline of Lew, weaver, against Richard Okley of Witney, dyer, for 4s.; charges 4d. (2)

                      Same against Thomas Bedwell the elder for 4s.; charges 4d. (2)

f.25v   Richard Yate of Witney against Leonard Yate, tucker, for 39s. 10d.; charges 4d. (3)

                      Same against Dennis Ficate for 3s.; charges 4d. (3)

                      Peter Sheppard of South Leigh, weaver, against Josias Peasse for 11s. 4d.; charges 4d. (3)

                      Md. 13 Nov. 1600 Henry Fipes of North Leigh, deceased, and William Fipes of North Leigh, husbandman, against Robert Whytar of Woodstock for 33s. 4d.; charges 4d.

f.26r   31 March 1600. Whereas it is decreed by us whose names are underwritten, at the appointment of the Worshipful Mr Edmund Bray, esq., that we should allow out of the lands and goods of Peter Johnson, the son of William Johnson deceased, as we should think fit for the keeping of the child begotten of the said Peter Johnson on the body of Mary Bewe, that the said Mary Bewe should be paid the sum of £8 if it please God that the child should live the term of eight years after the date hereof. That is to wit, 20s. a year at the four usual feast days, on 24 June next coming 5s., on 29 Sept. 5s., on 21 Dec. 5s. and on 25 March 5s. until the eight years be expired, if the child shall live so long, and Mary is to discharge the town of the child

---

[95] There was no parliament in 38 Eliz. (1595-6). In the parliament of 1593 three subsidies and six 15ths and 10ths were granted by the Act 35 Eliz.c.13. The fifth and sixth of these were to be collected in 1595 and 1596. There is no particular of account for these for Bampton Hundred in the P.R.O.

aforesaid. The bailiffs are to have the paying of the money quarterly for the relief of the child. The said Mary shall have a bed, a pair of sheets, a coverlet, a kettle and a skillet. Witnesses: [signatures of] Leonard Box, umpire, Thomas Webley, bailiff, Richard Box, John Bishoppe, Richard Humfreys, John Times; [marks of] Mr Edward Tirey, serjeant of the ewrey, Humfrey Yorke.[96]

f.26v　Tipplers licensed by the Justices for this present year, on the other side of the book: Roger Coxe, Robert Taillar alias Cakebred, William Cakebred, Henry Harpar, Thomas Townsend, Edward Handes, Richard Diton by Mr Laurence Tanfelld and Mr Edmund Bray, esqs.; William Heines, William Emanes by Sir Anthony Cope and Mr Edmund Braye.

Order: Md. taken at the court on the other side of the leaf. Tipplers to sell in and outdoors one full quart of good and wholesome ale on pain of 3s. 4d. for each default.

f.27r　Court held 17 Oct. 1600. Peter Rankill and William Hunte were elected and chosen bailiffs, being there accompanied by Thomas Webley and William Clempson the previous bailiffs, Mr Clarke, Richard Humfrey, Walter Dallton, Mr Thomas Cave with the constables Steven Colliar and Henry Whighte and others.

Wardsmen: John Hartley for Paternoster Row Ward, Nicholas Huchines, John Richardson, Walter Linley, Robert Taillar: sworn.

Cardenars: John Birkat, James Hickes: sworn.

Ale tasters: Nicholas Maior, William Ives: sworn.

Cloth searchers: Nicholas Gonne junior, John Willye junior: sworn.

Leather sealers: Edward Handes, Nicholas Stratton: sworn.

Agreed: between George Kempe and John Birkat before the bailiffs that Birkat to pay 3s. 4d. on 21 Dec. next and so every quarter following until the whole debt of 40s. be fully satisfied.

f.27v　Md. 30s. was delivered to the bailiffs by Mr Thomas Taillare, which was given to the use of the town of Witney in the year 1600 by Mr John Attwell, parson of 'Cornwell', to the use of the poor artificers and craftsmen of the borough.[97] The bailiffs are to deliver this sum to their successors and this to continue for ever.

f.28r　Court held 14 Nov. 1600 by the bailiffs with Mr John Clarke, the constables, the sergeant and others.

Actions of debt : Thomas Polle of Witney, chandler, against George Kempe of Witney for 18s.; charges 4d. (1)

　　　　Robert Tayllare of Witney, clothier, against George May of Witney for 4s. 11d.; charges 4d. (1)

Action of account: William Shelle, blacksmith, against Katherine Wright of

---

[96]　Perhaps Box is called an umpire because he had arbitrated on the settlement. The sergeant of the Ewrey was a royal officer but Tirey was also a tenant of the bishop; see Misc. Je I/1,f.40v. Edmund Bray who appointed the men was a Justice of the Peace.

[97]　Probably the county of Cornwall and not the Oxfordshire village; see below, p.206.

Witney, widow, for 14 weeks service at 10d. the week, whereof he has received 18d. and there remains for his demand 10s. 2d.; charges 4d. (1)

f.29v Collectors for the poor: William Bishope and Henry Goylles were elected at the court on the other side of the leaf for the present year 1601.[98]

Chamberlain: Thomas Handes was appointed chamberlain at the same court and the sum of 38s. 4d. was delivered to him.

Action of debt : Md. 15 Dec. [1600] Thomas Humfris of Witney, baker, against Richard Mace of Abingdon [Berks.,] for 10s.; charges 8d.

f.30r Court held 1 Dec. 1600 by the bailiffs with Mr John Clarke, Walter Daulltone, Thomas Webley, Henry Whighte and others.

Actions of debt : Edmund Petey, clothier, against Richard Knowlles for 24s.; charges 4d.

Robert Betartone of Purton, Wilts., against Thomas Shawe, butcher, for 13s. 4d.; charges 4d.

William Tirke of Witney, broadweaver, against Thomas Shawe the elder, butcher, for 8s.; charges 4d.

f.30v Paul Grenaway of Curbridge, wheeler, against Thomas Freman of Witney, butcher, for 4s.; charges 4d.

Richard Smyth, yeoman, against Robert Stevenes for 10s.; charges 4d. (1)

Action of account: Md. 8 Jan. [1601] Nicholas Turnar of South Leigh, shepherd, against Robert Wylliamsone of Black Bourton, gent., for 30s.; charges 8d. (1)

f.31r Md. a possession: given 29 Nov. 1600 by the bailiffs by an especial deed from Leonard Yate the father and Leonard Yate the son of two messuages and tenements situated in Corndell commonly called Corn St. with all appurtenances, to the use of William Emanes and Mary Emanes his wife and their heirs for ever, Leonard Yate the father and Leonard Yate the son making no claims to the messuages aforesaid. Witnesses: [signatures of] Peter Rankill, bailiff, Thomas Cave, John Clarke, George Box; [marks of] William Hunte, bailiff, John Richardsonne.[99]

f.31v Actions of debt : Robert Jholly of Birmingham, Warws., against William Nelson, saddler, for 39s. 11d.; charges 4d.

Richard Yate, son of Leonard Yate senior, against Leonard Yate of Witney, tucker, for 39s. 11d.; charges 4d. (2)

Peter Shepard of South Leigh, weaver, against Josias Perse of Witney for 11s. 8d.; charges 4d.

f.32r Court held 9 Jan. 1601 by the bailiffs with Mr John Clarke, William Clempson, the constables, the sergeant, Thomas Handes and others.

Actions of debt : William Clempson of Witney, mercer, against Robert Surell, haberdasher, for 20s.; charges 4d. (1)

Agnes Tayllar of Witney, widow, against Richard Knowles, son of John Knowles, for 6s. 4d.; charges 4d. (2)

[98] Presumably the court of I Dec. on f.30r; f.29 is blank.
[99] For the final concord on this transaction see CP 25(2) 197 Hilary 43 Eliz.

John Craftes of Hailey, yeoman, against Roger Wilksheare of Witney, shoemaker, for 39s. 11d.; charges 4d. (2)

f.32v Agreed: between Mr Bailiff Rankell and Richard Hodson that Hodson should pay Bailiff Hunte for the use of Rankell 6d. a week until the whole debt of 12s. 4d. is paid.

f.33r Court held 6 Feb. 1601 by the bailiffs with William Clempsone, Henry Whight, constable, and others.

Covenanted servant: Josias Tassell son of Richard Tasse [sic] late of Reading, Berks., received ten pence in earnest and with the consent of his aunt Ursula Rankyll confessed himself bound to Peter Rankill of Witney, clothier, for the term of ten years from 25 March next to be taught the occupation of a broadweaver. During the said term Tassell to perform the duty of an apprentice in all points; he is not to be taken with any manner of deceit or falsehood during his apprenticeship. To be found etc. [as on p.83; no correction clause]; at the end of the term 13s. 4d. wages and double apparel. Witness: [mark of] Josias Tassell.

f.33v Action of debt : Md. 12 Feb. 1601 Robert Fallknar of Witney, broadweaver, against John Weaynman of Lew, gent., for 23s. 8d.; charges 8d.

Action of account: Md. 20 May [1601] Henry Tirey of Witney, plasterer, against Richard Denne of Hanborough, 'wotmell' maker, for 3s. 8d.; charges 12d.

f.34r Court held 20 March 1601 by the bailiffs with William Clempson, John Linley, Henry Whighte, constable, and others.

Actions of debt : Md. 2 April 1601 [100] Mr Thomas Yate of Witney, gent., against Thomas Cowlgrove of New Woodstock, baker, for 13s. 4d.; charges 8d. Agreed.

Md. same day Richard Robynson of the Field [i.e. Leafield], tailor, against Richard Hareys of Minster Lovell, husbandman, for 39s. 11d.; charges 8d.

f.34v Covenanted servant: 5 April 1601 [101] Thomas Wryte, son of Henry Wright of Witney, broadweaver, deceased, received seven pence in earnest according to the statute herein provided and confessed himself bound to William Tirke of Witney, broadweaver, for seven years from Easter next to be taught the occupation of a broadweaver as an apprentice; to keep etc. and not to lend etc. [as on pp.158, 165]; at the end of the term 6s. 8d. wages and double apparel. Witnesses:[signature of] Henry Lewes; [marks of] Thomas Wrighte, Richard Lewes.

Action of account: Md. 20 May 1601 Nicholas Cooke, senior, of Oxford against Anthony Breyent of Chipping Faringdon, Berks., chapman, for 25s.; charges 12d.

f.35v Action of debt : Md. 23 May 1601 Thomas Persone of Witney, blanket maker, against Robert Horne of Hailey, carrier, for 14s.; charges 12d.

---

[100] Given as 1610 in Ms, presumably in error.
[101] Given as 1610 in Ms, presumably in error.

f.36r   Court held 17 April 1601 by the bailiffs with Mr John Clarke, Richard Humfris, John Collyar with the constable and others.

Actions of debt : Edith Walle, widow, against Robert Raibone of Witney for 4s.; charges 4d.

John Wyllye of Witney against William Daube of Witney, butcher, for 20s.; charges 4d. (2)

William Shelle, blacksmith, against Richard Masone for 2s. 6d.; charges 4d. (2)

f.36v   Agreed: Md. 14 May 1601 between John Raynowlles of Glastonbury, Somerset, innholder, and Thomas Shawe, butcher, and Robert Fauknar, broad-weaver, both of Witney. Fauknar agreed to pay Raynolles the sum of 28s. and thereupon received 2d. as assumpsit of the days set, that is to say on 30 June next 8s., on 2 Nov. next 10s. and on 3 Feb. next 10s. It is also agreed that if any of these days is broken by Shawe or Fallknar the sum is to be doubled to Alice Raynowlles or her assigns, Shawe and Fallknar both being bound in assumpsit.

Action of debt : John Richardson of Witney, tailor, against Richard Michell, broadweaver, for 18d.; charges 4d. (1)

f.37r   Court held 21 May 1601 by the bailiffs with Nicholas Gonne, William Brigfelle, Walter Daullton, the constable and others.

Actions of debt : William Brigfellde of Witney, yeoman, against Charles Elyfecke of Witney, broadweaver, for 16s. 6d.; charges 4d. (1) Agreed.

Richard Haskines of Witney, yeoman, against William Heynes of Witney for 12s.; charges 4d. (1)

William Shelle of Witney, blacksmith, against John Breyan for 6s.; charges 4d. (1)

f.37v   Md. a possession: taken 31 March 1601 by William Hunte, bailiff, of William Bringfeild of Witney, yeoman, by his attorney Roger Wilsheir, for the consideration specified in a certain deed dated 26 March 1601, of a messuage or tenement with appurtenances lying in Corn St. between the tenement of Leonard Yate on the west and that of Giles Bringfeild on the east, then in the occupation of Bringfeild's daughter Marie Falkner, to the use of the said Marie Falkner to whom quiet possession was immediately delivered. Witnesses: Peter Rankell bailiff, William Maior sergeant, the constables and John Harteley and John Richardson, wardsmen, and others.

f.38r   Md. a possession: taken 15 Sept. 1600 by William Hunte, bailiff, of Henry Harpar of Witney, victualler, of one messuage or tenement with court, garden, backside and other easements lying on the east side of the High St. between the tenement of Thomas Larden, tailor, now in the tenure of John Boullte, tailor, on the north and the tenement of Roger Leddg on the south; to the use of Thomas Handes of Witney, his heirs and assigns. The possession was given by the bailiff according to a deed delivered by Hunte to Handes according to the custom of the borough of Witney in the presence of the constable, William Maior, sergeant, Robert Tayllar and John Richardson, wardsmen, William Clempson, Richard Hathway, Richard Maior with others.

f.39r   Covenanted servant: 2 July 1601 William Vallanes, son of Owen Vallanes late of

Hanborough, broadweaver, deceased, received six pence in earnest and confessed himself bound to Richard Brice, broadweaver, after the manner of an apprentice for six years from Whitsun next to be taught the occupation of a broadweaver. To keep his master's secrets worthy to be kept;' to be found etc. [as on p.83; no correction clause]; at the end of the term 20s. wages and double apparel. Witnesses: [signature of] John Stanford; [mark of] William Vallanes.

f.40r   Court held 17 June 1601 by the bailiffs with Mr John Clarke, Thomas Cornishe, Thomas Webley, Thomas Cave, Nicholas Gonne, Richard Box and others.

      Actions of debt : Thomas Willshere of Witney, shoemaker, against Richard Okley of Witney, dyer, for 3s.; charges 4d. (2)

            John Butlar of Shifford, yeoman, against George Ward of Witney, metalman, for 6s.; charges 4d. (2)

      Agreed: between Thomas Person and Robert Horne that Horne is to pay William Hunte, bailiff, 8s. on 29 June next. (2)

f.40v   Action of debt : Richard Johnson against James Hickes of Witney, butcher, for 3s.; charges 4d. (2)

      Actions of account: Thomas Robines of Witney, labourer, against John Thomas of Witney, metalman, for 13s. 4d.; charges 4d.

            Edmund Young of Aston, narrow weaver, against Roger Babbe of Witney for 7s. for one narrow loom. Agreed.

f.41r   Court held 10 July 1601 by the bailiffs with Mr Tayllar, the constables and others.

      Actions of debt : Edmund Petye of Witney, clothier, against Nicholas Burnell of Witney, labourer, for 5s.; charges 4d. (2)

            George Freman of Campden, Gloucs., tucker, against Humfrey Becham of Witney, tucker, for 7s.; charges 4d. (2)

            Md. 29 July 1601 Elizabeth Baker of Witney, widow, against John Wyllyames of Woodstock, baker, for 20s.; charges 8d.

f.41v   Action of account: Md. 27 Nov. [1601] Walter Daullton of Witney, mercer, against Thomas Smyth of Eynsham for six and a half stones of tallow; charges 8d. This action drawn by Thomas Wilshear.

f.42r   Covenanted servant: Md. covenant witnessing that 13 Sept. 1601 Henry Goulld son of Henry Goulld of Witney, broadweaver, for and in consideration of 10s. [sic] in hand paid to his father by Nicholas Harrys of Witney, broadweaver, bound himself to Harrys for six years from 29 Sept. next to be taught the occupation of a broadweaver. To keep his master's secret and perform all covenants belonging to an apprentice; to be found etc. [as on p.83; no correction clause]; at the end of the term 26s. 8d. wages and double apparel. Witnesses: [signature of] Richard Maior; [marks of] Henry Gould, Richard Fishar.

f.43r   Court held 25 Sept. 1601 by the bailiffs with Walter Daullton, Thomas Clempson, Thomas Cornysh, the constables and others.

      Actions of debt : Richard Hamar against John Shaw for 12d.; charges 4d.

            Richard Fishar of Stanton [Harcourt] against John Ashat, coverlet weaver, for . . .

f.44r Court held 5 Oct. 1601.

Order: all those men who have been bailiffs of the town of Witney and are still living are to attend all future courts, lawful warning having been given the day before by the wardsmen, to accompany and assist the bailiffs of Witney in their court on pain of 5s. for default. The like for inferior officers on pain of 2s. 6d. for default without some lawful excuse made to the bailiffs then being. Witnesses that this was done by general consent: [signatures of] William Dyer, steward at this court, Thomas Box, Phillip Boxe, John Lynley, Thomas Webly, Peter Rankle, William Clempsone, John L . . ., Hew Rackes, James Hodsone, Thomas Willsheire, Walter Dalton, E[dward Bird?] [marks of] Thomas Cornish, William Hunte, Thomas Hands, John Clarke, Richard Box.

f.44v Tipplers licenced by the Justices: Roger Cox, William Cakebred, Robert Cakebred, Edward Handes, Widow Lovyll, Thomas Townsende, John Thomas by Mr Edmund Bray and Mr Laurence Tanfelld, esqs.; William Emanes, Richard Diton by Mr Edmund Bray and Sir Anthony Cope; William Heines by Sir Anthony Cope and Mr Laurence Tanfelld.

f.45r Court held 9 Oct. 1601 by Thomas Box and Thomas Cornishe, bailiffs, with others of the masters of the borough accompanying them.

Constables: John Boshop, Thomas Pessley: sworn.

Wardsmen: Robert Birkarstaffe for Paternoster Row; John Workhouse for the West Ward; Michael Mockson for the East Ward; John Harris for beneath the bridge; John Horswell for the Middle Ward: all sworn.

Ale tasters: William Ines, George Day: sworn.

Cardenars: John Birkat, John Robinsonne: sworn.

Leather sealers: Nicholas Strattone, Edward Hanndes: sworn.

Cloth sealers: Nicholas Gonne, John Willie: sworn.

f.45v Action of debt : Md. 19 Oct. 1601 Bartholomew Cordywell of Witney, broad-weaver, against Andrew Chaulline of Lew for 13s. 4d.; charges 8d.

f.46r Covenanted servant: 9 Oct. 1601 George Parate, son of Simon Parate of Eastleach Turville, Gloucs., deceased, received eight pence in earnest and confessed before the bailiffs himself bound to Mr John Clarke for eight years from 29 Sept. last past to be taught the occupation of a broadweaver as an apprentice. To be found good and wholesome bread, meat and bedding and all other things fit for an apprentice and to be given at the end of the term 26s. 8d. wages and double apparel. Witness: [signature of] George Parate.

f.46v Action of debt : Henry Rankle against Richard Maior for 39s. 11d. (1)

f.47v Covenanted servant: 31 Oct. 1601 John Trindall junior received seven pence in earnest and confessed before the bailiffs himself bound to his father John Trindall senior for seven years from 29 Sept. last past to be taught the art and science of a mason or rough layer. To fulfil all the covenants belonging to an apprentice; to be found etc. [as on p.83; no correction clause]; to be given by his master at the end of the term all manner of working tools belonging to the occupation and double apparel. Witnesses: [signature of] Richard Maior; [marks of] John Trindall, John Champnes.

f.48r   Court held 30 Oct. 1601 by the bailiffs with Mr John Clarke, Walter Daullton, William Hunte, William Clempson, the constables, John Martine, Richard Box, Henry Rankell and others.

Actions of debt : Roger Lane of 'Rodson' [i.e. Radstone, Northants.,], yeoman, against John Baker, broadweaver, for giving his word for Richard Horn for 39s. 11d.

                Same against the same for 26s. 9d.; charges 8d.

                Robert Fallknar of Witney against Roger Wilksher of Witney for 11s. 4d.; charges 4d. (1)

f.48v   John Wylly senior of Witney against Henry Lewes of Witney 20d.; charges 4d.

f.49r   Court held 27 Nov. 1601 by Thomas Cornish, bailiff, with other masters of the borough, Mr John Clarke, Thomas Taylor, Thomas Webley, with Thomas Pessly, constable, and others.

Collectors for the poor: William Yemanes and Philip Box elected.

Actions of debt : John Baylly of Milton against Richard Ockley, dyer, for 25s,; charges 4d.

f.49v   Martin Johnson of Ducklington, yeoman, against Roger Wryte of Witney for 5s.; charges 4d. (2)

                Same against Henry Lewese for 10s.; charges 4d. (2)

                Same against Robert Stevenes for 9s.; charges 4d. (2)

                Same against Michael Moxonne, glover, for 3s. 8d.; charges 4d. (2)

                Same against Alexander Barat for 6s.; charges 4d. (2)

                Same against Bennet Pirye for 9s.; charges 4d. (2)

                Same against Mary Patrick for 3s.; charges 4d.

                Same against Widow Horne for 16s.; charges 4d. (2)

f.50r   A note of the subsidies of Witney made in 1601.[102] First for lands: William Hunte, £5; Roger Whellar £2 [*cancelled*]; John Barnabe £1; Thomas Carter £2; William Brigfelld £1; Humfrey Yorcke £1 [*cancelled*]; Edward Ashfeld £2; John Bishop £2; John Shawe £1; Andrew Bird £1; Thomas Box £6; Richard Humfres junior £1 [£4 *crossed out*]; Thomas Handes £2; William Yemanes £1; John Lynley £1; [*cancelled*]; William Bukingame £1; Leonard Yate, the son of Leonard Yate £2; Leonard Yate, the son of Thomas Yate £6; Thomas Poole £1. In goods: Richard Clempsonne £5 [£6 *crossed out*]; Peter Rankill £4; Henry Rankill £3 [£5 *crossed out*]; Thomas Cave £4; Nicholas Gonne £5; Richard Box £4; Thomas Webley £4; William Clempson £4; Richard Hasskines £3; Robert Cakebred £3; Walter Daullton £5; John Clarke £9; Thomas Cornish £5; Thomas Taillor £5; Eliz. Byshippe £3 [*cancelled*]. Sum total £17 12s. [i.e. amount levied on assessement]

---

[102]   The particular of account for this subsidy is E 179/163/398. There are numerous differences between the two lists. In E 179 entries for Roger Whellar, Humfrey Yorke, John Lynley, Richard Clempsonne and Eliz. Byshoppe are not cancelled, Richard Humfres junior is assessed at £4, and Henry Rankill at £5; Thomas Poole is not listed, and there is an additional entry for Robert Baker at £1.

f.51r   Court held 18 Dec. 1601 by the bailiffs with Peter Rankill, William Hunte, Thomas Hanndes, John Lynnley and others, William Clempson, Richard Haskines.

Actions of debt : James Hearing of South Leigh, husbandman, against William Fathry for 6s.; charges 4d. (2)

Nicholas Gonne of Witney against Michael Mocksam of Witney for 5s.; charges 4d.

Richard Birey of Chipping Norton, mercer, against Josias Pearse of Witney for 4s. 10d.; charges 4d. (3) Agreed.

f.51v   Md. 18 April 1602 William Hemes of Witney seized upon such goods as were in his custody for a certain debt of Thomas Lardine late deceased of 8s. 4d.

f.52r   Court held 8 Jan. 1602 by the bailiffs with Thomas Webley, William Clempson, Richard Hasskines, John Boshop, Thomas Pessley and others.

Actions of debt : Richard Cunstabull of Cogges, husbandman, against Henry Whight of Witney, broadweaver, for 19s.; charges 4d. (1)

George Dickson of Langley against Mark Russell of Bampton Mill for 4s.; charges 8d.

f.53r   Court held 5 Feb. 1602 by the bailiffs with Mr John Clarke, William Hunte, William Clempson, Richard Hasskines, John Boship, Thomas Hanndes and others.

Actions of debt : Robert Fullknar of Witney against Andrew Chamline of Lew for 5s. 4d.; charges 4d.

Thomas Cokarill of Chipping Faringdon, Berks., against Thomas Dyten of Witney, broadweaver, for 7s.; charges 4d.

Md. 8 April 1602 Thomas Poole of Witney, chandler, against Thomas Smith of Eynsham, tanner, for 30s.; charges 8d. (2) This action was drawn in 28 May and the debt discharged with charges by Henry Goylles.

f.53v   Distraint: Md. 24 March 1602 distrained on behalf of Mr Bailiff Box on the goods of George May of Witney, glover, for rent due to Box the day and date above written for the whole previous year to the value of 16s. 8d., in the presence of John Boshap, constable, Richard Hasskines, Humfrey Yorke, John Harris, Nicholas Whitting and others, that is to say six dozen and nine white tawed sheep skins, one great kettle, one possnet, one brass candlestick, one hanging pot [a pair of pell hooks *crossed out*].

f.54r   Court held 5 March 1602 by the bailiffs with Mr John Clarke, William Clempson, Richard Hasskins, Mr Thomas Tayllar, Thomas Pessley, constable, and others.

Amerced: John Workhouse, John Horssowll, John Harris, Michael Mocksame, wardsmen, 12d. apiece for want of appearance at this court.

Action of debt : Md. 28 March 1602 Richard Ockley of Witney, dyer, against Thomas Egarly of Hardwick, carrier, for 25s.; charges 8d. (3); pledge Henry Goylles.

f.54v   Md. 12 April 1602 James Banting of Northmoor, tanner, exchanged one sorrel mare, with a bald face and four white sets, for one bay mare, brand marked on the near buttock with a crow's foot and marked with the same on the further shoulder, with Thomas Webley of Witney, clothier.

Book 20s.

f.55r Court held 14 April 1602 by the bailiffs with William Hunte, John Lynnlley, the sergeant, the wardsmen and others.
Actions of debt : Richard Morton of Fairford, Gloucs., husbandman, against Peter Ridar of Witney for 3s.; charges 4d. (2)
Same against Ellis Welles of Witney for 18d.; charges 4d. (2)
William Heines of Witney against Richard Ockley of Witney for 3s.; charges 4d. Agreed.

f.55v Same Richard Morton against William Fauthry of Witney, mason, for 3s.; charges 4d.
Richard Gylles of Witney against Roger Rackley of Witney, glover, for 6s.; charges 4d.
Nicholas Launce of Eynsham against Thomas Shawe of Witney for 20s.; charges 4d.
Leonard Yate of Witney, tucker, against Edmund Petty of Witney for 10s.; charges 4d.

f.56r Court held 7 May 1602 by Thomas Cornish, bailiff, with Walter Daullton, John Boshope, Thomas Pessley and others.
Action of account: Md. 24 May 1602 John Thomas of Witney for the spoiling of one helling or coverlet against James Jenkines for 10s.; charges 8d.
Actions of debt : Thomas Brigfells of Newland, husbandman, against John Cartar of Witney for 30s.; charges 4d.

f.56v Md. 26 May 1602 by William Furnisse senior of Oxon. [sic] against John Williamson of Minster Lovell, gent., for 15s.; charges 8d.

f.57r Court held 28 May 1602 by the bailiffs with William Hunte, William Clempson, Thomas Pessley, constable, and others.
Actions of debt : Mr Bailiff Thomas Box against George May, glover, for 16s. 8d.; charges 4d. This action was drawn between the parties abovesaid. Paid.
Christopher Cottes of Witney against Humfrey Jacate, loader, for 20s.; charges 4d. (1)
Mr John Clarke against William Honne of Witney, slater, for 5s.; charges 4d.
Humfrey Jacate against Roger Willshear of Witney, shoe-maker, for 22s.; charges 4d.

f.57v Action of fugitive: Md. 22 June 1602 John Brown of Newland, tailor, against Christopher Jeffris of Witney and his late wife . . . for 5s. 6d.; charges 8d. The weight of a pot taken for a distress was 12½lb.
Actions of debt : Richard Samson of Kidlington-on-the-Green against Gawain Baker of Witney, bellfounder, for 10s. 4d.; charges 8d.
Edmund Gunys of South Leigh, husbandman, against William Fauthrey of Witney, mason, for 7s. 11d.; charges 4d.

f.58r   Court held 18 June 1602 by the bailiffs with Mr John Clarke, William
Clempson, James Hoddson and others.

Covenanted servant: Anthony Larden, son of Roger Lardine, broadweaver,
with consent of his father confessed in court that he received nine pence in
earnest and bound himself to Nicholas Gonne of Witney for nine years
from 24 June next to be taught the occupation of a tailor as an apprentice; to
keep etc. and not to lend etc. [as on pp.158, 164] neither to do, procure or
cause to be procured hurt to his master but with all speed to warn him
thereof; at the end of the term 3s. 4d. wages and double apparel.

f.59r   Actions of debt : Richard Biry of Chipping Norton, mercer, against Josias Perse
of Witney, tailor, for 2s. 8d.; charges 4d.

Thomas Radbourne of Stanton Harcourt, husbandman,
against Mr Wyllyamson of Minster Lovell, gent., for 10s. 3d.; charges 8d.

Henry Harbar of Curbridge against James Hikes of Witney,
butcher, for 11s. 6d.; charges 4d.

Thomas Gonne late of Wilcote against Josias Perce of Witney,
tailor, for 4s.; charges 4d.

f.59v   Md. 6 Nov. 1602 by Alice Dyten of Witney and Robert
Whood of Witney against . . . Emanes of Filkins, slater, for 4s. 9d.; charges
8d.

f.60r   Court held 23 July 1602 by the bailiffs with Richard Box, Walter Daullton,
William Clempson, Henry Rankill, Roger Willsheare.

Actions of debt : Md. 26 Sept. 1602 Thomas Brise of Witney, tucker, against
John Peerse of New Bridge Mill, tucker, for 4s.; charges 8d.

John Willyar of Bampton, mercer, against Josias Peerse of
Witney, tailor, for 3s. 9d.; charges 4d.

Md. 28 Oct. 1602 Andrew Steward of Hanbury, Worcs.,
against William Genes of . . ., Worcs., for 8s.; charges 12d. Agreed.

f.60v   Md. possessions: taken 29 Nov. 1602 by Thomas Box and Thomas Cornish,
bailiffs,[103] by virtue of receipt of a twig and a turf of ground, of Thomas
Yate of Standlake, yeoman, of one plot of ground 40 feet wide, 60 feet
long, being butted and bounded, to build a messuage or tenement thereon,
near Woodgreen Hill between the tenement of the said Thomas Yate on the
west and the close of the same on the east, butting on Newland Lane, the
which close of land being now in the occupation of Henry Gowllde and the
house in the use of Thomas Yate; to the use of Jeremy Saundars of North
Leigh, slater, to have and to hold to him, his heirs and assigns for ever,
paying 4d. a year to Yate, his heirs and assigns, when it shall be due and
payable to the chief lord of the manor. The which possession was recorded
in one poll deed made from the former deeds of Thomas Yate. Witnesses:
John Bishop and Thomas Pessely constables, William Maior sergeant, John
Horsoulle and Michael Moxon wardsmen, Robert Yate son of James Yate,
Richard Maior, Robert Whode, William Whodde, William Cannyng the
younger and others.

[103]   Thomas Taylor and Henry Rankell were now bailiffs in fact.

f.61r   taken 4 Oct. 1602 by Thomas Box and Thomas Cornish,
bailiffs, of Richard Kinge of the City of London, grocer, of one messuage
or tenement on the east side of the High St. in Witney, between the
tenement of Agnes Lucas, widow, on the north side and the tenement of
Hugh Hill now in the occupation of John Cartar on the south side; to the
use of Oliver Garddinar of the City of London, grocer, to hold all the
premises and appurtenances, that is to say the hall, parlour, chambers,
solars, backhouses, garden or gardens, court, backside, orchard and one
grass close butting on the river Windrush. Possession was made by the
bailiffs, by virtue of a deed between King and Garddinar, according to the
ancient custom of the borough. Witnesses: John Bishop and Thomas
Pessley constables, William Maior sergeant, John Horssowld, John
Workhouse, Michael Moxon, Richard Maior, Giles Pallmar and Robert
Pallmar, wardsmen, with others.

f.61v   Tipplers licensed by the Justices: Roger Cox, William Cakebred, Elizabeth
Lovyll, John Thomas, Edward Handes, Widow Ditten, Henry Harpar,
Thomas Townsend, John Collyar licenced by Mr Edmund Bray and Mr
Laurence Tanfelld; William Yemanes, Richard Ditene's wife [cancelled],
William Hennes by Mr Edmund Bray and Sir Anthony Cope; Thomas
Hankes, Robert Cakebred by Mr Edmund Bray and Sir William Spenssar;
Thomas Fallknar by Sir Richard Waneman and Mr Edmund Bray.

f.62r   Court held 22 Oct. 1602 by Thomas Tayllar and Henry Rankill, bailiffs, with
Mr John Clarke, Thomas Clempson, Roger Willshear, William Brigfelld
and others.
Constables: Henry Gylles, Henry Whight: sworn.
Wardsmen: Steven Brice, John Seay, Humfrey Becham, John Times, John
Wyllye: sworn.
Cloth sealers for all narrow cloth, friezes and all other such cloth as shall be sold
in the market: Nicholas Gune, John Willye: sworn.
Leather sealers: Edward Handes, Nicholas Stratton: sworn.
Ale tasters: George Deye, William Eynes: sworn.
Cardenars: John Birkat, John Robinson: sworn.

f.63r   Covenanted servant: Thomas Burnell, son of Thomas Burnell, deceased, with
the consent of his friends received nine pence in earnest and bound himself
in court before the bailiffs to Robert Bickarstaffe of Witney, shoemaker, for
nine years from the date above to be instructed in the occupation of a
shoemaker as an apprentice; to keep etc. and not to lend etc. [as on
pp.158, 165]; Bickerstaffe is to receive the rent of one tenement for the term
of nine years and at the end of the term to give Burnell 10s. wages and
double apparel. Witnesses: [marks of] Thomas Burnell, John Welles,
Thomas Kimbell.

f.64r   Court held 12 Nov. 1602 by Thomas Tayllar, bailiff, with Mr John Clarke,
Thomas Box, Richard Box, William Clempson and others.
Action of debt : William Heines of Witney, victualler, against John Shawe of
Witney, tucker, for 20s.; charges 8d. (1)

Actions of debt : Andrew Chamllin of Lew against Robert Fallknar of Witney for 3s. 4d.; charges 8d. (1)

Thomas Vickares of Thame, husbandman, against Robert Fallknar of Witney, broadweaver, for 28s.; charges 4d. (1)

f.64v   Richard Clempson of Abingdon, Berks., mercer, against John Laraunce of Witney, glover, for 9s. 5d.; charges 4d.

John Shewarye of 'Cockarupe' [i.e. Cokethorpe], yeoman, against Thomas Cartar of New Mill for 4s. 8d.; charges 8d.

f.65r   Court held 10 Dec. 1602 by Thomas Taillar, bailiff, with Thomas Cornysh, Walter Daullton, Roger Wilksher, Henry Goylles, Mr John Clarke, William Clempson, John Boshop.

Collectors for the poor: John Harlly and Giles Brigfeld were elected.

Action of debt : Md. 5 Jan. 1603 John Ellys of Hardwick, tailor, against Thomas Alldar of Hardwick for 38s. 11d.; charges 12d.

f.66r   Md. a possession: taken 24 Dec. 1602 by Thomas Taillare of William Hunte senior of Witney, cardmaker, of two messuages or tenements situated on the west side of the High St. between the tenement of Thomas Handes on the south and the tenement of Robert Fallknar on the street called Crundall St. alias Corn St. on the west, which tenements then being in the tenure of Robert Surrell, haberdasher, and the aforesaid William Hunte; to the use of Roger Hunte, youngest son of the said William, to hold the two tenements with all appurtenances, viz. the halls, parlours, chambers, shops, solars, kitchens, stables and all other buildings with the backsides and gardens and one acre of land lying in the West Crofts at the back of Corn St. on the north between the 'yarndayll' of Thomas Handes on the south, by virtue of a deed poll drawn from the principal deeds of the property. Witnesses: Henry Gilles, constable, William Maior, sergeant, John Willy junior, wardsman, Roger cox, John Bircat and others.

f.67r   Covenanted servant: Md. covenant witnessing that 30 Dec. 1602 William Salley, son of Richard Sally of Witney, deceased, received four pence in earnest and bound himself to Peter Rankill of Witney, clothier, for four years from 21 Dec. last past to be taught the occupation of a broadweaver after the manner of an apprentice. To keep his master's secrets worthy to be kept, not to marry and to do his duty like a faithful and true servant; to be found etc. [as on p.83; no correction clause]; at end of the term 20s. wages and double apparel. Witnesses; [signatures of] Richard Drinkwater, Richard Maior; [mark of] William Salye.

f.67v   Action of debt : Md. 23 June 1603 Richard Harte of South Leigh, yeoman, against Robert Williamson of Twelve Acres [Eynsham] or Minster Lovell, gent.,[104] for 21s. 4d.; charges 12d.

f.68r   Action of fugitive against William Barnay, glazier, under written.

Actions of debt : Md. 28 Feb. 1603 Henry Walker of Witney, blacksmith, against William Barnay, glazier, for 21s.; charges 4d.

John Seye of Witney against the same for 14s.; charges 4d.

Robert Fallknar against the same for 6s. 8d.; charges 4d.

---

[104]   See below, p.206.

f.68v　　　　　　　Md. 18 July 1603 Richard Constabull of Cogges, husbandman, against Anne Voulles, widow, for 3s. 4d.; charges 12d.

William Marchante of South Leigh, labourer, against Roger Whillar of Witney, carpenter, for 3s. 9d.; charges 8d.

Mr Thomas Yate, gent., against Richard Humfray of Witney, yeoman, for 20s.; charges 8d.

f.69r　Court held 4 March 1603 by Thomas Tayllar, bailiff, with Mr John Clarke, Roger Willsheare, Henry Gilles, constable, Richard Humfrys and others.

Action of fugitive: Md. 15 April 1603 Francis Johnson of Witney, carpenter, against Gavin Baker late of Witney, bellfounder, for 20s.; charges 8d.

Covenanted servant: 15 May 1603 William Russill, son of Robert Russell of Witney, broadweaver, received four pence in earnest and by the advice and

f.69v　　　consent of his father bound himself,to Richard Brice of Witney for four years from 29 Sept. next to be instructed in the occupation of a broadweaver as an apprentice. To keep his master's secrets lawful to be kept, to avoid taverns and alehouses except on his master's business and not to marry; to be found etc. [as on p.83; no correction clause]; at the end of the term 20s. and double apparel. Witnesses: [signature of] Richard Maior; [mark of] William Russell

f.70r　Md. a possession: taken 30 June 1603 by Thomas Taillar senior of Thomas Brian of Witney, broadweaver, of one messuage or tenement situated on the north side of Crondall St. alias Corn St. between the tenement of John Lusskie, gent., then in the tenure of Thomas Butlar, slater, on the west side and the tenement of William Wodord, yeoman, then in the tenure of Bartholomew Cordiwell, broadweaver, on the east side; to the use of Robert Baissley of Witney, broadweaver, to have and to hold with all the appurtenances, viz., the hall, chambers, solars, shop and backside garden or close or orchard, according to the deeds made between them. Witnesses: the bailiff, Henry Gilles, constable, William Maior, sergeant, and others.

f.71r　Court held 9 Sept. 1603 by Thomas Taillore, bailiff, with Mr John Clarke, Thomas Cornish, William Clempson, William Hunte and others.

Actions of debt : Francis Knight of Swinford Verey in Cumnor, Berks., yeoman, against Richard Okley of Witney, dyer, for 5s.; charges 8d.

John Archar of Witney, miller, against Anthony Ebessworth of Witney, dyer, for 5s. 8d.; charges 8d.

f.71v　Amerced: Md. 6 Oct. 1603 William Barney, glazier, 3s. 4d. for a bloodshed on Sebastian Walker.

f.72r　Court held 7 Oct. 1603 by Andrew Bird and Walter Daullton, they having been chosen bailiffs on 3 Oct., with Mr John Clarke, Mr Thomas Taillar, Mr William Dyare, William Hunte, Richard Box, William Clempson and others.

Constables: James Wates, Richard Bishope: sworn.

Wardsmen: Thomas Hakes for Paternoster Row; John Robines for the Middle Ward; Simon Cusser for the West Ward; Edward Boulles for the East Ward; John Daullton for beneath the bridge: all sworn.

Ale tasters: Nicholas Maior, George Deye: sworn.

Cloth sealers for all manner of cloth: William Purssar, George Deye: sworn.
Leather sealers: Nicholas Straten, Edward Handes: sworn.
Cardenars for flesh and fish: John Birkat, John Robinsson: sworn.

f.72v Action of debt : Md. 20 Oct. 1603 Agnes Rosse, daughter of Steven Rosse of New
Yatt, Witney, tailor, against Henry Slatford of North Leigh, yeoman, for
4s. 4d.; charges 12d.

Md. of purchase: 25 Nov. 1602 Agnes Ringe of Cogges, widow, bought of
Michael Monke of Cogges one brown tagged heifer, star on the forehead,
cropped under the near ear, price 33s. 4d., for the use of Joan Becke. Monke
to discharge Agnes, her heirs, executors or assigns from all former bargains.
Witnesses: [signatures of] Thomas Broke, Richard Maior; [mark of] Michael
Monke.

f.73r Assessment for the subsidy[105] of the borough of Witney, assessed by John Clarke,
Thomas Taillor, Thomas Box, Richard Box, William Clempsson in the
year 1603. In lands: Thomas Box £6; William Hunte £4; Thomas Cartar £1
[cancelled]; John Barnabe £1; Edward Ashfeld £2; John Bishope £1; John
Shawe £1 [cancelled]; Andrew Birde £1; Richard Humfrey senior £1
[cancelled]; Richard Humfrey junior £1; Henry White £1; Thomas Handes £2;
William Yemanes £1; William Buckingame £1; Leonard Yate son of Thomas
Yate £4; Thomas Poolle £1; James Wates £2; In goods: Richard Clempson
£5; Peter Rankell £4; Henry Rankell £3 [£5 crossed out]; Thomas Cave £4;
Edith Goone £3 [£5 crossed out]; Richard Box £4; Thomas Weblley £4;
William Clempsson £4; Richard Haskines £3; Robert Cakbred £3; Walter
Daullton £5; John Clarke £9; Thomas Cornishe £5; Thomas Taillor £5.

f.74r Court held 25 Nov. 1603 by the bailiffs with Thomas Taillor, William
Clempson, Thomas Handes, William Hunte, Thomas Webley, Mr Leonard
Yate, Richard Humfree, Richard Boshope and others.

Collectors for the poor: Henry Brigfelld and Edmund Budde were elected.

Action of debt : the whole body of the town at the suit of Thomas Webley,
William Clempsson and others, plaintiffs against Steven Colliar and Henry
White, broadweavers, for 20s.; charges 4d. (2)

Action of detinue: Mr William Barfote of South Leigh, clerk,[106] against Robert
Surell of Witney for one felt [hat] value 5s.; charges 4d. (2)

f.74v Covenanted servant: 30 Nov. 1603 Alice Fluraunc, daughter of Edward Fluraunc
late of Witney, clerk, received nine pence in earnest and confessed herself
bound to William Hunte and Christian his wife for nine years from the day of
these presents, to do such business as her master and dame shall appoint,
using them well and truly in word and deed. They are to provide her with
good and wholesome bread, meat, drink and bedding linen, woollen hose
and shoes and all other things fit for such a servant to wear as well in sickness
as in health and for wages at the end of the term one gown and a petticoat for
Holy Days and another gown and petticoat for working days fit for such a
servant to wear with other necessary linen. Witnesses: [signature of] E.
Byrd; [marks of] Alice Fluraunc, Andrew Bird, bailiff.

[105] Granted by Act 43 Eliz. c.18 (1601)
[106] Curate of Stanton Harcourt in 1604: Oldfield, Clerus Oxon.

f.75r Court held 15 Dec. 1603 by the bailiffs with Thomas Tayllor, James Wattes, constable, Thomas Cornish, John Clark, William Clempsson and others.
Actions of debt : Mr John Clarke of Witney, clothier, against Leonard Yate, tucker, for 10s.; charges 4d. (1)
Same against Roger Whellar of Witney, carpenter, for 5s ; charges 4d. (1)
Thomas Kirsson of South Leigh, husbandman, against Roger Whellar, carpenter, for 6s. 2d.; charges 4d. (1)

f.75v Md. 24 Dec. 1603 Thomas Poolle of Witney, chandler, against Charles Bowell of South Leigh, baker, for 6s. 8d.; charges 8d. (1)
John Alldar of Aston against William Willtone of Witney, cooper, for 2s. with the entrance of the action.
Action of fugitive: William Maior, sergeant, against Robert Rabon of Witney, 'aquayty man' for 3s. 6d.; charges 8d.

f.76r Court held 20 Jan. 1604 by the bailiffs with Mr John Clarke, Richard Humfris, Richard Bishop, William Clempsson, Edward Bird, Thomas Willshere, Thomas Webley.
Action of debt : Md. 27 Jan. 1604 Alexander Barat of Witney, broadweaver, against Charles Ellyfekes of Witney for 14s.; charges 8d.

f.77r Court held 17 Feb. 1604 by the bailiffs with Thomas Cornish, William Clempsson, Richard Humfrys, Thomas Hannse and others.
Action of debt : Md. 2 April 1604 John Walbrig of Burford against William Barney of Brighthampton [in Standlake], glazier, for 10s.; charges 8d.

f.78r Court held 16 March 1604 by the bailiffs with Roger Willsher, James Wates, William Clempsson, Richard Bishope and others.
f.78v Md. of purchase: 3 May 1604 Thomas Webley of Witney bought one 'gressilld ronde' gelding, brand marked on the near shoulder, 'hallpenid' on the near ear,[107] of Robert Forde of Brize Norton for £3 6s.

f.79r Court held 6 April 1604 by Walter Daullton, bailiff, with Thomas Webley, William Clempson, William Hunte, James Wats, Richard Bishope and others.
Action of debt: Md. 19 April [1604] John Sellwood, deputy for Richard Sellwood of 'Etone' [i.e. Water Eaton?], yeoman, against Roger Collyar of Ashford Mill, miller, for 12s.; charges 8d. Agreed and paid.

f.80r Court held 27 April 1604 by Walter Daullton, bailiff, with Mr Okines, Thomas Cornishe, William Hunte, Thomas Willsher, Thomas Taillor, Thomas Cave and others.
Action of debt : William Asstine of South Leigh, husbandman, against Robert Barre of South Leigh, yeoman, for 10s.; charges 8d. Agreed.
f.81r Covenanted servant: 18 May 1604 Robert Tirey, son of Henry Tirey of Witney pargeter, received seven pence in earnest and confessed himself bound to

[107] i.e. grey, stout, brandmarked and cropped on the near ear.

William Tirke of Witney, broadweaver, for seven years from 24 June next to be taught the occupation of a broadweaver as an apprentice; to keep etc. and be found etc. [as on p.83]; at the end of the term 10s. wages and double apparel. Witnesses: [signatures of] Robert Tiry, William Turck, Richard Maior.

f.82r   Court held 8 June 1604 by the bailiffs with Thomas Cornishe, James Wates, constable.
Amerced: Thomas Hankes, Edmund Boullte, Simon Cussor, John Daullton, 6d. apiece for want of appearance. At the court on 28 Sept 1604 Edmund Boullte and John Daullton were amerced for the like.

f.82v   Action of fugitive: Md. 11 Aug 1604 William Cakebred of Witney, broadweaver, against William Wood, surgeon, for 4s. 6d.; charges 8d.

f.83r   Court held 6 July 1604 by the bailiffs with Thomas Cornishe.
Actions of debt : Thomas Heines of Burford, linen draper, against John Trindall of Witney, mason, for 5s.; charges 4d.
             John Templlar of Burford against William Farthrey, mason, for 9s. 4d.; charges 4d. Agreed and paid.
             John Powell of Witney against John Trindall of Witney for 25s.; charges 4d.

f.83v   A note of the subsidy granted in 43rd year of our most Sovereign Lady Elizabeth.[108] In land: Thomas Box £6; William Hunte £4; John Barnabe £1; Edward Ashfelld £2; John Boshop £1; Andrew Bird £1; Henry White £1; Richard Humfrey junior £1; Thomas Hanndes £2; William Yemanes £1; Leonard Yate son of Thomas Yate £4; Thomas Poolle £1; James Wattes £2. In goods: Richard Clempson £5; Peter Rankell £4; Henry Rankell £3; Thomas Cave £4; Richard Box £4; Thomas Webley £4; William Clempson £4; Richard Haskines £3; Robert Cakbred £3; Walter Dallton £5; John Clarke £9; Thomas Cornish £5; Thomas Taillor £5.

f.84r   Court held 12 Aug. 1604 by Walter Daullton, bailiff, with Thomas Cornish, Richard Bishop constable, Thomas Taillor, William Hunte and others.
Actions of debt : William Cakbred of 'Lunder', [i.e. London], clotherworker, against Richard Cartar of Witney, husbandman, for 3s. 4d.; charges 4d.
             Md. 22 Aug. 1604 John Sellman of Witney, carpenter, against Thomas Willyames of Hailey, husbandman, for 6s.; charges 8d. Agreed and paid.

f.84v   Md. 4 Oct. 1604 Robert Heyat, deputy of Michael Kelle of Minster Lovell, against Thomas Lord of Claywell [in Ducklington], husbandman, for 6s. 8d.; charges 8d.

f.85r   Court held 28 Sept. 1604 by the bailiffs with Mr John Clarke, William Clempsson, Thomas Cornishe, Thomas Tailor and others.
Actions of debt : Giles Stevanes of Hatherop, Gloucs., miller, against William Fautheray of Witney for 8s.; charges 12d.

108   Granted in 1601 by Act 43 Eliz. c.18; cf. p.182.

Susan Barford, servant to Thomas Hankes of Witney, against Robert Wryte of Witney, blacksmith, for 2s.; charges 4d.

f.85v Names of the victuallers or alekeepers within the borough of Witney licensed by the Justices: Roger Cox, Thomas Hanks, Elizabeth Lovill, Sebastian Wallker, Thomas Willsher, William Cakbred, Christopher Ford, William Yemanes, Agnes Collyar (non), Robert Cakbred (non), James Wates, Thomas Townssend, Richard Bude, William Heines (non), Henry Harpar, Edward Hands, Thomas Humfrey, Thomas Bedewll senior, Joan Fissher (non), Mary Tirey [non *crossed out*].[109]

f.86r Court held 5 Oct. 1604 by Richard Box and James Hodsson, then being chosen bailiffs, with Walter Daullton, Andrew Bird, Thomas Taillor, Thomas Cornish, Richard Humfrey, William Clempsson and others.

Constables: William Yemanes, Thomas Persson: sworn.

Wardsmen: Robert Hamwell, Ellis Handsse, Thomas Beddowll, Christopher Forde, William Ockley: all sworn.

Cardenars: William Peney, James Hikes: sworn.

Cloth sealers: George Dey, William Purssar: sworn.

Ale tasters: Henry Walkar, John Birckate: sworn.

f.87r Court held 26 Oct. 1604 by the bailiffs with Mr John Clarke, William Clempson, the constables, Thomas Handes, Thomas Webley.

Actions of debt : Richard Harris of Witney, glover, against Richard Haskines of Witney, clothier, for . . .; charges 4d. (2)

     Md. 15 Nov. 1604 Robert Frannssis of Ducklington, glover, against Phillip Purssones of Shilton, yeoman, for 20s.; charges 8d.

Action of fugitive: Md. 12 Nov. 1604 Simon Cussor of Witney, baker, against James Jhoans, broadweaver, for 15s. 9d.; charges 8d. (2)

f.87v Action of debt : Md. 11 Jan. 1605 by Thomas Edmones of Hardwick, husbandman, against Robert Bollock of Hardwick, miller, for 16s.; charges 8d.

f.88r Court held 16 Nov. 1604 by James Hodsson, bailiff, with Mr John Clarke, Thomas Webley, William Hunte, William Clempsson, William Yemanes and others.

Court held 7 Dec. 1604 by the bailiffs with the constables, the sergeant, Thomas Persson, William Yemanes, William Hunte, Richard Haskines, William Maior and others.

Actions of debt : Mr Bailiff Box against Andrew Chalin of Witney for 14s.; charges 4d. (2)

     Md. Thursday [27] Dec. 1604 John Dall of Oxford against Benedict Padge of Faringdon, Berks., for 20s.; charges 8d.; pledge John Hartley, ironmonger. Agreed.

f.88v Chamberlain: at the court on 7 Dec. 1604 William Yemanes was elected and 10s. 6d. was delivered to him.

[109] 'Non' may refer to the non-production of licences or the non-appearance of the licensees.

Actions of debt : Md. 6 Feb. 1605 William Borsslen of Standlake, miller, against William Speke of Burford for 3s.; charges 12d.

William Pallmar of shoemaker, against John Goodmansse of Kencot, yeoman, for 16s.; charges 12d.

William Selly of Ascott against . . . Flechar of Brize Norton, yeoman, for 4s.; charges 12d.

f.89r	Court held 11 Jan. 1605 by the bailiffs with Mr John Clarke, Richard Humfrey, William Clempsson, William Hunte, Thomas Hannds, William Yemanes, Thomas Persson and others.

Actions of debt : Elizabeth Lovell against Elizabeth Hankes, widow, for 12s.; charges 8d.

Robert Tannar of Curbridge, yeoman, against John Willy junior for 5s. 2d.; charges 4d.

f.90r	Covenanted servant: 13 Jan. 1605 James Griffen, son of Thomas Griffen of Witney, labourer, received twelve pence in earnest and confessed himself bound covenant servant or apprentice to Thomas Pearson of Witney, clothier and broadweaver, for twelve years from 29 Sept. 1603 to be taught the occupation of a broadweaver. To fulfil all points of covenant fit for an apprentice, not to neglect anything in his master's business with only the lawful leave of his master, not to use taverns and alehouses, not to marry; to be found etc. [as on p.83; no correction clause]; at the end of the term

f.90v	20s. wages and double apparel. Witnesses: [signatures of] William Clempson, William Yemans, Giles Bryngfeld, Richard Maior; [marks of] James Griffine.

Action of debt : Md. 7 March [1605] George Burdssen of Crawley, husband-man, against Margary Sallter of Witney, widow, for 10s.; charges 12d. (1) Agreed and paid.

f.91r	Court held 1 Feb. 1605 by the bailiffs with Mr John Clarke, Richard Humfrey, Thomas Cornish, William Clempsson and others.

Covenanted servant: William Maior, son of Nicholas Maior late of Witney, labourer, received eight pence in earnest and by the advice of his mother confessed himself bound to Thomas Pesseley of Witney, broadweaver, for eight years from 2 Feb. last past to be taught the occupation of a broad-

f.91v	weaver as an apprentice;* not to do or procure hurt or damage to his master but with all speed to warn him thereof;* to keep etc. [as on p.158];

f.92r	at the end of the term 20s. wages and double apparel. Witnesses: [signatures of] Richard Box, John Clarke, William Clempson;[110] [marks of] William Maior, James Hodsson.

Court held 20 [02 in Ms] Feb. 1605 by the bailiffs with Mr John Clarke, William Clempson, William Yemanes constable and others.

Action of debt : Steven Rosse of New Yatt, Witney, tailor, against Thomas Humfrey of Witney for 3s. 4d.; charges 8d.

Six later covenants employ the clause between asterisks. Clarke's and Clempson's signatures may be marks. Clarke had made his mark before but signed later; see pp.174, 190.

f.92v   Court held 14 March 1605 by the bailiffs with Thomas Cornish, William
          Clempson, William Yemanes and others.
              Action of debt : Md. 1 April 1605 Richard Ockley of Witney, dyer, against
          William Robarts of Brill-on-the-Hill, Bucks., for 39s. 11d.; charges 12d.

f.93r   Covenanted servants: 25 March 1605 Richard Audsley, son of Henry Audsley of
          Barton-on-the-Heath [Warws.], and Matthew Perks, son of Edward Perks
          of Chipping Sodbury, Gloucs., deceased, received nine pence and eight
          pence in earnest and confessed themselves bound to Henry Rankill of
          Witney, clother and broadweaver, for nine and eight years from the day of
          these present to be taught the occupation of broadweavers as covenanted
          servants or apprentices; to keep etc. and not to hurt etc. [as on pp.158, 186;
          with correction; no clause re absence]; at the end of the term 20s wages each
          and double apparel. Witnesses: [signatures of] Edward Busbe, Richard
          Maior; [marks of] Richard Audsley, Matthew Perks.

f.94r   Same day John Warine, son of Gray Warine late of
          Witney, and Robert Patarick, son of Hugh Patarick of Witney, deceased,
          received nine pence each in earnest and confessed themselves bound to
          Henry Rankill of Witney, clothier and broadweaver, for nine years each
          from the day of these present to be taught the occupation of broadweavers
          as covenanted servants or apprentices; to keep etc; and not to hurt [as on
          pp.158, 186, with correction; nothing re absence]; at the end of the term
          20s. wages and double apparel. Witnesses: [signatures of] Edward Busbe,
          Richard Maior; [marks of] John Warine, Robert Patrick.

f.95v   25 April 1605 Robert Champnes, son of Sacrey
          Champnes of Sutton, in Stanton Harcourt, husbandman, received seven
          pence in earnest and confessed himself bound to Bartholomew Cordiwell
          of Witney for seven years from the day of these present to be taught the
          occupation of a broadweaver. To be found etc. [as on p.83; no correction
          clause]; at the end of term 20s. wages and double apparel. Witnesses:
          [signatures of] William Cakbred, James Rowlland, Richard Maior; [mark
          of] Robert Champnes.

f.96r   Court held 5 April 1605 by the bailiffs with Mr John Clarke, Thomas Webley,
          Thomas Cornish, William Clempson, William Yemanes and others.
              Actions of debt : Henry Stubes of Witney against Elizabeth Russell of Witney
          for 3s. 6d.; charges 8d.
                            Leonard Martine of the Field [i.e. Leafield] against Thomas
          Hewllat of Witney, carpenter, for 4s.; charges 8d.
                            Thomas Bedoull senior against Roger Whillar of Witney,
          carpenter, for 5s. 4d.; charges 8d.

f.96v   Covenanted servants: 1 May 1605 Roger Atkines, son of Thomas Atkines of
          Witney, glover, received eight pence in earnest and confessed himself
          bound to Leonard Taillar of Witney, shoemaker, for eight years from the
          day of these present to be taught the occupation of a broadweaver as
          covenanted servant or apprentice. To serve truly and justly as becomes a
          servant, not to neglect his master's business without lawful leave; to be
          found etc. [as on p.83; no correction clause]; at the end of the term 2s.
          wages and double apparel. Witnesses: [signatures of] Leonard Yate,

Richard Maior; [marks of] Roger Atkines, John Daullton, John Dicksson.

f.97v   25 March 1605 Robert Stevenes, son of John Stevenes of Witney, deceased, received eight pence in earnest and by the advice of his mother Joanne Stevenes and of his friends confessed himself bound to Giles Brigfield of Witney, broadweaver, for eight years from the day of these present to be taught the occupation of a broadweaver after the manner of an apprentice; to keep and not to hurt etc. [as on pp.158, 186; no clause re absence]; at the end of the term 26s. 8d. wages and double apparel Witnesses: [signature of] Richard Maior; [marks of] Robert Stevenes, Edward Burnill.

f.98v   Court held 26 April 1605 by the bailiffs with Thomas Webley, Mr John Clarke, Thomas Cornishe, Walter Daullton, Henry Rankill, the constables and others.

Actions of debt : John Trindall of Witney, mason, against William Fauthrey of Witney, mason, for 15s.; charges 8d. Agreed before Mr Bailiff Box, Mr Clarke and William Hunte that Fauthary to pay 1s. a week after Whitsuntide for ten weeks and the other 5s. to be paid between then and Easter 1606.

Md. 2 May 1605 Richard Birey of Chipping Norton, linen draper, against William Hibard of Lew for 13s. 4d. Charges 12d.

f.99r   Covenanted servants: 24 June 1605 Robert Alltaffe of Cogges, son of William All taffe of Cogges, yeoman, received seven pence in earnest and confessed himself bound to Thomas Webley of Witney, clothier and broadweaver, from 24 June next to be taught the occupation of a broadweaver after the manner of an apprentice; to keep etc. [as on pp.158, 186, with correction; nothing re absence]; Alltaffe also agreed and covenanted before his father to serve Thomas Webley one whole year after the expiry of the term and received one penny in earnest. For his several years Webley to give Alltaffe £3 wages. Witnesses: [signatures of] Robert Alltaffe, Richard Maior, William Alltaffe.

f.100r   Same day Hugh Rosse, son of Steven Rosse of New Yatt, tailor, bound to John Hunte of Witney, clothier and [as Alltaffe above but without covenant for extra year]; at end 20s. wages and double apparel. Witnesses: [signatures of] Daniel Stanfurd, Richard Maior; [marks of] Hugh Roose, John More.

f.101r   John Fearman, son of Thomas Fearman of Crawley, husbandman, received ten pence in earnest and confessed himself bound to John Hoursoull of Witney, broadweaver, for ten years from Pentecost next [St Philip and St James, i.e. 1 May, crossed out], to be taught the occupation of a broadweaver as an apprentice; to keep etc. [as on pp.158, 186; with correction; nothing re absence]; at the end of the term 16s. wages and double apparel. Witnesses: [signatures of] Robert Beachume, Richard Maior; [marks of] John Fearman, Walter Cowell, Thomas Hewlate. Md. agreed after the confessing of this covenant that Frearman should serve Horsoull's wife Marian for the remainder of the term if Horsoull dies within the said ten years, provided she continues in her husband's trade.

f.102v   Richard Slatter, son of Michael Slatter of Witney, broad-

103r weaver, received eight pence in earnest and confessed himself bound to Peter Rankill of Witney, clothier, for eight years from 29 Sept. 1605 to be taught the occupation of a broadweaver; to keep etc. and not to hurt etc. [as on pp. 158, 186; with correction; nothing re absence or matrimony]; at end of the term 26s. 8d. wages and double apparel. Witnesses: [signatures of] Richard Maior, Walter Dolton; [mark of] Richard Slattar.

Md. of purchase, 6 June 1605 Thomas Deanne of Cogges bought of Walter Heiford of 'Cockarape' [i.e. Cokethorpe?] two kine, one of them with a brown tagged ear and the other with a red whole ear, price £5.

f.104r Court held 17 May 1605 by Richard Box, bailiff, with Mr John Clarke, William Yemanes, constable, William Hunte, William Clempsson, Richard Haskines and others.

Action of debt : Richard Haskines of Witney, clothman, against . . . Blomyer of Hatherop, Gloucs., for 6s.; charges 12d.

f.104v Covenanted servants: 25 March 1605 Abraham Robines, son of John Robines of Witney, labourer, received eight pence in earnest and confessed himself bound to Henry Rankell of Witney, clothier and broadweaver, for eight

f.105r years from the day of these present to be taught the occupation of a broadweaver as an apprentice; to keep etc. and not to hurt etc. [as on pp. 158, 186, with correction; nothing re absence]; to avoid fornication in his master's house; at the end of the term 20s. wages and double apparel. ['Agreed and freed with Mr Henry Ranckle's consent,' *added in a different hand on f.104v*].

f.105v 24 June 1605 William Tipper, son of Robert Tipper of Ludgershall, Bucks., received seven pence in earnest and confessed himself bound to Robert Baysselay of Witney, broadweaver, for seven years from the day of these present to be taught the occupation of a broadweaver as an apprentice. To keep his master's secrets lawful and honest, to fulfil his master's commandments during his term, avoid fornication within his master's house, not to marry, not to make any privy contract during his term, not to play at dice, cards or other forbidden games, not to lend his master's goods to any man without permission; to be found etc. [as on p.83]; and at the end of the term 20s. wages and double apparel. Witnesses: [signature of] Richard Maior; [marks of] William Tipper, Francis Yempe, Roger Wryte.

f.106v 28 June 1605 Timothy Greene, son of Paul Greene of Burford, broadweaver, deceased, received seven pence in earnest and confessed himself bound to Thomas Smarte of Witney, broadweaver, for seven years from the Feast of St. John the Baptist [24 June], the day of these present, to be taught the occupation of a broadweaver as an apprentice; to keep and not hurt [as on pp. 158, 186 nothing re absence]; to keep his master's commandments and avoid fornication in his master's house, at the end of the term 6s. 8d. wages and double apparel. Witnesses: [signatures of] Nicholas Whithorn, Richard Maior; [marks of] Timothy, Green, Walter Johnssonne.

f.108r Court held 19 July 1605 by the bailiffs with Thomas Cornish, William

Clempssonne, William Emannes, constable, Peter Rankill, Thomas Taillor and others.

Actions of debt : Henry Brooke of Witney, broadweaver, against William Purnell junior, broadweaver, for 4s. 3d.; charges 8d. (1)

                Richard Box against Thomas Wyan, broadweaver, for 4s.; charges 8d. (1)

f.109r Court held 9 Aug. 1605 by the bailiffs with Mr John Clarke, Thomas Cornish, William Clempson, the constables and others.

Court held 13 Sept. 1605 by the bailiffs with Mr John Clarke, Thomas Webley, the constables and others.

Action of debt : Md. 19 Sept. 1605 Thomas Cootmore of Brize Norton, husbandman, against John Hall of Brize Norton, husbandman for 20s. 2d.; charges 12d.

f.109v Covenanted servant: at the court on 4 Oct. 1605 Giles Goulding of own assent and by the counsel of many friends and in consideration of ten covenant pence put himself apprentice to Thomas Poole of Witney, chandler, for ten years from 29 Sept. last to be taught the occupation of a chandler, for ten found etc. [as on p.83; no correction clause]; at the end of the term 20s. wages and double apparel. Witnesses: [signatures of] John Clarke and Thomas Webley, bailiffs.

f.110r Court held 4 Oct. 1605 by Mr John Clarke and Thomas Webley, bailiffs, with Thomas Cornish, William Clempson, James Hodson, Thomas Taylor, Thomas Marten and Robert Taylor, constables.

Wardsmen: John Harris for Paternoster Row; John Lawrance for the West Ward; Richard Humpheris for the Middle Ward; Alexander Gardner for beneath the bridge; Richard Wesson for the East Ward.

Cardenars: James Hickes, William Peney.

Ale tasters: John Bircott, Henry Walker.

Cloth sealers: George Day, William Pursser.

Leather sealers: Edward Hannes, Nicholas Stratten.

Md. of debt: William Maior confessed himself indebted to Richard Box for 2s. 8d., to be paid to Box to the use of Mr Knight at the rate of 6d. a week until the debt be satisfied.

f.110v Names of the victuallers and alehouse keepers allowed within the borough of Witney by the bailiffs, the constables and the general consent of our neighbours: Roger Cox, Elizabeth Lovill, Thomas Willsheire, William Cakebred, William Yeomans, David Evans, Agnes Colliar, Robert Cakebred, James Wattes, Mary Terrye, Thomas Townsend, William Heines, Thomas Humpheris, Edward Hanns, Henry Harper, Widow Bedoll, Richard Ockley, Simon Ensor all licensed by Mr Edmund Braye and Sir Laurence Tanfeild.

f.111r Court held 29 Nov. 1605 by the bailiffs with Richard Box, William Clempson, James Hodsonne, Thomas Marten, constable, and others.

Collectors for the poor: Andrew Hodsonne and William Box gave their account for the past year. There remained 21s. 5½d. in the poor man's box. They were re-elected to the office for the following year and the money was delivered back into their hands.

Actions of debt : Richard Haskins of Witney, clothier, against P . . .

Mr John Clarke and Thomas Webley, bailiffs, against Richard Maior of Witney, broadweaver, and William Yeomans of Witney, tailor, for 30s.; charges 4d. (3)

f.111v Covenanted servants: John Tooley, son-in-law [i.e. stepson] of Gregory Shepheard of Witney, broadweaver, with the assent of his father-in-law and self and in consideration of eight covenant pence confessed to put himself apprentice to William Basley of Witney from the Feast of St. . . . Apostle next for eight years to be taught the art of a clothier; to be found etc. [as on p.83; no correction clause]; at the end of the term 26s. 8d. wages and double apparel.

f.112r   John Willobie, son of Humphrey Willobie of North Leigh, husbandman, with the assent of self and father and in consideration of seven covenant pence confessed to put himself apprentice to James Hodsonne of Witney, clothier from the Feast of St. . . . for seven years to be taught the occupation of a broadweaver; to be found etc. [as on p.83; no correction clause]; at the end of the term double apparel.

f.112v Court held 21 Dec. 1605 by the bailiffs with Thomas Taylor, Thomas Cornish and the constables.

Actions of debt : Richard Berrie of Chipping Norton, linen draper, against Thomas Carter of Witney, tucker, for 15s.; charges 4d.

Same against Richard Banning of Witney, broadweaver, for 1s. 11d.; charges 4d.

Same against Roger Willsheire of Witney, shoemaker, for 2s. 5d.; charges 4d.

Richard Wesson of Witney, mercer, against William Haines of Witney, victualler, for 13s. 4d.; charges 4d.

f.113r Court held 17 Jan. 1606 by the bailiffs with Mr Thomas Cave, Thomas Taylor, Thomas Cornish, Leonard Yate, William Clempsonne, James Hodsonne, Richard Box, Thomas Martin, constable, and others.

Agreed: by general consent of the bailiffs and the rest of the company there present that Thomas Taylor, Mr Thomas Cave, Richard Box, Thomas Cornish, John Horne of Hailey and Edward Bowman and Thomas Smyth, constables of Hailey, should have the disposing of the £40 delivered to them on 16 Jan. 1606 by the gift of one George Tompson, late of Bampton, deceased. to the use and relief of the poor inhabitants of Witney and Hailey for this present year. [Cancelled.]

Action of debt : Robert Tayler alias Cakebred against Nicholas Gune of Witney, tailor, for 10s.; charges 4d. (3)

Agreed: at the same court in the public assembly there Messrs. Thomas Taylor, Thomas Cave, Richard Box, Thomas Cornishe, John Horne and Edward Bowman, inhabitants of the town and parish of Witney, were by the common consent of the same assembly thought fit to be joined with the bailiffs of Witney and the constable of Hailey for the disposing of the £40 given and bequeathed by George Tomson late of Bampton, yeoman, deceased, to the poor of Witney and Hailey and to that purpose were then and there elected and chosen.

f.113v Court held 7 Feb. 1606 by the bailiffs with Thomas Cornish, William Clempsonne, Richard Humpheris, James Hodson, Thomas Martine, constable, and others.
Action of debt : Robert Bedoll of Witney, baker, against Hugh Walker of Witney, labourer, for 3s. 6d.; charges 4d. (2)

Court held 28 Feb. 1606 by the bailiffs with William Clempsonne, Thomas Martin, constable, and others.
Amerced: according to the order set down by the jury on 6 Oct. 1601 Richard Wesson, Richard Humpheris, Alexander Gardener, wardsmen, John Birckett, Henry Walker, ale tasters, 2s. 6d. apiece for want of appearance at the court.
Actions of debt : Elizabeth Lucas of Witney, servant, against Thomas Humpheris of Witney, innholder, for 5s. 6d.; charges 4d. (1)
            Md. 6 March 1606 Thomas Daniell of Burford, collar maker, against John Hampson of Broadwell, woollen draper, for 30s.; charges 12d. (3)

f.114r Court held 21 March 1606 by the bailiffs with Thomas Taylor, Thomas Cornish William Clempson, Richard Box, James Hodsonne and others.
Actions of debt : Richard Clempson of Abingdon, [Berks.,] mercer, against Richard Healer of Witney, broadweaver, for 10s. 6d.; charges 4d. (3)
            Same against John Powell of Witney, mason, for 2s. 3d.; charges 4d. (3)

Court held 2 May 1606 by the bailiffs with Richard Box, William Clempson, Thomas Martin, constable, and others.

Court held 23 May 1606 by the bailiffs with Thomas Cornish, William Huntt, Thomas Martin, constable, and others.
Actions of debt : Richard Wesson against William Heines of Witney, victualler, for 39s. 6d.; charges 4d. (3)
            William Heines of Witney, victualler, against Richard Wesson of Witney, mercer, for 6s. 5d.; charges 4d. (3)
            Richard Wesson against William Heines for 2s. 10d.; charges 4d. (3)
            Robert Tanner of Curbridge against Richard Maior of Witney, broadweaver, for 4s.; charges 4d. (3)
f.114v   Richard Clempsone of Abingdon, [Berks.,] mercer, against Henry Brinfeild of Witney, broadweaver, for 2s. 6d.; charges 4d. (3)
            Md. 29 May 1606 Mr . . Arsbasson of Burford, gent., against Ambrose Turby of Newton [in Buckland?], Berks., yeoman, for 2s. 1d.; charges 8d.

Md. 5 June 1606 John Haynes of Burford, mercer, against Richard Maior of Witney, broadweaver, for 4s. 6d.; charges 4d.

Thomas Standish of Eynsham Mill, miller, against Henry Stutter of Hanborough, labourer, for 9s.; charges 8d.

John Henynes of Burford, mercer, against Richard Maior of Witney, broadweaver, for 4s. 6d.; charges 4d. (3)

Richard Clempson against Greogory Shepheard of Witney, broadweaver, for 14s. 2d.; charges 4d. (3)

f.115r Subsidy men inhabiting within the borough of Witney and their assessment.[111]
In land: Thomas Box £6; William Huntt £3; John Barnabie £1; Edward Ashfeild £2; Andrew Byrd £1; Richard Humpheris junior £1; Thomas Hannes £2; William Yeomans £1; Thomas Yate, gent., £4; Thomas Poole £1; James Wattes £1; Henry Whitte, fuller, £1; Richard Haskins £1; James Hodsonne £1; Thomas Pearson £1. In goods: Richard Clempsonne £5; Peter Rankell £4; Henry Rankell £3; Thomas Cave £4; Richard Box £4; Thomas Webley £5; William Clempsonne £4; Robert Cakebred £3; Walter Daulton £5; John Clarke £9; Thomas Cornish £5; Thomas Taylor £5.
Assessors of the above rates: John Clarke, Thomas Webley, Richard Box, William Huntt.

f.115v Court held 20 June 1606 by the bailiffs with Thomas Martin, constable, William Clempsonne, Walter Daulton with others.
Actions of debt : Richard Clempsonne of Abingdon [Berks.], mercer, against Andrew Byrd of Witney, butcher, for 27s. 6d.; charges 4d. (3)

Same against John Thomas of Witney, metalman, for 2s. 8d.; charges 4d. (3)

Court held 18 July 1606 by the bailiffs with William Clempsonne, Richard Box, Thomas Cornish, the constables and others.
Actions of debt : Richard Berrye of Chipping Norton, mercer, against John Powell of Witney, mason, for 8s. 11.; charges 4d. (3)

Same against Henry Lea of Witney, husbandman, for 6s. 5d.; charges 4d. (3)
Assize of bread: the bread of Robert Hanwell was weighed and found too light by one ounce and a half.

f.116r Court held 15 Aug. 1606 by the bailiffs with the constables, William Clempsone, William Yeomanns, Thomas Hannes, John Butler.
Actions of debt : Richard Clempsonne of Abingdon, Berks., mercer, against George Deye of Witney, broadweaver, for 8s.; charges 4d. (3)

Same against Richard Ocley of Witney for 7s.; charges 4d. (3)

Nicholas Gun, tailor, against Robert Rybone of Witney, tailor, for 4s. 1d.; charges 4d.

Court held 12 Sept. 1606 by the bailiffs with Thomas Cornish and others.
Action of debt : Elizabeth Lovill of Witney, victualler, against Alice Wells of Witney, widow, for 2s.; charges 4d. (3)

[111] Probably for one of the three subsidies or the six 15ths and 10ths granted to James I by Act 3 Jas.I c.26.

Action of debt : Md. . . . Sept. 1606 Thomas Cornish of Chipping Norton, mercer, against George Burgin of Eynsham, butcher, for . . .; charges . . . .

f.117r Court held 10 Oct, 1606 by William Clempsonne and Thomas Hanns, bailiffs, with John Butler and John Tymms, constables, John Clarke, Thomas Box, Richard Box, Thomas Cornish, William Huntt, James Hodsonne, Henry Brooke, Richard Humpheris senior, James Wattes, Thomas Webley.

Wardsmen: Edward Gardiner for the East Ward; William Hunt junior for Paternoster Row; Simon Pearson, weaver, for the Middle Ward; John Huntt for the West Ward; William Townsend for beneath the bridge.

Ale tasters: Bartholomew Cordewell, Nicholas Stratten.

Cardeners: John Bircott, James Hickes.

Leather sealers: Thomas Sexton, Leonard Taylor.

Cloth sealers: George Deye, William Purser.

Md. the sum of £40 given and bequeathed by the late George Tompsonne of Bampton, yeoman, was delivered to the bailiffs. Then, in the assembly there present, Thomas Taylor, Thomas Cave, Richard Box, Thomas Cornish, John Horne and Edward Bowman, inhabitants of the town and parish of Witney, were by common consent thought fit to be joined with the bailiffs of Witney and the constable of Hailey of disposing of the said £40 for the year following. And also 27s. for the use of the same money to be distributed to the poor of Witney and Hailey on 23 April next according to the effect and true meaning of Tompson's will.

f.117v Actions of debt : Mr John Clarke against Henry Whitt, weaver, and Anthony Ebsworth, dyer, for 20s., being part of the money given by George Tompson; charges 4d. (3)

Thomas Cotterell of Ramsden, labourer, against Robert Whood of Witney, cooper, for 4s. and a new pair of shoes: charges 4d. (3)

Robert Redbande of Stanton Harcourt, husbandman, against Edward Hanns of Witney, shoemaker, for 12s.; charges 4d. (3)

Marie Patrick of Witney, widow, against Roger Wryght for 2s. 6d.; charges 4d. (3)

Md. 19 Oct. 1606 Elizabeth Beverley, wife of James Beverley of Wallingford, Berks., duly appointed deputy of her husband, against William Nellson of Witney, saddler, for 8s. 11d.; charges 4d. (3)

f.118r Court held 1 Nov. 1606 by the bailiffs with Richard Box, John Clarke, James Wattes, John Tymmes, constable, Thomas Webley, John Butler, Henry Brooke.

Actions of debt : Thomas Pearsonne of Witney, clothier, against Ellis Hanns of Witney, shoemaker, for 13s. 11d.; charges 4d. (2)

John Archer of Witney, miller, and John Sea of Witney, joiner, against Sebastian Walker of Witney for 10s.; charges 4d. (2)

William Hunte junior of Witney, cardmaker, against Henry Walker of Witney, blacksmith, for 6s. 8d.; charges 4d.

Edward Ellis of Standlake, clerk, against Thomas Carter of Witney, tucker, for 11s. 6d.; charges 4d. (3)

Thomas Willsheire against the same for 9s.; charges 4d. (3)

Court held 5 Dec. 1606 by the bailiffs with Thomas Webley, Richard Box, Richard Haskins, the constables and others.

f.118v Action of debt : Richard Haskins of Witney, clothier, against Anthony Ebsworth of Witney, dyer, for 22s.; charges 4d. (3)

Collectors for the poor: Andrew Hodsonne and William Box presented their accounts for the previous year. There remained 41s. 3d. in the poor men's box which was delivered into the hands of Thomas Poole and Richard Weston, then chosen collectors for the ensuing year.

Actions of trespass: Md. 11 Dec. 1606 Thomas Woode of Stanton Harcourt, yeoman, against Marton Redbande of Standlake, yeoman, for detaining 30s. of Woode's money; charges 7d.; pledge Robert Cakebred.

Md. same day Richard Parme of Eynsham, yeoman, against Martin Redbande of Standlake, yeoman, for detaining unjustly 17s. 6d. of Parme's money; charges 6d.; pledge Robert Surrell.

f.119r Court held 16 Jan. 1607 by the bailiffs with Thomas Webley, Thomas Cornish, John Butler, constable, and others.

Md. of agreement: whereas Richard Clempson of Abingdon, [Berks.,] mercer, entered an action of debt against Andrew Byrd for 27s. 6d. Byrd now promised to pay Clempson the full sum of 20s. on 1 May next. Witnesses: [signatures of] William Clempson bailiff, Thomas Wilsheire; [marks of] Andrew Byrd, Thomas Hanns bailiff.

Victuallers licensed by the justices: the following came and showed their licences for the keeping of their victualling or selling ale: Thomas Townsend, Roger Cox, James Wattes, Robert James, Thomas Willshere, John Sea, all licensed by Sir Laurence Tanfeild kt.

f.119v Actions of debt : Thomas Cornish of Chipping Norton, mercer, against John Trindor of Witney, mason, for 3s. 3d.; charges 4d.

Same against Robert Bechum of Witney, broadweaver, for 7s.; charges 4d.

Same against John Tooley of Witney, tailor, for 5s. 8d.; charges 4d.

Same against James Hartt of Witney, mason, for 7s.; charges 4d.

Same against Hugh Walker of Witney, labourer, for 6s.; charges 4d.

Same against Josias Peirce of Witney, 'paritor', for 7s.; charges 4d.

Md. 5 Feb. 1607 Richard Pratt of the Field [i.e. Leafield] labourer, against Henry Allen of Witney, mason, for 5s.; charges 4d.

f.120r Court held 13 Feb. 1607 by the bailiffs with John Clarke, Thomas Webley and the constables.

Assize of bread: Nicholas Stratton and Bartholomew Cordwell, ale tasters and weighers of bread, returned Leonard Goode, baker, for making his bread light by two and a half ounces in a penny white loaf.

Action of debt : Md. 26 Feb. 1607 Tobias Snowsill of Lew, husbandman,

against Henry Rathbone of Brize Norton, gent., for 26s.; charges 8d. (2);
pledge John Butler.
Actions of debt : Md. 12 March 1607 Robert Hanwell of Witney, baker, against
Richard Shad of Woodstock, chandler, for 9s.; charges 7d. (3); pledge
Thomas Shawe.

Md. same day Thomas Yate of Witney, gent., on behalf of
Henry Hebden of London, gent., against Henry Ranckell of Witney,
clothier, for 20s.; charges 4d. (2)
Action of trespass: 12 March 1607 Richard Smyth of Witney, yeoman, against
Anthony Stainton of Bampton, tailor, because Stainton impounded and
unjustly from 5 March 1607 withheld one sow colour white, eight sucking
pigs, nine barrels, one twig basket, two long poles and four posts to the
value of 39s. 11d. and thereupon he brings his suit.

f.120v Court held 13 March 1607 by the bailiffs with John Tymes, constable, Thomas
Cornish, Thomas Webley, Thomas Yate, gent., and others.
Action of debt : Md. 2 April 1607 John Gobbet of Hanborough, yeoman,
against Edward Smyth of Enstone, butcher, for 30s.; charges 8d.

Court held 10 April 1607 by the bailiffs with John Butler, constable, and others.
Thomas Chamlin of Lew, mason, came and testified on oath that Henry
Rathbone of Brize Norton, gent., promised Tobias Snowsill of Lew that he
would pay him whatsoever money he should earn out of the coal pit of
Lew[112] and that the sum of 26s. was due to him before he was discharged
out of the said work. John Harris likewise testified the same on oath. Harris
also testified that the residue of the said sum of 26s. Snowsill earned after
Chamlin left his work, which likewise was before they were discharged
of the said work.

Court held 8 May 1607 by the bailiffs with John Clarke, Thomas Webley,
Thomas Cornish, Thomas Yate, Richard Box, John Butler, constable.
Action of debt : Richard Box against William Wilton of Witney, cooper, for
3s., charges 4d.
f.121r Bond for performance of covenant re settlement: Md. 10 May 1607 William
Goodgame of Witney, carpenter, bound himself in the sum of £20 that he,
his executors or assigns, shall sufficiently discharge, save and keep
harmless the inhabitants of Witney of and from all charges of encumbrances
that may arise against them by reason of Ann Endoll, daugher of Thomas
Endoll of Brize Norton, shepherd, with Margaret his wife who was
delivered of her, Ann Endoll, within the house of the said Goodgame on 9
May 1607. Witnesses: [signatures of] Thomas Willsheire; [mark of]
William Goodgame.

---

[112]   For the case see also above, p.195. Coalpits Farm on the borders of Lew and Bampton is a
modern post-inclosure farm which may commemorate some such diggings, but as Langford
noted in the 19th century there is no other evidence save this reference in the court book: Top
Oxon. d 211, p.85.

f.121v Court held 5 June 1607 by the bailiffs with the constables and others.

Covenanted servants: in court William Caning, son of Joan Caning of Witney, widow, with his mother's consent and in consideration of six covenant pence confessed himself bound as an apprentice to Richard Rankell of Witney, broadweaver, for six years from 1 May 1607 last past; to be found etc. [as on p.83; no correction clause]; at the end of the term 26s. 8d. wages and double apparel. Witnesses: [signature of] William Caning; [mark of] Richard Rankell.

f.122r   6 June 1607 Thomas Smyth, son of Richard Smyth of Hailey, yeoman, came before the bailiffs and by the force of seven covenant pence and with the advice and consent of his father and his grandfather Steven Brice of Witney, gent., acknowledged himself bound as apprentice to Thomas Webley of Witney, clothier, for seven years from 25 March last past; to be found etc. [as on p.83; no correction clause]; at the end of the term double apparel. Witnesses: [signature of] Thomas Webley, Thomas Smith.

f.122v Court held 31 July 1607 by the bailiffs with Thomas Cornish, Thomas Yate, John Butler, constable and others.

Action of debt : Jane Clarke of Bampton, widow, against Bartholomew Cordewell of Witney, broadweaver, for 9s.; charges 4d.

Court held 21 Aug. 1607 by the bailiffs with Thomas Cornish, John Butler, constable, and others.

Actions of debt : Thomas Cornish of Chipping Norton, mercer, against Richard Beardes of Witney, broadweaver, for 10s.; charges 4d.

                Same against Roger Fale of Witney, labourer, for 14s. 5d.; charges 4d.

Md. 11 Sept. 1607 Judith Dyer, wife of Robert Dyer of Weald, husbandman, came before William Clempsonn, bailiff, and confessed that one Bartholomew Cordewell of Witney, clothier, bought of one Jane Clarke of Weald, widow, three tods of wool wanting 3 lb., price 4d. the lb., in all 27s., which money Cordewell promised to pay Clarke on the Monday in Easter week last.[113]

f.123r Court held 18 Sept. 1607 by the bailiffs with John Clarke, Thomas Taylor, Thomas Cornish, Richard Box, John Tymes, constable, and others.

Actions of debt : Richard Haskins of Witney, clothier, against Robert James of Witney, butcher, for 9s. 4d.; charges 4d. (3)

                Same against John Workhowse of Witney, tucker, for 5s.; charges 4d. (1)

                Same against Francis Ympe of Witney for 2s. 5d.; charges 4d. (1)

                Robert Clever, servant to Henry Payne of Cogges, against Roger Wheeler of Witney, carpenter, for 20d.; charges 4d. (3)

---

[113]   See above, 31 July 1607.

Action of debt : Md. 30 March 1609 Nicholas Cooke of Oxford, skinner, against William Veysey of Burford for 2s. 6d.; charges 7d.[114]

f.123v Court held 9 Oct. 1607.

Victuallers licenced by the Justices: Thomas Towndsend, David Evans, Edward Hanns, James Wattes, John Sea, William Yemans, Sebastian Walker, Nicholas Gune, Simon Ensor, Roger Cox, Henry Harper, Thomas Willsheire by my Lord Chief Baron; Robert Bedoll by my Lord Chief Baron and my Lord Bishop; Robert Cakebred by my Lord Chief Baron and Mr Bray.

f.124r Court held 9 Oct. 1607 by Thomas Yate and Henry Brooke, bailiffs, with John Clarke, Thomas Taylor, Walter Dawlton, Thomas Webley, William Clempsonne, Thomas Hanns, James Hodsonne, Roger Willsheire, Nicholas Shorter and Thomas King, constables, and others.

Wardsmen: Edward Hawkins for Paternoster Row; Henry Humpheris for the Middle Ward; John Hartt for the East Ward; Thomas White for beneath the bridge; Nicholas Deye for the West Ward.

Ale tasters: Nicholas Stratten, John Workhowse.

Leather sealers: Thomas Sexten, Leonard Taylor.

Cloth sealers: Richard Angell, Robert Wyley.

Md. the sum of £37 10s. was delivered to the bailiffs with one bond for the receipt of £2 10s. from Francis Ympe, being the money that was given by the will of George Tompson late of Bampton. Thomas Taylor, Thomas Cave, Richard Box, Thomas Cornish, John Horne and Edward Bowman, inhabitants of Witney, were by the common consent of the assembly thought fit to be joined with the bailiffs of Witney and the constable of Hailey for the disposing of the £40 in the year following and were then elected and chosen. They were also to admininster 30s. for the use of the same money to be distributed to the poor of Witney and Hailey on 23 April next according to the effect of George Tompson's will, and 7s. 6d. out of John Birckoot's house, which is of the gift of Mr Richard Ashcombe, gent., deceased.[115]

f.124v Actions of debt : Thomas Hanns senior of Witney, butcher, against Anthony Ebsworth, dyer, for 30s. 7d.; charges 4d. (3)

      William Freeman of Wood Eaton, miller, against Robert Surrell of Witney, felt maker, for 34s.; charges 4d. (3) Agreed.

      Henry Gardner of Witney, fuller, against Michael Moxam of Witney, glover, for 2s. 6d.; charges 4d. (3) Received of this 6d. 6d. paid.

      Md. 30 Oct. 1607 by Richard Joyner of Witney, shepherd, against Adrian Williams of Witney for 6s. 6d.; charges 4d. (3)

f.125r Will of George Tompson of Bampton, yeoman. In the name of God, Amen. The sixth day of June in the first year of the reign of our Sovreign Lord James, by the grace of God of England, France and Ireland and of Scotland king, Defender of the Faith etc. [1603], I, George Tompson of the parish of

---

[114] Entry in a different hand.
[115] For the bequests and wills see above, pp.xxviii–ix.

Bampton in the county of Oxford, being sick of body but of perfect remembrance, blessed be Almighty God, do make and ordain this my last will and testament in manner and form following. First I commend my soul into the hands of Almighty God my Creator etc. Item I give to the poor people of Witney and Hailey £40 to be paid and delivered to the bailiffs of Witney and the constable of Hailey for the time being within six months before Michaelmas [29 Sept.] next after my decease. And for the disposition thereof, first my will and desire is that such order be taken by the discretion of the bailiffs of Witney and the constable of Hailey for the time being, with the advice and consent of six others, the honest inhabitants of the said limits, which shall be thought and esteemed in public assembly of the parishioners of Witney to that purpose most intimated and held, tendering the benefit and good of the poor, so that my legacy be not at any time diminished but kept whole in stock and employed from time to time for ever, to the best use and profit of the poor aforesaid: so as that £10 thereof shall be lent out freely from year to year by the said bailiffs, constable and inhabitants aforesaid, to four young occupiers and beginners, that is to say 50s. apiece, they taking good security of them that the said stock be not diminished. And my will is that no one party shall have the use thereof above one whole year, except upon good causes to be liked by the most part of the bailiffs, the constable and the inhabitants before specified, and absolutely no man to have the use of any part thereof above two years but then it shall be lent out again, as before, to others and so to continue for ever. As for the other £30, my will is that the bailiffs and constable with the inhabitants aforesaid shall use and employ [it] at their discretion to the best use and profit they can of the poor of Witney and Hailey aforesaid, so that the stock be always kept whole and undiminished, the profit yearly upon St George's Day [23 April] shall be distributed to the poor aforesaid and thus to continue yearly forever.[116]

f.125v Grant of probate to Joanna, widow of George Tompson, and William Hanckes, 4 Feb. 1603.

f.126r Court held 30 Oct. 1607 by the bailiffs with John Clarke, William Clempsonn, Richard Humpheris, Roger Willsheire, Thomas King, constable, and others.
Presented: for misdemeanours committed Sunday 25 Oct. last at unlawful hours as follows: Hugh Walker and Young Just at Robert Bedoll's; Thomas Hickes, Robert Meares and Roger Wheelar at . . . Layghton's; Anthony Ebsworth, William Purnell and William Cusse at Edward Busbye's; Hugh Hill, Michael Moxam and William Brignfeild at Robert James's.
Actions of debt : William Clempsonne against Richard Ockley of Witney, dyer, for 20s.; charges 4d. (3)
          Md. 19 Nov. 1607 Edith White of New Yatt, widow, against John Tooly of Witney, tailor, for 20d.; charges 4d. (3)
          Md. same day Annys Craftes of Witney, widow, against John Moore, broadweaver, for 3s. 4d.; charges 4d. (3)

[116] Part only of Tompson's will. He made other bequests to other parishes.

Md. 13 Nov. 1607 John Clarke and Thomas Webley delivered into the hands of Thomas Yate and Henry Brooke, then bailiffs, the sum of £6 13s. 4d., being the use of £100 bequeathed by Richard Ashcombe late of Curbridge, gent., deceased, to be employed to the profit of the poor of Witney aforesaid.

f.126v Covenanted servants: at the court on 30 Oct. 1607 Thomas Collett, son of Alice now wife of . . . Sealey, broadweaver, with his own and mother's assent and in consideration of seven covenant pence acknowledged himself bound apprentice to Nicholas Shorter of Witney, dyer, for seven years from 1 Nov. next to be taught the occupation of a dryer; to be found etc. [as on p.83; no correction clause]; at the end of the term 20s. wages and double apparel.

f.127r   at the court on 20 Nov. 1607 John Toolie, son-in-law [i.e. stepson] of Gregory Sheepheard, broadweaver, with the consent of his father-in-law and in consideration of seven covenant pence acknowledged himself bound apprentice to Henry Brooke of Witney, vintner, for seven years from 30 Nov. next to be taught the occupation of a broadweaver which Brooke now uses; to be found etc. [as on p.83; no correction clause]; and to be given at the end of the term 13s. 4d. wages and double apparel.

f.127v Court held 20 Nov. 1607 by the bailiffs with Thomas Cornish, William Clempsonne, Thomas Hanns, James Hodsonne, Richard Heskins, Richard Bishop, Nicholas Shorter, constable.

Covenanted servants: William Madock on the receipt of seven covenant pence acknowledged himself bound apprentice to Henry Brooke of Witney, vinter and broadweaver, for seven years from 24 Nov. next, to be taught the occupation of a broadweaver; to be found etc. [as on p.   ; no correction clause]; at the end of the term double apparel. Crossed [out] with the consent of both parties 18 Sept 1609 by me Thomas Willsheire. [Signature of] William Madockes; [mark of] Henry Brooke.

f.128r   28 Nov. 1607 Nicholas Gyles came before the bailiffs and in consideration of two covenant pence and with the consent of his mother Alice Gyles and John Horswell his late master confessed himself bound apprentice to Nicholas Coules, broadweaver, for two years from 21 Dec. next to be taught the occupation of a broadweaver; to be found etc. [as on p.83; no correction clause]; at the end of the term 20s. wages and double apparel. Witnesses: [marks of] Nicholas Cowles, Nicholas Gyles.

f.128v Action of debt : Md. 10 Dec. 1607 Richard Cooke of Burford, blanket maker, against Thomas Willes of Croscombe, Soms., for 35s.; charges 8d.

Court held 11 Dec. 1607 by the bailiffs with John Clarke, Richard Box and others.

Actions of debt : Francis Darby of Crawley, yeoman, against Thomas Shawe of Witney, butcher, for 7s. 6d.; charges 4d.

Joan Aiers against Roger Wilsheire of Witney, shoemaker, for 30s.; charges 4d.

Md. 31 Dec. 1607 Thomas Bodie of Hanborough against Edward Tryndor of Oxford, wheeler, for 12s. 4d.; charges 8d.

Court held 8 Feb. 1608 by the bailiffs with Thomas King, constable, Thomas Cornish and others.

Action of debt : John Harrys, shoemaker, against Roger Wright for 2s. 8d.; charges 4d.

f.129r Md. a possession: taken 4 Jan. 1608 by Richard Cullen M.A. by virtue of a letter of attorney from Edmund Lyllie D.D. of Oxford and Mr Thomas Yate and Henry Brooke, then bailiffs, of one messuage or tenement situated in Witney with the River Windrush on the north side and Mill Lane on the south, late in the tenure of William Critchley, gent., with one curtilage and other things specified in an indenture made between Lyllie and John and Maximilian Pettey; to the use of John and Maximilian in their proper persons according to the tenure and form of the said deed. Witnesses: [signatures of] Thomas Yate, bailiff, Thomas Kinge, constable, Thomas Willsheire, Henry Humfrey, wardsman, Richard Maior, sergeant; [mark of] Henry Brooke, bailiff.

f.129v Covenanted servants: 17 Jan. 1608 Richard Baker in consideration of six covenant pence and with the consent of his father-in-law [stepfather] William Shepheard and of Bartholomew Cordewell his late master, came before two bailiffs and confessed himself bound apprentice to John Huntt of Witney, clothier and broadweaver, for six years from 25 April next to be taught the occupation of a broadweaver; to be found etc. [as on p.83; no correction clause]; at the end of the term 20s. wages and double apparel. Witnesses: [signature of] John Hunt; [mark of] Richard Baker.

f.130r   29 Jan. 1608 Timothy Willsonn in consideration of seven covenant pence and with the consent of his uncle Robert Willsonn, parson of Lockinge, Berks., and of his own free will came before Henry Brooke bailiff and confessed himself bound apprentice to John Clarke of Witney, clothier, from the day and date hereof for seven years to be taught the occupation of a broadweaver; to be found etc. [as on p.83; no correction clause]; at the end of the term double apparel. John Clark, Timothie Willsone.

f.130v   31 Jan. 1608 Anthony Larden in consideration of three covenant pence and with the consent of Nicholas Gune, tailor, his late master, and of his own assent came before Henry Brooke, bailiff, and confessed himself bound apprentice to John Richardes of Witney, tailor, for three years from the date hereof until 24 June 1611 to be taught the occupation of a tailor; to be found etc. [as on p.83; no correction clause]; at the end of the term 3s. 4d. wages and double apparel. Witnesses: [marks of] John Richardes, Anthony Larden.

f.131r   14 Feb. 1608 Thomas Buller alias Barber, son of Alice Buller of Witney, widow, in consideration of seven covenant pence and with the advice of his mother and own assent came before Bailiff Brooke and confessed himself bound apprentice to Andrew Hodsonne of Witney, broadweaver, for seven years immediately ensuing to be taught the occupation of a broadweaver; to be found etc. [as on p.83; no correction clause]; at the end of the term 13s. 4d. wages and double apparel. Witnesses: [marks of] Andrew Hodsonn, Thomas Barber.

f.131v Action of debt : Md. 18 Feb. 1608 Gregory Shepheard of Witney, broadweaver, against Bartholomew Daie of Finstock for ten bushels of barley; charges 7d.

Court held 19 Feb. 1608 by the bailiffs with Mr John Clarke, Richard Box, William Clempsonne, Thomas King, constable, and others.
Actions of debt : Edward Hawkins of Witney, butcher, against Ann Yate of Witney, widow, for 8s.; charges 4d.
John Moore, broadweaver, against Alice Wells, widow, for 3s. 4d.; charges 4d.

Court held 18 March 1608 by the bailiffs with Thomas King, constable, Thomas Cornish, William Clempsonne, Thomas Webley.
Action of debt : Md. 7 April 1608 Walter Dawlton of Witney, mercer, against Christopher Byrd of Bampton, butcher, for 39s. 11d.; charges 8d.

f.132r Court held 8 April 1608 by the bailiffs with Thomas King, constable, Thomas Cornish.
Action of debt : Robert Surrell, felt maker, against John Workhowse, tucker, for 5s.; charges 4d. (3)
Md. John Birckot brought in 5s. for his half-year's rent due 25 March last and paid the same to the bailiffs.[117]

Court held 22 April 1608 by the bailiffs with Mr John Clarke, Walter Dawllton, William Clempsonne, Thomas Webley, Thomas King, constable, and others.
Md. George Tompson's money: £15 in cash and bonds for receipt of £25 were delivered to the bailiffs, viz. Robert Bedall £5, Matthew Horne £5, Thomas Bryan £5, James Hickes £2 10s., Adrian Williams £2 10s., [Richard, Edward crossed out] Bud [no sum], Edward Byrd £2 10s. Thomas Taylor, Thomas Cave, Richard Box, Thomas Cornish, John Horne and Edward Bowman were chosen fit men to join the bailiffs and the constable of Hailey to hold the money and to pay it to the inhabitants of Witney and Hailey at or in the town hall of Witney in and upon the Friday before 23 April next. Also delivered to the bailiffs 15s., part of the use of the money aforesaid, to be distributed to the poor of Witney and Hailey on 23 April next. [Signature of] Thomas Yate; [mark of] Henry Brooke.
f.132v Action of debt : Md. 22 April 1608 Richard Wesson against Isaac Saunders, slater, for 4s. 10d.; charges 4d. (3)
Md. a possession: given by deed dated 6 April 1608 by Richard Tack alias Tacket of Lew, shepherd, of his two tenements with the courts, gardens, backsides and all appurtenances situated in Witney on the north side of Corn St. between the tenement of Thomas Webley, clothier, on the east side and that of Philip Cakebred to the west, to Henry Wheeler, carpenter, for consideration of £13. Witnesses: [signatures of] Thomas Yate, bailiff,

---

[117] For a town house.

Thomas King, constable, Richard Maior, Thomas Willsheire: [mark of] Henry Brooke, bailiff.

f.133r Md. a possession: given 11 April 1608 by Henry Rankle of Witney, clothier, by his attorney Walter Dawlton of Witney, mercer, of all his messuage or tenement in Witney on the east side of the High St. between the tenement of Giles Palmer on the north side and that of Richard West on the south, with all houses, edifices, buildings, backsides, orchards, gardens and closes thereto belonging and all other things mentioned in one deed dated 5 April, to Walter Flude and Frances Bridges of Adderbury to have and to hold according to the meaning of the said deed and as by one letter of attorney made for Rankle to Dawlton for the true execution of hereof under his hand and seal dated 11 April.[118]

Witnesses: [signatures of] Thomas Yate, bailiff, Richard Maior, Thomas Willsheire; [mark of] Henry Brooke, bailiff.

f.133v Court held 12 May 1608 by the bailiffs with Thomas Cornish, Thomas King, constable, and others.

Actions of debt : Richard Johnsonne against Thomas Mukehill for 9s.; charges 4d.

Same against William Dytten for 3s.; charges 4d.
Same against William Wilton for 5s.; charges 4d.
Same against Ann Radree, widow, for 4s.; charges 4d.

f.134r Md. a possession: given 28 May 1608 by William Cakebred of London, cloth-worker, Edward Cakebred of Witney, broadweaver, and Elizabeth his wife, of one messuage or tenement in Witney on the west side of the High St. between the tenement of Elizabeth Beck alias Lovill on the south and the close of Marie Harecourte, widow, on the north, with all houses, edifices, buildings, gardens, orchards and closes belonging, late in the tenure of Robert Bickerstaffe, shoemaker, Edward Hawkins, butcher, and Elizabeth Beck alias Lovill, to Robert Cakebred of Witney, innholder, for consideration of £40 paid to Bickerstaffe, Hawkins and Beck alias Lovill by Robert Cakebred and by virtue of a deed dated as above.

Witnesses: [signatures of] Thomas Willsheire, Edward Hawkins.[119]

f.134v Court held 3 June 1608 by the bailiffs with William Clempsonne, Thomas Hannes.

Actions of debt : Richard Berry of Chipping Norton against John Powell, mason, Thomas Hewlett and Leonard Taylor alias Morris for 6s.; charges 4d. (3)

Same against Anne Legg, widow, for 2s. 4d.; charges 4d.
Same against William Sheepheard for 2s. 4d.; charges 4d.
Same against Thomas Gillam for 20d.; charges 4d. (3)
Same against Roger Wheeler for 4s. 4d.; charges 4d. (3)

[118]   For the final concord on this transaction see CP 25 (2) 339 Easter 6 Jas.I.
[119]   For final concord see ibid. This tenement was later given to the town charities: see above p.xxix, and O.R.O. TC III.

Actions of debt : Thomas Cornish against Thomas Taylor, mason, for 7s. 6d.; charges 4d.

Md. 20 June 1608 Christopher Wheeler against Thomas Poole, chandler, for 7s. 4d.; charges 4d.

Md. 29 June 1608 Avery Terald of Hagbourne, Berks., yeoman, against Charles Bowell of Stanton Harcourt for 25s.; charges 8d.

f.135r Court held 1 July 1608 by the bailiffs with John Clarke, Thomas Cornish, William Clempsonne, William Yeomans and others.

Action of debt : Md. 28 July 1609 [*rectius* 1608?] by Ralf Longworth the younger of Woolsham Mills, yeoman, against William Chawney of Minster Lovell Mill for 26s.; charges 8d.

Court held 29 July 1608 by the bailiffs with Thomas Cornish, William Clempsonne and others.

Md. of sale: 4 Aug 1608 Robert Surrell of Witney, felt maker, sold in the market one grey ambling mare with a bald face to Richard Heskins of Witney, clothier, for £5; vouchers for Surrell,[120] Justinian Goode and Thomas Upperton. [Signature of] Justinian Goode; [mark of] Thomas Upperton.

Actions of debt : Md. 25 Aug. 1608 Thomas Cornish of Chipping Norton, mercer, against Thomas Wyam of Witney, broadweaver, for 7s. 6d,; charges 4d.

Md. same day Thomas Bowdley of Curbridge against Thomas Jefferis of Witney, shoemaker, for 27d.; charges 4d.

f.135v Court held 2 Sept. 1608 by the bailiffs with Thomas Cornish, William Clempsonne and others.

Action of debt : Md. 20 Sept. 1608 by Thomas Poole, chandler, against Thomas Humpheris of Witney, innholder, for 26s. 8d.; charges 4d.

Court held 30 Sept. 1608 by the bailiffs with Thomas Cornish, John Clarke and others.

Distraint: a pot of Francis Impe's distrained for a debt of 2s. 5d. with the court charges at the suit of Richard Heskins was appraised at 3s. 4d. by John Harte, Henry Walker and others.

f.136r Md. a possession: given 5 Oct. 1608 by Walter Flude of Adderbury, gent., and Frances Bridges of Adderbury, gentlewoman, of one half of their messuage in Witney to Henry Paine of Cogges, gent., according to the tenor of a deed date 20 June 1608. Witnesses: [signatures of] Thomas King, bailiff, John Hart, constable, Thomas Willsheire.

Action of debt : Md. 27 Oct. 1608 Edward Camden of Minster Lovell against William Hobbins alias Chawney of Minster Lovell, miller, for 10s.; charges 8d.

---

[120]   i.e. that he sold the mare.

f.137r Court held 7 Oct. 1608 by Thomas Cornish and Thomas King, bailiffs, with
Mr William Duckit esq., Thomas Yate, gent., Henry Brooke, William
Clempsonne, Thomas Hanns, John Harte and William Ockley, constables,
James Wattes.
Wardsmen: Thomas Kimble for Paternoster Row; John Williams for the West
Ward; Nicholas Shorter junior for the Middle Ward; Robert Wyley for the
East Ward, Thomas Constable for beneath the bridge.
Ale tasters: John Birckot, Nicholas Shorter.
Leather sealers: Edward Hanns, Thomas Sexten.
Cloth sealers: Richard Angell, John Wyley.
Md. John Bircoot delivered to the bailiffs 5s. for his half-year's rent due 29 Sept.
last.[121]

f.137v Covenanted servant: 1 Nov. 1608 Bartholomew Baker in consideration of five
covenant pence and by the advice and consent of his mother Elizabeth
Sheepheard, wife of William Sheepheard of Witney, broadweaver, and
own assent confessed himself bound apprentice to Thomas Webley of
Witney, clothier and broadweaver, for five years from the date hereof to be
taught the occupation of a broadweaver; to be found etc. [as on p.83; no
correction clause]; at the end of the term double apparel.
Witnesses: [signature of] Thomas Webley; [marks of] Bartholomew Baker,
Elizabeth Shepheard.

f.138r Court held 4 Nov. 1608 by the bailiffs with John Clarke, Henry Brooke, John
Harte, constable, and others.
Actions of debt : William Cleevely of Alvescot, yeoman, against William
Cakebred of Witney, broadweaver, for 13s. 4d. [27 *crossed out*]; charges 4d.
          William Hunte of Witney against William Box of Witney,
broadweaver, for 3s. 6d. [7s. 8d. *crossed out*]; charges 4d.
          Same against Robert Basley, broadweaver, for 7s. 6d.; charges
4d.
          Md. 31 Nov. 1608 William Scot of Burford, mercer, against
William Stephens of Witney, shoemaker, for 6s.; charges 4d. (3)

Court held 9 Dec. 1608 by the bailiffs with Thomas Taylor senior, William
Ockley and others.
Collectors for the poor: John Hunte and John Harris, glover, elected.
f.138v Action of debt : Md. 18 Dec. 1608 Walter Jefferis of Witney, blacksmith, against
Thomas Upperton of Cogges, husbandman, for 29s.; charges 8d.

Court held 13 Jan. 1609 by the bailiffs with Henry Brooke and others.
Actions of debt : John Harper of Witney, yeoman, against Nicholas Shorter
junior, dyer, for 4s.; charges 4d. (3)
          Roger Willsheire against Francis Johnsonne of Witney,
labourer, for 10s.; charges 4d. (3)
          Same against Thomas Saunders for 5s. 6d.; charges 4d. (3)

[121]   For a town house.

Covenanted servant: Annis Craftes, widow, confessed before the bailiffs and the
assembly there present that her son Nathaniel Craftes with her consent put
himself apprentice to Nicholas Withorne for nine years from 24 June 1605
to be taught the trade of a broadweaver and that Nathaniel received nine
pence in earnest in the presence of Richard Purnell, broadweaver. [122]

f.139r Court held 3 Feb. 1609 by the bailiffs with John Clarke, Thomas Webley,
Henry Brooke and others.

Court held 10 March 1609 by the bailiffs with John Harte, Thomas Willsheire
and others.
Actions of debt : James Watts against John Workhowse of Witney, tucker, for
6s.; charges 4d.
Md. 30 March 1609 Nicholas Cooke of Oxford, skinner,
against William Veysey of Burford for 2s. 6d.; charges 7d.
Md. 31 March 1609 Thomas Poole of Witney, chandler,
against Richard Healer of Witney, broadweaver, for 20s.; charges 4d.

f.139v Court held 21 April 1609 by the bailiffs with John Clarke, Thomas Taylor,
Thomas Yate, Thomas Webley, Richard Box, Henry Brooke, Walter
Dawlton, John Harte, constable, and others.
Md. George Tompson's money: Thomas Yate and Henry Brooke delivered to
the bailiffs £22 10s., part of the money given by George Tompson.
Thomas Taylor, Thomas Cave, Richard Box, Thomas Webley, John
Horne and Edward Bowman were chosen to join the bailiffs and Roger
Wearing the constable of Hailey for disposing of the money not yet
brought in as well as the £22 10s. The bailiffs have agreed to pay the sum of
£22 10s. at or in the town hall of Witney on the Friday next before 23 April
1609. [Signature of] Thomas King; [mark of] Thomas Cornish.
f.140r 20s. was delivered to the bailiffs for the use of the money aforesaid. Thomas
Yate and Henry Brooke delivered to the bailiffs the sum of 30s. being the
gift of a parson in Devonshire to be employed to the profit of the poor of
Witney aforesaid. [123]
Actions of debt : Richard Martin of Faringdon, Berks., felt maker, against
Thomas Gillam of Witney, tailor, for 12s. 6d.; charges 4d.
Md. 4 May 1609 William Woodleafe of Oxford, yeoman,
against Edward Williamsonne of Twelve Acres in Eynsham, gent., for
14s.; charges 7d.
Md. 12 May 1609 Richard James, butcher, against William
Hill for 2s. 8d.; charges 8d.

Court held 12 May 1609 by the bailiffs with Walter Dawlton, Henry Brooke
and others.

[122] The only entry of this kind where the mother appears and where the covenant money
was said to have been paid in the presence of someone other than the bailiff.
[123] Presumably the parson from Cornwall, see above, p.169.

Md. George Tompson's money: £5, part of George Tompson's money, was delivered to the bailiffs.

Actions of debt : Md. 19 May 1609 John Russell, miller, against William Hill for 3s. 10d.; charges 7d.

f.140v   Md. 16 June 1609 Henry Lyfallie of Minster Lovell, husband-man, against Nicholas Cowles of Witney, broadweaver, for 14s. 6d.; charges 4d.

Court held 30 June 1609 by the bailiffs with Henry Brooke, Thomas Webley, Walter Dawlton and others.

Action of debt : Thomas Brindie of Hardwick against Thomas Gillam of Witney, tailor, for 2s.; charges 4d.

f.141r Covenanted servants:[124] William Busbie in consideration of six covenant pence and with the counsel of his friends and own assent confessed before the bailiffs himself bound apprentice to Richard Box of Witney, clothier, for six years from . . . [blank] to be taught the occupation of a broadweaver; to be found etc. [as on p.83; no correction clause]; at the end of the term double apparel.

f.141v   Anthony Greenward in consideration of seven covenant pence and with the counsel of his friends and own assent confessed before the bailiffs himself bound apprentice to Richard Box of Witney, clothier, for seven years from 25 March 1608 to be taught the occupation of a broadweaver; to be found etc. [as on p.83; no correction clause]; at the end of the term double apparel.

f.142r   John Warren in consideration of . . . [blank] covenant pence and by counsel of his friends and own assent confessed before the bailiffs himself bound apprentice to Richard Box, clothier, for . . . [blank] to be taught the occupation of a broadweaver; to be found etc. [as on p.83; no correction clause]; at the end of the term double apparel.

f.142v Court held . . . July 1609 by the bailiffs with Thomas Taylor, Henry Brooke, William Dyar, James Wattes, John Hart, constable, and others.

Actions of debt : Md. 3 Aug. 1609 Thomas Wright in the name of Andrew Walle of Brize Norton against Christopher Rawlins of Charlbury for 30s.; charges 7d.

Md. same day Andrew Walle of Brize Norton by his attorney Thomas Wright of Burford against Christopher Rawlins of Charlbury for 30s.; charges 7d.

f.143r Covenanted servant: 31 July 1609 Leonard Rybone, son of Robert Rybone, late of Witney, tailor, in consideration of eight covenant pence and with the counsel of friends and own assent acknowledged before the bailiffs to put himself apprentice to George Barret of Kirtlington, tailor, for eight years from . . . to be taught the occupation of a tailor; to be found etc. [as on p.83; no correction clause]; at the end of the term 20s. wages and double apparel. Witnesses: [marks of] Leonard Rybone, George Barret.

[124]   The date at the top of the folios is illegible but presumably these are covenants of 1608/9.

f.143v Action of debt : Md. 17 Aug. 1609 Thomas Brookes of Bampton against
Christopher Byrd of Bampton, butcher, for 28s. 9d.; charges 7d.

Court held 25 Aug. 1609 by the bailiffs with John Clarke, Thomas Webley,
Walter Dalton, John Hart, constable, and others.

Md. a gown of Thomas Gillam's wife was appraised by John Bircote, Robert
Wyly and Nicholas Whithorne at 16s. for the debt due to Richard Martyn
and one Thomas Grindie.

Actions of debt : Md. 9 Sept. 1609 Robert Surrell against William Hollowaye
of South Leigh, blacksmith, for 20s.; charges 7d.

Md. 21 Sept. 1609 William Tylar of Aston Ingham,
Herefordshire, husbandman, against Thomas Collishow of Chimney,
yeoman, for 39s. 11d.; charges 7d.

Md. same day William Page junior of Stow-on-the-Wold,
Gloucs., cooper, against John Harper of Witney, yeoman, for 23s.; charges
4d.

Court held 22 Sept. 1609 by the bailiffs with John Clarke, Walter Dawlton,
Richard Box, Thomas Hanns, the constables and others.

f.144r Court held 6 Oct. 1609 by Thomas Taylor and James Wattes, bailiffs, with
John Clarke, Thomas Webley, Richard Box, Thomas Cornish, Walter
Dawlton, Thomas King, Andrew Hodsonne, William Bishop alias Martyn
and others.

Wardsmen: William Bazeley for Paternoster Row; Walter Lynlie for the West
Ward; Humfrey Beacham for the Middle Ward; Henry Gardner for beneath
the bridge; Robert Palmar for the East Ward.

Ale tasters: John Birckate, Nicholas Stratton.

Leather sealers: Robert Bickerstaffe, Thomas Sexten.

Cardenars: Thomas Shawe, Nicholas Hutchins.

Cloth sealers: George Deye, William Pursser.

Action of debt : Peter Rider against Francis Ympe for 19s. 6d.; charges 4d.

f.144v Md. a possession: granted at the court held 6 Oct. 1609 by the bailiffs and
other inhabitants of Witney whose names are hereunto subscribed to
William Bazeley and Ursula his wife of all that tenement, garden and
backside now in Bazeley's tenure situated in Corn St., to have and to hold
for the term of 21 years from 29 Sept. last past, paying 20s. rent per annum
by equal portions on 25 March and 29 Sept, and all charges arising out of
the premises to the king, the chief lord and the commonwealth; they are to
maintain the premises and are not to let it or any part thereof without leave
of the bailiffs and their successors and other the inhabitants of Witney. By
us: [signatures of] Thomas Taylor, bailiff, John Clarke, Richard Box,
Thomas Webley, William Bishopp, Thomas Kinge; [marks of] James
Wattes, bailiff, Andrew Hodsonne, Thomas Cornish, Henry Brooke.

f.145r Actions of debt : Md. 16 Oct. 1609 William Symons against William Hunte for
29s.; charges 4d.

Md. 19 Oct. 1609 Nicholas Gune against Thomas Gillam for
2s. 2d.; charges 4d.

Court held 27 Oct. 1609 by the bailiffs with Mr William Ducket, esq., Roger Willsher, Thomas Webley, Thomas Cornish, Thomas King, Andrew Hodsonne, constable, and others.

Actions of debt : William Gould of Hailey against Anthony Ebsworth for 28s.; charges 4d.

Md. 2 Nov. 1609 Thomas Craftes of Hailey, clothier, against John Brafeild of Northampton, glover, for 30s.; charges 7d.

Md. 9 Nov. [1609] Richard Farmer against James Hickes for 19s. 6d.; charges 4d.

Court held 17 Nov. 1609 by the bailiffs with William Martyn, constable, Henry Brooke, Thomas King, Thomas Webley, Roger Willsheire, John Clarke, Walter Dawlton.

Actions of debt : John Hamsheire of Crawley against Anthony Ebsworth of Witney, dyer, for 39s. 11d.; charges 4d.

f.145v   Md. 20 Nov. 1609 John Coussens of Marcham, Berks., yeoman, against Sebastian Walker of Witney, blacksmith, for 7s. 8d.; charges 4d.

Court held 8 Dec. [1609] by the bailiffs with Thomas Webley, Henry Brooke, Phillip Box and others.

Actions of debt : William Brooke of Lew against Thomas Shawe of Witney, butcher, for 20s.; charges 4d.

Md. 14 Dec. 1609 Robert Wright, blacksmith, against John Russell of Minster Lovell for 10s. 9d.; charges 7d.

Court held 12 Jan. 1610 by the bailiffs with John Clarke, Henry Brooke, John Harris, Andrew Hodsonne, constable, and others.

Action of debt : John Wylie senior, tailor, against Esau Collier of Witney for 11s.; charges 4d.

John Russell promised to pay Robert Wright 6s. 8d. in full satisfaction of his debt aforesaid.

Actions of debt : Md. 8 Feb [1610] Giles Brinfield against Bartholomew Cordwell for 2s. 6d.; charges 4d.

Md. same day John Hampsheire against Anthony Ebsworth for 39s. 11d.; charges 4d.

f.146r Covenanted servant: . . . 1609 [?] Henry Boult, son of John Boult of Newland, Cogges, broadweaver, in consideration of three covenant pence and by the advice and consent of his father and own assent, acknowledged before one of the bailiffs himself bound apprentice to Thomas Webley of Witney, clothier, for three years from 21 Dec. to be taught the occupation of a broadweaver.

f.146v Court held 9 Feb. 1610 by the bailiffs with Thomas King, William Bishop, constable, and others.

Actions of debt : Thomas Box against Robert Keep for 31s.; charges 4d.

Md. 15 Feb. 1610 Richard Mayade of Eynsham, husbandman, against Thomas Bryan of Witney, clothier, for 22s. 9d.; charges 4d.

Md. 24 Feb. 1610 Thomas Humpheris against Richard Bishop for 39s.; charges 7d.

APPENDIX

List of Bailiffs of Witney

		Date of election or [first appearance]	Ref. in Court Books
John Peny	Roger Legge	26 Oct. 1538	i.1r
John Peny	Roger Legge	10 Oct. 1539	i.4r
Thomas Tayler	Richard Umfrey	8 Oct. 1540	i.6r
Richard Umfrey	Robert Tempull	7 Oct. 1541	i.8r
Robert Temple	William Bouysshyp	6 Oct. 1542	i.11v
	Marten		i.15v
Robert Temple	William Marten	[14 March 1544]	i.16r
Leonard Yate	Thomas Ryng	23 Oct. 1544	i.17v
[year missing]		[see ff. 18v to 19r]	
William Box	John Peny	15 Oct. 1546	i.19r
Roger Legge	Thomas Taylor	[7 Oct. 1547]	i.20v
Thomas Taylor	John Raynkell	[. . 5 Oct. 1548]	i.25r
William Byshoppe	Thomas Yate	2 Oct. 1549	i.29r
Thomas Rynge	Walter Jones	10 Oct. 1550	i.31r
Thomas Ringe	William Brynkefeld	9 Oct. 1551	i.34v
William Brigfeild	William Burde	21 Oct. 1552	i.41r
Phillip Boxe	John Lawrans	20 Oct. 1553	i.46r
Richard Umfrey	Matthias Penny	5 Oct. 1554	i.51r
Thomas Taylor	Walter Jones	[3 Jan. 1556]	i.58v
Leonard Yate	John Barnaby	[30 Oct. 1556]	i.63v
Thomas Ringe	Thomas Colier	20 Oct. 1557	i.65r
(d. by May 1558)			
Thomas Yat	Walter Jones	4 Nov. 1558	i.70r
Thomas Yat	Walter Jones	[20 Oct. 1559]	i.72v
Thomas Taylor	Philip Boxe	11 Oct. 1560	i.74r
Thomas Taylor	Richard Beckynshaw	10 Oct. 1561	i.81r
Harry Jones	Thomas Bysshop	23 Oct. 1562	i.84r
Leonard Yate	William Huchyns	8 Oct. 1563	i.86r
Thomas Hanckes	William Ellmar	6 Oct. 1564	i.90r
Humfrey Malen	Richard Hyet	5 Oct. 1565	i.94v

John Lawrence	Thomas Clemson	4 Oct. 1566	i.100v
Thomas Taylor	Harry Jones	10 Oct. 1567	i.106v
Philip Box	Peter Ranckell	1 Oct. 1568	i.111r
Giles Jones	Philip Boxe	21 Oct. 1569	i.114v
Leonard Yate elder	William Ryng	13 Oct. 1570	i.117v
Thomas Bishoppe		10 Oct. 1571	i.125v
	Thomas Yate	14 Dec. 1571	i.128r
William Hutchyns	Nicholas Ifeelde	17 Oct. 1572	i.133r
William Ellmore	Richard Humfrey	9 Oct. 1573	i.141v
Thomas Hanckes	William Harris	9 Oct. 1574	i.151r
Thomas Taylor	Nicholas Gunne	7 Oct. 1575	i.160v
Henry Jones	Peter Ranckell	5 Oct. 1576	i.169v
Philip Boxe	William Ring	4 Oct. 1577	i.175v
Leonard Yate	John Barnaby senior	10 Oct. 1578	i.183v
Thomas Yate	Peter Ranckell	9 Oct. 1579	i.191v
Thomas Bysshoppe	Richard Jonson	7 Oct. 1580	i.199v
Philip Boxe	Leonard Yate	13 Oct. 1581	i.208v
John Stampe	Nicholas Gunne	5 Oct. 1582	i.215v
Henry Jones	Thomas Taylor younger	4 Oct. 1583	i.224v
Leonard Yate elder	Richard Clempson	6 Oct. 1584	i.229v
Richard Humfrey	Thomas Boxe	8 Oct. 1585	i.238v
John Clarcke	Peter Ranckell	7 Oct. 1586	i.246v
Thomas Bisshoppe	Roger Willsheere	6 Oct. 1587	i.251v
Mr Thomas Yate	Thomas Walters [until June 1589]	11 Oct. 1588	i.259v i.f.263v
Philip Boxe	Mr Thomas Yate	10 Oct. 1589	i.266v
Thomas Taylor	Nicholas Gunne	9 Oct. 1590	i.272v
Henry Jones	Walter Dallton	8 Oct. 1591	i.280v
Leonard Yate	Richard Clempson	6 Oct. 1592	i.285v
John Clarke	Thomas Boxe	5 Oct. 1593	i.290v
Leonard Yate senior, gent.	Richard Humfrey	4 Oct. 1594	i.298r
Richard Jonson	Henry Ranckell	10 Oct. 1595	i.304r
Thomas Taylor	Thomas Cave	8 Oct. 1596	i.313r
Walter Daullton	Richard Boxe	7 Oct. 1597	i.327r
John Clarke	Richard Boshope als. Marten, tucker	6 Oct. 1598	i.341r
Thomas Webley	William Clempsonne	12 Oct. 1599	ii.f.7r
Peter Rankill	William Hunte	17 Oct. 1600	ii.f.27r
Thomas Box	Thomas Cornishe	9 Oct. 1601	ii.45r
Thomas Tayllar	Henry Rankill	22 Oct. 1602	ii.62r
Andrew Bird	Walter Daulton	7 Oct. 1603	ii.72r

Richard Box	James Hodsson	5 Oct. 1604	ii.86r
Mr John Clarke	Thomas Webley	4 Oct. 1605	ii.110r
William Clempsonne	Thomas Hanns	10 Oct. 1606	ii.117r
Thomas Yate	Henry Brooke	9 Oct. 1607	ii.124r
Thomas Cornish	Thomas King	7 Oct. 1608	ii.137r
Thomas Taylor	James Wattes	6 Oct. 1609	ii.144r

INDEX OF PERSONS

References on consecutive pages are run together to save space. There may be more than one entry for a name on the page.

Occupations are given in this index but place and date are only given when needed to distinguish individuals of the same name. Such identifications can often only be tentative and it is advisable to consult the text where date, occupation and place can be found.

Not all of the many variations in spelling of surnames are given and the text should be consulted. The most familiar and the most used spelling in the text and the most unusual variations have been noted and cross-referenced. Variations of 'y' for 'i' and vice-versa and the doubling of letters and the addition or omission of final 'e' or 'es' have not always been noted in the index but can be found in the text.

Common abbreviations are used for Christian names and the full spelling can be found in the text. Unlike the surnames the christian names in the text have been modernized.

Other abbreviations used are: bkr. baker; blksm. blacksmith; bp. bishop; brdwr. broad-weaver; butch. butcher; carp. carpenter; ct. court; cvt. svt. covenanted servant; d. died; dau. daughter; draper, woollen draper; fam. family; fl. flourished; husb. husbandman; jnr. junior; lab. labourer; m. married; mkr. maker; shep. shepherd; snr. senior; svt. servant; tpl. tippler; vctlr. victualler; w. wife; W. Witney; wid. widow; wvr. weaver; yeo. yeoman.

The list of Bailiffs has not been indexed.

Aberstoke, Ralph, 1
Able, Abley, Hably, Rd. 8–12
  Wm. smith, lxviii, lxxxiii, 1, 7
Abraham, Rbt. 87, 160
  Wm. 93
Abreck, Edw. carp. 49, 53
Absten, Abstyne *see* Austen
Adams, Geo. upholder, 114
  Hy. upholsterer, 157
  Thos. 32
Adeane, Deene, Margett, 16
  Rd. yeo., Horton, 16, 72, 123
  Rd. husb., Sandford, 16
  Rbt. xlix, 16, 23, 28
Aiers *see* Ayres
Alder, Alldar, Jn. 183
  Margery, 27
  Thos. 180
Aliphexe *see* Ellyfecke
Alldworth, Jn. tanner, Wantage, 45
  Jn. yeo., Aston, 139
Allen, Allan, Alyn, Geo. brdwr. 102
  Jane, w. of Geo. 133
  Leo. 25
  Hy. cvt. svt. mason, 157, 195
  Hy. sawyer, 29–31, 44–5, 49, 55, 72, 77, 81
  Nich. 3, 9, 12, 16, 18, tpl. 22, 24

  Rbt. 102
  Thos., Eynsham, 71
  Thos. of W. 29, 33, 140
  Wm. blksm., Ducklington, 94, 104
  Wm. of W. 23–4, 110
  fam. lxv, lxvii
Alltaffe, Rbt. cvt. svt., son of Wm. 188
  Wm. yeo. 188
Andrews, Androsse, Androw, Ayndros, Nich. 60
  Rd., Aston, 37
  Rd. sawyer, lxviii, 19
  Thos. brdwr. 130
  Thos. sawyer, lxviii, 1, 2, 4, 6, 19
  Wm. lxxvii, 19, 26, 33–4, 39
Angell, Rd. 198, 205
Appowall *see* Powell
Archer, Archar, Jn. miller, 181, 194
Arden, Wm. royal Clerk of the Market, xxvi, 16
Arndayll, Wm. salter, 154
Arnold, Edw. shoemkr. 129, 132
  Eliz. svt. 96
  Wm. 27
Arsbasson, Mr. gent. 192
Ashat, Asshett, Jn. coverlet mkr., wvr. 118, 135, 148, 159, 163–4, 173

115–17, 130, 133–7, 143, 150, 163–4, 167, 173, 179
Wm. mercer, lxix, lxxxii, lxxxiv, 126, 137, 141–2, 144, 148, 155–6, 163, 169–87, 189–95, 197–200, 202–5
Wm. shoemkr. xxxii, 112–13, 117
fam. xlix, lxiv, lxxxiv
Clennard, Wm. tucker, 146
Cley see Clay
Clynche, —, husb. 97
Cock, Hew, 47
Wm. 34
Cockes, Cokkes see Cox
Cockrell, Cockarill, Hy. yeo. 122
Thos. 176
Coke see Cook
Coles, Colles, Coules, Cowles, Chris. brdwr. 166
Edw. 108
Edw., Shipton, 118
Edw. yeo., Leafield, 149
Gratian, husb. 86
Jn. alias Barnes, 78
Jn. yeo. 77
Nich. brdwr. 47, 56, 59, 80, 82, 94, 106, 109–10, 115, 118, 125, 130, 132, 200, 207
Colgrove, Cowlgrove, Rd. 26
Thos. bkr. 171
Collett, Alice m. (2) — Sealey, 200
Thos. cvt. svt., son of Alice, 200
Collier, Coliare, Agnes, vctlr. 185, 190
Esau, 209
Jn. (several?), clothier, tucker, mercer, tpl. lxxiv, lxxix–lxxxi, 27, 29, 32, 40, 43–4, 50, 56–9, 61, 63, 70, 74, 76–7, 79, 84–7, 90, 104, 106, 113, 115–6, 120–2, 134, 137–8, 140, 143–4, 147, 172, 179
Jn. vintner, 101, 115
Rog. miller, 183
Steph. (fl. 1549), fuller, brdwr. lxxx, 153–6, 169, 182
Steph. (d. 1639), butch. lxxxiv
Thos. (fl. 1544–69), clothier, lxviii, lxxxi, 20, 24–7, 29, 33, 42–3, 48–9
Thos. (fl. 1580–87), chandler, fishmonger, 93, 97, 100, 103–4, 110, 113–14, 117
Tim. husb. 166
fam. lxii, lxxxiv
Collishaw, Thos. yeo. 208
Collpepar, Coullpepoar, Walt. Mr. Justice, 163
Collsborne, Jn. lab. 66, 77, 85–6, 100, 103, 120, 132

Collydon, Hy. 13
Collyns, Cyprian, 32–3
Jn. 3–4
Rd. 163
Thos. 83
Wm. 1
Constable, Cunstabull, Rd. husb. 176, 181
Thos. plasterer, lxxxiii, 205
Cook, Coke, Cookes, Couk, Kooke, Hy. husb. 100
Jas. butch. 54
Joan see Jones
Jn. husb., Bladon, 146
Jn. of W. 5, 7–8, 16, 18, 23, 25–6, 29, 32, 34, 37, 40, 42–3, 45
Jn. sawyer of W. 107
Jn. yeo., Hanborough, 147
Nich. skinner, 171, 198, 206
Ralph, husb. 133
Rd. 125
Rd. blanketmkr., Burford, 200
Rd. husb., Signet, 168
Rog. miller, 129
Thos. brdwr. lxvn, lxxix, 25, 31, 48
Wm. 164
fam. lxv, lxvii, lxxix
Cooper, Rog. miller, 129
Cootmore, Thos. husb. 190
Cope, Ant. cvt. svt., son of Rbt. 110
Ant., Sir, Justice, 146–7, 159, 163, 169, 174, 179
Rbt. minister, 110
Cordwell, Cardewell, Cordywell, —, 39
Barth. brdwr., clothier, 105, 140, 155, 158, 174, 181, 187, 194–5, 197, 201, 209
Joan, wid. 132, 141, 145
Wm. bkr., tpl. 54–5, 60, 62, 65, 70–1, 74–5, 82, 86, 90–1, 94, 102, 104, 106, 109, 115, 120, 126
Wm. (another?), 160
Cornbury, Lord, see Hyde
Cornish, Mgt. see Bishop
Thos. mercer, lxiii, lxxxiv, lxxxix, xc, 173–5, 177–87, 189–98, 200–6, 208–9
fam. lxiv
Cosborne, Jn. 1
Cossam, Thos. carter, 137
Cosyns, Cossen, Coussens, Edm. 24
Jn. husb. 89
Jn. yeo. 209
Cotes, Cotyse, Chris. brdwr., clothman, 104, 114–16, 125, 138, 146, 155, 177
Nich. brewer, 147–8, 154

Loovestie, Rbt. lab. 136
Lopton, Lupden, Wm. 3–6, 18, 20–2, 24
  Walt. *alias* Bolchar, 38
  Wm. 23, 26
Lord, Lorde, Rd. tailor, 138
  Thos. husb. 184
Louyll, Lovell, Lovill, Eliz. wid., tpl. 159,
  163, 174, 179, 185–6, 190, 193
  see also Beck
Lowdall, Wm. 21
Lowe, Rbt. 11, 14
  Thos. 2
  Wm. 10
Lucas, Agnes, wid. 179
  Eliz. svt. 192
  Jas. wvr. 104
  Mich. cvt. svt., son of last, 104
Luddyatt, Edw. 16
Lugg, Cicely, w. of Thos. 108
  Thos. lab. 108
Luker, Thos. yeo. 163
Lun, Jn. 3
  Lupden *see* Lopton
Lusskie, Jn. gent. 181
Lydall, Jn. chapman, 77
Lyffoley, Lyfallie, Lyfe Holye, Geo. husb.
  158
  Hy. husb. 145, 207
Lygon, Rd. lxv
Lyllie, Edm. 201
Lynley, Linley, Lynnlley, Jn. brdwr. 92, 97,
  101, 121, 123, 160, 171, 174–7
  Walt. 169, 208
Lysson, Wm. clk. 7
Lyvingstone *see* Levinstone

Mabbat, —, 131
Mace *see* Mate
Machyn, Ant. wvr. 96
Madock, Wm. cvt. svt. 200
Magood, Maygood, Jn. glover, 36, 38, 48,
  77, 84, 89, 90, 118
Maior, Mager, Major, Mayior, Meger,
  Agnes, 116
  Jn. *alias* Humphris *see* Humphrey
  Jn. shoemkr. 148
  Margery, w. of Jn. 148
  Nich. xxi, 27, 32, 37, 39, 40, 43, 46, 54, 58,
    60, 74, 76, 79, 82, 86, 90, 93, 104–6, 116,
    120, 123, 127, 131, 133–4, 142, 153, 158,
    169, 181
  Rd. brdwr. xxi, xlvi, 59, 90, 104, 106, 108,
    122, 126, 151, 154, 160n, 163, 165, 167,

172–4, 178–82, 184, 186–9, 191–3, 201,
  203
  Wm. (fl. 1503–56), xxi, 1, 2, 12–15, 18,
    20–1, 24
  Wm. the younger, (fl. 1553–c.1604), xxi,
    xxv, 18, 25–6, 32, 45, 60–3, 69, 71, 78,
    82, 99, 105, 111, 114, 118, 121–3, 125–6,
    128, 131, 142–3, 146, 149, 151, 155–6,
    168, 172, 178–81, 183, 185
  Wm. cvt. svt., son of Nich. lab. 186, 190
  fam. xxi
Makepeace, Geo. xxxiv, 160–1
  Rd. cvt. svt., son of Wm., xxxiv
  Wm. 141
Malen, Malyn, Maylyn, Humph. brewer,
  draper, tpl. lxxii, lxxxiv, 8–12, 16, 19,
  22, 25, 29, 32, 39, 42, 48–9, 52, 57–8,
  60–1, 63–8, 70, 73–5, 79, 90
  Wm., Ducklington, 48
  Wm. of W. 10, 14, 21, 28, 37, 39, 43
Marbleston, Margett, 16
Marchante, Wm. lab. 181
Marcheras *see* Margeris
Margeris, Marcheras, Margeyes, Mariges,
  Annese, 15
  Cuthbert, tailor, 52–8, 73, 84, 105–6, 109
  Joan, wid. 68, 70, 90–1
  Jn. 65, 74
  Randall, brewer, tailor, tpl. lxviii, lxxv,
    1–5, 8–14, 18, 19, 21–9, 32–9, 43–5, 49,
    50, 59, 61
Margetes, Jas. cvt. svt., son of Martin, 31
  Martin, 31
Margeyes *see* Margeris
Marlborough, Duke of, *see* Spencer, Spencer-
  Churchill
Marle, Thos. tailor, 125
Marlow, And. cvt. svt., son of Thos. 95
  Thos. tailor, 95
Marriatt, Jn. smith, lxxxiii
  Nich. 129
Martin, Jn. 2, 22
  Leo, 187
  Rd. feltmkr. 206, 208
  Thos. barber, yeo. 29, 42, 131, 156
  Thos. jnr. 131, 190–3
  Wm. svt. 94
  fam. lxii
  see also Bishop *alias* Martin
Mashorader, Edm., vicar of Shilton, 24, 42
Mason, Rd. 172
  Wm. 23
Mate, Mace, Rd. 170

Rudlande, Geo. plumber, 142
Rugg, Hy. 15
Russell, Russill, Eliz. 187
　Jn. miller, 161, 207, 209
　Mark, 176
　Rbt. brdwr. 181
　Wᴵᴵᴵ. cvt. svt. 181
Rybone see Raybone
Rydge see Rudge
Rydle, Rydley, Rydy see Ridley
Rydsdale, Wm. miller, 130
Ryman, Thos. glover, 182
Ryme, Mgt. svt. 36
Ryng see Ring
Ryvar, Damyan, carp. 126

Sadlare, —, yeo. 157
Sagar, Geo. brdwr. 62, 77, 86
　Rbt. 12
Saley, Sally, Saly, Eliz. wid. 142
　Ellys, 41
　Jn. 2
　Margery, wid. 128
　Rd. 180
　Rbt. clothmkr., fuller, 32, 37, 39–41, 52,
　　58, 60, 63, 65, 70, 73–4, 79–81, 85, 93,
　　99, 106
　Thos. 110
　Wm. cvt. svt. son of Rd. 180
Sallter, Margary, wid. 186
Sally see Saley
Samson, Sampson, Rd. 177
　Rbt. gent. 102
Sanders see Saunders
Sanng, Wm. 166
Saton, Jn. 1
Saunders, Sanders, Sawnders, Isaac, 202
　Jeremy, slater, 178
　Jn. 14, 19, 20, 22
　Nich. husb. 75
　Thos. 205
Savage, —, glover, 112
Savery, Ant. 53
　Rd. mercer, 40, 44, 46–7, 50–1, 53, 62, 64,
　　71, 74–5, 80–2, 84, 88, 90–2, 94, 97–9,
　　103, 106, 108, 111, 116, 119, 121
　Rbt. cvt. svt. 134
Sawgares, Rbt. 22
Sawnders see Saunders
Saxton, Saxtene, Wm. husb. 146, 148
Scargill, Skargell, Skargill, Jn. tailor, 46, 47,
　81, 85, 88–9, 104
　Mgt. 6

Scargyn, Skargyn [?Scargill], Jn. tailor, ?1, 3,
　4, 51, 85, 96
Sclatter see Slatter
Scopam see Skopam
Scott, Cuthbert, vicar of W., 68
　Wm. mercer, 205
Sea, Seay, Seye, Jn. joiner, vctlr. lxxxiii, 133,
　159, 179–80, 194–5, 198
Sealbe, Rbt. husb. 146
Sealey, Selly, Wm. brdwr. 186
　see also Collett
Secoll, Secoole, Rbt. lxxvi
　Thos. brdwr. 129
　Wm. 38, 42, 44
Sellman, Jn. carp. 184
Sellwood, Jn. 183
　Rd. yeo. 183
Selly see Sealey
Selpe, Wm. smith, 17
Serle, Francis, gent. xiv, 127
Sewell see Shewell
Sexten, Sexton, Thos, 194, 198, 205, 208
　Walt. husb. 88
Shad, Rd. chandler, 196
Shale, Mary, wid. 117, 119
Sharp, Jn. 72
　Jn. husb., S. Leigh, 105, 125, 128
　Thos. 23–4
Shaw, Agnes, Anne, Annes, wid., tpl. lxxxv,
　40–3, 46, 51, 60, 65, 67, 70, 74, 76, 90,
　94
　Jn. tucker, 114, 140, 155, 173, 175, 179,
　182
　Rd. butch. lxxxv, lxxxix, 44, 50, 52, 56,
　69, 74, 76, 78, 80, 87, 108, 115, 130–2,
　141, 143
　Thos. (d. c. 1564), butch., tpl. 19, 22, 25,
　27, 29–30, 32–5, 37
　Thos. (fl. 1572–1609), cvt. svt. butch., tpl.
　xlix, lxiii, 61, 67, 86, 106, 113, 116, 131–
　3, 139, 143, 149, 152, 156, 160, 164, 168,
　170, 172, 177, 196, 200, 208
　Wm. draper, 95
　fam. lxxxiv
Shawle, Mary, w. of Wm., 41
　Wm. 41
Shealer, Jn. chapman, 70
Shelle, Wm. blksm. 169, 172
　Wm. svt. 162
Sheowell see Shewell
Shepard, Sheepheard, Shepperd, Eliz. 17
　Eliz. (another), 205
　Geo. brdwr. 200

Rbt. lxxx
Webbe, Ant. husb. 159
  Eliz. wid. 88
  Jeremy, 35
  Jn. svt. lxxv, 50
  Rd. brdwr., clothier, lxviii, lxxv, lxxix,
    lxxxi, 1, 2
  Thos. yeo. 94
Webley, Anne see Petty
  Thos. brdwr., clothier, xc, 140, 142, 144,
    149, 153–6, 158, 163, 169–70, 173–7,
    182–5, 187–8, 190–1, 193–8, 200, 202,
    205–9
  fam. lxiv
Webster, Thos. sawyer, 115, 125
Weekes, Edw. gent. 142
Wellar, Welar, Justinian, 153–4, 156
  Rog. 14
Wells, Alice, wid. 193, 202
  Ellis, brdwr. 135, 149, 159, 165, 177
  Jn. 179
Welshman, Walensis, —, xlviii
Wenman, Waneman, Waynman, Weayn-
    man, Ann, w. of Rd. see Bushe
  Augustine, 25
  Emmote see Hervey
  Francis, gent. 109, 112, 131
  Hy. woolman, lix, lx
  Jn. gent., Lew, 171
  Jn. stockfishmonger, London, lix
  Rd. merchant of the Staple, woolman, lii,
    liv, lix–lxi, lxvii, lxviii
  Sir Rd. justice, 179
  Rd. son of Thos. gent. 94
  Sir Thos. M.P., Caswell, lx
  Thos., Elmley, 25
  Thos. gent. Witney Park, xlix, lxxvi, 16,
    48
  fam. xxxix, liii, lv, lix–lxii, lxviii, lxix,
    lxxv, lxxxvi, lxxxviii
Wesson, Rd. mercer, 190–2, 202
West, Jn. husb. 89
  Jn. gent. 166
  Rd. 203
  Thos. clothier, 147
  Thos. mercer, 133, 136, 141, 143, 146, 154
Wested, Geof. yeo. 66
Westley, Jerome, saddler, 128
Weston, Rd. 195
Wether, Jn. 3
Wethered, Wm. 30
Wever see Weaver
Wheeler, Wheyllar, Whillar, Whyller, Chris.

204
  Ed. see Dodeswell
  Hy. carp. 202
  Jn. lii
  Mgt. 6
  Rog. (d. 1602), carp. lxxxix, 24, 31, 34, 41,
    50, 54, 70–1, 102, 106, 109, 118, 154,
    159, 175
  his w. and grandson, lxxxix
  Rog. jnr. carp. lxxxix, 79, 181, 183, 187,
    197, 199, 203
  Thos. lxxxix
  Ursula, dau. of last, 154
  fam. lxxxiii
Wheley, Jn. 41, 45–6, 50
White, Whight, Whitt, Whyte, Edith, wid.
    199
  Hy. brdwr., tucker, 156, 158, 163, 167,
    169–71, 176, 179, 182, 184, 193–4
  Jn., Bp. of Winchester, xiii
  Mgt. 1
  Margery, wid. 138
  Rbt. 36
  Thos., Charlbury, 37
  Thos., Cogges, 146
  Thos. lab. of W. 94, 114, 198
  Wm. svt. 19
Whithorne, Nich. 189, 206, 208
Whitsyd, Whightsyde, Hy. 162–3
Whitting, Whytyng, Nich. 176
  Rd. lab. 68
Whitton, Reynold, tpl. 159
Whode, Whood, Rbt. cooper, 178, 194
  Wm. 178
  see also Hood
Whytar, Rbt. 168
Whytley, Jas. cvt. svt., brdwr. 35, 49, 62
Wickes, Wyckes, Nich. yeo. 155
  Wm. gent. 76
  Wm. shep. 68
  Wm. yeo., Curbridge, 99
  Wm. yeo. of W. 80, 91
Willes, Thos. 200
Williams, Wyllyams, Adrian, 198, 202
  And. yeo. 134, 140
  Awdwen, yeo., Astall Leigh, 117
  Awdwyn of W. 127–8
  Edw. 202
  Jn., Mr., bkr., New Woodstock, 145, 173
  Jn. clk., Great Faringdon, 92
  Jn. tailor, Burford, 105
  Sir Jn., Thame, lx
  Jn. wiredrawer of W. 122, 124, 126, 133–6,

INDEX OF PLACES

Individual townships are indexed separately and under the main component of their name. Oxfordshire places are indexed without the county identification but other places are identified by the counties to which they belonged before 1974.

M.M.

INDEX OF SUBJECTS

This is mainly an index of the Introduction, where cross references to the text are given.
Specific trades and occupations are grouped under the entry 'trade'; court officers are grouped
under 'officers'. Cross references to persons and places are to those particular indexes.

see Bishop *alias* Martin, Bushe, Cely,
Fermor, Hood, Midwinter, Wenman,
Wilmot
woolwinder *see* Roberts
wotmell maker *see* Deane
tumbril, xi
turn *see* courts

undertenants, xxviii, lviii, 67

vagabonds, vagrants, xxii, lviii
vestry *see* Banbury, Witney

wages, xxxiii, xxxviii, xxxix, xli
see also servants
warping house, li, lxxiv, lxxix
warrant of the Peace, 11
waste, bishop's, *see* Witney
wearing apparel, lxxxvii
broadweavers', 6
servants', xxxiii, xxxiv, 96, 113
weaving shops *see* Witney
weights and measures, xvi, xxiii
widows, xc
wills, xxv, xxvi, lv, lvii–lx, lxii–lxvii, lxix–
lxxii, lxxvi, lxxix–xci

administrators, 19
executors, xli, 57
nuncupative will, xiv, 127
overseers, 91
Tompson's will, 198–9
see also inventories
windows, glass, l, li, lxxii
wool, purchase, 197
supplies, xlviii, lxxiii, lxxv–lxxviii
wool trade, xvi, liii, lix, lxi, lxiii
see also trades
wool types (coarse, fell, fine, fleece, middle), lxxiv, lxxvii–lxxix
yarn, lxxiv, lxxv, lxxvii–lxxx
wool patentee, lxxvi
workhouse *see* Witney Bridewell
workmen, lxvi, lxxix

yarn *see* linen, wool
yeld hall *see* Witney
yeomen, xxxix, xlvi, lxxvii
local, lxxii, lxxiii
wealth of, lxxxvi, lxxxvii, lxxxviii